GOD REVEALS HIS <u>GLORY</u> [<u>DOXA</u> – TRUE IDENTITY]

By Dr. James V. Holland

Texas Sisters Press, LLC

God Reveals His Glory [Doxa – True Identity]

ISBN: 978-1-952041-34-1 - hardcover
ISBN: 978-1-952041-35-8 - paperback

©2021 James V. Holland

All rights reserved. No part of this publication may be reproduced, stored in a retrieval system, or transmitted in any form or by any means, electronic, mechanical, recording or otherwise, without the prior written permission of the author.

Published by Texas Sisters Press, LLC. Lufkin, TX U.S.A.

This book is designed to provide information and motivation to readers. It is sold with the understanding that the publisher is not engaged to render any type of psychological, legal, or any other kind of professional advice. The content is the sole expression and opinion of its author, and not necessarily that of the publisher. No warranties or guarantees are expressed or implied by the publisher's choice to include any of the content in this volume. Neither the publisher nor the individual author shall be liable for any physical, psychological, emotional, financial, or commercial damages, including, but not limited to, special, incidental, consequential or other damages. Our views and rights are the same: You are responsible for your own choices, actions, and results.

Texas Sisters Press, LLC.
2021

Dedication

Philippians 2:5-11

"For let this mind be in you which also is in Christ Jesus, who is the Deity of Heaven and being revealed in the identity of man; humbled Himself having become obedient until death, even the death of a cross.

Therefore `Ĕlôhîym highly exalted the Christ and gave Him a name above every name that at the name of Jesus every knee should bow; of those in heaven and those of earth and those under the earth. And every tongue should confess that Jesus Christ is Lord, to the <u>*glory*</u> [<u>Doxa</u> – the apparent true identity of Deity] of the Father."

In the Book of Genesis: God commissioned Abraham, Isaac, and Jacob/Israel to create a Spiritual Nation from the whole world. In the New Testament Gospels; as Christ was ascending to His Throne of Life in heaven, He again commissioned His Disciples to go into the whole world to finish His ministry of salvation and He is with us to the end of the world.

Now, God Himself, is pleased to dedicate His Book to bless every one of His children who have the mind of Christ, who faithfully serve Him as His ministering Spirits with His Word of Truth – the only light that can penetrate the darkness of death.

PREFACE

Proverbs 1:7, "The *fear* [Yir`âh – fem. Heb. Noun from root word Yârê, meaning absolute terror, dreadful; a positive feeling of awe, reverent trembling] …of the Lord is the *beginning* [Rê`shîyth – fem. Heb. Noun meaning the first in place, time (creation of time), order, rank; the supreme head] …of knowledge."

It is of vital importance to God that every person in this world has knowledge of the truth that captures the mind toward belief in Him as the supreme authority of Life and exercises that belief by faith in Him as Savior. It is imperative that every person learns to be obedient to God's authority so that He can teach us to live our spiritual life by the power of His righteousness. His righteousness is the power of His Throne of Timeless Life that cannot die. It is this power that destroyed the curse of death to keep man in the grave and will completely destroy the power of death to ever exist again. My life has been and will continue to be a journey of developing this proper relationship with God by learning to reverence Him as the personal, supreme authority of "The Living God".

I didn't know anything about the Person of God as a small child, but my sister was a Christian and because of her I knew in my heart there was a Spiritual Being of infinite goodness. So, at the age of six I went looking for Him at the Baptist church near my home. I was directed to a Sunday school class and what I found was a teacher speaking so fast I couldn't understand anything he said and ten other boys just sitting around killing time by carving on the wooden chairs. I was extremely disappointed. I did not return to a church until eight years later when I was invited to go with my school friends.

One night at a revival service I asked my friends how to be saved. They told me all I had to do was go down to the front, join the church and be baptized. That was easy enough, but I felt there was more to it. I wanted to please God with my life, so I began working as hard as I knew how to meet my own expectations of what a Christian should be. It wasn't long before I began to receive praises for my new "Christian" life. I had mixed emotions about that. On the one hand it confirmed my belief that the way to be saved was to live a life pleasing to God; but on the other hand, I knew I was a fraud. I wasn't as good a person as people thought I was. I decided my standard of goodness was not the right way to please God. By the time I was eighteen I had completely turned away from trying to please Him.

I spent two years on a college campus with very poor results. I did construction work for several years and then served a tour of duty in the Air Force. My father died while I was stationed in France, so I returned home to help my mother. I moved back into the church scene and became friends with a retired Baptist Missionary. At his urging, I was "licensed" to preach the gospel. I worked at several jobs for three years and then enrolled at East Texas Baptist College as a ministerial student. I attended one semester and quickly learned that there is one thing most ministers and I had in common, the lack of money.

I got a job as a counselor for emotionally disturbed boys at the Dallas Businessmen's Boys Club. The camp was sponsored partly by the Dallas Cowboys and the Green Bay Packers annual preseason football games. It was an exciting time in my life to meet all those famous sports figures. But all the money in the world could not deliver these boys from the tragedy of human life under the control of death. These emotionally disturbed boys could not function in society; so, the boys and counselors lived year-round in tents isolated in a remote area of East Texas.

God used my work with these boys to open my eyes to how weak the human being is as purely a fleshly being. No matter what medical term is used to classify human behavior (drug addiction is now called a "disease"), these boys knew exactly what they were doing and the more evil is rewarded, the more they loved it. I learned a very crucial lesson which strengthened my resolve to know God: people under the curse of death do not have the power to change themselves. God is the only power which can do that.

I began my studies at Dallas Baptist College on a Presidential Scholarship from the First Baptist Church of Garland, Texas. The school gave me a full academic scholarship after this first semester. Professor Ray Milligan acquired a government grant at the end of my junior year for a summer trip to East Africa. In addition to class requirements, my wife and I were commissioned to make television documentaries for Texas colleges and high schools. In Uganda, we encountered the Godless, pagan world of the blood thirsty army of Idi Amin. I gained a new respect for God because of His protection in very perilous situations. God gave me an understanding that He had important plans for my life, and He would guide me to accomplish them. It is always a tremendous blessing to give God control of my mind when He awakens me in the morning hours.

I loved the college and I had confidence in and admiration for my professors. The scriptures became the open door for me to gain knowledge of the God I had been seeking all my life. I was deeply impressed with the genuineness of the spiritual character of many of the ministerial students and realized that it was sorely missing in mine.

One evening in March 1970, I was maneuvering my way through the freeway traffic in down-town Dallas, when I heard God's voice. This was the first of many times that God has addressed me personally. God said with authority, "James, you are lost." I stopped my car on a side street and had a Damascus road experience with God. He said, "You know a lot about Me, but you are not saved because you do not have a personal relationship with Me as your Lord." I felt the power of God's love for me and I had a head-over-heels experience of falling in love with Him. With an over-whelming feeling of joy, I thanked Him profusely for forgiving me of my sins and delivering me from the curse of death. I knew in my mind that if God had not spoken to me, I quite possibly would never have been saved. I made top grades in my studies of the Bible but in reality, I was not grasping the true concept of the message of the Bible. I was President of the Ministerial Alliance of the first graduating class of the college, preaching in churches every Sunday and on Thursday nights at the Dallas Rescue Mission. But when God spoke to me, I realized I was still the teenage boy trying to please God by my works. From that moment of God taking control of my mind, I was acutely aware of the Holy Spirit blessing everything He was leading me to do.

The Lord spoke again in His quiet voice to me and my wife. He had plans for us to return to Africa as missionaries. My training would require pastoral experience and a seminary degree. I graduated from College on a Friday night in May 1970. At that time two men came to me and said God had selected me to pastor their church. I moved to my first pastorate the next day and started my studies at Southwestern Baptist Theological Seminary the next September.

God placed me in this particular pastoral position of leadership to learn a very important lesson. The church is the body of Christ (Spiritual Israel) and the Holy Spirit is the presence of God in this body. There was a very powerful presence of the Spirit which accomplished God's will. He restored broken lives and brought a continuous revival spirit which in eighteen months brought one hundred and thirty people to Jesus for their salvation. God taught me in a powerful way that He had made Himself known to the whole community through this one little local church. In so doing, He had reestablished the credibility and character of the church that had been destroyed in the past. <u>Because of the Holy Spirit</u>, my pastoral ministry at this church will always remain in my mind as a very happy time with people I will love dearly for the rest of my life.

I continued to work with the Baptist Foreign Mission Board through this time to get an appointment but was turned down as being unqualified. This was difficult for me to accept because I was anxious to get back to Africa. I learned the value of Godly patience from the wise counsel of Air Force Major General Robert Preston Taylor. He was the only Protestant Chaplin to survive the Bataan death march, the hell-ships and was a POW in Japan and Manchuria *(See the Appendix for information on his book <u>DAYS OF HOPE AND DAYS OF GLORY</u>). God was teaching me in His own quiet way to wait on Him while He was preparing the way for me to learn even more about the authority of His throne. I had to learn the wisdom of trusting God in absolutely everything. I had no idea that my forthcoming missionary career would involve walking with Him through the perils of six civil wars.

The Lord terminated my ministry at this church just two weeks before my last semester of seminary. I didn't have a place to live or have any financial income. The Lord had already acted to open doors for me to move into new student housing on the Seminary campus and to work for the campus maintenance department. At the end of those two weeks my wife got her master's degree in education and delivered our first child. *Almost at the same time.

I fully expected the Lord to get my appointment with the Baptist Mission Board when I graduated in December of that year but again God had other plans. General Taylor knew that I was not ready, so he wrote a letter and sent it to several churches. I moved into the parsonage of a church in Virginia within a week after my graduation. Then before I could even unpack, I received a request to pastor a Baptist church in Taos, New Mexico. If I had received the request a week earlier, I would have been torn by indecision. I decided to stop second guessing the Lord's long-range plans and learn to live in the joy and provision of His everyday presence.

My wife and I and our five-month-old son were welcomed into the hearts of some of the most precious, loving people on earth. I have often wished that it had been possible for this ministry to never end. I would have loved to spend my life with those delightful people. We cherish them as great saints of God's Kingdom of Life.

The critical issue of God's ministry to this church was for me to learn how to value (respect) the individual identity of human beings as decision makers. All people struggle within themselves to break free from the human dilemma of bondage to death. I had nothing but respect and love for every member of this church body; but God could not bless this church because it was under the control of an individual with awesome power over the church and ever person's personal life. God placed me there to reveal His spiritual battle to unify it under the sole authority of the Holy Spirit. It was God doing the work that only He could do. He placed me there to stand in His place and be His voice to bring the truth to light. It was a painful experience for the whole church, but God made it His church and infused it with His spiritual power to make it a continuing light that cannot be extinguished. It was God Who was working in every person's heart and mind to surrender their lives to Him and they gave Him the glory that is His alone.

God was ready now to use my wife and me as foreign missionaries. We wanted to return to Uganda, Africa, because there seemed to be such a powerful need for us to minister to that war torn land. But once again the Lord had other plans for us. I felt it strange that the Mission Board was appointing others to that country but would not appoint me. The Board suggested instead the need for us to go to Angola, Africa; a country I didn't know even existed. We had no inkling of how wonderful "God's assignment" would turn out to be.

Angola had been engaged in a civil war since 1960. The first Baptist missionary couple (Harrison and June Pike) had been working alone for over ten years and in that time, God was using them to bring about one of the greatest evangelistic movements of this era. God had prepared them for this work by taking them through the purifying fires of many years of service in the country of Brazil. God added another family (Curtis and Betty Dixon) with a similar mission experience gained in Brazil, and a journeyman (Tress Miles) to serve as the mission secretary. One other family (Bert and Virginia Sutton) had been appointed to Angola, as agriculture evangelists; but they were required to spend one year in language school in Lisbon, Portugal. Ironically, my family would arrive in Angola the same time as this family because my wife and I were permitted by the government to study Portuguese in the capital city of Luanda. In God's infinite wisdom, He assembled His choice of people He could use in the brief time we were allowed to work in the holocaust that would engulf that country.

My family was met at the Luanda airport at 2:30 A.M. on 28 December 1974. The resident missionary Harrison Pike was leaving at 6 A.M. on a trip to Carmona; a city in the north where the fighting had been the worst. He was going to hold an ordination service in the back yard of the house where I was assigned to live after language school. God started a church there with 6883 people He had delivered through the horrors of the war. It would be the first Protestant religious service allowed by the Catholic controlled government in sixteen years. I told him, "You are not going without me!" Within a few hours of arriving in a country unknown to me; I began to form a powerful bond of love, precious friendship and the highest respect for the powerful leadership of this man I relevantly call "Moses". All of our mission families cherish the bond of friendship developed by our service to one another in those difficult days of civil war. God truly blessed us with people He had chosen for this purpose.

That fateful day of our arrival in Angola was the beginning of a new awakening for me. I was engulfed in the experience of living every day by the authority of God's throne of Life. The area within the walls around my house was crammed shoulder-to-shoulder with an unknown multitude of people singing and rejoicing in the glory of God. Pickup trucks driving around town would hold fifty-plus people singing the praises of God. The crowd overflowed into the streets. This crowd outside the walls of my yard was estimated to be about three thousand people. There was no way to actually count their number. Fifteen more new churches were organized in that district in the following months with more than a thousand to a church. I was amazed at the magnitude of God's power to reach out into the hidden recesses of that vast land in the midst of the on-going war and save thousands upon thousands of spiritually lost people. We never arrived at a village for a worship service without a large group walking beside our car, singing the praises of God.

The African pastor of this church (Garcia Benedito) had been tortured nearly to death. He had to watch as his twenty-five-year-old son was fed alive to crocodiles and his eighteen-year-old grandson was beaten to death (I met him when they started with his feet to work their way up his body); all because this man abdicated his position of their King (about six million people) and refused to stop preaching the gospel. His son admonished him at the time of his death; telling him that the people needed Jesus more than he needed him. I asked this Godly man his response to all that had happened to him. He simply said with a broken heart, "The people who do these things are in the darkness of death. They do not know what they do".

This African man's love for God is the power of His Righteousness which enabled him to suffer for Christ, as Christ suffered for man. The truth of God's presence in this world is revealed by His character, which is the light of truth shinning in His people in the darkness of this world. I became acutely aware that the people creating the chaos that greatly affects our lives are in the darkness of death and have the desperate need of God's salvation. God's Righteousness is the standard I expect of myself; not to be saved, but because I am saved. God commands us to be His light shining in the darkness even when under the threat of our own death. Standing in the presence of that Godly man, I realized I had come a long way from that day when a disappointed six-year-old boy could not find God.

Many people did not survive the war. Angola (twice the size of Texas) was rated eighty percent on the worlds suffering index; meaning eighty percent of the people were either killed or maimed. Viet Nam only ranked thirty-five percent. Those who did survive would only give God the glory for it. One such witness was an old blind man. It was revealed that he had lived alone in the forest for two years after being separated from his family in a battle. He told how God fed him every day and protected him from the lions and snakes. Others told of how God had protected them from the crocodiles when they had to cross the rivers at night to escape the army attacking them.

In my years of military experience in the French/Algerian civil war and in the missionary experiences of my wife and I in Africa and Mexico; we were witnesses to the slaughter of an untold number of people in six bloody civil wars. No person in this world is safe from the tyranny of Satan's warfare with God. We give witness that every day we live; it is by God's grace and for His purpose. Praise God with great joy for your experience of living in this world as God's holy people.

There were very few Bibles available for the large number of people hiding in the jungle in Angola. Pages of the few Bibles available were distributed as best they could be in such a vast area. Every person memorized every page they could get. My co-pastor (Garcia Benedito) came to me one day and asked me to express the heartfelt thanks of his people to every Christian in America for supplying everything our mission was giving to his people. But the one thing they needed more than anything else was complete Bibles. The people were hungry to know more about the God who saved them than the one page they had memorized. With tears in his eyes, he asked me, "Do you think Baptist in America would have some Bibles we could use?" Unknown to either of us, the Lord had already answered his prayer. God had already worked through Harrison Pike to open the first Baptist bookstore in Angola. Ask and you shall receive from the bounteous storehouse of God. I will never forget the joy on their faces to get all the Bibles they wanted. *That bookstore is Gods continuing presence to reveal Himself to these people.

Every day was a new experience of God's grace. Warfare was a very powerful, constant, destructive presence; but I did not personally feel threatened or alarmed by it. I was captured by two communist backed soldiers and told (I had a rifle barrel against the back of my head and another on the right side) to drive to a place for my execution. I had a powerful sense that God was in control of the situation; so instead of showing fear, I simply drove around town and witnessed to the soldiers in French and Portuguese (which I spoke very little of either). My only real concern was to keep watch on my house where my wife and son were barricaded under a mattress. A violent gun fight was taking place in my yard and the surrounding area and God was simply keeping me occupied until the fighting stopped. When the battle ended, I told the soldiers to go home to their families and I was going home to mine; and they got out of my car without a word. (However, a sniper shot a man off a 9th floor balcony just as I got home.)

The apex of God's work to teach me the most important lesson of my life occurred as the fighting in Luanda had escalated to a very dangerous level that would soon require our evacuation. Jonas Savimbi, the leader of UNITA, one of the military factions was to hold a meeting in Luanda at the historic First Baptist Church. The English-speaking congregation at that time consisted of the Baptist missionary families, the skeleton crew left at the American Consulate and a number of English-speaking nationals. Curtis Dixon and I were at the church with about three hundred nationals (Portuguese speaking congregation) awaiting the arrival of Savimbi, when the building was attacked by the pro-communist army (MPLA) under the control of Agustino Neto.

The outside of the church building suffered heavy damage but not one bullet or mortar shell came through a window. Soldiers burst through the front door carrying machine guns. One put his gun to my head and pulled the trigger, but nothing happened. Then God spoke but I was the only one who could hear Him. He said, "James, I did not bring you here to die. I will keep you safe if you will give me your permission." It seemed incredible at the moment that He wanted me to demonstrate to the soldiers my trust in His authority. I burst out laughing with a sense of relief and thanked God for allowing me to watch Him work; with the full understanding that this really was the power of His presence. For the next thirty minutes or so God scared the living fool out of those soldiers. They couldn't shoot me and try as hard as they could with their combined forces, they couldn't move me or take my camera away from me. God gave me the ability to speak some limited Portuguese and I told them they were not soldiers, but thieves. I was not going outside the building and they could not have my camera. Then God spoke again. He said, "Can you understand the culture of these men? They cannot leave here without some kind of victory." The soldiers came in again and demanded the film out of my camera. I did not want to give it to them because I had been taking their pictures. God spoke again, this time with a very authoritative voice. He said, "I told you to give these men a back door to escape this place. I have prepared an opportunity to deal with them later under different circumstances and they will know Who I Am." I apologized to the Lord for acting against His Will and asked His forgiveness for acting so selfishly as to take over the work He was doing. I immediately stripped the film out of my camera to expose it. I couldn't believe men loaded down with so much armament could move so fast. I can only imagine the story those men had to tell; and to pray for a newborn faith in God the next time they met Him.

The soldiers departed in a cloud of dust, but God had more to say to me. He explained that He was giving me two spiritual gifts which would glorify Him alone. I could not use them to serve myself because He could only put them into effect by my sacrificial obedience to His will. The first gift is faith to walk so close to Him that I became a partner with Him; to have such an intimate relationship with Him that we are of the same mind. The purpose of this gift is that it enables me to see Him and know Him by the experience of walking with Him. This is what God wants me to reveal to other people who have not learned to see Him. Our salvation is not "pie-in-the-sky, by-and-by". It is the presence of His Throne of Life at work in our physical lives to make us spiritually alive. God has not revealed Himself to be Biblical doctrines, or a creed, or four spiritual laws to be obeyed. He is the Holiness of Life that cannot die; and this power of timeless spiritual life is His salvation gift to man. A gift we can receive only by faith.

My gift of faith has been absolutely necessary for God to accomplish His Will for my life. Every ministry God has commissioned me to do have been specific job assignments to accomplish a specific result. Through it all God has been faithful to fellowship with me every day. I look forward with great anticipation for Him to awaken me in the night to instruct me and counsel me. The effectiveness of this gift has been revealed to me a number of times when folks tell me that in a short time of my ministry with them, they had learned more about the Lord than they had learned in their whole lives. This gift has also blessed me rhetorically because the Holy Spirit produces a deep sense of joy in my heart when I am in the presence of every other person who also is blessed with the presence of Jesus.

The second gift from the Lord is my ability to love people as sinners under the burden of death and not be judgmental of them. This gift is purely the work of God's Spirit to overcome our prejudices that belittle people. It does not matter what people believe or if they have any religious belief at all; the Spirit opens the door to their minds for His people to be accepted and welcomed to speak with them. Sometimes it is for their salvation; sometimes it is for the Lord to release them from Satan's grip that produces nothing but the character of death. No matter what God does or why He does it; every time it is a witness to the depth of His love for man. The enormity of this gift has been revealed by the number of people whose minds have been opened to receive me and God's message to then. I have witnessed God's salvation for Catholic priests, Jews, Buddhists, Presidents of nations, and the rich and the poor. Twice in my pastoral ministry the Lord has awakened me in the middle of the night to go see a man I did not know (one in Texas and one in Washington State). When I got to their homes, I found they knew my name and were waiting for me to get there. Both made professions of faith and I buried these two of God's Saints the very next week. My mind is always praising God for Who He is as a *saving God*. But my heart also weeps for the untold number of people who will always remain blind to such love. I can never thank God enough for knowing my heart before I was even born and for preparing the time on a Dallas freeway when He would be welcomed with great joy to speak to me for my own salvation.

Everything about this preface brings me to the point of why I am writing this book. The Lord woke me about 2 A.M. one morning with a new assignment. Thus far my service to Him had been through individuals and the local church. He wanted to expand the revelation of Himself to a much larger world. He directed me to write a book in a prescribed manner which allows

Him to speak through His own written words. The Bible has the single subject of God's personal revelation of who He is as a Kingdom Power of Timeless Spiritual Life. He is the sole revelation of truth and His Spirit is the only power that can reveal truth to the human mind.

My only experience of writing was my doctoral thesis; child's play compared to this book. He had to erase everything I had ever learned about Him from the teaching of men and the English language; to have an open mind to comprehend the meaning of the scriptures in the original languages of Hebrew and Greek. The revelation of God in this book is purely His use of His own words. It is simply allowing God to discipline our minds to hear what the Holy Spirit is teaching through the scriptures He has already written (not what men copy from other English translations). Its purpose is to open the minds of English-speaking people to the deeper meanings of the Hebrew and Greek (both dead languages). I pray for those who read it; that all will be as disciplined by the Holy Spirit to study it as God has disciplined me to write it.

My everyday learning experience with God has opened my mind to see His work in both heaven and earth. He involved me in His great spiritual movement in Angola, Uganda, Kenya, The Republic of South Africa, Botswana, Mexico and Brazil; and to build a missionary training center in Kohima, the capital city of Nagaland, India. My beloved friend, Dr. Phuvey Dozo is God's personal witness that in 1959, God converted 800,000 headhunters to be His most powerful evangelists (all Baptists) for the conversion of many people in India and the surrounding countries.

God has blessed my life with forty-one years of pastoral ministry in the States of Texas, Virginia and Washington and the fourteen years it has taken to write this book. I found that many Hebrew and Greek words are a combination of words and I had to find the root word for each one of them to understand their meanings combined in one word. And now, I pray that you will be blessed in your life as you grow in the grace and knowledge of the Living God. Do not be satisfied with anything less than walking in the light of Jesus and learn what only God can teach you.

God bless every person who reads this book.

Dr. James V. Holland

God Reveals His Glory [Doxa – True Identity]

Table of Contents

PREFACE	3
INTRODUCTION	13
Chapter 1	31
GOD'S REVELATION OF HIS KINGDOM RULE	31
BY GOD'S NAME	31
BY THE CREATION OF TIME	34
BY THE NECESSITY FOR CREATION	39
BY THE SEVEN REVELATIONS OF SANCTIFIED LIFE	41
Chapter 2	57
GOD REVEALS THE KINGDOM RULE OF DEATH	57
THE SERPENT	57
THE DECEPTION OF THE SATANIC LIE	60
Chapter 3	63
GOD REVEALS HIS JUDGMENTS ON DEATH	63
DEATH'S CURSE ON SATAN	64
DEATH'S CURSE ON THE WOMAN	66
DEATH'S CURSE ON ADAM	71
DEATH'S CURSE ON THE FIRST GENERATION OF MAN FROM ADAM TO NOAH	72
Chapter 4	77
THE SECOND GENERATION OF MORTAL MAN	77
NOAH	77
GOD'S COVENANT WITH MORTAL MAN	78
THE FORMATION OF CIVILIZATIONS	79
Chapter 5	83
CREATION OF SPIRITUAL ISREAL: THE PEOPLE OF GOD	83
ABRAHAM	83
ISAAC	99
ISAAC'S DESCENDANTS	100
MOSES	109
Chapter 6	133
GOD IDENTIFIES SPIRITUAL ISRAEL AS HIS HEAVENLY PEOPLE	133
GODS SANCTIFICATION OF HIS PEOPLE	133
GOD'S HEAVENLY CONSTITUTION TO GOVERN SPIRITUAL ISRAEL	139
GOD'S TEMPLE	155
Chapter 7	171
GOD REVEALS HIMSELF BY PROPHESY	171
Chapter 8	183

GOD DESTROYS DEATH BY HIS PRESENCE	183
EPIPHANEIA – THE SACRIFICIAL LAMB OF GOD	183
PHANEROO - THE HOLY SPIRIT	237
THE DEITY OF HEAVEN SPEAKING TO MAN	237
APOKALUPSIS – THE KING OF KINGS GLORIFIED FROM HEAVEN	249

Chapter 9 261

GOD'S FINAL JUDGMENT ON DEATH	261
THE RULE OF CHRIST	261

Chapter 10 273

THE FINAL STATE OF GLORIFIED HUMANITY	273

EPILOGUE 287

BIBLIOGRAPHY 293

APPENDIX 294

EXODUS FROM ANGOLA	295
BOTSWANA	308
MEXICO	314

INTRODUCTION

The invisible, intangible *Spiritual Being of Deity* [`Ĕlôhîym] has revealed Himself to be the sole creator and authority over the existence of all life; physical and spiritual. He reveals His supreme authority to be His perfect holy character of righteousness: His Kingdom Rule of Life that cannot die. This Rule of Life is given to redeemed man for his salvation. It will be the only thing that survives His judgment on death revealed in Revelation 21-22.

By His personal power of *love* (Agape - John 3:16), God exacted His judgment of justice on death and to make an atonement for the death of humanity. By His own sacrificial death of the soul of man [God's personal presence as the Messiah], He took all the sins of humanity upon Himself (atonement) and entered Hades for three days. By resurrecting Himself from the grave, He revealed His identity of the Living God Who rules heaven and earth. His heavenly Kingdom of Life in action on earth destroyed the power of death to hold humanity in the grave. The salvation of the human being belongs solely to God; not to the human race which has no life in it, nor the power in any form to change it.

God's power to restore all of humanity to His Kingdom of Spiritual Life is a free gift. Until God returns to this earth for judgment on all the powers of death (the Apokalupsis); the *Holy Spirit* [Phanaroō - John 21:1, the breath of God] is God's continuing presence on earth to reveal the truth of His salvation to the mind of every person. God reveals Himself to the whole world to restore His timeless Spiritual Life to all mankind; but every individual person must make a personal decision to believe it or reject it. Every human being who will commit themselves to God by *faith* [a verb – the activity of the mind to believe the truth that Jesus is Lord; and to *repent* (make a confession to God that death rules his life) and call upon the name of Jesus to save him with the full assurance that God now rules his life]. God has made salvation so simple that every person can receive it by the faith of a small child; but every person who rejects this revelation of salvation from God, will perish under His judgment on death.

God has chosen to communicate His identity of a saving God (His mind) through the Scriptures with the power of His Spirit to reveal its truth to the mind of man (I Cor.2). The Bible is God's infallible revelation of His Kingdom Rule of Life; to completely remove death so that it cannot be a memory in the human mind in God's perfect heaven or even have the remote possibility of ever existing again. God's final and greatest revelation (Revelation 22:5) will be when there is no longer the need for Him to be revealed by His Life-giving power of Deity; the Creator, Jesus (Huios), and Holy Spirit. It is only when He has completely destroyed death (Rev.20) that He will appear to the saints in heaven in His timeless presence as the One God [`Ĕlôhîym – Hebrew and Theos – Greek] on His throne as He was in the beginning before creation (Genesis 1:1).

Adam was the first man created with the spiritual life of God's Throne. His mind was holy and pure in thought as a heavenly creation in God's image. He had the freewill to trust and love God, and to be His decision maker on earth. The intangible power of death became the ruling power over the whole human race when Adam turned his face away from God. The whole history of man under this authority of death has been his unbelief and perversion of the truth.

God 's purpose is to reveal His identity as the only Deity that exists, and to restore His Kingdom Rule of Timeless Spiritual Life to the entire human race. But He has to do it (1) in the darkness of death's rule of the human mind, and (2) reveal Himself to His creation that has absolutely no knowledge of Him.

I John 1:5-7

"And this is the *message* [Aggelia - The singular message from God. This Greek word is only used twice; this verse and 1John 3:11.] …we have heard from Him and *announced* [Anaggeliō – to tell in return what was heard from heaven] …to you that God is *light* [Phōs – revelation of truth that is kindled in heaven and cannot be quenched on earth; it produces only joy and happiness], …and in Him there is no *darkness* [Skotia – unhappiness; this word is not sin but the consequence of sin] …at all. If we say that we have fellowship with Him and yet *walk* [Pěripatěō – a manner of living; to deport oneself] …in the *darkness* [Skotos – to be restrained by the night; to do the evil works of the darkness, to be ruled by the kingdom of death], …we lie and do not practice the *truth* [Alēthia – The reality pertaining to an unveiled appearance of Holy Spiritual Life; it is an appearance of truth that is revealed clearly before the eyes of man in the Deity of Jesus, the Christ—the Messiah]; …but if we walk in His light as He Himself is in the light we have fellowship with one another and the *blood* [Haima – Lev. 17:11 'For the life of the flesh is in the blood.` The blood of Jesus was offered as a sacrifice for the atonement of sin and the restoration of spiritual life in man.] …of Jesus: His [Huios –The Deity of Jesus the Christ is God's revelation of His holy presence in human flesh] …*cleanses* [Katharizō – This does not mean to be washed physically, i.e., free from things that kill the flesh. It means to be free from the curse of death: to restore spiritual life that was lost.] …us from all sin."

I John 3:7-8

"Little children let no one deceive you; the one who practices *righteousness* [Dikaiosunē –conformity to the power of God's justice; the essence of God's pure love] …is righteous, just as He is righteous; the one who practices sin is of the devil; for the *devil* [Diabolos – The angel who slandered God in the holiness of heaven. He continues to act in this manner on earth to separate people from God.] …has sinned from the beginning. Jesus *appeared* [Phaneroō – The divine revelation by the Holy Spirit to make the true saving work of Jesus known to the human mind.] …for this purpose, that He might *destroy* [Luō– to loose something that is bound; to loose man from his bondage to death] …the works of the devil."

The Bible is God's Self-Revelation of His *Glory* [Doxa–The true identity of the Kingdom Rule of Life. It is revealed as "The Kingdom of Heaven/Kingdom of God – the rule of God's heavenly Throne". God's glory is His work of opening heaven to see Him in His radiant holiness and to feel His heartbeat of Love for His greatest creation – Man.]. God glorifies Himself by the communication of His living *Word* [logos–Jesus, the Christ; is the living, spoken

God Reveals His Glory [Doxa – True Identity]

revelation of the mind of God to man (I Cor. 2:1-13)]. God's Word reveals what is impossible for man to know; that God's heavenly kingdom rule of life present in this world of darkness is the only power which can destroy the kingdom of death. Belief in The Word of God (Jesus) is the heavenly authority of truth which overcomes the distortion of the satanic lie and its power over the human mind. II Cor. 5:17, "If any man is in Christ, he is a *new* [Kainos – Qualitatively different identity] …*creature* [Ktisis - recreated spiritual life to be God's heavenly children surrounding His Throne of Life.]." This was God's purpose for creating Adam in His Image.

*God's conversion of humanity from death to His timeless Life is His true identity of Deity – the creator of all life. His message to humanity is the inerrancy of His Word. Anyone who perverts His Word perverts His identity.

Revelation 22:18-19
"I testify to everyone who hears the *words* [Logos – the intelligence of God's mind to reveal Himself] …of the *prophecy* [Propheteia – God's revelation of His Deity in this world for the total destruction of death and the restoration of man to timeless spiritual life] …of this *book* [Bibliŏn – the scroll of writing which God has written as the Book of Life; God's revelation of His saving work only through Himself – the Lord Jesus Christ]:

if anyone adds to them (the salvation of man by human design, or Christ plus the works of man), God shall add to him the plagues which are written in this *book* [Biblos – God's revelation of His Kingdom Rule of Life for the salvation of man].

and if anyone takes away (perverts God's Word to make salvation through Jesus to be of none affect) from the words of the *book* (Biblos) of this prophecy, God shall take away his part from the *Book of life* [Biblos Zōe – the spiritual life God gave to Adam; which is what Christ restores to man; distinguished from bios (physical life)]

and from the *holy* [Hagios – sanctified, consecrated to the service of Deity, sharing in God's purity] …*city* [mētrŏpŏlis – the inhabitants which comprise the community of the redeemed; those given spiritual birth from heaven by God's authority. It is all the people of the world whose minds have been purified from the rule of death so as to be incapable of sinning and to never even remember its existence; then and only then can glorified man live in the holiness of God's throne of Life.] … which are written in this book."

*These verses reveal the mind of God toward any and every person who perverts His Glory – His Self-revelation of His true identity. God (Jesus) speaks directly to this issue of men making themselves superior teachers to His word with human inspired precepts:

Matthew 10:1
"And having *summoned* [Proskaleō – God's call for lost humanity to come to Him for salvation. It is used in this verse in the middle voice; God's Divine call to entrust men with His authority for the preaching of His Gospel message.] …His twelve disciples, He gave them *authority* [Exousia – God's permissive power/strength {executive right/might to act in accordance to His Will}] …over unclean spirits, to cast them out, and to *heal* [Therapeuō – to heal miraculously/to rescue/to bring to safety; the primary use of this word is the action of the physician's watchful attendance of the sick/to be a manager in God's house (not a slave or domestic servant but a free man who solicitously looks after his masters affairs] …every kind of disease and every

kind of *sickness* [Malakia - softness/weakness/deny spiritual identity{the power of death to weaken the human mind to reject God's Throne of Life and regard life as purely physical}]."

Matthew 10:5-7
"These twelve Jesus *sent out* [Apostellō – to be sent forth on a certain mission to bless a certain group of people with the message of God which has the power to save from death] ...after instructing them, saying, 'Do not go in *the way* [Hodos – a road to a particular people] ...of the *Gentiles* [Ethnos – the whole race of mankind under the curse of death; referred to as one nation] ...and do not enter any city of the Samaritans; but rather go the *lost* [Apollumi – life that has been permanently destroyed; killed; perished] ...sheep of the house of Israel.

And as you go, *preach* [Kerussō – to be a herald of the gospel; to proclaim the victory of Christ's salvation] ...saying, The *Kingdom of heaven* [Basileia ton Ouranos – an abstract noun denoting the sovereignty, royal power and dominion of God's Throne of Life. Jesus used both the {kingdom of heaven} and the {kingdom of God} to mean the same sphere of God's rule of life over death in heaven and on the earth. The Spiritual Kingdom Rule of Life that God has brought through His Own Deity to rule the human mind must be acknowledged as God's Kingdom Rule over death and is voluntarily received by every human being of the whole world. *Every human being is the same to God. All are sinners condemned to death and all must be redeemed to God's timeless spiritual life through Christ – God's anointed Savior.] ...is *at hand* [Eggizō– to bring near in a transitive and intransitive sense of motion. God's kingdom Rule of Timeless Life that governs all of heaven has been *brought from heaven* by the Messiah– Christ to rule on the earth in all redeemed humanity.]. This redemptive work of God cannot end until the last person on earth who can be redeemed, is redeemed.]"

Daniel 2:44
"And in the days of those kings (rule of human kingdoms in Daniel's vision; Jesus was brought forth in the rule of Rome) the God of heaven will set up a kingdom which will never be *destroyed* [Châbal – bring to ruin by the kingdom of death which has destroyed humanity.]."

Daniel 7:13-14
"I kept looking in the night visions and behold, with the *clouds of heaven* ['Anan – an Aramaic word found only in this single verse of scripture; it means that which covers heaven from sight/what God has not revealed.] ... *The Deity in Human Form* was coming, and He came up to the Ancient of Days and was presented before Him. And to Him was given *dominion* {the absolute rule of `Ĕlôhîym over all life in heaven and the earth}, *Glory* {the true identity of `Ĕlôhîym as the saving God} and a *kingdom* [Malkûw – Aramaic for the sovereign rule of a foreign king – God's Heavenly Throne of Spiritual Life] ...which is not ruled by the *kingdom of death* [Malkâh - Hebrew for the rule of a foreign queen–the weakness of human flesh]."

Death began in heaven (Lucifer/and angels), but God established His rule of Spiritual Life on the earth by the power of the man (Adam); that all the *peoples,* ['Am – all of mankind restored to the spiritual life of God through the Christ] ...*nations*, ['Ummâ - Aramaic – singular for a particular tribe of people. It is translated plural nation(s), meaning every single person of a tribe taken from the entire tribe of man] ...and men of every tongue (language).

God Reveals His Glory [Doxa – True Identity]

I Peter 2:9

"But you are a chosen race, a royal priesthood, a Holy Nation, a people for God's own possession, that you may proclaim the Excellencies of Him who has called you out of darkness into His marvelous light."

Matthew 15:1-11, God reveals His truth that every person who perverts His Word by human precepts: does not have a God or a Savior.

"Then some *Pharisees* [Pharisaiŏs – religious separatist; those who set themselves apart as the only people of God.] … and *scribes* [Grammatos – (Syn. Nomikos – Lawyers); ones skilled in the human interpretation of God's law given in the Old Testament.] …came to Jesus from Jerusalem, saying, 'Why do your *disciples* [Mathētēs - pupils, learners who could not speak in a manner of superiority to their instructor. These men identified themselves with Jesus by their rule of conduct.] … *transgress* [Parabainō - the guilt of stepping out of line; a moral decision to act contrary to what is taught as holy] …the *tradition* [Paradŏsis –precepts of men which were taught as the Law of God; teachings which replaced the moral teaching of God] …of the **elders* [Presbus– (Numbers 11:16-17) Seventy men who were the spiritual leaders of the Hebrews who God delivered from Egypt. God selected them to help Moses bear the burden of spiritual leadership for the teaching of the Law given on Mt. Sinai.

For they (Christ's disciples) do not wash their hands when they eat bread. And Jesus answered and said to them, 'And why do you yourselves transgress the commandment of God for the sake of tradition? For God said, 'Honor your Father and Mother, and He who speaks evil of Father or Mother, let him be put to death`.

But you say, 'Whoever shall say to his father or mother, anything of mine you might have been helped by has been given to God, he is not to honor his father or mother'. And thus, you *invalidated* the word of God (made it to be untruth) for the sake of your tradition.

You hypocrites, rightly did Isaiah prophesy of you, saying, 'This people honor Me with their lips, but their heart is far away from Me. But in **vain** (Exodus 20:7), do they worship Me, teaching as *Doctrines* [Didaskalia – what is taught by the authority of the teacher; *only God can write Biblical doctrines/ truth for teaching] …the *Precepts* [Entaima – commandments which emphasize the authority of the one commanding] …of men`. He called the multitude to Him and said to them, 'Hear, and understand; not what enters unto the mouth *defiles* [Koinoō – pollutes, makes unclean] …the man, but what proceeds out of the mouth, this defiles the man`."

Jesus identified the precepts of the Jews as Satan's powerful deceptive work to turn the entire nation away from understanding the true identity of the Messiah. The precepts of nationalistic Israel invalidated the true identity of Jesus to have Him murdered by the hated Roman civil government. Jesus condemned the precepts of the Sanhedrin in these verses in Matthew 15.

In this present day, the precepts of Dispensationalism/Fundamentalism designed by John Nelson Darby, H.A. Ironside, C.I. Scofield and others who call themselves "learned professors and authors of books", have taken over the world. They have distorted the scriptures in their effort to create a special dispensation for nationalistic Jews to be saved apart from God's salvation of all other people of the world.

Revelation 20 is the continuing revelation of the Apokalupsis given in I Thessalonians 4:17. It gives us the complete revelation of what it means for Jesus to bring God's judgment at His coming from heaven to destroy this place of death's rule and take all His saved people (Romans 10: 11-13, Jews and Gentiles are the same to God; all are sinners and all are saved by faith in the person of God – Jesus the Messiah) unto Himself for His iron rod rule of righteousness in the Rule of Christ {Rev.19:15}.

In I Corinthians 15, God will transform *mortal* [Thanĕtos – to die a natural death. Until Jesus returns all human beings will die a natural death whether saved or not; for in this world their *souls* (life of the body) are under the rule of death (the death of the grave)] …to *imperishable* [Aphthartos – not under the rule of death. The spirits of all the Saints in the presence of Jesus (those who come with Him from Paradise and those believers on earth at His coming) will not be subject to the power of death to sin.]….and keep *immortal man* [Athanasia – God's people He has redeemed to timeless spiritual life since the beginning of time] …unto Himself for the Rule of Christ to finalize God's complete destruction of Death.

These Greek words in I Corinthians 15 are God's revelation that death will have absolutely no power in the presence of Christ's Rule until it is His purpose to reveal the very last vestige of created life that can still turn away from Him. The Saints (redeemed Jews and Gentiles) will worship Jesus face to face just like the Angels do before the Throne of God. They will not be subject to the power of death (which will still be present) until Satan is released from the pit to reveal the true mind of Gog and Magog/Reubenites (I Chronicles 5:1). *See the exegesis of Revelation 20 and the section of the revelation of Jesus by prophesy.

This is God's final judgment on death. He will separate and cast into Hades those Satan deceives to turn away from Him. Following the Great White Throne Judgment; Satan, the fallen angels, death, Hades and all the human spirits that are in it; will be thrown into the lake of Fire. God will have purified the minds of every redeemed human being in the history of the world so not even one of them will remember it. *(If they remember it, they will go back to it.) It will then be impossible for death to ever exist again. This completes God's planned judgment on death and His creation of the perfect heaven of Revelation 21-22, ruled completely by the sinless mind of God. This is God's guarantee that death can never exist again.

Every world religion is a precept of Satan's creation. God's word is clear that the Holy Spirit is the presence of God to give every person in the world the same responsibility and opportunity to believe in Christ to be redeemed to the spiritual life of God. Not one single person who will ever live on this earth is exempt from God's judgment for salvation. On the negative side, not one single human being who rejects God's salvation in Christ will escape Hades, the Great White Throne Judgment, and the Lake of Fire. God did not write human precepts, nor has He taught even one single word of all the "isms" that men use to define religions and denominations.

Jesus made it very clear that every person and every religious belief which perverts the identity of God by teaching precepts they claim to be the true doctrines of the Bible, and by acting as a superior authority to God by enforcing these precepts on the minds of all the population of the world; will perish by God's judgment. Anyone can believe in these human precepts if they wish; but everyone who teaches or preaches that a precept is Biblical Doctrine will find themselves under judgment for perverting the Prophecy of Jesus as revealed by the Holy Spirit.

God did not create His kingdom rule of spiritual life as a dispensation for different people. This is a precept created by men. Beware of what Jesus said to the Jews in Matthew 15:9, "But in vain do they worship Me".

Apostasy takes many forms; from creating the precepts of world religions to the distortion of the Bible by false translations. The Discovery Channel on television broadcasted programs directed by Simcha Jacobovici, Kenneth Hanson (author of Secrets from the Lost Bible) and Rabbi David Wolpe from Sinai Temple in Los Angeles. These men reject the validity of the Bible as myths. Example: the parting of the Red Sea and Jesus identity as the Deity of God, they say Jesus was a disillusioned man who thought he was a god.

Satan is saturating the world with the worship of aliens; gods whose purpose is to save the world from destruction. The development of computer graphics has made science fiction characters to be real life heroes in the minds of children. These are examples of Satan's relentless work to destroy the true identity of God and assume that identity as his own. This is his work to bring this world to be the total habitation of death.

It is incredible that since Adam and Eve, the whole world believes the satanic lie. But then, is it so hard to believe when our children are taught by Walt Disney (an atheist) that witches are real and good; and the church joins the world teaching that Christmas and Easter are simply pagan holidays celebrated by Santa Claus and Peter Rabbit?

Another distortion of God's word is the practice of enforcing the meaning of modern-day English words upon the Hebrew, Aramaic, and Greek of the Bible. The following are examples.

The Hebrew word `aleph (the first letter of the Hebrew alphabet) is used 525 times in the Old Testament as a causative, a multiplier to signify a large unknowable number (such as a large herd of animals) and is symbolized in writing by the head of a cow. The word R^{e}bâbâh [from râbab - a really huge abundance, to multiply by the myriad; to represent an uncountable number] …is used four times. This word Rĭbbôw [myriad – an indefinite large number] is used six times. Every Hebrew word meaning an indiscernible number; specific words God used to uncover the magnitude of His glory were all translated in the King James Bible by the definitive English word "thousand". The word Mê`âh [a multiplier to indicate a large, indefinite number] is used twenty-eight times. It is translated every time in the King James Bible as "hundred".

The Greek word muriŏi [an indefinite number; meaning an unknowable number] is used thirty-one times in the New Testament. Every time it is translated "thousand" or "millennium" in English Bibles. The Old Testament Hebrew uses fourteen multipliers. Jesus preached to the "multitudes" [Ŏchlŏs – a very large unknown number, or throng of people]. Jesus said in John

10:10, "...I came that they might have life, and might have it <u>*abundantly*</u> [Perissos– an emphatic superlative to anything known by the human mind]."

The King James Bible and The New American Standard Bible say in I John 3:15, "Everyone who hates his brother is a murderer." *Everyone* is a multiplier that encompasses the unknowable number of the whole world. The NIV says, "Anyone", and the Scofield Bible and the Thompson Chain-Reference Bible says "whosoever". These two latter words relate that "somebody" (one or more) might be guilty of murder, whereas "everybody" encompasses the unknowable totality of the human race. God used multipliers throughout the Bible to reveal the magnitude of His Deity and power. The most significant and purposeful occasion is found in Revelation 20:1-6.

Revelation 20:1-2

"And I saw an angel coming down from heaven having the key to the abyss and a great chain in his hand. And he laid hold of the dragon, the serpent of old, which is the devil and Satan; and bound him for a [χίλια{chiliŏi} – a multiplier to designate the timeless rule of Christ. It is used thirty-two times in the New Testament. The King James Bible incorrectly translates this multiplier as "thousand or millennium".]

God uses [chiliŏi] to impress upon our minds the concept that Jesus will destroy the <u>Môw'êd</u> (worship) of Satan by the breath of His mouth at His coming from heaven and will seal him in the abyss so that the power of death cannot rule the minds of God's resurrected Saints in His timeless rule.

['Ετη{ĕtŏs} - Ĕtŏs and Ĕniautŏs are Greek words which correspond to the Hebrew word Shânâh, used 377 times to signify a relationship of the moon and the seasons of a religious lunar year as designated times for the worship of God] …. Ĕtŏs is incorrectly translated in King James English as "years of the Roman solar calendar". Ĕtŏs is not the time of an English solar year (chronological time will cease to exist at the Apokalupsis of Christ); but the timeless presence of God for the saints to worship Him face to face and finalize the complete removal of death.

God wrote *chiliŏi ĕtŏs* (timeless worship) in the context of the Apokalupsis to mark the <u>Rule of Christ</u> over all His saints in the timelessness of His presence when death will have no power until Satan is released to reveal the very last vestige of created life that will turn against Him. Death began at the Throne of God and it will end at the Rule of Christ. Death and everything under its power will be permanently removed by the Lake of Fire. Then and only then can God reveal the heavenly city He has created especially for His Spiritual children.

Another example of the scriptures distorted by the English language is the use of the word "kill" for the Hebrew and Greek words– "murder", which God uses to identify the human mind empowered by the curse of death. The scope of this error is revealed in the exegesis of Exodus 20:13.

The babbling of human languages fosters even more confusion to the Bible. People write and rewrite their own versions of the Bible to say what they want it to say. Thus, religions are created by men to give themselves the identity of spiritual rulers over all other people. Four English words were inserted in the Lord's Prayer which totally changed what Jesus said concerning the Kingdom of God.

God Reveals His Glory [Doxa – True Identity]

The entire Bible is the revelation of God's mind as He envisioned everything before He actually created it (Genesis 1:1-2). His Spirit inspires His words to be understood by the whole human race. Many people who teach and preach the Bible are not always led by the Holy Spirit and what they teach is not always a true revelation of God. They agree that the Bible is the Word of God, but they make the message of the Bible a matter of their personal interpretation (precepts). Thus, the Person of God ceases to be what He revealed Himself to be and becomes solely the perverted personal property of each person's religious beliefs (theological precepts, denominations and world religions).

An example of this is found in Ephesians 5:21-24. The American Standard Version reads "…and be *subject* [Hupŏdĕiknumi – place yourself beneath others to exhibit an inferior position] to one another in the *fear* [Phobos – reverent obedience to the authority of holiness] …of Christ. Wives; be *subject* [Hupotassō – to place oneself in a dependent position to a superior power] …to your own husbands, as to the Lord. For the husband is the head of the wife as Christ also is the head of the church; He himself being the Savior of the body. But as the church is *subject* [Hupotassō – a dependent position to a superior power] …to Christ, so also the wives to their husbands in everything."

*Notice the different Greek words and different translations of the NIV, Thompsons Chain Reference and the Greek Interlinear, as opposed to The American Standard.

"*Submit* [Hupotassomenoi – have a spirit of humility and a servant attitude to demonstrate the character of Jesus. *we receive God's salvation only by submitting our will to His] …yourselves one to another in the *fear* [Phobos – reverent obedience to the authority of holiness] …of God. Wives *submit* [Hupotasseste – Yield your will to God's appointed *spiritual principality*. Do not resist or supersede the rightful place of one who has the God given responsibility to take care of you;] …yourselves unto your own husbands, as unto the Lord. For the husband is the *head* [burden bearer; the caretaking responsibility given to Adam over all of God's creation, *including Eve*] …of the wife even as Christ is the *head* [burden bearer] … of the church; and He is the *Savior* [Sōtēr – deliverer, sustainer and preserver] …of the *body* [Sōma – Adam was created with physical life (soul) that was ruled by the heavenly power of spiritual life (pneuma). God has perfected the relationship between the man and his wife so that they are one single physical and spiritual body in submission to Christ. The righteousness of God that rules over every human being (male and female) identifies them together as the mystic body of Christ (the church).]. …Therefore, as the church is *subjected* [Hupotassetai – placed in a subordinate position to the Deity of Christ], so let the wives be to their own husbands (submissive to the spiritual principality established by God)." *see God's judgment on Eve for her transgression against creation.

The concept of subjection and submission are vital to our understanding God's revelation of salvation and of Rev. 20; God's revelation that every sanctified human being will have a heavenly existence as a spiritual being that is totally unified in submission to the iron rule of God's Throne of Life. *God's mind is the only ruling authority in His newly created heaven.

This is God's assurance that death can never exist again. Opposition to this submissive relationship of the mind to the Spirit of God to rule human life is the power of death ruling the mind.

If you claim a saving relationship with Christ by submitting your life to Him; then He will gather you together with every person of the entire history of this world of death to worship God face to face in a holy environment where death will have no power. In this rule of Jesus, you will be subjected to the iron rule of God's righteousness. At the proper time Jesus has finished His work of perfecting our obedience to His Heavenly Kingdom Rule, then death will again be given the power to reveal those who still have a mind to reject God's righteousness (Reubenites). This is God's final judgment on death. The disobedient angels, Satan, every disobedient human being, Hades and Death itself will cease to exist in the Lake of Fire. There will be no death in God's perfect heaven because there will be only *ONE MIND*. Every created being in His presence (man and angels) will be absolutely submissive to His mind; the iron rule of God's righteousness that is so Holy it cannot die.

That is why God says, "be holy as I am holy". That is the Kingdom of Life that God is perfecting in our lives in every moment of our existence in this world. If God cannot destroy His greatest enemy in this world; He loses every one of us. He is winning that battle in every person who will be subject to His authority and is submissive to obey His every command.

This word "submission" is the revelation of God's authority to govern our minds as spiritual beings and puts an end to the power of death that makes us nothing more than flesh. It identifies God's people with the humble attitude of obedience to Gods rule of righteousness for a voluntary peaceful relationship with all people. "Submit to one another out of holy reverence for Christ." "Wives submit to your husbands as to the Lord." "As the church submits to Christ, so also wives submit to your husbands in everything."

The distinction between these two words "subject and submit" are critical to our understanding of "living under the law of the flesh - death" and "living as ones free from the rule of death". The following is a simple illustration: every person driving a vehicle is subject to the laws of the civil government. The law for driving in a school zone is set at a specific maximum speed limit. If you break that law, you are subject to a fine. Because you are subject to the penalty doesn't mean that you will obey the law, especially if there is no policeman to hold you accountable to the law. People who live with this attitude of the flesh have no respect for the law and contempt for the people whose job is to enforce the law. People who submit themselves to obey the laws that govern physical life do so because it is an act of obedience to the righteousness of God. They have no fear of the laws of man because there is no penalty for obeying God's laws.

God has given us laws and every human being is subject to the authority of God to enforce those laws. In Romans 6:23, God wrote two laws in one verse. "The wages of sin is death". Every person is subject to this law because every person is ruled in the flesh by the power of death to be evil in our actions. God's second law in this verse is "But the free gift of God is timeless life in Christ Jesus our Lord." This law is the revelation of God's authority to transform us from being slaves to the rule of death; to become obedient servants to God's rule of life. The entire sixth chapter of Romans reveals that Jesus was submissive to the righteousness of God to become subject to the rule of death; so, He could destroy the power of death and free us to be alive as holy spiritual beings. God is teaching us that absolute submission to His iron rod rule of righteousness creates a holy people who rule with Him in His perfect, holy Throne of Life in heaven. The perfect example of people who will not be submissive to God is the Reubenites (Gog and Magog – people who will not submit their mind to God's rule will be thrown into the Lake of Fire.) of Revelation 20:7-9.

There are a multitude of people in the world today who claim the Bible says nothing against homosexuality, lesbianism and same sex marriage. They are ignorant to the truth of what God said in Leviticus 18:22, "You shall not lie with a male as one lies with a female; it is an abomination." And Romans 1:26-28, "For this reason God gave them over to degrading passions; for their women exchanged the natural function for that which is unnatural. And in the same way also the men abandoned the natural function of the woman and burned in their desires toward one another; men with men committing indecent acts and receiving in their own persons the due penalty of their own error. And just as they did not see fit to acknowledge God any longer, God gave them over to a depraved mind, to do those things which are not proper."

In Genesis 2:22-25, God revealed the creation of a wife for Adam. The King James translation of the word ['Ishshâh] (verses 22-23) is "woman" – simply a human female constructed from the human male. But in verse 24 this same word is translated as "wife" because of her special relationship with Adam to be fruitful and multiply. Every woman is a female but not every woman is a wife. Eve – Adam's wife was created for God's purpose of a helpmeet to him for the purpose of the reproduction of the human race. Verse 3:20, her name "Eve" means "mother of all the living".
Genesis 2:24, "For this cause a man shall *leave* ['Äzab – to be set free from the physical parent/child relationship; to fulfill God's commandment to be fruitful and populate the earth with spiritual beings created in the image of God.] ...his father and his mother and shall cleave to his wife; and they shall become *one flesh* [Bâsâr – a unique living body that is both physically and spiritually related to God for the purpose of reproduction.]" In Genesis 1:27, Adam was created a holy spiritual being in a body of flesh. Human reproduction enables God to continually create new human life that is ruled by His Spirit.
Human beings are given both physical and spiritual life by a blood relationship with their father; and a physical relationship with their mother as the one specially made to give them "birth". The sexual relationship of a man and a woman outside the purpose of marriage is adultery and fornication. The "marriage" of a man and a man, or a female and a female is impossible. It is a perversion of God's creation of the human being (*not created an animal – but a heavenly being) and will be judged accordingly by the Deity of God.

God is the only one who can give us the true understanding of scripture. The Apostle Paul spoke to this issue in I Corinthians 2:4-5, "My message and my preaching were not in persuasive words of wisdom but in demonstration of the Spirit and of power that your faith should not rest on the wisdom of men but on the power of God."
God did not reveal salvation to be a precept of a religious organization. It is only by God's conversion of a human being's mind from the power of death; to the power of life through

His own kingdom power of Life that cannot die - Christ. Because salvation is the power of God's redemptive work to save every person who will believe in Him by the power of faith; He saves every human being who will call upon Hs name. God is not an ignorant bumpkin who does not know how to speak to humanity. But as clear and simple as He has made it, the message is still received and believed by only a remnant of the human race. Jesus told people they have ears to hear words, but they do not have a mind to understand spiritual truth.

Beware of what you teach about Jesus as it is written in modern languages and beware of what human authorities teach you about Jesus. What people cling to as the truth of God is nothing more than the Demonic inspired precepts of men. Satan has been doing this since Eve.

God's revelation of His Deity in this world (Epiphaneia) is to destroy death. Jesus was God's revelation of His identity of a saving God incarnate in human flesh {His grave clothes; the sacrificial death of the soul; the life of the physical body} and He said over and over again, "look at Me, and you see God" and "look at the works I do, and you see God".

The power of God's salvation is revealed by the act of Christ to take His judgment of death upon Himself. This was revealed by God's Passover. All the people who give their life to Christ are free from God's judgment. Purified by the blood of Christ; God's free gift is His timeless spiritual life that identifies us as His heavenly children living in human flesh.

Many people today have a Bible which uses the English word "Love". These verses reveal the Person of God to be a passionate and compassionate being. The emotion of "love "is the primary driving force of God's mind for the salvation of the whole world, but it is not revealed by this English word that is defined simply as a fond, tender feeling; to like very much. This one English word is used for each of the Hebrew and Greek words which have a multiplicity of meanings which reveal the holy character of God. The result is we cannot "see Jesus" because we cannot grasp the true character of God. God is *love* [Agapē – The identity of God that defines Him as Deity. It is revealed by its actions of empowering all life with His holy identity that can do nothing but good. God's love seeks the welfare of the whole human race and sacrificially provides what is needed without recourse to self. God's Passover (His removal of His judgment of death which keeps His people – Spiritual Israel /Christians - in the grave) is the revelation of Agapē.].

I John 4:7-8

"*Beloved* [Agapētoi – one who is loved by God], …we should *love* [Agapōmen – a direction of the will to find one's joy in something (an object that is loved); used of God's love toward man and vice versa] …one another, for *love* [Agapē - a word not found in classical Greek, but only in scripture; it is God's revelation of Himself as One who makes every sacrifice to give what He deems is needed to bless the one in need. It is the essential nature of God's mind. This is falsely translated as "charity" in King James English, meaning benevolent love. One can be charitable and still give people absolutely nothing that meets their needs] …is from God; and everyone who *loves* (Agapē) is *born* [Gennaô – the impartation of God's timeless life to the believer by the Holy Spirit] …of God and knows God. The one who does not *love* (Agapōn– to possess the mind of God) … does not know God, for God is *love* [Agapē]."

God Reveals His Glory [Doxa – True Identity]

The primary law of God means believers are to *love* (Agapē) God above all and demonstrate His character of *love* (Agapētoi) toward all people, because this is the revelation of His righteousness (power of God's kingdom of Life that cannot die). God's *Love* (agape) is to be the driving force which controls the mind of a spiritual person (Spiritual Israelite/Christian). Romans 12:9, "Let *love* (agape) be without hypocrisy." All other forms of love (Philĕo, Eros) come from the human mind. Romans 12:10, "Be devoted to one another in *brotherly love* [Philadelphia – the love of Christians for each other]." The first and second laws of God say if you genuinely *love* (Agape) God, then you must also genuinely *love* (agape) your fellow man. Like the Holy Spirit revealed to Jesus' disciples in John 21; God knows the truth about what kind of love controls every person's mind.

This Greek word "*love*" (Agape) is explicit in its pertaining to God. It defines Him as the power of Deity to extend salvation to man by His grace (the power of a sound mind to act righteously). But to humanity under the curse of darkness, *love* is [Eros - the self-serving power to love self, the world, sin, the lust of the flesh, and etc.]. The human mind under this curse of death cannot begin to comprehend the concept of *love* (Agape) as the emotion of God to be a saving God. To the human mind taught to *love* (Eros) only self from birth; the concept of being loved (Agape) by God, or loving other people as yourself, or the command to love your enemies; appears to be ridiculous. Man, under the curse of death is blind to the true image of God because the identity of God as *"love"* (agape) is not known to them from their experience of living.

The only way this word "*love*" (agape) can communicate the true revelation of the person of God is by His sovereignty of revelation. This means God cannot be known as a saving God unless He reveals Himself in the power of love for the lost. When the lost man realizes God's *love* (agape) is not the hypocritical self-serving practice of people (Eros), but the fact that he is personally and sacrificially loved by God; then he can return that love.

II Corinthians 5:14-15, the power of God's *agape* is to restore man to His heavenly identity.
"For the Agape of Christ *controls* [Sunechō – to be one mind] …us, having *concluded* [Krinō – to make a judgment, a decision] …that one *died* [Apothnēskō – to make atonement for the sins of the human race] …for all, therefore all died; and He died for all, that they who *live* [Zaō – timeless spiritual life of God] …should no longer live for themselves, but for Him Who died and *rose again* [Egeirō – the resurrection of the dead from the grave to be a living being] …on their behalf.

The human mind driven by the curse of death is enamored in its shell of unbelief also because scripture is the progressive revelation of God's plan for the world.

I Corinthians 2:7, 10-13
"We speak God's wisdom in a *mystery* [Musterion – something locked up so that it cannot be fully revealed]; …the hidden wisdom which God predestined before the ages.

For to us God revealed them through the Spirit; for the Spirit searches all things, even the depths of God. For who among men knows the thoughts of a man except the spirit of the man, which is in him? Even so the thoughts of God no one knows except the Spirit of God. Now we have received, not the spirit of the world but the Spirit who is from God that we might know the things freely given to us by God, which things we also speak, not in words taught by human wisdom but in those taught by the Spirit (Phaneroō), combining spiritual thoughts with spiritual words."

Hebrews 1:1-3, discloses God's final revelation to the world; that His salvation is through Sonship. The experience of belonging to God as His Son/children is by spiritual birth. This means God's destruction of death ruling the mind, enables Him to restore (resurrect) man to His original sinless character of spiritual life as was given to Adam made in God's image as a spiritual being.

The Greek language has two words which define the single English word "son". Human beings are *born* [Ginomai– given life by means of a physical birth]. Teknon is the Greek word for the physical birth of human beings. This author is a "Teknon" of his mother and father.

In John 3, Jesus introduced the concept of another kind of birth, "…unless a man is *born* [Gennaō – to be given life] …*again* [Anōthen– {*ano* – above; and *then* - denoting from}; the complete meaning is: "given life from his Father above." Only God can recreate spiritual life in a spiritually dead human.] …he cannot *see* [Oida– to know experientially] …the Kingdom of God [Basileia – the royal dominion of God's rule of heavenly life]."

Nicodemus was dumb struck. He could not conceive of the possibility of such a thing as a human concept of birth being given twice nor could he believe it is possible for a human being to be "born – Gennaō" with God as his father. Jesus responded in verses 5-6, "…unless one is *born* (Gennaō) of *water* (God created the earth as the domain of physical man from the water of the expanse) … and the *Spirit* [Pneuma – the breath of God. Adam's body was created from the earth, but his spiritual life came from the throne of God] …he cannot enter into the Kingdom of God. That which is born of the *flesh* [Sarx–the human being corrupted by the kingdom of death] …is flesh, and that which is born of the *Spirit* [Pneuma – the breath of God] …is spirit (the identity of God on His throne)." Spiritually dead humanity must be given a new spiritual life from God. This "Teknon" writing this book has been recreated to the identity of God by the Deity Who creates all life.

John 1:1-18 reveals that the Deity of God (Jesus) who came into the world is the [Monogenēs Huios Theos – one and the same Deity of God in essence and number. Jesus cannot be a Teknon (a physical person who is given life by virtue of a human father), but *Huios* {the presence (Parousia) of the very Deity of God who gives life}; the one who gives man a spiritual birth to be related to God as "*children of God*" [Tekna Theos (John 1:12)]. The concept of a spiritual birth for man is related in Romans 8:14, "For all who are being led by the Spirit of God, these are *sons of God* [HuioiTheou – one and the same identity with God by one and the same perfect character of righteousness that cannot die; timeless spiritual life given through Jesus, the Deity of God."

John 10:30, Jesus said, "I and the *Father* [Patēr – ʾĔlôhîym: the divine essence of Deity is called Father because He is the creator of all life] …are *one* [Hen – one and the same essence of Holy Spiritual Life. Jesus is <u>Hen</u> and also <u>Heis</u>- one by numerical count. <u>God is One Single Spiritual Deity</u> – Who reveals Himself by three manifestations of His Deity to restore humanity to His Holy Image {the human race was created for this purpose} and to completely destroy the power of death.]."

In the story of Jesus' birth; Luke 2:7, "And she brought forth her *first-born son* [Prŏtotokos Huios – the pre-eminence of the human race which exists for the sole purpose to die and be raised from the dead.]. Jesus yielded His physical body to death and was raised from the dead by His own authority. *God created the human race for His purpose of destroying the power of death in every individual person and redeeming each one to His timeless Spiritual Life,

In Luke 2:11, "for today in the city of David there has been *born* [Tiktō – to bring forth Jesus, the Huios of God] …for you a Savior, who is Christ the Lord." Jesus, the {Huios – Deity} of God, was not *born* [Ginomai – a Teknon of Mary and Joseph]. The Huios - Deity of God; timeless Spiritual Life was [Tiktō–brought forth from the womb of a woman in the visible body of a human being. Adam was created a heavenly spiritual being in God's image. Christ restores us to His image with His holiness that cannot die.

Revelation 21:6-7,

"And He who sits on the throne said to me, 'It is done. I am the Alpha and Omega, the beginning and the end. I will give to the one who thirsts from the spring of the water of life without cost.

He who overcomes shall inherit these things, and I will be his God and he will be My [<u>Huios</u> – human beings recreated by God to be His heavenly children that gives off the light of God's holiness]." *Angels cannot do this.

God (Theos) is not a (trinity) of physical or spiritual gods, the Greek mythology of a multiplicity of gods. This human precept has been ingrained in the minds of men to the point that they will defend it with their lives.

<u>God {'Ĕlôhîym - Theos} is One Timeless Spiritual Deity</u>: **I AM THAT I AM** - who reveals Himself to man by three distinct and purposeful kingdom powers of His Deity to destroy the spiritual kingdom of death**.** He can do that only in His creation (earth) where the darkness of death is given its power over man and man has no knowledge of Him.

<u>'Ĕlôhîym is Omnipotent</u> – The infinite power of all life. This power reveals His authority of Deity to create and destroy spiritual and physical life in heaven and the earth as the ruling creator on His Throne of Life. This power of Deity created man a Spiritual Being in His Image; humanity without the light that shines in heaven. He issued the command; Matthew 23:9, "Do not call any man on earth your Father; for One is your Creator, He who is in heaven."

God created man in the weakness of a physical body that would succumb to the power of death. He gave that body a soul, which is the life that animates the body in physical action. The body and the soul perish in the grave. But He gave man His Spirit of Life that animates his mind to produce the character of God. It is this <u>Spirit</u> that is restored to Life as His timeless heavenly children which will live in His heavenly presence (not as His shadow, but the light of His Holiness).

Every physical man is born a body, soul and Spirit. He is not three separate beings. Thank God for that; and thank Him also for the revelation that God is One Spiritual Deity of infinite holiness and love to redeem humanity from death to His Holy Spiritual Life

'Ĕlôhîym is Omnipresent – The power of Deity to reveal Himself as a Timeless Spiritual Being present in heaven <u>and</u> in His creation outside of heaven. His Omnipresence reveals His authority of Deity to destroy the power of death ruling in the angels in heaven <u>and</u> in His creation of man under His judgment of death. He identifies His Deity in the <u>*form*</u> [morph– appearance of God without His heavenly light.] …of man as the [Huios Theos – One and the same identity of 'Ĕlôhîym by His sinless character and Omnipotent authority to destroy the power of death to hold man in the grave (Christ – Messiah).

He did this because as the ruling authority of His Throne of Life; He had removed death from His heavenly presence to be destroyed only where He had given it authority to rule. By His Deity as the Christ, He redeemed man to be the Spiritual Children of God [His temple; His dwelling place; His image.]. He will reveal His Deity of the Christ a second time by His appearance from heaven to bring about the complete destruction of death and the creation of a heavenly dwelling especially prepared for His children.

'Ĕlôhîym is also Omniscient – The infinite knowledge of all things in heaven and in His creation. Sinful man cannot know the Holy God of heaven unless He reveals Himself to the mind of man by the movement of His Spirit**.** His Spirit reveals His power of salvation is in His <u>*presence*</u> [Parousia – the power of His Deity; Christ doing the work that only God can do].

I Corinthians 2

"And when I (the Apostle Paul) came to you brethren, I did not come with superiority of <u>*speech*</u> [Logos – the spoken revelation of human intelligence.] …or of <u>*wisdom*</u> [Sŏphia – the highest intelligence of man] …proclaiming to you the <u>*testimony*</u> [Marturiŏn – the truth that God has made evident] …of God; for I determined to know nothing except Jesus Christ and Him crucified. And I was with you in weakness and in fear and in much trembling.

And my <u>*message*</u> [Lŏgŏs–the expression of God's mind; the revelation of Divine Truth] …and my <u>*preaching*</u> [Kērugma – as a verb; it means the act of proclaiming the gospel of salvation. As a noun; it means the revelation of the substance of the gospel of salvation] …were not in persuasive <u>*words of wisdom*</u> [Logos Sŏphia – highest intelligence of man] …but in demonstration of the <u>*Spirit*</u> [Pnĕuma – the strength, vigor and force of God's mind to move upon the human mind] …and of <u>*power*</u> [Dunamis – the miraculous authority of Deity to speak to the mind of man], …that your <u>*faith*</u> [Pistis – conviction of the human mind to the revealed truth of God] …should not rest on the wisdom of <u>*men*</u> [Anthrŏpŏs – anything of human origin] …but on the power of <u>*God*</u> [Thĕŏs – Greek word for the one true Deity. It is the same as the Hebrew word; 'Ĕlôhîym].

Yet we do speak wisdom among those who are <u>*mature*</u> [Tĕlĕiŏs–the mental capacity, integrity and virtue of man brought to completion as it was intended by his creation of a spiritual being in God's image]; …a wisdom, however, not of this age, nor of the rulers of this age who <u>*are passing away*</u> [Katargĕō – entirely useless]; …but we speak God's wisdom in a <u>*mystery*</u> [Mustēriŏn – That which can be made known only by divine revelation and is made known in a manner and at a time appointed by God, and only to those who are illumined by His Spirit.], …the hidden wisdom which God <u>*predestined*</u> [Prŏŏrizō – to limit to a fore ordained time; to mark out beforehand] …before the *ages* [Aiōn – before the creation of time; in this present context it identifies the timeless Messianic rule of Christ in this present existence of mortal man and beyond it in His timeless rule of heaven] …to our *glory* [Dōxa – the nature and acts of Christ to reveal His true identity as the Creator of His spiritual children]; …the wisdom which none of the rulers of this age has understood; for if they had understood it they would not have crucified the Lord of glory; but just as it is written, 'Things Which Eye Has Not Seen And Ear Has Not Heard, And Which Have Not Entered The Heart Of Man, All That God Has Prepared For Those Who Love Him.' For to us God revealed them through the Spirit; for the Spirit searches all things, even the depths of God.

For whom among men *knows* [Ĕidō – to understand by the perception of the mind] …the thoughts of a man except the spirit (the activity of the mind for thought) of the man, which is in him? Even so the thoughts of God (wisdom of Deity) no one knows except the Spirit of God.

Now we have received not the spirit of the world (the wisdom of man), but the Spirit *Who is God*, that we might know the things *freely given* [Charizŏmia – to bestow a favor unconditionally; for God it is to remove His judgment of death and replace it with His gift of life.] …to us by God, which things we also speak, not in words taught by human wisdom, but in those taught by the Spirit, *combining* [Sugkrinō – to judge one thing by its connection to another] …spiritual thoughts (the Mind of Deity) with spiritual works (the actions of Deity).

But a *natural* [Psuchikŏs – a person who yields everything to the human reasonings of the soul (lives purely as a physical being), never thinking of his need for the higher power of God] …man does not accept the things of the Spirit of God; for they are *foolishness* [Mōria – absurdity; moronic] …to him, and he cannot understand them, because they are *spiritually* [Pněumatikōs – non-physical; pertaining to Deity] …evaluated as a great treasure.

But he who is *spiritual* [Pněumatikŏs – non-physical; regenerated to the Spiritual life of God] …treasures all things, yet he himself is treasured by no man. For who has known the *mind* [Nŏus – the power of Devine righteousness revealed by His Holiness] …of The *Lord* [Kuriŏs – the supreme authority of Deity that cannot die] …that we should instruct Him? But we have the *mind of Christ* [Christŏs – the Deity of the "Nŏus- Temple of God" in human form; anointed for the removal of His judgment of death on the human race to be the Spiritual Children of God.]."

God's first appearance in human form was His authority of Deity to redeem man to spiritual life. His continual presence in human life is the Holy Spirit who illuminates Christ in the minds of men and calls them to Him for a conversion of their minds. The entire book of I John reveals the intensity of this spiritual battle between God and Satan for the spiritual life of every human being. It reveals the personal involvement of God's spiritual children in this battle.

*Note to the reader of this book. God's purpose for it is to give you a true understanding of Who He is; who you are; and who He created you to be. The structure of this book is meant to involve your mind as a witness to God's revelation of His mind to completely destroy the power of death. You are a spectator to His working in the minds of people through the ages to create a personal, saving relationship with Him; and you will witness the interaction of God on His Kingdom Throne of Life in heaven with the Christ and the Holy Spirit on earth.

You will also see the majority of the human race arguing with Him and hating Him to the point of trying to kill him. You will see the deceptive power of Satan upon the human mind for every person to be his/her own god. They will all be without excuse on judgment day because they are guilty of committing the unpardonable sin of rejecting the revelation of Jesus the Christ; given by the Holy Spirit.

    I pray that you will come to the realization that God loves you beyond any comprehension of your mind and is speaking to you - personally; that He can transform your Spirit from death to His timeless life.

Chapter 1

GOD'S REVELATION OF HIS KINGDOM RULE

BY GOD'S NAME

Genesis 1:1
"In the beginning *God* [`Ĕlôhîym] **created** the heavens and the earth."

Genesis is a Hebrew word meaning the origin of the generations of a lineage. The book of Genesis reveals the timeless Deity of God is the creator of all life in heaven and the earth; and it is of vital importance because it reveals Him to be the origin of the generations of man created in His image (His lineage). Every verse in the Bible was written for God's purpose of unveiling His identity to man. No man can know the truth about his own life until he can know the truth about the governing power of all life. No man can know that truth unless God reveals it to him.

The context of God's name in Genesis 1:1, reveals Him to be the Sovereign Spiritual Deity whose existence is purely the power of Timeless Life that cannot die. Three words in verse one is of vital importance to God for the purpose of His self-revelation. The word "beginning" is the declaration that God existed as the determinative Supreme Being before He had any use for time. Revelation 1:8, "I am the Alpha and the Omega, says the Lord God, who is and who was and who is to come, the Almighty." This sovereignty of existence was revealed to Moses when He asked for the name of the God of Israel's fathers; Exodus 3:14, "And God said to Moses, 'I AM WHO I AM`; and He said, 'Thus you shall say to the sons of Israel, I AM has sent me to you`."

The word "created" reveals God to be the life-giver; the only one who animates all life in heaven and all-natural life of our creation. Revelation 4:11, "You are worthy, our Lord and God to receive glory and honor and power, for you *created* [Kitzō – to produce from nothing] ... all things, and by your will they were created and have their existence." God shaped His message to the world through Jesus, the Christ (for man to see God) and designed the creation of a spiritual people of the whole world in His image; Spiritual Israelites / Christians; true descendants of Abraham, Isaac and Jacob/Israel. God does not simply create things; but everything created or destroyed is for the purpose of knowing His identity as the only kingdom power of life that cannot die.

The first two verses of Genesis reveal God to be the architect or designer of a creation which reveals His identity (glorifies Him) in its most minute details. If everything we are to know about the Deity of God is revealed simply by His actions of creating things, then the Bible is nothing more than God's autobiography. The truth is**:** The Bible is the voice of the Living God empowered to reveal His *Glory* [Doxa – true identity of Deity] to the human mind. Why?

Because the genesis of God reveals Him to be the Father (creator) of timeless life he loves the most: man.

It is God's name itself that is the focal point of these verses and it is the focal point of the entire Bible. The name is `*Ĕlôhîym* [This is a plural masculine noun which is used both as singular and plural. Its sole meaning is the divine ruler, the sovereign judge]. `Ĕlôhîym usually takes a singular verb; in this case, created. There is no implication in this plural noun to identify God as a multiplicity of beings. He is not a physical being, but one Spiritual Being Who reveals Himself by His planned purpose to destroy the kingdom of death and restore humanity to its created purpose as Children of God. `Ĕlôhîym is translated in the Greek Septuagint as "Theos – One God". The plural of Theos is "theon – the name for pagan gods". The singular of `Ĕlôhîym is `Ĕlôwahh – pagan god.

God's purpose in the use of this name is to enforce upon the human mind His identify as the singular (unique), supreme authoritative ruling power of Life. There is no kingdom power or being in heaven or in the created universe which can stand in God's place or sit on His Throne of Life. *(See the first article of God's Constitution in Exodus 20.) Absolutely everything is under His sole authority and the judgments of His throne will be obeyed. If God commands something to exist that does not exist; then it comes into existence. At the time God is finished with His creation; at His command it will cease to exist as if it never existed. By His command, spiritually dead humanity is restored to the authority of His kingdom of Life because He created it to be so.

Hebrews 1:8-9, the defining power of God's Throne of Life is *righteousness* [Dikaiosunē – God's own conformity to the highest standard of justice. It is the state of purity commanded by God to withstand His test of judgment]. This means that it is absolutely impossible for there to be the minutest trace of evil in God's person. He is the epitome of holiness; the power of Life that cannot die. This is what separates God from all other life. If there is even that minutest trace of evil in God, then He would be the kingdom power of death. Death is anti-life. It is a power that destroys everything it controls. God is the power for Timeless Life, which is His supreme power over death.

God gave His judgment that man was created with His gift of life. God gave a righteous judgment; Romans 3:23, "All have sinned and fall short of the *glory of God* [Doxa – recognition of the true identity of God]." God gave another righteous judgment; Romans 6:23, "For the wages of sin is death, but the free gift of God is timeless life in Christ Jesus our Lord." God gave another righteous judgment; Romans 4:3, "For what does the Scripture say? Abraham believed God and it was reckoned to him as righteousness."

God's righteous judgment was that Abraham was separated from the authority of His throne of Life because of Abraham's obedience to the power of death. Abraham obeyed the authority of God's righteous command to believe in Him; and by God's righteous judgment, Abraham was restored to God's righteousness (God's authority of Timeless Life).

Abraham was the first man in the genealogy of Noah in which God reveals His creation of a holy, sanctified people He creates in His image (Spiritual Israelites / Christians; Descendants of Jacob - Israel). Every single human being can be redeemed from the curse of death and be restored to Spiritual Life, but only because of the righteous justice of `Ĕlôhîym. Every human being who obeys His command to believe {Faith} in Him is transformed to His heavenly identity by His command.

Every word of the Bible is the righteous judgment of God's justice to reveal His glory and is to be believed and obeyed. His judgment is decreed in Psalm 111:10, "The *fear* [Yir`âh – Holy reverence] …of the Lord is the *beginning* [Rê`shîyth – foundation] …of *wisdom* [Chokmâh – the full range of human knowledge of God] …A *good* [Tôwb – beneficial, joyful, fruitful] …understanding have all those who *do* [`Âsâh – ethical obligation to obey; to fully accomplish] …His commandments; His *praise* [T^ehillâh – a technical musical term for a song which exalts God] …is timeless."

This name `ĔLÔHÎYM is the *glory* [Doxa - true identity of God]. Before God created anything at all, His righteous judgment decreed that everything is accountable to Him. He is the judge of the very thoughts of your mind. All other kingdoms are devised by the mind of Satan and fallen man which are not real kingdoms at all. Every angel or human being who rejects His authority will submit to it at His designated time of judgment. Be sure of this fact; everything will submit to His supreme power of Life at its designated time.

`Ělōhîym is the embodiment of Spiritual Life. He, alone, has the total knowledge of all things and is singularly responsible for the complete removal of death. He accomplished this great feat by His own Deity {Christ/Huios} in the place He created for death to rule. No created life in any form can rule in His place.

John 1:1-4

"In the *beginning* [Archē - the first and only ruling power in existence] …was the *Word* [Logos – intelligence of God's mind (truth) that could be understood by the human mind] …and the Word (Jesus) was with God, and the Word was God. He was in the beginning with God. All things came into being by Him, and apart from Him nothing came into being that has come into being. In Him was life, and the life {Christ – the shining light of the holiness of God} was the light of men."

John 1:14

"And the *Word* [Logos – the spoken revelation of the mind of God to man for his redemption] became flesh – Jesus the Christ; and He dwelt among us and we beheld His glory; true identity of the only One brought forth from the Deity of God, full of grace and truth."

John 3:16

"For God so loved the world that He gave His only {begotten - visible form} [Huios– Christ; one and the same Deity of God anointed to destroy the kingdom rule of death] …that whoever believes in Him should not perish but have timeless life."

John 3:36

"He who believes in the {Huios - Christ} has timeless life; but he who does not obey the {Huios – Christ} shall not see life, but the wrath of God abides on him."

The entire Bible is the progressive revelation of `Ělōhîym's Kingdom Rule of Life over everything that exists. His righteous judgment predetermined that death would rule over the created natural order of man. He also predetermined to restore lost humanity to His kingdom rule by the authority of His own (Parousia – presence of His Deity); to bring death and everything under its domain to its permanent end in the lake of fire; and to create a spiritual domain where it is absolutely impossible for death to ever exist again. That timeless day of rest will come when the last individual person of the human race is purified by His holiness. God made this righteous judgment before He actually created anything, and it will be exactly as He has decreed.

The Bible is `Ĕlôhîym's voice to every individual human being. It is His assurance that man is not ignorant of the judgments of His kingdom rule of life, because it is through man restored to spiritual life in His Image that He achieves His purpose of timeless life of absolute purity. What God designed in His mind in Genesis 1:1-2, is completed in Revelation 21-22 when His Mind will be the sole ruling power over all created life. There is no death in the Deity of God.

BY THE CREATION OF TIME

Genesis 1:1

"In the *beginning* [Rê'shîyth – the first in place, time, order, or rank; the beginning of a fixed point of time; the initial act of creating time] …`Ĕlôhîym created the heavens and the earth".

An as yet undisclosed power (Death) had come into existence in God's dwelling place. Beginning is God's announcement of His predetermined purpose to create time as the confine outside of the timelessness of heaven for the total and complete destruction of this kingdom power. The creation of time means that everything in heaven and everything in His creation is under God's authority to reveal His sovereignty of life and it is the first and primary revelation of His mind. There are a number of Hebrew words for time and they all reveal God as the rule of rightness in His creation to bless humanity as spiritual life under His authority.

Ecclesiastes 3:1

"There is an *appointed time* [Z^{e}man – to be determined, to be fixed, a prescribed time for occurrence] …for everything. And there is a *time* ['Êth– a feminine singular noun derived from Ad, meaning the right time, the proper time for occurrence. It describes three principal situations: 1) regular events, 2) the exact time for an unrecurring event, and 3) a set time which demands God's presence] …for every *event* [Chêphets – pleasure, delight, wish, desire] …under heaven."

Z^{e}man is the sovereign judgment of God that He has created humanity for the purpose of bringing glory to Himself. God had an appointed time to meet this author on a Dallas freeway in March 1969. His purpose was to make his lost spiritual condition known to him. Z^{e}man is the appointed time that God commissioned him for every work of his ministry. It was His appointed time that He would again speak to him for the purpose of changing the direction of his life, from the pastoral ministry to a writer. In Jeremiah 29:1-11, God had an appointed time to place believing Israel in Babylon to change the mindset of its rulers. Z^eman is the revelation of God which gives us assurance that our lives are not guided by fate, but the benevolent Will of our creator.

‘Êth is the righteous judgment of God that every moment of our time is His time. It gives God joy to do exactly what needs to be done to take care of us at the precise moment it is needed. Psalm 31:14-15, King David said, "Because you are my God, my *times*(‘êth) are in your hand." At the precise moment this author was in mortal danger caused by civil wars, he knew God's power of Life was there to deliver him. One time was most memorable; he was at a point of exhaustion from Satan's relentless warfare. For the twinkling of an eye, he stood in the presence of God. It was a white light of pure holiness and love beyond any human comparison or ability to describe. Since that moment he has never again been controlled by Satan's power of fear. Whatever the situation of the moment; God's creation of ‘êth assures us that it is His will for us to live in the perfect peace of His care.

Hosea 10:12
"Sow with a view to righteousness, reap in accordance with kindness; break up your fallow ground, for it is *time* (‘êth) to seek the Lord until He comes to rain righteousness on you."

God predetermined that a specific time is given for us to make a judgment on our unbelief. It is the point in which we choose Life. This point of time in which we are saved is a gift from God's love because it is what we need and is the reason He created us. He designed us for this purpose and this moment of birth into His timeless kingdom of Life, and all of heaven rejoices over it.

II Corinthians 6:2
"For God says, 'at the *acceptable time* [Dektos – a verbal adjective with the meaning of the perfect participle, passive of dechomai; to accept or decide favorably, to make a favorable decision of the will. It is used to point us to the sacrifice of Christ to specify it as the object of divine approval and our approval. It is used with elements of time such as Kairos (necessity of the task at hand) and Ĕniautŏs (the time of worship which God has pleasure in, which He Himself has chosen)]…I listened to you, and on the *day* [Hēmera – existence of God's presence for His judgment of timeless life as opposed to existence in spiritual darkness; the coming of Christ as the timeless presence of life]…of *salvation* [Sōtēria – deliverance, preservation]…I *helped* [Bŏēthĕō – to give aid, relief from a burden]…you`; behold, now is the *acceptable time* [Euprosdektos – God's designated opportunity to accept the affirmation of belief; the time for His grace to save; the positive necessity of the task at hand]…behold, now is the day of salvation."

Dektos is the righteous judgment of God for man to be saved by the action of his own free will. Dektos is the judgment of God for His Spirit to bring us to make a "faith" decision. Faith is the only act of righteousness on our part that is acceptable to the Kingdom of Righteousness; for transforming us from death to Life. Faith is our unshakable knowledge of God as the perfect judge of righteousness to save. The criterion for placing our faith in Him is the truth of God's own sacrifice (the Messiah) to atone for our sins. God calls His Kingdom of Salvation the "Kingdom of David" because he was a man of righteousness, a man after God's own heart. David is the example of faith that God expects of every person to be saved. Romans 10:9-11, "…if you confess with your mouth Jesus as Lord and believe in your heart that God raised Him from the dead, you shall be saved; for with the heart man believes, resulting in righteousness, and with the mouth he confesses, resulting in salvation. For the Scripture says, 'Whoever Believes In Him Will Not Be Disappointed`."

<u>Kairos</u> is used with Dektos to denote God's own designated objective or action in response to our decision of faith. His predetermined judgment before He created anything is that the human being will be converted from death to life by His power of Life. (<u>Dektos</u>–the time He gives us the required knowledge of Himself which will bring us to believe in Him and turn away from death), and (<u>Kairos</u> - His predetermined immediate response to our faith to restore us to His Kingdom of Life**)**.

Kairos declares the absolute authority of God's heavenly actions in this world of man to destroy the power which separates all life from Him. God entered the realm of *time* (<u>Chronos</u>) in fulfillment of His promise to be the Messiah. Galatians 4:4, "But when the *fullness* [<u>Plērōma</u> – the completion of a particular time before ordained and appointed] …of the *time* (<u>Kairos</u>) came, God sent forth His {<u>Huios</u> – <u>Christ</u>}, brought forth of a woman, born under the Law." Before God created anything (Genesis 1:1), His judgment of time on the power of death had declared His Will to literally bring it to pass. The Christ came at the specific *appointed time* (Z^eman) God predetermined. It was the only time in the history of the world which afforded Him the ability to literally destroy death's power of separation by submitting to it Himself. The Christ, being the revelation of heavenly Deity abiding in human flesh; *resurrected* (restored) Himself to His Deity of `Ĕlôhîym that was His before all things were created in heaven. The righteous judgment of His timeless Kingdom of Life demanded it. It revealed His absolute power over death that began in heaven.

Ephesians 1:1-8
 "Paul, an *apostle* [<u>Apostolos</u> – An ambassador of God; the office instituted by Christ to be a witness of Him before the whole world.] …of Christ Jesus by the *will* [<u>Thelêma</u> – The suffix {-ma} indicates something that is the result of the will. God's Will is not a demand but an expression or inclination of pleasure towards the object which is liked; that which pleases and creates joy. It signifies God's gracious disposition towards something.] …of God, to the *saints* [<u>Hagios</u> – Holy, set apart to the service of Deity; sharing in God's purity and abstaining from earth's defilement.] …who are at Ephesus, and who are *faithful* [<u>Pistos</u> – trustworthy, steadfast to one's word of promise] …in Christ Jesus:
 Grace to you and *peace* [<u>Eirēnē</u> – the absence or end of strife; a state of untroubled, undisturbed well-being; the new relationship between man and God brought about by the atonement for sin.] …from God our Creator – the Divine Life; Father of man by creation and new spiritual birth.] …and the Lord Jesus *Christ* [<u>Christos</u> - The proper name for the anointed High Priest of God.]

Blessed [Eulogētnos – to speak well of God {to eulogize God}] …be the God Who has blessed us with every *spiritual* [Pneumatikos – man restored to spiritual life by the authority of God] …*blessing* [Eulogia – to declare as indwelt by God and is thereby fully satisfied {God's eulogy of man}] …in the heavenly places in Christ,

just as He chose us in Him before the foundation of the world that we should be holy and *blameless* [Amōmos – a technical word to legally designate the total absence of internal blemish] …before Him.

In love He *predestined* [Proorizō–to determine or decree beforehand {in this verse the placing of those who are born of God into their proper position before Him},] …us to *adoption as sons* [Huithe- sia – the greatness of divine love to make a stranger, such as a sinner to be a real son of God by spiritual birth.] …through Jesus Christ to Himself, according to the kind intention of His will,

to the *glory* [Doxa – to recognize the true identity of God] …of His *grace* [Charis – the absolute freeness of the loving-kindness of God to man] …which He *freely bestowed on* [Charitoō - to be acceptable, highly favored to receive His love] …us in the *Beloved* [Agapaō - indicates the specific direction of the will to find one's love in the person of God].

In Him we have *redemption* [Apolutrōsis – God paid the ransom price to deliver man from the curse of death] …through His *blood* [Haima – blood is the substantial basis of life. Christ sacrificed His blood {God's Passover} as a covering for His covenant of salvation by the forgiveness of sin.] …the *forgiveness* [Aphesis – the putting away of sin and the deliverance of the sinner from its power] …of our *trespasses* [Paraptōma – this word is used of both great and serious guilt, and generally of all sin, unknown and unintentional] …according to the riches of His grace which He lavished upon us."

Acts 1:7

"It is not for you to know *times* [Chronos – the succession or measurement of moments, the length of time] …or *epochs* (Kairos) which the Father has fixed by His own authority."

Chronos is God's allotted measurement of the rule of death revealed by the history of man under its curse. God's judgment on the kingdom of death is that it will not have a permanent existence like His own kingdom rule of life. Both its beginning and its end are under His authority. Death can rule only in the darkness of the expanse and only over the physical life of creation. Chronos began at the instant Adam (God's decision maker on earth) yielded his mind to the satanic lie. It is in the confines of chronos that `Ĕlôhîym reveals Himself to be a saving God by His grace. Our salvation is the predetermined judgment of God; that man be restored to a spiritual life of righteousness that is permanent (like God; it is timeless, outside the realm of time). Chronos will cease to exist when Christ reveals Himself from heaven (the Apokalupsis) to rule over immortal man (humanity not ruled by death). It will have served its purpose when God no longer has a use for creation as the place of death.

Daniel 12:5-7

"Then I, Daniel, looked and behold, two others were standing, one on this bank of the river and the other on that bank of the river. And one said to the man dressed in linen, who was above the waters of the river, 'How long will it be until the end of these *wonders* [Pele`– the extraordinary aspects of how God deals with His people]? ...And I heard the man dressed in linen (silk), who was above the waters of the river, as he raised his right hand and his left toward heaven, and swore by Him who is timeless life that it would be for a *time* [Môw`êd – the festive gathering of a religious assembly; a designated gathering of people for worship]...*time* [Môw`êd]...and *half a time* [P^{e}lag – Aramaic for dividing something in half], ... and as soon as they finish shattering the power of the holy people, all these events will be *completed* [Kâlâh – accomplished]."

Môw'êd is God's predestinated time to worship. The first Môw'êd is recorded in Genesis 1:14, when God declared that man would worship Him for the creation of the luminaries. Môw'êd is also God's judgment for Satan's rule over the human race in its corrupted state. This last Môw'êd of Satan is the designated *last days* [Eschatos –the time when the development of God's plan of salvation is brought to a close.] It is the gathering of lost humanity to worship him as a "god". God designated this *time* [Z^{e}man] to identify all those who reject the rule of God; to identify them with the lawless character of death. This Môw'êd will end with the abomination of desolation; the designated time God gives Satan to rule in the human heart [the temple of God] that rightly belongs to God. This rule of death will completely destroy the human race. God will end it {P^{e}lag} like He did in the day of Noah, when only a remnant is left.

The authority God gives to Satan is to bring the power of death (tribulation) upon the human race. This is God's final effort to save those who will be saved; to identify the sheep by the character of God and to identify the goats by the character of death. Those who cling to Christ, glorify Him by their faith. Many of them will glorify God as martyrs (witnesses) to His kingdom of life. The Môw`êd of Satan will be completely destroyed by the greater power of God's glory; the light of God's presence (Revelation 19: the Apokalupsis of the Christ). This begins the Môw'êd of Jesus` rule over His sinless people (I Corinthians 15).

The Môw`êd of Christ. The predetermined Rule of Christ will be the timelessness of God as it was before the *beginning* [Rê`shîyth – the initial act of creating time]. The purpose of the Rule of Christ will be for God's final judgment on death. Death began in the presence of God's heavenly rule; it will make its final claim upon man in the presence of Christ's rule. After the Great White Throne Judgment, God will then throw Death, Hades, and all unsaved humanity into the lake of fire (Revelation 20). This is God's final act of cleansing heaven and earth of any and all life that could possibly turn away from Him again. Then and only then, can God create the new and perfectly holy heaven of Revelation 21-22.

God's creation was formed in His timelessness as it is in heaven. His creations of time are His revelations of His absolute control over everything that transpires within the confines of the existence of man. The same God Who ruled on His throne of Life before He created time; rules over everything He created for the purpose of totally destroying the existence of death; and His timelessness will continue to rule after He has finished with time.

BY THE NECESSITY FOR CREATION

Genesis 1:1-2
"In the beginning `Ĕlôhîym created the heavens and the earth. And the earth was formless and void, and darkness was over the surface of the deep; and the Spirit of `Ĕlôhîym was moving over the surface of the waters."

Created [Bârâ` – to form, to make, to produce, to bring an object into existence out of nothing]. This word is the revelation of God that it is impossible for anything physical or spiritual to exist that He does not make. The physical creation cannot make itself, nor can any kind of life evolve from what does or does not exist. Absolutely everything was created to perfection (sinless) in the mind of `Ĕlôhîym; for the purpose of destroying the curse of death.

Heavens [Shâmayin – noun which means: (1) to be lofty (sky above the earth); and (2) the abode of God. This second connotation has no limits; it is infinity. It magnifies the glory of God as the over-whelming power of rightness and goodness. This is the realm of spiritual life; of God and angels; of God as light and pure holiness]. God's abode is not a physical location; it is the timeless infinity of His omnipresent Holiness.

It was in the presence of God's infinite holiness that death was born in the mind of Lucifer. The heavens in this verse are both the physical expanse (space/sky) which God created to contain the darkness of death for the purpose of destroying it, and the spiritual heaven of God's holiness. God has the full authority to exercise the same power of His will in the glory of His throne and in the unholy darkness of the expanse. But the kingdom rule of death has no authority to exercise its power anywhere but in the darkness of the expanse and this only when God allows it. Death had no authority to rule in creation until Adam turned his face away from God. God's authority was given to Adam as a heavenly decision maker; and he made the choice for death to rule when he ate the fruit of the Tree of The Knowledge of Good and Evil.

Earth [`Erets– an often-used noun which specifically means the physical planet of earth as the abode of lost humanity.] It is used to contrast and emphasize the ruling authority of the unholy over the holy. This unholy place will cease to exist at the Apokalupsis of Christ.

Was [Hâyâh – to exist, to become, to happen; what was unseen because it existed only in God's mind until His design would become completely finished]. What God designed in His mind could only exist by His power to create from nothing.

Formless and Void [Tôhûw – emptiness, unreality, absolutely nothing what-so-ever]. Before God began the creation of physical life, the new heaven and earth existed only in the sovereignty of His mind. What He sees is not just what He will make, but its purpose and the details of every life form in His creation from beginning to end.

Darkness [Chôshek – obscurity, misery, falsehood; a state which is diametrically opposite of light. It refers many times to death and the darkness of the grave]. The creation of a new heaven and the earth reveal they both exist in God's mind for His purpose.

The creation of a new heaven reveals the abode of God would again be holy, for He separated it from the ungodliness of darkness which He contained in the expanse. God rules over the holiness of His abode and over the darkness contained in the expanse.

The new heaven of God's purified holiness is His designated authority for the spiritual life of His throne to be the ruling power over the authority of the darkness as well. What death destroys God makes new. What God makes new will never again be subject to death's power.

Before God actually created anything, He reveals that the totality of everything He would actually create is under the timeless rule of His kingdom power of rightness and absolutely nothing else. Death has no power in the timeless rule of God; only in the physical confines of time (Chronos) created for that purpose. Darkness can rule only when and where God permits.

"Darkness was over the surface of the _deep_ [T^ehôwm or T^ehôm – an abyss; a surging mass of deep water as the ocean; an inexhaustible subterranean water supply]; …and the _Spirit_ [Rûwach – the creative Word of God; the air put in motion by the divine breath of God] …was moving over the surface of the _waters_ [Mayim – the original basic substance for physical life to exist in the expanse]."

God's revelation of His mind to envision creation from beginning to end reveals that it is in the place of darkness (the expanse) where He would destroy death by entering into it Himself. The battle for the supremacy of spiritual life over death could not be fought in the purity of heaven. The total destruction of death could only take place in the arena where it would be given domination to destroy spiritual life.

This power of darkness is so strong that man under its power rejects even the concept of a heavenly God such as `Ĕlôhîym. It is where man is totally blind to the truth of God that he can be saved by the spiritual power of faith in the light that God shines upon him. It is where `Ĕlôhîym is not known that His Spirit would unveil Him as the redeemer; the Christ, the purifying power of heaven; the fountain of _living water_ [Châyâh – to exist, to make alive, the source of life]. *The Living Bread of the Lord's Prayer is Gods never ending presence to give us Life.

I John 5:6
"And who is the one who over-comes the world, but he who believes that Jesus is the [Huios – Christ; the Deity of God Who gives Life] …of God? This is the one who came by water (physically) and the blood (sacrifice of Jesus Christ); not with the water only, but with the water and with the blood."

John 3:5-6
"Jesus answered, 'Truly, truly, I say to you, unless one is _born_ [Gennaō– given physical life by God] …of _water_ [Hudôr – the essential element of physical life] …and the _Spirit_ [Pneuma – breath of God] …he cannot enter into the kingdom of God. That which is born (given life) of the flesh is flesh and that which is born (given new spiritual life by the Deity of heaven) is timeless spiritual life of God`.'"

Revelation 21:6
"And He said to me, 'It is done. I am the alpha and the omega, the beginning and the end. I will give to the one who thirsts from the _spring_ [Pēgē – fountain; an inexhaustible source of life] …of the _water_ [Hudôr] of _life_ [Zōe – Spiritual life of God] …without cost`.'"

Revelation 22:1,
"And He showed me a river of the water of Life, clear as crystal, coming from the throne of God and of the Lamb."

Mark 1:9-11
"And it came about in those days that Jesus came from Nazareth in Galilee and was *baptized* [Baptizō – to immerse or submerge in water; symbolic act of total identification with life from God] …by John in the Jordan. And immediately coming up out of the water, He saw the heavens opening and the Spirit like a dove descending upon Him; and a voice came out of the heavens: 'You are My Beloved Huios (God's Deity), in You I am well-pleased`.'"

The inexhaustible water of heaven in this verse (Genesis 1:2) is God's revelation that He Is Life and His life would be poured out upon humanity by the sacrifice of His blood {Luke 22:20, "And in the same way (as the bread) He took the cup after they had eaten, saying, 'This cup which is poured out for you is the new *covenant* [Diathēkē – the disposition a person makes of his property in prospect of death; God's witness that *His Timeless Life* would be dispensed to His children] …in My blood`.'"

Leviticus 17:11, "For the *life* [Nephesh – Man is not merely a physical being like animals. He has a spirit which was made in the image of God and is the object of God's love.] …of the *flesh* [Bâsâr – created physical life that is the habitation of God] …is in the blood, and I have given it to you on the altar to *make atonement* [Kâphar – to cover, to expiate, to make reconciliation, to cancel, forgive] …for your souls (*sins of the body*); for it is the blood by reason of the life that makes atonement."

BY THE SEVEN REVELATIONS OF SANCTIFIED LIFE

THE FIRST REVELATION

Genesis 1:3-5
"Then God said, 'Let there be light`; and there was light. And God saw that the light was good; and God separated the light from the darkness. And God called the light day, and the darkness He called night. And there was evening and there was morning, one day."

Let there be [Hâyâh – to breathe, to exist. It refers to the timelessness of God; His ever-present existence as the kingdom rule of Life]. God's revelation of Himself is His identity as a saving God (light). This word is His judgment that Life will be the superior ruling power in His new creation in contrast to the ruling power of death. He must make it clear that death is the most powerful ruling force outside of Himself. This force of death is clearly revealed by its authority over Lucifer, the holiest of all the angels in heaven; and it would be given authority to put Christ in the grave. Jesus surrendered Himself (soul; the life of the body) to this authority for the death of the grave; but the righteous judgment of God would resurrect Him (restore Him to the glory of His identity as the ruler of spiritual life).

This word declares God's revelation that spiritual life created in His image (MAN) will be subject to the death of the grave; but His judgment is to resurrect him (restore man to his original relationship with God) by the power of Jesus' name; the permanent timelessness of His own kingdom rule of timeless life. Jesus' resurrection destroyed the power of death to permanently keep man in the grave.

Light [`Ôwr – a masculine noun meaning enlightenment; the glory of God shining in the darkness. The first *light* (morning) that dispels the darkness of death is the good news of God's salvation. It is spiritual life that is the shining glory of heaven and it is to be the dominate force in human existence.

God's first enlightenment(day) is the revelation of His Deity in creation as the kingdom power of life to penetrate the darkness of death and destroy it. It is in the confines of the expanse where darkness is the ruling power; that God creates the existence of heavenly life that is not under the rule of death. The rule of the evening is overcome by the greater power of the morning. Death had no authority in God's creation to twist any form of life from God's control; until God gave its power to the satanic lie and its resultant power over the human race. Darkness is the power to twist life away from God's throne; *light* is the power of God to restore that lost life to His rule with His authority by which it can never again be taken away.

John 1:3-4

"In Christ was *life* [Zōe – the highest principle of spiritual holiness that cannot die] …and the life was the *light* [Phōs – light of the day, which is never kindled nor quenched, for it is of itself] …of men, and the light *shines* [Phainō – to appear, to be conspicuous by its brightness] …in the *darkness* [Skotia – unhappiness, the consequences of sin] … and the darkness did not *comprehend* [Katalambanō – to take possession of or apprehend] … it."

In 1976, this author was taken a quarter mile underground at a copper/nickel mine in Selibi-Pikwe, Botswana. He was overwhelmed by the power of the darkness. He discovered that total darkness defuses light and renders it totally useless. He could not see his hand right in front of the light on his helmet. The mine operator led him to a tunnel where there were powerful lights, and the walls were painted with white paint. Even these lights could work only where the beams were reflected by the white paint. Later that day the Lord led him to John 1:1-5 and revealed to his mind that the truth of God's salvation in the Christ is the enlightenment of heaven reflected in the purity of God's own Deity: Jesus is the only "daytime" (spiritual light - truth) which can penetrate the darkness of death. The holiness of God is reflected in His own Deity to enlighten man in the darkness of his mind. The darkness of evening (death) is overcome by the light of the morning (The Holiness of Deity).

Good [Tôwb – righteous; the right virtue of moral goodness in contrast to immoral evil. It is beneficial, pleasing, pleasant, joyful, and precious]. What God sees in His mind is the creation of life in the expanse that is not under the rule of death.

The earth (the place of death) is under His righteous rule until His judgments are completed. He sees everything created with the authority of life from His throne. He sees the salvation of human life under His kingdom rule and He sees the seventh day (revelation) when He has brought death to its final destruction in the lake of fire; and the creation of a different kind of heaven where death can never exist again. {What He envisions is the entire spectrum of His creation fulfilling the purpose for its existence; to restore to His authority of timeless life, that which twists itself out of His hands}.

John 10:27-30

Jesus said, "My sheep hear My voice, and I know them, and they follow Me; and I give timeless life to them and they shall never perish; and no one shall snatch them out of My hand. The Deity Who has given them to Me is greater that all; and no one is able to snatch them out of His hand. I and the _Father_ [the ruling power of `Ĕlôhîym on His Kingdom Throne of Life] …are _one_ [Heis – one in number; and Hen - the same essence of Deity]. God on His Throne, God in this physical world as Jesus, and the Holy Spirit; are all one single Spiritual Being (`Elohiym) revealing His presence (Parousia) to destroy death and create new spiritual life.]."

Separated [Bâdal– to disjoin, sever, to distinguish between two diverse things]. God's righteous judgment(revelation) was to distinguish between good and evil, light and darkness, death and life, the power of death's rule and the power of God's rule. The two cannot co-exist. Evil is the controlling power over the good in this place of death, but God is the greater power to overcome all evil with His own goodness.

The darkness had already become the controlling power over Lucifer and an untold number of angels. History has proven this truth that men love darkness more than light. Romans 3:23, "For all have sinned and fall short of the glory of God." The entire book of Proverbs is God's instructions for man to have the wisdom of God to know the difference between good and evil and to choose Him as the controlling power for the goodness of spiritual life. In God's creation, spiritual life is distinguished from death by His superior authority of righteousness which cannot die.

God called the light _Day_ [Yôwm–this word occurs 2,355 times in the Old Testament. It is God's self-revelation of His presence and the sovereignty of His kingdom of life to create new life. God created time and cannot be subject to any form of time. What He does with light/day (God's presence) gives meaning to His creation as life completely under His control. "_Light_" is the revelation of God's glory; the truth which overcomes the darkness of death {the evening becomes the morning}.

Psalm 118:24, "This is the "day" (Yôwm) which the Lord has made; let us rejoice and be glad in it." This word does not have anything to do with time (Chronos), but God's appearance as the Christ. It is the "daytime" (revelation) of God's glory working the power of His Kingdom of Life to take away the sins of the world.

In Genesis 2:1-4, the six days of creation are connected to the timelessness of God as the sovereign power of life to create life. The creation of the angels took place in the timelessness of God and so were the revelations of creation in chapters one and two. They are not numbered as the progression of time (Chronos), but each day is "_a day_," a specific revelation of the presence of _"light"_ (the glory of God which is distinguished from the darkness) to accomplish a specific judgment of His sovereign kingdom of life over the darkness.

In verse 4, the entire six days (six revelations of God's kingdom rule of life) are revealed to be *"the day"*; as one single revelation of God's judgment. Each judgment of creation in chapter one is upon the *darkness* (evening)resulting in God's rule of *life* (light/morning). The seventh day is the final judgment of God; not to create, but to establish worship of Him by man restored to spiritual life in the timelessness of His presence. There is no reference of "there was evening and there was morning" because the darkness of death will no longer exist. There will only be "morning "in His timelessness. God will be at rest (the cessation of revealing Himself as Savior). His judgments will have accomplished their purpose (death will be totally destroyed and every saved human being will worship Him in the glory of His timeless presence).

God called the darkness *night* [Layil – that which twists itself away from a controlling power to be its own authoritative power; death]. Night(darkness) and day(light) are understood to be the two distinct powers of death and life. Death twists life way from God's authority. Day is the shining glory of God's greater authority to restore life under the control of death to His timeless kingdom rule of Life that cannot die. In God, there is no darkness at all.

THE SECOND REVELATION

Genesis 1:6-8

1:6 "Then God said, 'Let there be an *expanse* [Raqiya– a masculine noun from Raqa; to expand by hammering. Raqa means to spread something out by pounding it to make a thin plate as an overlay. It was used for pounding out a piece of gold to overlay an idol. God pounded out the space which we call the universe] …in the midst of the waters and let it *separate* [Badal – to disjoin, to distinguish diverse things]. …the water from the waters."

Under the influence of Greek scholars, the translators of the Septuagint translated Raqiya with Stereoma "firmament". The King James Version followed this translation and the Latin Vulgate followed suit with "firmamentum". These translations tell you nothing about God. However, Isaiah 40:22 says, "God *stretched out* (Raqiya) the heaven like gauze."

1:7 "And God *made* [`Asâh – to do, to fashion a created object. Bârâ and `Asâh alternate in the account of creation; Bârâ conveys the thought of creation ex-nihilo; while `Asâh is broader in scope and deals with refinement to completion of what God creates from nothing. `Asâh and Raqiya give credence to the archeologist's proof that creation was not accomplished in six twenty-four-hour days of chronological time {which did not even exist until Adam sinned}, but in the timelessness of God. Psalm 136:5, 'Give thanks to Him who made (`asâh) the heavens with *skill* {Tâbûwn – infinite wisdom of a craftsman`}] `….the expanse and separated the waters which were below the expanse from the waters which were above the expanse; and it was so."

1:8 "And God called the expanse *heaven* [Shamayim or Shâmeh– unused Hebrew root words that mean 'to be lofty, the sky, the physical universe we allude to as the heavens`.] … And there was evening and there was morning; a second day."

The creation of the expanse was to separate the abode of physical life and the power of death to this thin band of darkness; removed from the abode of God where only holiness can exist. This second revelation of creation is: death cannot escape its limitations nor work its kingdom power in the holiness of God's abode where it originated in the mind of Lucifer. The vastness of space reveals the magnitude of God as the infinity of spiritual life which cannot be captive to any kingdom power. The magnitude of space bedazzles our imagination; but that is nothing compared to the glory of God (spiritual life) which cannot be limited to the confine of physical space.

THE THIRD REVELATION

Genesis 1:9-13
"Then God said, 'Let the waters below the heaven be gathered into one place, and let the dry land appear'; and it was so. And God called the dry land earth and the gathering of the waters He called seas; and God saw that it was good. Then God said, 'Let the earth sprout vegetation, plants yielding seed, and fruit trees bearing fruit after their kind, with seed in them, on the earth'; and it was so. And the earth brought forth vegetation, plants yielding seed after their kind, and trees bearing fruit, with seed in them, after their kind; and God saw that it was good.
And there was evening and there was morning, a third day (revelation of God)."

The formation of the earth is *dry ground* [Yabbâshâh–to be dried up, completely without moisture; dry land in contrast to bodies of water.] ...*formed* (`Asâh) by God's control of the waters. He *gathered* the waters [Miqvêh – this masculine noun has the basic meaning of confident expectation. Its root word is [Qâvâh; to bind together by twisting so as to be enduring.] The word picture God has painted is that of condensing water of the expanse in one place; the sea is one body. God created the whole planet of earth by binding the water outside the border of dry land (one single continent). The earth was not only the first planet of God's creation, but also the only planet with water and plants; life sustained by God.

The dry ground and the sea He called *earth* [Erets–the physical planet as opposed to the heaven which surrounds it. It is the habitation of man as a physical being.]. The dry ground *appeared* [Rââh – to look at intellectually as to perceive and experience]. The earth was designed and fashioned in the mind of God. It did not fashion itself by billions of years of evolutionary process. What was visible only in God's mind became a reality for Him to accomplish His purpose of sustaining spiritual life in the expanse. It was the first planet God created and is the only living planet in the expanse. Everything has its own DNA created by the mind of God (natural law). It produces plants *yielding* [Zâra'–to be fruitful] ...*seeds* [Zera'–offspring, posterity, family, race, semen] ...after their kind. This physical source of life can reproduce only physical life and it does so without fail. The God of the kingdom of life revealed Himself to be the only authority for life to exist. The human being is totally dependent upon the unchanging rightness of God's rule for both his physical and spiritual existence.

This third revelation of God is the truth that the power of the darkness is the destruction of life. It has absolutely no power to create any form of life. Heaven and earth are a single unit for God's kingdom rule of life. No life can exist in heaven or on the earth except that which comes from the judgment of God's kingdom rule of life. Likewise, in this timelessness of God, nothing can die except by God's judgment. Everything pertaining to the earth was created living and by God's design, produced more life. Death had no power to destroy any life on the earth until the appointed time for it to rule over Adam. All the life God created was holy and death could not transgress God's laws of righteousness.

THE FOURTH REVELATION

Genesis 1:14-19
"Then God said, 'Let there be lights in the expanse of the heavens to separate the day from the night, and let them be for signs, and for seasons, and for days and years; and let them be for lights in the expanse of the heavens to give light on the earth; and it was so. And God made the two great lights, the greater light to govern the day and the lesser light to govern the night; He made the stars also. And God placed them in the expanse of the heavens to give light on the earth, and to govern the day and the night, and to separate the light from the darkness; and God saw that it was good. And there was evening and there was morning, a fourth day."

God's fourth revelation of Himself as the ruler of all life was the creation of a light source to _govern_ the earth [Memshâlâh – dominion, rule, and power. This word expresses the sovereignty of God and the scope of His rule over the earth to create a visible separation of powers]. He created a _greater light_ [Mâ`ôwr – a luminous body which gives off light from within itself (sun); to govern the physical day time of man by the revolution of the earth; else it would burn up.] and a _lesser light_ [the moon which can only reflect light from the sun to govern the nighttime; man will not be in total darkness].

Then God created the stars that fill the expanse (sky). I Corthinians 15:40-41, "There are heavenly bodies and earthly bodies, but the glory of the heavenly is one and the glory of the earthly is another. There is one glory of the sun, and another glory of the moon, and another glory of the stars; for star differs from star in glory."

The creation of the sun and the moon are for _signs_ [`Ôwth – miraculous proof of spiritual sovereignty; confirmation of God's covenant for Spiritual Life to exist on earth.]. God's sovereignty and the scope of His rule over the earth are revealed by the creation of the sun to specifically give physical light and heat to the earth. The glory of the sun reveals the presence of God to dispel the ever-present darkness of the expanse; and the presence of God as "the light of the world "to remove the ever-present spiritual darkness of death. The glory of the sun and the moon reveal the unchangeable truth that human life will never be left alone in the power of the darkness of death; it will always be in the heavenly light of God.

God's presence in earthly life is clearly revealed by the luminaries which are also for _seasons_ [Môw'êd– appointed festive gatherings of religious assemblies; the lunar calendar God created for the sons of Jacob to worship Him in recognition of His power of Life. He is the goodness of life which rules over the evil of the spiritual darkness which separates life from its creator.

The luminaries are a constant reminder that the power of God's throne of Life is a constant presence to accomplish His will. This word "seasons" does not mean man is to worship the luminaries (paganism), nor to measure time by counting a certain number of days (solar time), but by the recurring festivals to worship the living God by the light of spiritual truth. Man is a creation of life that is entirely submissive to the holiness of God's kingdom rule of Life, not the rule of the darkness.

The luminaries are a witness to the passing of time (chronos) for God to fulfill His will for this planet earth (the Apokalupsis of Christ will remove the earth as the habitation of death). When Christ returns for Gods' final festival for worship; He will establish His timeless rule when the luminaries are gone, and He will be the light.

The fourth revelation of God (day) is the fact that His glory is His sovereign ruling power over the darkness that pervades the earth. It is always visible and never ceases to give spiritual and physical life; for He alone is the light of the world and the new heaven for man. This is the reason God commands His people to praise Him for the luminaries when they gather to worship. *Note the hymns which praise God for creation.

THE FIFTH REVELATION

Genesis 1:20-23
"Then God said, 'Let the waters teem with swarms of living creatures, and let birds fly above the earth in the open expanse of the heaven`. And God created the great sea creatures and every living creature that moves; with which the waters swarmed after their kind and every winged bird after its kind; and God saw that it was good. And God blessed them, saying, 'Be fruitful and multiply, and fill the waters in the seas, and let birds multiply on the earth`. And there was evening and there was morning, a fifth day."

The fifth revelation of God is an expression of His holiness and the holiness of everything He creates. God populated the sea and the sky with *living* creatures [Chay- Hebrew adjective from Châyâh; life which is intrinsically good (sinless)]. The great *sea creatures* [Tannîyn–huge sea creatures. This word was used in the Old Testament to show the Lord's power over His creation. It is not to produce fear in their minds, but trust in God because man is a superior being to rule over all God's creation.] …and every living (devoid of death) creature was good [Nephesh–a breathing creature; oxygen is the life of the body for both the sea and land creatures.]. God blessed all He created [Bârak - to bend the knee, to kneel down in submissive worship. Everything God created was in absolute submission to His Kingdom rule of Life; devoid of death].

It is clearly revealed that every form of life God created is sacred to Him and can only be subject to His law of righteousness. This character of sinlessness was the power of natural life before death was given its authority to rule. All-natural life was created with the capacity to die at the appointed future time. But death could not gain its kingdom rule over the earth through sanctified natural life; it did not have the capacity to sin or change its identity in any form or composition.

God designed every species of life to have its own unique identity and to fill the sea and cover the earth. The skeletal remains of dinosaurs and other huge animals have been found all over the modern world because the earth was one single continent at creation. This author was personally involved in the uncovering of dinosaur tracks at Glen Rose, Texas, with verified human footprints in them. Some creatures seem to have been created in certain small areas that later became unique to a particular continental land mass (see the division of the earth in Genesis 10:25). No species evolved from another species and everyone ate the herbs from the earth. Dinosaurs, sharks, lions, tigers, snakes and every meat-eating species were created holy. There was no such thing as prehistoric carnivorous animals. Many became carnivorous when their nature was changed to be wild by the curse of death that was God's judgment on Satan in Genesis 3:14. This same holiness of life revealed in creation will again be the only ruling power of all life when Jesus reveals Himself from heaven for His timeless rule. The lion will lay down with the lamb and the child will play with the asp because death will cease to have power over life.

The fifth revelation of God (day) is the glory of His Deity to create the pureness, holiness, and sacredness of His Throne in every form of physical life created in this natural world. Sinlessness is a witness to the character of God and is revealed by total submission to His sovereign rule. Death had no power over any form of natural life which existed by the authority of God's throne.

This revelation is God's future witness to the sacredness of human life restored to Him by the authority of Christ's redemption. Salvation is God's recreation of spiritual life that will never again be under death's authority. Life is sacred to Him and He expects His holy character to be the glory of His light shining in the darkness of this world.

THE SIXTH REVELATION

Genesis 1:24-25
"Then God said, 'Let the earth bring forth living creatures after their kind: cattle and creeping things and beasts of the earth after their kind'; and it was so. And God made the beasts of the earth after their kind, and the cattle after their kind, and everything that creeps on the ground after its kind; and God saw that it was good."

These verses pronounce God's judgment for natural life to multiply and populate the _earth_ [`Erets – the dry ground; the physical planet where all-natural life is created]. …All the living creatures: the _beasts_ [Chay–the quickening of life that is intrinsically good] …have been identified by the power of God's throne of life. No created life on this planet could break God's natural laws for procreation and God said that it is good. These verses set the stage for God to create a being of this world for the purpose of possessing the holiness of spiritual life (Adam) to rule over all God's creation and to populate the earth with the holiness of God.

Genesis 1:26a King James translation of the Bishop's Bible:
"Then _God_ ['Ĕlôhîym– Divine ruler, the sovereign judge; one single omnipresent Spiritual Deity] …said, 'Let us make man in our image, according to our likeness."

This is one of many verses in the KJV where only parts of Hebrew words were translated, and some words were not translatable at all. English Bibles copied the King James and reiterated the **human precept** that God is a multiplicity (Trinity) of Spiritual Beings (Greek Pantheism, which is the violation of Gods revelation in Exodus 20:1-7). The words "us and our" are not in any of these verses.

The Hebrew Interlinear Bible translates these words as "heavens"; which simply means the authority of Deity to create man a heavenly Spiritual Being. Up to this point He has revealed

His Deity as one single power of Spiritual Life that is unknowable to man. The critical issue of this verse is not to be guilty of reading something into it that is not revealed in the text.

This is the correct translation of this verse: "God said He created man from nothing to a completed form; a particular spiritual representative figure of God according to His original pattern." This verse is the first of God's progressive revelation that it is only by His presence in creation that He can reveal the timeless ruling power of His Kingdom of Life on earth as it is in heaven. Adam was the first man created with spiritual life; the Christ would be the second Adam to reveal Himself as the saving God.

The progressive revelation of the identity of God as a single omnipresent Spiritual Power of Deity is to destroy death; revealed by His life giving actions of a (1) Creator – Progenitor of life, Caretaker, Authoritative power of life]; (2) Huios Theos - (Christ) the presence of 'Ĕlôhîym revealed by His sinless righteousness to remove His judgment of death upon every human being He restores to spiritual life ; and (3) Holy Spirit [Ra´ăvăh – the breath of God which moved upon the waters for the creation of all life, the power which enables man to know the mind of God, to communicate the life changing truth of God's salvation to the human mind, the violent exhalation of life/breath from God to reveal Himself to every human being in His creation.].

It was God's plan formulated in His mind in Genesis 1:1-2 and revealed in this verse; that He would destroy death and totally remove it from existence through the wisdom of His ruling power of life given to man created in His Image. God is the only power that can destroy death and He has to do it in the place where death is given authority to rule the human mind.

When the supreme ruling power of 'Ĕlôhîym has finished His task of the complete removal of death so that it can never exist again, then there will no longer be the need to see Him as Creator, Christ and Spirit. His greatest revelation to man will be in a perfect heaven ruled by One Mind**:** the mind of the Single Spiritual Deity of Ĕlôhîym (Revelation 22:5 which reveals nothing in English but is God's greatest revelation in Greek).

Genesis 1:26b
"Let God *make* [`Âsâh – to make something complete, to fashion(design) something to have its unique identity. It is used alternately with Bârâ` (to createex-nihilo/from nothing). `Âsâh is broader in scope and deals with refinement. Its emphasis is on fashioning a created object to perfection] ...*man* [`Âdâm – mankind in the collective sense; as a proper noun it is the first man God created; it is the spiritual life of God which makes it superior over the rest of creation] ... in God's *image* [Tselem- shadow; a representative figure of God which maintains the essential nature of God's Throne of Life without the glory that shines from within God.] ...according to God's *likeness* [D^emûwth–resemblance, model, to pattern something after an original].

God is a single spiritual being, with the mind and power of timeless life. Adam was a single heavenly spiritual being with a God conscious mind and a *soul* (life that animates the physical body) *neither God or man is a trinity of beings); ...and let them (mankind) *rule* [Mâshal – to have Godly superiority] ...over the fish of the sea and over the birds of the sky and over the cattle and over the earth, and over every creeping thing that creeps on the earth."

God created man a freewill spiritual being with all the authority of His own kingdom of life to be His holy family (Hebrews 1, specifically says that man is a superior power of life to the Angels and will rule with Him in a perfect heaven designed for this purpose).

His purpose for man was to be His Godly power of righteousness to rule over the earth. Man reflects his identity with his creator by the inherent authority of the mind to *rule* [Râdâh – to tread down as a winepress with the feet; to be the master] ... and *subdue* [Kâbash – bring into submission; keep under bondage] ...the totality of the natural life of the world.

Having the mind of God; the righteousness of God's throne was the moving, motivating force of man's mind and character. Man was accountable to the ruling power of God's throne to act righteously (sinless) toward all created life. He was not an animal of the natural world, but a spiritual being of heaven accountable to the higher laws of God's righteousness. God gave man this awesome power of His Throne of Life to be a Godly being on earth; that he would be God's decision-making power on earth for either God or death to rule over him.

As long as Adam was obedient to the mind of God, he could eat of the tree of life. If he chose to live by the authority of his own mind, he could eat of the tree of the knowledge of good and evil. To do so, he would cease to be ruled by the mind of God and would become a slave to the ruling power of the kingdom of death.

Genesis 1:27

"And God *created* [Bârâ` – to originate something which does not exist; only God can do this]...man in His own image, in the image of God He created him; *male* [Zâkar–maleness; to bring God to remembrance (Spiritual power of God in physical life); from the primary root {Zâkah - to be transparent, clean, pure of heart, holy}; God's sinless righteousness is the predominate spiritual power that rules the mind and the actions of man's physical life]...and *female* [Nᵉqêbâh– this word is used for the female sex; whether of man or animals. It identifies all created life to be physical flesh with the power of reproduction (Adam was created from the earth with the God given power for reproduction; a power the angels do not have). Adam {Man} was created a heavenly spiritual being in a fleshly body] ...He created them (the human race)."

These words Male and Female in this verse have nothing to do with gender. Adam was not created a bi-sexual being and the human female sex was not created (Bârâ`) as was Adam and all animal life. The human female was {`Âsâh – manufactured from the preexisting body of Adam}. This word *female* comes from the primary root word [Nâqab – meaning to puncture, to perforate, blaspheme, bore a hole, curse, pierce, to strike through].

Adam was created to accomplish one purpose: to submit his spirit, his soul and his body of flesh as one single identity to the authority of God. He was created male (image of God with the ability to be totally spiritual minded) and female (weakness of the flesh with the ability to be totally fleshly minded).

God designed the human race with free will. The angels (sexless spiritual beings) were created with the same Godly power of choice in the timelessness of heaven. This verse reveals every human being is born with the strength of spiritual life and the weakness of physical life. Spiritual life was lost to the rule of death by the weakness of the flesh (man chooses to become a sinner and falls short of the glory of God).

This spiritual life at Adams creation is restored to all human beings who choose to repent; turn away from death and turn to God to be their supreme Lord of Life. This is God's salvation plan for man: to resurrect a spiritual being which reflects the true character of God.

Genesis 1:31
"And God saw all that he had made (created holy), and behold, it was very good. And there was evening and there was morning, the sixth day (Sixth Revelation).

This verse is not the conclusion of the creation of man. It is the revelation of God's approval for creating man primarily as a heavenly spiritual being with a temporal life on earth. The seventh revelation (2:1-3) is injected following this verse to reveal the end result of God's work is for spiritual man to have a permanent life with Him in the holiness of heaven where there is no death. This is revealed in Revelation 21-22 as the result of God's perfect work to destroy death so that it can never exist again and will never be remembered by the human mind; because God's mind will be the only authority to rule heaven.

THE SEVENTH REVELATION

Genesis 2:1
"Thus, the *heavens* [Shâmayim – (plural) (1) the realm of the sky which surrounds the earth (the expanse which contains the universe), and (2) the abode of God] …and the *earth* [`Erets – the physical planet, the abode of man] …were *completed* [Kâlâh – (past tense) brought to an end, consumed, destroyed, vanished, ceased, nothing is left to be done. *This is an all-or-nothing word. Absolutely everything God planned in Genesis 1:1-2 to destroy the kingdom of death is completely finished and it is removed as if it had never existed] …and all their *hosts* [Tsâbâ`- The heavenly and global army of God amassed to fight God's battle for the total destruction of death]."

Genesis 2:2
"And by (by means of) the *seventh day* [Yŏwm – God's revelation of the holiness of His kingdom rule of righteousness (timeless rule)] … God *completed* [Kâlâh –terminated] …His *work* [Me lâ`kâh– The principal meaning is deputyship, ministry, service, employment; to dispatch someone as a messenger, a herald. The general sense is an ambassador representing someone who sent him. The Messiah was God's final and perfect revelation of His finished work. He reveled Himself to be the truth, the light of the world, and the kingdom of life. It does not mean the toilsome, laborious side of the physical work of man, but the act of sacrificing His life for the sake of all of humanity. God's final work is to save only the remnant of humanity which will not turn away from Him] …which He had *done* [`Âsâh – created; fashioned] …and He *rested* [Shâbath – to desist from exertion, to cease, to leave off, to come to an end of work, to bring work to a stop.] …on the seventh revelation from all His work (Me lâ`kâh) which He had done (`Âsâh)." *God's redemptive work to destroy death in the confines of man will be completed; and therefore, there is no need to continue.

This verse reveals God's plan for the creation of His holy spiritual life in man from its creation in the world to the final resurrection of sanctified man to a purified heaven; is to free man from the curse of death to establish His rule as the King of Kings and Lord of Lords.

Matthew 26:27-29, "And when He had taken a cup and given thanks, He gave it to them saying, 'Drink from it, all of you; for this is My blood of the covenant, which is poured out for many for forgiveness of sins. But I say to you, I will not drink of this fruit of the vine from now on until that day when I drink it new with you in My Father's kingdom`.'"

Matthew 28:18-20, "And Jesus came up and spoke to them saying, 'All authority has been given to Me in heaven and on earth. Go therefore and make disciples of all the nations, baptizing them in the name of the Father and Jesus and the Holy Spirit, teaching them to observe all that I commanded you; and lo, I am with you always, even to the end of the age`.'"

Genesis 2:3,
"Then God *blessed* [Bârak – to kneel in worship; to be empowered by God for continued existence] …the seventh revelation (day)and *sanctified* it [Qâdâsh – to pronounce clean holy, consecrated to God, the sphere of what is sacred; totally devoid of sin and death] …because in it he rested (desisted) from all His work which God had created and made."

The <u>Seventh Day</u> is the revelation of God's creation of a new heaven that is so holy death cannot exist there (Rev. 21-22). God created earth for man to have a temporary physical existence. He will create a new heaven for man redeemed to spiritual life free from death, to worship Him in the pureness and holiness of His timeless presence. God blessed heaven with a multitude of spiritual children endowed with His Throne of Life.

God's blessing upon the seventh revelation is His assurance that the totality of believing man has a permanent place of worship before His heavenly throne. The seventh revelation (the absolute rule of God on His throne**)** is realized in His final and most glorious revelation (Rev. 22:3-5). When death cannot even be a memory and it is impossible for death to ever exist again, then God will no longer be revealed as the triune saving God. He will appear on His throne as the one ruling power of `Ĕlôhîym…Revelation 1:8, "I am the Alpha and the Omega says the Lord God, who is and who was and who is to come; the Almighty".

Genesis 2:1-3, makes it very clear that the seven days(revelations) of creation are not twenty-four-hour days of chronological time. They are the progressive revelation of God as the King of Glory to establish His rule of timeless life in the place (expanse) where He gives death its authority to rule. This revelation began with the formulation of His plan in His mind (Genesis 1:1-2), which ends in the completion of His kingdom work when He throws fallen angels, death, Hades, and every human being whose name is not found in the book of life into the lake of fire which is the second death (Revelation 20:14-15). The Seventh Revelation (the number for the perfect ruling power of God on His throne of life as it was before death entered His presence) is God's judgment that man cannot experience the glory of His perfect heaven until everything of

God Reveals His Glory [Doxa – True Identity]

the first six revelations is completed to the point of nonexistence. The authority of the seventh revelation is God's judgment that the redemption of man and the utter destruction of death are finished. God will cease to be revealed as the saving God; and will be revealed only as the spiritual being of 'Ĕlôhîym as He was before He created anything (Revelation 21-22).

God revealed Himself to be the power of the Throne of Life by the seven revelations of His light overcoming the darkness. Six times "there was evening and there was morning", but His most glorious revelation is the seventh. Here there is no evening, only the holiness of timeless spiritual life.

SIXTH REVELATION CONTINUED

The sixth revelation for the creation of mankind is not complete without the disclosure of Adam as both a spiritual and a physical being. Genesis 2:4-25 is the revelation of Adam as a physical being through whom God completes His work of completely destroying His enemy: death that began in the mind of Lucifer.

Genesis 2:4-9
"This is the *account* [Tôwlᵉdah – origin of the generation of man (God's lineage): derived from Yâlad (to bring forth children)] …of the earth when they were created, in *the day* [Yôwm – the sixth revelation of the timeless sovereignty of God] …that the Lord God made earth and heaven. Now no shrub of the field was yet in the earth and no plant of the field had yet sprouted, for the Lord God had not sent rain upon the earth; and there was no man to cultivate the ground. But a mist used to rise from the earth and *water* [Shâqâh – irrigate] the whole surface of the ground.

Then the Lord God *formed* [Yâtsar – to squeeze into shape, to be distressed; a technical potter's word to mold clay into a desired form; it is used to express God's "planning" or "preordaining", according to His divine purpose] …*man* [`Âdâm – a noun referring to mankind in the collective sense; also, a proper noun meaning the first man created] …of *dust* [`Aphâr – fine dust as blown by the wind (dust cannot evolve or mutate) …

God made man a physical being that could perish; cease to exist]…from the *ground* [`Ădâmâh – red soil of the earth, topsoil, humus living soil that supports life; owned and cultivated by God to be sinless]…and breathed into his *nostrils* [`Aph– a noun used figuratively to express emotions; the character of God as a righteous being: love, peace, mercy, forgiveness, etc.]…the *breath* [Nᵉshâmâh – breathing; the frailty of man as a living soul (life of the body)] …of *life* [Chay – to exist as a sacred, sinless being]… and man became a *living being* [Chay Nephesh– these words stand for the entire person as (1) a Body: the presence of a unique physical identity of man, (2) a Soul: the temporal life which animates the body, and (3) a Spirit: the timeless existence of Godly life which demonstrates the holy character of God.

Man was created a physical being with the power of spiritual life to act according to the character of God, and a spiritual being to fellowship with Him in the light of His presence. It is impossible to separate the creation of man from his heavenly creator. They are an inherent part of one-another. God identified Himself to man as "I AM". Man has the right to identify himself in the same manner as a spiritual being *outside of the realm of heaven*.

And the Lord God planted a garden toward the east, in Eden; and there He placed the man whom He had formed. And out of the ground the Lord God caused to grow every *tree* ['êts – wood that produces fruit]…that is *pleasing* [Châmad – to desire, to covet] …to the sight and *good* [Tôwb – beneficial; an important meaning is moral goodness as contrasted with immoral evil]…for food; the *tree of life* ['êtsChay – life on earth that has its source from God]…also in the midst of the garden, and the *tree of the knowledge* ['êtsDa`ath – intelligence gained through the physical senses purely for the purpose of serving the will of the flesh]…*of good* (Tôwb) *and evil* [Ra`– inability to come up to good standards which will be of benefit; unethical, immoral activity]."

Genesis 2:10-14 places the Garden of Eden just south of the present-day city of An Nasiriyah, Iraq. The ancient temple of Abraham is located there (Ur of the Chaldeans) and is still in use by the Moslems. They claim it is the birthplace of their religion as descendants of Abraham and Hagar. It is only fitting that the Garden of Eden was both God's place for the fall of man and the formation of a man-made world religion that does not just deny Him but hates Him.

Genesis 2:15-17
"Then the Lord God took the man and placed him in the Garden of Eden to *cultivate* [`Âbad – to labor, toil, to make weary, fatigued, to be enslaved] …it and *keep* it [Shâmar – to guard; to protect with great care]. And the Lord God *commanded* [Tsâvâh–the picture of a superior giving an order to a subordinate. God gives an order that is to be obeyed without question] …the man, saying, 'From any tree in the garden you may eat freely; but from the tree of the knowledge of good and evil you shall not eat, for in the day that you eat from it you shall surely *die* [Mûwth– to bring to death; to be separated from God] `."

Some people think of the Garden of Eden as the epitome of paradise. But in truth it was here that God acquainted Adam with the reality of life as a physical being. Adam was not created to be a loafer or a beggar. He had a strong body for labor and a mind with a good work ethic. He was to be a husbandman, a steward for diligent management of the soil and all the animals. In verses 2:9 and 16, Adam was encouraged to satisfy the natural need of food for his body from God's bountiful resources. Everything he needed for this purpose was provided for him in Eden. Also in this garden were two trees which served a different purpose. The Tree of Life was there to feed his spirit and empower him with the righteousness of God. He was commanded to eat freely of this tree and be totally satisfied with his timeless relationship with God. The only thing God required of Adam was obedience to the authority of His kingdom rule of righteousness.

God Himself must be obedient to righteousness to be the Holy Living God. It is exactly what was required of Him when it was time for Him to come into this world as the second Adam (the sinless Christ). Absolute obedience to the throne of God is what identified Jesus as being "One" with God, the Huios – one and the same deity, revealed by the same perfect sinless character. Like Adam in the garden and the saints under the Rule of Christ. (Revelation 19:15, sinless humanity will be under the iron rod rule of righteousness (the Mind of God) as they will be in God's perfect heaven (Revelation 21-22) where death cannot exist.)

Philippians 2 reveals that Jesus emptied Himself (gave up the glory which identified Him as God) and took on the *form* [Morphē – total identity / appearance of a servant in the likeness of man]. The message of the Sixth Revelation is God's plan to create a spiritually empowered being like Himself which would be a servant to His purpose for the destruction of death. Even under the power of the curse of death, man is the only created being which God endowed with the ability to be restored to His glory by obedience to His command of faith.

Hebrews Chapter One reveals that God honors man with a higher place before His throne than the angels. Revelation 21:6-7, "And He said to me, 'It is done. I am the Alpha and the Omega, the beginning and the end. I will give to the one who thirsts from the spring of the water of life without cost. He who overcomes shall inherit these things, and I will be his God and he will be My *Son* [the heavenly relationship of man to God as His spiritual children with the same holy Spiritual Life`]."

The other tree in the garden would produce a vastly different result. Adam was commanded not to eat of it because that *day* [Yôwm –The revelation of God's creation of chronological time: time that has a beginning and an end to measure His judgment on the kingdom power of death.] …that you eat from it, you shall surely *die* [Mûwth – to be separated from the power of life; for man it is the death of both spiritual and physical life]. The event of Adams disobedience (Genesis 3:6) began God's judgment upon man as a mortal (controlled by death), physical creation. Adam and Eve immediately lost the blessed joy of fellowship with God. They then lived-in fear of God; they hid from Him and tried to justify themselves by speaking nothing but lies to Him.

*Some theologians have an adamant belief that death was not God's original plan for the human being. They believe Adam was simply warned that death was the penalty for disobedience to God's command. Death became the ruling power over him only because he ignored God's warning. Thus, it was necessary for God to restore humanity to His kingdom rule of timeless life, not by the righteous rule of justice of His throne of life, but purely by His grace.

This author does not believe this human precept. God's grace was predetermined for the redemption of man before He actually created anything. It is His inherent justice for the redemption of man to again be a spiritual being by the authority of Christ – his redeemer. This must be man's choice.

God put the two trees in Eden for His purpose of giving man his freewill choice. He could continue to be God's heavenly image of a spiritual being; or he could choose to be nothing but a perishable fleshly being. God continues to give humanity the same choice – through Christ we can go to heaven as a spiritual being or we can choose to be nothing but flesh that will be consumed in the lake of fire.

Genesis 2:18-25
"Then the Lord God said, 'It is not good for the man to be alone; I will *make* ['Ashah – to produce by design] … him a helper suitable for him`. And out of the ground the Lord God formed every beast of the field and every bird of the sky and brought them to the man to see what he would call them; and whatever the man called a living creature that was its name. And the man gave names to all the cattle and to the birds of the sky and to every beast of the field, but for Adam there was not found a helper suitable for him.

So, the Lord God caused a deep sleep to fall upon the man, and he slept; then He took one of his ribs and closed up the flesh at that place. And the Lord God *fashioned* [Bânâh – to manufacture or construct a new object by adding to existing material] ...the rib which He had taken from the man and brought her to the man. And the man said, 'this is now bone of my bones, and flesh of my flesh; she shall be _called_ [Qârâ` - the basic meaning is to enunciate a specific message. It is addressed to a specific recipient and is an act of sovereignty over the thing which is being named. Adam (the image of God) would rule over his own body; his body would not rule over him*(for the wife to rule over the husband is the same as the flesh ruling over the spirit. This is anathema to God.)] ..._woman_ [`Ishshâh– this word identifies the human female to be God's designed helper to the physical male sex for the propagation of the human race; because she was taken out of _Man_ [`Îysh – Adam, a specific male; created maleness (Zâkar) as opposed to femaleness (N^{e}qêbâh). ` Adam was created with the strength of a heavenly spiritual being in the weakness of the flesh and Eve was made the weakness of the flesh with the strength of God's spiritual life.

For this cause a man shall _leave_ [`Âzab – to be set free; to leave behind] ... his father and his mother (spiritual and physical guardians) and shall cleave to his _wife_ [`Ishshâh–one specific female] ...and they shall become _one flesh_ [Bâsâr – one body; a living creature submissive to God's authority for His Spirit to rule over the flesh.]. ...And the man and his wife were both naked and were not _ashamed_ [Bûwsh – disgraced by sin]."

The Sixth Revelation (day) is God's judgment for death to be the ruling authority over all life on earth. God designed man (the spiritual representative of God's throne) to be the spiritually empowered decision maker to accomplish this judgment. This Revelation is indicative of man created holy, sinless; but he becomes the self-ruling power of the flesh. Six is the number for man; 666 is the number for the total Godlessness of man as the ruling power of death on the earth and God's judgment on humanity in the days of Noah; and the Apokalupsis of the Christ.

Chapter 2

GOD REVEALS THE KINGDOM RULE OF DEATH

THE SERPENT

Genesis 3:1
"Now the *serpent* [Nâchâsh – a hissing enchanter] …was craftier ['Âruwm– meaning to be smooth, to form cunning plans, to deal subtly] … than any *beast* [Chay – the intrinsic goodness (sinlessness) of natural life] …of the *field* [Sâdeh – a plain; open country where animals roam free] …which the Lord God had *made* [`Asâh – to create, to refine by design]."

Chapters one and two of Genesis reveal nothing about the darkness because they are the revelation of the holiness of life and God does not glorify evil. It is not until chapter three that the revelation is given of the presence of angels; spiritual beings with heavenly authority, preexistent to the darkness and the creation within it. The magnitude of God's rule of life in His abode is greatly enhanced by the identity of these spiritual powers which served Him before there was even a need for creation. The revelation of the evil serpent in the Garden of Eden and the angels which prevented Adam and Eve from remaining in the Garden of Eden; identify them as key figures in the spiritual warfare being waged in the heaven of God's abode and the darkness of the expanse. Revelation 12:9, "And the great dragon was thrown down, the serpent of old who is called the devil and Satan, who deceives the whole world; he was thrown down to the earth, and his angels were thrown down with him."

Genesis chapter three continues God's silence as to the identity of the evil angel. He is simply introduced as the Nâchâsh (poisonous serpent which kills) which brought about the fall of man, by the power of a lie to the mind of sinless man. This revelation of God now shifts from His timeless rule in heaven to the historical account of man's life in the flesh (God's judgment on death within the confine of chronological time). To fully grasp the identity of the serpent and its spiritual implications we need to examine the only two names for angels given in the scriptures. These names are descriptive of them according to their purpose and their power.

SARAPH

Isaiah 6:1-7
"In the year of King Uzziah's death, I saw the Lord sitting on a throne, lofty and exalted, with the train of His robe filling the temple. *Seraphim* [Plural of Sârâph – a poisonous, fiery (the glow of God's holiness), flying serpentine form] …stood above Him, each having six wings; with two he covered his face, and with two he covered his feet, and with two he flew. And one

called out to another and said, 'Holy, Holy, Holy is the Lord of hosts, the whole earth is full of His glory'. And the foundations of the thresholds trembled at the voice of him who called out, while the temple was filling with smoke. Then I said, 'Woe is me, for I am ruined because I am a man of unclean lips; for my eyes have seen the King, the Lord of hosts`! Then one of the seraphim flew to me with a burning coal in his hand which he had taken from the altar with tongs. And he touched my mouth with it and said, 'Behold, this has touched your lips; and your iniquity is taken away and your sin is forgiven`'." {The fire from the altar is the purifying power of holiness.}

This scripture passage indicates the Seraphim to be the highest ruling authority, the most noble and holiest of all the angels, not only by their superior appearance but most importantly by their position of hovering above God and His throne. Their chief duty is to glorify His holiness. Their voices shook the foundations of the thresholds of the heavenly temple when they shouted His holiness. Their own holiness is the same character as the throne they serve. The appearance of being on fire is the radiating holiness of God's own glory. The connotation as poisonous emphasizes the ability to kill (wars in heaven; to bring death into existence by the power of their mind). The fallen angels and man are the only powers outside of God with this power. It proved to be disastrous for a Sârâph to take the glory (identity of God) for himself, but it was God's foreordained will for it to be so when He created them. It is the same with the creation of man. A Union soldier in the American civil war aptly identified mankind as "killer angels".

The only scripture which infers the identity of the serpent in the Garden of Eden is Isaiah 14:12-15. In the context of these verses, God uses the typology of the earthly king Nebuchadnezzar who twisted himself loose from God's kingdom rule. God had used his kingdom power to exact His judgment on unbelieving Judah. When Judah's captivity was finished and the remnant of believers was allowed to return to Jerusalem, then God turned His wrath upon the Babylonian king for transforming his rule from good to evil.

Isaiah 14:12-15

"How you have *fallen* [Nâphal – a violent circumstance to fall away or be overthrown] … from *heaven*, [Shâmayim – height; the sky or abode of God] … O *star of the morning* [Shining one] … son of the *dawn* [descendant – the intimate relationship of the first-born son, blessed by the father]! *(This part of verse 12 in the King James Bible is translated as, "How art thou fallen from heaven, O *Lucifer* [Shining one –holiness of God], son of the morning") … You have been cut down to the *earth*, [`Erets – the planet earth as opposed to heaven] … you who have weakened the nations! But you said in your heart, 'I will *ascend* [`Âlâh– to be exalted]…to heaven; I will raise my *throne* [Kiççê – figurative seat of honor]…above the stars of *god*, [`Êl – Hebrew masc. noun emphasizes might, power; the name of pagan gods in the ancient Near East] …and I will sit on the mount of *assembly* [Môw`êd –time God created for man to worship Satan] …in the recesses of the *north* [Tsâphôwn – dark, gloomy, hidden place; from (Tsâphan – a secret place hidden by covering it over until it is revealed.)]. …I will ascend above the heights of the clouds; I will make myself like the *Highest* [`Elyôwn – the over whelming majesty of pagan deity`] … nevertheless, you will be thrust down to *Sheol*, [Sh^e`ôl – Hades, hell, place of the dead without recourse to God] … to the recesses of the *pit* [Bôwr– dungeon; grave]."

What happened to this Seraph? In his fall, he is no longer the outward shining glory of holiness and perfect purity. In an instant, he no longer reflected the holiness of God's Throne of Life; but the deceitfulness of a deadly poisonous serpent (the inherent power of the kingdom of death). He turned the light of Glory away from God to shine upon himself. It is now a light that he can see only in his mind. It distinguishes one's self to be greater than God. It is the power of the mind to exalt self as a god and belittle God or deny His existence.

In that moment when this Seraph surrendered himself to self-glorification so as to be God, he sought to remove `Ělôhîym as his judge. In that instant, the epitome of holiness became the epitome of evil, the kingdom power of Death directly opposite of Life. `Ělôhîym's superior judgment was passed upon him and the timeless nature of God was taken from him. Now he is timeless darkness. He is no longer the holy Seraph of heaven, but (Genesis 3:1) the <u>serpent</u> (Nâchâsh – a poisonous snake which kills). He has the power of the <u>serpent</u> (Nâchash – to cast magic spells by sorcery) and he is the master <u>serpent</u> (Nachash – one who practices the occult).

The glorious Saraph which magnified the <u>glory of God</u> (true identity of God) now magnifies <u>his own glory</u> (true identity of death). "The shining one" is now <u>Satan</u> [Satan as – adversary; one who comes between two powers to separate them. It is a collective word for the power of death]. …<u>Devil</u> [Diabolos – evil power. Devil and Satan have the same meaning]. In Matthew 4:3, Satan is called the <u>tempter</u> [Peirazō – one who entangles a person to sin, to act contrary to God's will].

I John 3:8

"The Devil has sinned from the beginning. The Christ appeared for this purpose that He might destroy the works of the Devil."

II Peter 2:4 and 9

"For if God did not spare angels when they sinned but cast them into hell and committed them to pits of darkness, reserved for judgment.… Then the Lord knows how to rescue the <u>godly</u> [Eusebēs – one who reverences and worships God] …from temptation and to keep the unrighteous under punishment (Hades) for the day of judgment."

CHERUB

Genesis 3:24

"So, He drove the man out; and at the east of the Garden of Eden He stationed the <u>Cherubim</u> [Plural of K^erûwb–to bless, to praise, and to adore; an order of angels below the seraphim which serve God with holy reverence.]."

Cherubim are servants of God in heaven and to the created world. They have a composite appearance of heaven and earth. They are described in Ezekiel 1:5-21 as spiritual beings having human bodies and hands, four wings, four faces (man, lion, ox, and eagle), feet like a calf, they had the appearance of being on fire, and they had a wheel within a wheel beside them covered with eyes (the spirit of the being is in the wheel) which enabled them to travel at lightning speed in any direction without moving their heads. Their functions were to guard the tree of life to keep Adam and Eve from the Garden of Eden (Genesis 3:22-24); to serve the purposes of the throne of God (Ezekiel 10); and to show God's majesty (II Samuel 22:11). Their images were placed on the mercy seat (Exodus 25:18-22), on the Temple veil (Exodus 26:31), on the curtains (Exodus 36:8), and in the Temple (I Kings 8:6-7). The angel speaking to the virgin Mary in renaissance paintings is that described in Ezekiel 10, and is identical with the UFOs modern man claims are aliens from another planet.

THE DECEPTION OF THE SATANIC LIE

Genesis 3:1-6

"Now the *serpent* [Nâchâsh – poisonous snake, enchanter] … was craftier than any beast of the field which the Lord God had made (sinless beings). And he said to the woman, 'Indeed, has God said, "You shall not eat from any (every) tree of the garden"? ` And the woman said to the serpent, 'From the fruit of the trees of the garden we may eat; but from the fruit of the tree, which is in the middle of the garden, God has said, "You shall not eat from it or *touch* it [Nâga' - to lay the hand upon something. This is not a negative word in itself, but for humanity to touch what is holy is the same as striking God and incurs His judgment. Exodus 19:12, God sanctified believing Israelites, but the unbelieving Israelites were commanded not to touch Mt Horeb under the pain of death"] `. … And the serpent said to the woman, 'You surely shall not die! For God knows that in the day you eat from it your eyes will be opened and you will be like God, knowing good and evil`. When the woman saw that the tree was good for food, and that it was a delight to the eyes, and that the tree was desirable to make one wise, she took from its fruit and ate; and she gave also to her husband with her, and he ate."

The serpent the woman was talking to was not a snake (a sinless beast of the field; for no life God created on earth was yet under the curse of death). The poisonous serpent was the fallen seraph, Satan. The woman demonstrated no fear of talking to him because she was acquainted with the magnificent sight of angels. There is nothing in scripture to indicate that Satan's appearance was changed from his heavenly form to a snake upon the ground, or a human figure in a red suit with horns on his head and an arrowhead shaped tail, or the grotesque ghoul in the movies.

Satan's power is in the perversion of the mind; he knows how to twist the truth of God's word to be a lie so that it will be believed. It was by his subtle design that he proposed a theological question to Adam's wife (made from the flesh of man) instead of to Adam who was created a spiritual being in the image of God. She had not yet been made when God gave His commands to Adam about the Tree of Life and the Tree of the Knowledge of Good and Evil. She did not have first-hand knowledge to God's instructions for righteousness and was not meant to take God's place as Adam's spiritual teacher. She was a creation of the flesh and did not have the spiritual mind of God to recognize Satan's deception.

The woman's response to Satan's question was from the perspective of her fleshly mind that was purely self-serving; and perverted God's command (Verse 3:3, "God has said, 'You shall not eat from it, or touch it, lest you die. `)." Her response opened the door for Satan to assert himself as a greater spiritual power than God. With great authority he blasphemed God by distorting His word (Verse 3:4, "… 'You surely shall not die`!"). Satan proceeded to take the place of her spiritual teacher and told her itching ears what she wanted to hear (Verse 3:5, "For God knows that in the day you eat from it your eyes will be opened, and you will be like God, knowing good and evil.").

Satan's deceptive question accomplished its purpose. Her perversion of the truth revealed her belief that she (a creation of the flesh), was a spiritual authority equal to God. She made herself to be the judge of right and wrong. All she had to do was to act on her own authority and eat the fruit of the tree.

Genesis 3:6

"When the woman *saw* [Raah–to see intellectually, to perceive with the mind; to ascertain by inward authority]…that the tree was *good* [Tôwb – beneficial, pleasing to the senses]…for food, and that it was a delight to the eyes, and that the tree was *desirable* [Châmad – to covet; an inordinate, ungoverned, selfish desire]…to make one *wise* [Sâkal – to act purposely with the authority of God], …she took from its fruit and ate; and she gave also to her *husband* [`Îysh– an individual human man; one body with his wife; as opposed to Adam (the man created in the image of God). It is derived from the root word `Ĕnôwsh - the weakness or frailty of mankind in general as a fleshly being. This was God's purpose for creating Adam. He was created a holy being to act as a Godly decision-making power of heaven. But like Lucifer did in heaven; he acted to please himself as a being superior to the ruling power of God, and in so doing would initiate the curse of death upon the human race.] …with her, and he ate."

Satan did not have any problem revealing the ruling power of death over the fleshly centered mind of the woman. Adam should have been more difficult to deceive. He was created with the mind of God [spiritual life of God's throne]. He enjoyed a blessed fellowship with God and the angels. It was a natural thing for God to talk with him; to instruct him in righteousness. He was taught the absolute necessity for obedience to the rule of God and saw the holiness of the obedient Cherubim. He acted faithfully as a ministering spirit of righteousness over all the natural life of creation, which included the wife made from his own body. He had no fear of the spiritual powers that took care of him as long as he lived in reverent obedience to God. He lived in a relationship of perfect peace with God because there was nothing evil in his mind. He was given the command that disobedience to God's demand for righteousness would change everything, the loss of his image of God as a spiritual life, the loss of his relationship of peace with God, and his trust in the person of God. Adam had no reason to doubt the validity of God's commands because death did not exist as a kingly power over his own mind and he had never encountered any spiritual being that was disobedient to God.

Satan's entrance into Adam's idyllic world changed everything. He encountered a dazzling angelic being which acted contrary to everything he had been taught. This was a different kind of angel; this one spoke with the authority of God. Adam was face to face with death and he surrendered his discerning spirit of righteousness to believe him. Adam (the image of God) like the wife of flesh, died spiritually before he ate the fruit, she gave him. He died the instant he acted by the power of his mind to disobey the truth of God's word; to obey the lie of the kingdom of death. Adam's spiritual death transformed him from a Godly power of spiritual life (free from the power of death) to nothing more than the fleshly identity of the wife. She did not give the fruit to Adam (spiritual image of God); she gave it to her _husband_ [`Îysh – an ordinary human man; weakness of the flesh]. The human race did not die with the transgression of the wife; it died when the kingdom of righteousness ceased to rule the mind of Adam. He ate the fruit in defiance to the explicit command of God. * [The ruling power of death over the mind dictates the sinful actions of the flesh. Likewise, the ruling power of God's kingdom of Life dictates the righteous actions of a spiritual mind.].

There are three instances in scripture which define the kingdom of death to be the self-ruling power of the mind. (**1**) Lucifer, the Saraph in heaven and the angels which followed him;(**2**) Adam, the authority of God's kingdom rule of life on earth; and (**3**) the people resurrected to spiritual life;(Revelation 20) free from the rule of death for the worship of Christ at His second coming; people which pull away from God's rule of their minds (Gog – the leader of a people, and Magog – the whole tribe of people. This is the last vestige of created life that can turn away from God). All three live in the presence of God and all three turn away from God's kingdom rule. This reveals that a person's evil environment is not an excuse to sin and a holy environment is not a deterrent to sin. All three reject the ruling power of God's kingdom of life to place themselves above God. This event in Revelation 20 is God's final judgment on death and it is thrown into the Lake of Fire (God's final purification of heaven and earth).

Chapter 3

GOD REVEALS HIS JUDGMENTS ON DEATH

Genesis 3:1-7:24
    Genesis 3:1-6 marks the beginning of man as a *mortal* being (under the rule of death). It is also the beginning of chronological time; the historical framework for God to destroy the kingdom power of death. Chronological time and the rule of death will cease with the Apokalupsis of Christ; the authority of God's personal presence to rule over sinless man.
    Genesis 3:7-7:24 is the historical account of God's judgment on Satan, the woman, the man, and the generation of humanity from Adam to Noah. The character of death's rule which began in Adam and Eve gets progressively worse as the human population grows. The power of evil intensifies to the point that there are only eight people left who are righteous. The revelation of God for His destruction of death's rule over this generation of man is the execution of His judgment upon the whole human race which refuses to submit to His rule of righteousness.

Genesis 3:7-13
    "Then the eyes of both of them were *opened*, [Pâqach – to gain knowledge by sight; to be observant; to ascertain physical experience is superior to truth spoken by God] … and they knew that they were physically and spiritually naked; and they sewed fig leaves together and made themselves loin coverings. And they *heard* [Shâma – to hear intelligently, to give undivided attention] …the sound of the Lord God walking in the garden in the *cool of the day*, [Rûwch – breathing; air put in motion by divine breath; this is not a specific time of day but the movement of the Holy Spirit which revealed the presence of God.] …and the man and his wife hid themselves from the presence of the Lord God among the trees of the garden. Then the Lord God *called* [Qârâ– sustained summoning by a sovereign power to a specific individual to assert himself] …to the man, and said to him, 'Where are you`? And he said, 'I heard the sound of Thee in the garden, and I was *afraid* [Yârê`– the emotional and intellectual anticipation of harm; dread; fear (love is the power of life; fear is the power of death] … because I was *naked* ['êyrôm– physically nude; exposed; vulnerable] …so I hid myself`. And He said, 'Who told you that you were naked? Have you eaten from the tree of which I commanded you not to eat`? And the man said, 'The woman whom Thou gave to be with me, she gave me from the tree, and I ate`. Then the Lord God said to the woman, 'What is this you have done`? And the woman said, 'The serpent deceived me, and I ate`."

    Adam was created with the essence of God's holy authority of spiritual life. He had a true knowledge of God's identity because he enjoyed nothing but peace as he walked and talked with God in the light of His revelation of righteousness. Now he hides from God in the garden because He has separated himself from God. He was pure and innocent in the light of holiness, but now he is guilt ridden with fear in this darkness of the mind. He no longer had the spiritual identity of God. * In Christ, God restores this lost spiritual life to us with the peace of heaven, and He destroys the earthly power of fear.

God was not ignorant of Adam's actions. These verses are an anthropomorphic usage; God is described in human terms so that all of humanity can understand what He is saying to Adam (mankind in its mortal state). Adam did not have the foggiest idea of the consequence of his action. God asked Adam some poignant questions to elicit a confession of guilt. What He got from Adam was excuses. There was no repentance or remorse for his lawlessness. There was no acknowledgement of God's forgiveness and love for him. Adam had lost his reverent fear of God as his judge. He no longer worshipped Him with love and devotion for His rightness. He had lost every sense of accountability to God as the kingdom power of life. He had twisted himself away from the ruling power of life to be the master of his own life.

Death is a very powerful force which robs our mind of a true knowledge of God. The result of this is man's creation of gods that he can make with his own hands. Like Adam, every generation of man moves to the point where he is his own god. ***The whole Bible is God's work to restore humanities knowledge of His true identity (His glory), that all who believe in Him may be redeemed to His kingdom throne of life. In the end, what God had to do to this first generation of man He will do again to this present generation and He will do also to the rebellious generation of man in the Kingdom rule of Christ. Once God has completely removed every vestige of life in which death can rule, then it will be impossible for death to ever exist again.

DEATH'S CURSE ON SATAN

Genesis 3:14-15
"And the Lord God said to the serpent, 'Because you have done this, *cursed* [`Ârar - rendered powerless to resist] …are you more than all the cattle and more than every beast of the field; on your *belly* [Gâchôwn –to give issue; to gush forth as water; the source of life (birth). Lucifer could not produce the spiritual life of heaven as he sought to do by usurping God's throne of life. He can only produce the physical race of man governed by the evil kingdom of death. The curse {powerless to resist} is just as effectual for Satan as it is for all the physical life of the earth. God can remove the curse on man and the animals but not so for Satan] …shall you go, and *dust* ['Âphâr – dry earth; return to the earth; meaning to be eternally identified with the lowliness and fragility of fleshly human nature under the power of death; to die and return to the earth. Satan was created a Seraph with non-ending life; but now he is no different than physical life that will perish in the lake of fire.] …shall you eat all the *days* [Yôwm – The limits of chronological time God created to limit the power of death's rule on the earth.]…of your *life* [Chay – experiences of the body; limited physical existence] …And I will put *enmity* [`Êybâh – to be an enemy; to be hostile; to hate; Satan hates the fleshly human being] …between you and the woman and between your *seed* [Zera'- singular offspring; Satan has produced the lost human race as a singular body]…and her seed (Christ was brought forth from a woman); He shall bruise you on the *head*, [Rô`sh – chief leader, head of a family; Christ will totally remove Satan's

power over man]…and you shall bruise him on the <u>heel</u> ['Âqêb – mas. Hebrew noun meaning a victory achieved at a tremendous cost.

    Satan could deceive the minds of men, but he could not change the reality of the impossibility to control the mind of Jesus – when Lucifer rebelled against the rule of God, the full weight of God's authority to judge all created life fell on him and all life that he deceives.]."

    Lucifer was created to be the servant of God's throne and glowed with God's holiness. But he deluded his own mind to believe that he could twist himself away from the authority of God's rule so as to be superior to Him. Not only did he deceive himself, but he revealed death to be a latent power in the minds of a host of the Cherubim (fallen angels) as well.

    `Ĕlôhîym is the only real power of life. The judgment of His throne was to remove Lucifer from the holiness of heaven to the world created in the darkness of the expanse. It is in this world of flesh that God gave Lucifer (the head; the chief leader of the source of death) authority to be the deceiver. God's purpose was for him to reveal the latent power of death; first in the mind of the woman in the garden, then in the mind of the man who had a true knowledge of God. He is given this same power to bring the entire race of man to an end; and also, to expose the latent power of death in the minds of people at the end of the Kingdom Rule of Christ.

    God's judgment of removing timeless life from Lucifer is revealed in the curse placed upon him. The first part of this curse is that death became the ruling power over all life created on the earth. Animals that were created holy and sacred to God became wild and carnivorous. The snake became a hated, poisonous serpent. Instead of Lucifer being a glorious godly power worshipped on earth; he is equated with the hated snake and despised as more evil than all the wild animals. He is the epitome of the evil of death. He will never again be identified with the holiness of God; only as the Devil from the bowels of the earth for as long as God lets him live.

    The second part of the curse reveals that Lucifer and his <u>seed</u> [Zera` – singular; the entire mortal human race as a single unit from Adam] …will suffer God's judgment to totally remove every vestige of life from them. Lucifer relished his deception of the woman in the garden to produce mortal man, but God placed an <u>enmity</u> [hatred] between them; because she would also provide the fleshly delivery of <u>God's seed</u> [singular; the totality of the whole human race born to the kingdom of God by the second Adam; the Christ, is one single spiritual body].

    Lucifer hates the woman because he could not do anything about the birth of Christ. He is not a god in control of his own life; God controls it. In Lucifer's battle for survival, he will bruise (crush) <u>God's heel</u> [Jesus' death of the tomb], but God will bruise (crush) <u>Lucifer's head</u> (Lucifer and his kingdom power of death will perish in the lake of fire). Jesus' death was temporary because it was the death of the flesh, but Lucifer's death will be the complete and permanent end to the totality of his existence. God made him from nothing, and God will return him to nothing. *What God does to Satan He must do also to the totality of the human race that rejects Him.

DEATH'S CURSE ON THE WOMAN

Genesis 3:16
"To the woman He said, 'I will greatly multiply your *pain in childbirth* [`Itstsabown – worrisomeness, toil, hard work, sorrow. This word is used only for the pain at the moment of actually giving birth],…in *pain*[`Etseb – the discomfort of carrying a child from conception to birth]…you shall bring forth *children* [Ben – young one; from the root word Bânâh- to build or manufacture something from existing material(the woman gives birth to the child but she cannot give spiritual and physical life(actual life) to the child that can die in the womb; that life comes from the blood God placed in the semen – the seed of man.]…yet your *desire*[T^eshuwqah– this fem. Heb. noun means to stretch out after, to covet the role of the human male] …shall be for your husband and he shall *rule* [Mashal – to govern, to have dominion, to manage.] …over you`." *Eve usurped Adam's identity by eating the forbidden fruit; so, the husband is God's Spiritual principality in the marriage relationship.

The totality of God's judgment on the woman is upon her transgression of the purpose for her creation. She was made from Adam's body for the female purpose of reproducing mankind. She was physically designed to give birth to the body of a child for physical life]. Giving birth would become a painful experience under the kingdom power of death that rules this world. The most important aspect of giving birth to a child (a live birth) belongs to God and cannot be changed. The spiritual and physical life of every person begins at the moment of conception because the life is in the blood: She can contribute to the physical features of the child with x and y chromosomes, but she cannot give the child *LIFE*. This was not God's purpose for making her.

Leviticus 17:11
"For the life of the flesh is in the blood, and I have given it to you on the altar to make atonement for your *souls* (the sinful actions of the body); for it is the blood by reason of the life (the sacrificial death of the Messiah) that makes atonement."

Leviticus 17:14
"For as for the life of all flesh, its blood is identified with its life."

The blood (the life) of every human being comes from the sperm of the father; it does not come from the woman's egg, or from the placenta in the womb (*verified by medical doctors in Mount Pleasant, Texas). The woman (wife) was made from the body of the man and derived her physical and spiritual life from Adam's blood before death began. Every human being (including Eve) is a physical and spiritual descendant of Adam. The spiritual life that was given to Adam is safe in the righteousness of God. * It is passed on to every person born of a woman. It is only by the life in the blood that we are born safe in God's image with His character of righteous. God placed blood in every male sperm – life begins the instant a sperm penetrates a female egg that has no life in it. Every human being is born with the Spiritual Life given to Adam.

God Reveals His Glory [Doxa – True Identity]

It is not sin for a child to be born; for it is God who gave Adam his life blood and it is God who gives us our life blood (spiritual and physical life). We die physically at any time (even in the womb) because we are under the judgment of death. We cannot die physically if we do not have a physical life. Neither can we be "lost" spiritually if we are not born with spiritual life. Our spiritual life is put to death by our sins that separate us from God. God's salvation comes from the power of His blood to restore us to His Spiritual Life that cannot experience death a second time. Only God can transform a spiritually dead human to His Timeless Life.

The perfect illustration of this theological and medical fact is found in the birth of Jesus, the Christ. Gabriel, the chief messenger from God told Mary (a spiritually and physically chaste woman) that she would conceive in the womb by the Deity of God and bear a son. The Holy Spirit (God- not a physical being) would come upon her and the power of the Highest would overshadow her; and for that reason, the holy offspring shall be called the (Huios – Christ) of God (Luke 1:26-35). *This is the first revealed transplant of an existing embryo into the womb of a woman. Joseph had absolutely nothing to do with the inception of the life placed in her womb. Through a woman (created for this purpose), the Deity of God was [Tiktō –not born; but brought forth in human flesh].

The glory of God in His ability to reveal Himself as Life placed in the womb of Mary is the same glory of His ability to put life blood in the sperm of man. We are given this object lesson in conjunction with the birth of John, the son of Zacharias and Elizabeth.

Luke 1:7

"And they had no child, because Elizabeth was _barren_ [stĕirŏs– sterile; her eggs had an unnatural hard covering that could not be penetrated by the sperm] …and they were both advanced in years."

Luke 1:13

"But the angel said to him, 'Do not be afraid, Zacharias, for your petition has been heard and your wife Elizabeth will _bear_ [Gennaō – passive voice, to be born; mainly used of men begetting children (men give the baby life from the blood in the sperm)] …you a son, and you will give him the name John`."

Luke 1:37

"For _nothing_ [Pas – all things in their totality and each thing within that totality come into existence through God; and Rhēma – everything comes into existence by the all-powerful word or command of God] …will be impossible with God."

God removed the hard covering of Elizabeth's egg so her husband's sperm could enter it. Thus, God gave life to John, the forerunner of Christ. The totality of the human being reveals the glory of God as the kingdom power of Life. The birth of every human being is God's gift of life through the blood of Adam. The greater glory of God is the revelation that it is through His Own Blood [the blood sacrifice of the second Adam, Jesus the Christ] that we receive His greatest gift; the restoring of timeless spiritual life directly from God: the creator of all life (John 3:3).

God ordained marriage to be a commitment between a man and a woman for the purpose of God's spiritual protection upon the weakness of human flesh. God had given Adam authority to rule over everything God created with the power of physical life (flesh). This included the wife and God will never rescind this judgment. The wife was to be submissive to Adam's watch care because he was God's spiritual presence in this world. Because of the woman's transgression of God's purpose for making her, she twisted herself away from God's protection and placed herself under the destructive kingdom rule of death. It is a perversion of creation for a wife to rule over her husband and it is impossible for two males or two females to justify an immoral relationship by the sanctity of a marriage ceremony.

God's judgment on the wife is that her submission to this ruling power of evil does not negate the authority of God's throne of life. God's judgment on the wife is His revelation that her "desire– what she strives for, what she covets" is the security God provides by her submission to the spiritual principality of her husband's watch care. The wife's obedience to the spiritual principality of her husband's rule is her witness to the absolute rule of God's throne of life.

It is the wife's purpose from creation to give witness to the world under the curse of death that the flesh does not rule over the spirit. Our security for living in this world of death is the timeless rule of God's kingdom of life.

I Corinthians 11:7-9

"For a man ought not to have his head covered, since he is the *image* [Eikôn – a physical representation of the spiritual being of God) ...and *glory* [Doza –revelation of the true identity] ...of God; but the woman is the glory of man. For the man does not originate from the woman but woman from the man; for indeed the man was not *created* [Ktizō – to produce something tangible from nothing] ...for the woman's sake (glorify the flesh), but the woman for the man's sake (bare children which God can transform from death to spiritual life - that is a living witness to God's kingdom of life with His spiritually born children around His throne)."

Satan has done a deadly work with the confusion of male and female roles with the insulting and belittling identity given to men and the rule of women over men. American courts rule in the case of a divorce; is the mother of the children has absolute possession of the children. But the husband has to pay the bills. Disregard for God's command for the human male (the father) to rule over his own children, is the rejection of God's plan for the salvation of the world. The man was created in the image of God to be the spiritual presence of God; to teach his children and rule his home. It is through this spiritual message that God works His spiritual power of life for the salvation of all mankind. The man was not created for the woman's sake, but for God's revelation of His kingdom of life.

Psalm 8:3-6

"When I consider thy heavens, the work of thy fingers, the moon and the stars, which thou hast ordained; what is man that thou dost take thought of him? And the [Huios– Jesus; God in human flesh]; that thou dost care for him? For thou hast made him a little lower than God (Christ is God in the weakness of human form) and dost crown him with glory and majesty! Thou dost make him to rule over the works of Thy hands; Thou hast put all things under his feet." *The purpose for Christ in human form is to destroy the power of death in this world where the Deity of God is not known. The only power that can penetrate the darkness of death is the light of truth revealed in the Christ. God's salvation can only be by the conversion of the human mind from the darkness of death to the timeless rule of God's Throne of Life. Faith (a verb) is the power of the human mind to place human life in the hands of the Living God to do what only He can do.

The woman was made from the flesh of Adam for the purpose of producing human children. She was made for the sake of man; to give physical birth to mankind. God's purpose for the woman is that the Christ would come into this world in the flesh of a man; <u>brought forth of</u> a woman (<u>not born</u> from a human father). His mother and her husband were obedient to the commands of God for His protection and He was submissive to the authority given them for His care. When they searched for Him for three days and found Him in the temple, He revealed His primary obedience was to His heavenly Deity, who is the authority for all life. This is a condemnation upon every man who will not be a witness to God as his heavenly father and a condemnation upon every woman who belittles God's spiritual authority over her and destroys the minds of her children.

I Corinthians 11:3
"But I want you to understand that *Christ* [Christos – God's anointed high priest; the Redeemer] …is the *head* [Kephalē – superior spiritual principality and power in the hierarchy of God's throne] …of every *man*, [Anēr – male; spiritual power of God to rule over this world] …and the man (Aner) is head of the woman (wife), and God (the Father) is the head of Christ"

The sinlessness of Christ was revealed in His identity of the heavenly Deity; mankind's sinlessness is revealed in obedience to Christ; and the sinlessness of the woman (wife) is revealed in her obedience to the male (husband). This is the order for the spiritual principality which reveals God to be the sinless, righteous power of the throne of life. It is very difficult for people to surrender their lives to the authority of God if they cannot see His authority in the lives of the people who claim Him to be their Lord. Refusal of the woman to accept God's command to be obedient to the principality given to her husband is the same transgression as Eve in the Garden of Eden. Proverbs 25:24, "It is better to live in a corner of the roof than in a house shared with a contentious wife." Proverbs 19:13, "The contentions of a wife are a constant irritation." A henpecked husband (a domineering wife) is an abomination to God.

Ephesians 5:22-24
"Wives be *submissive* [Hupotassō– to place one-self in an orderly fashion; to voluntarily show one-self in proper relation to superiors (something that is demanded in the military)] …to your own husbands as to the *Lord* [Kurios – one who wields authority for good; contrast is (despotēs – slave master)]. …For the husband is the *head of the wife* [Kephalē–a superior spiritual principality] …as Christ also is *head of the church* [Kephalē]…He Himself being the Savior of the body (church). But as the church body is *submissive* (Hupotassō)to Christ, so also the wives to their husbands in everything."

I Corinthians 14:32-35 is another scripture passage which tells us God has ordained that He should reveal Himself by the authority He has given to principalities in heaven (the angels) and on the earth (prophets, apostles, teachers, spiritual gifts, husbands). The church body is submissive to the principality of Christ and the principalities within the church are submissive to one another to prevent confusion and strife. Each principality has a divine purpose that is empowered by submission to God (the superior principality of His kingdom rule of life). Every principality which acts contrary to its purpose are in direct rebellion to God (church splits, divorces, women pastors and deacons, and deacons ruling over the spiritual shepherd of the church) is an abomination to God and an attack upon His own Person.

I Timothy 2:11-15

"Let a woman *quietly* [Hēsuchia – silence] …receive instruction with entire *submissiveness* [Hupŏtagē –honor the order of spiritual principality] …But I do not allow a woman to *teach* [Didaskō – instruct by word of mouth] …or *exercise authority* [Authentĕō – dominate; usurp authority] …over a *man* [Anēr–the Hebrew word Male which identified Adam as the Image of God] …but to remain quiet. For it was Adam who was first created and then Eve. And it was not Adam who was deceived, but the woman being quite deceived, fell into *transgression* [Parabasis – an excessive negative act of the will toward a commandment; much more serious than (Hamartia – sin)] …But women shall be *preserved* [Sōzō – deliverance from danger, suffering] …through the bearing of children if they *continue* [Menō– to stand firm or steadfast; longsuffering or patience] …in faith and love and sanctity with *self-restraint* [Sōphrŏsunē – soundness of mind *(opposite of transgression against the rule of God's Spirit)]."

For the woman to usurp the position of a man to be a principality of the church (Pastor, Deacon, and teacher) is a violation of God's *law* [Nomos – the divine administration of the judgments of God's throne of righteousness]. There is no need for a woman to do this because the proper role of the wife in a marriage is a powerful and vital witness of obedience to God required by His servants and demonstrated by Jesus.

I Peter 3:1-2

"In the same way, you wives, be submissive [Hupotassŏ] to your own husbands so that even if any of them are *disobedient to the word* [Apeitheō – refusing to place themselves in subjection to Christ] …they may be won without a word by the behavior of their wives as they observe your *chaste* [Hagnos – pure, holy] …and respectful behavior."

I Peter 3:6-7

"Thus, Sarah *obeyed* Abraham [Hupakouō – to respectfully listen and follow directions] …calling him *lord* [Kurios – one who wields God's authority for good] …and you have become her children if you do what is right without being *frightened* by any fear [Phobeō– to fear revenge; burdened by guilt]. …You husbands, likewise, live with your wives in an understanding way, as with a *weaker vessel* [Asthĕnēs – without strength; flesh does not have the strength of the spirit] …since she is a woman (a special creation of human life to be the help-meet of Adam); and grant her honor as a *fellow heir* [Sugklēronomos – a personal equality based on an equality of possession] …of the grace of life, so that your prayers may not be hindered."

The curse God pronounced upon the woman's transgression of creation was not designed to make her a slave to man or to be of lesser value than the man. It was meant for the woman to voluntarily honor God's purpose for creating Adam first, and then Eve. Each one has a divine purpose that glorifies God.

DEATH'S CURSE ON ADAM

Genesis 3:17-24
"Then to Adam He said, 'Because you have *listened* [Shâma – to obey, to give heed] …to the voice of your wife and have eaten from the tree about which I commanded you, saying, "You shall not eat from it"; cursed is the ground because of you; in toil you shall eat of it all the days of your life. Both thorns and thistles it shall grow for you; and you shall eat the plants of the field by the sweat of your *face* [`Aph – masc. noun, breathing part of the body (part of the body that expresses anger, the nature of death)] …you shall eat bread till you *return* [Shûwb – to return to the place of departure, *to die*] …to the ground, because from it you were taken; for you are dust and to the dust you shall return`.

Now the man called his wife's name *Eve* [Chavvâh – life-giver; to bring forth physical life] …because she was the *mother* [`Êm – first physical mother of all future human beings] …of all the living. And the Lord God said, 'Behold, the man has become like one of Us (decision maker) knowing good and evil; and now, lest he stretch out his hand and take also from the tree of life and eat and live *forever* [`Ôwlâm – timeless; continuity without change] `; therefore, the Lord God sent him out from the garden of Eden to cultivate the ground from which he was taken. So, He drove the man out; and at the east of the Garden of Eden, He stationed the cherubim and the flaming sword (holiness of God) which turned every direction to guard the way to the tree of life."

Adam lived in the Garden of Eden in a blessed state of peace. Because he surrendered God's control of his mind to obey the persuasive words of Satan, he was condemned to live under the rule of death. Life would be a yo-yo of emotional and physical instability. He would eat the bread produced from the ground produced by his own labor. He would be dependent upon the good and bad conditions of the earth for his physical life.

Even though people born in this generation of Adam were given extremely long lives; they still faced the reality that physical life had an end. The curse of evil on the earth is the reality that it too, will come to an end. Every human being will lose the sanctified spirit of their birth to the cursed kingdom rule of death. Adam could never produce a child without a sin nature. Every person reveals their true identity as children of Adam by their sinful actions and will eventually die in their sins. Only God can make it possible for man to return to the spiritual power of life of Adam's creation. This could only be achieved by the second Adam – the Christ.

Adam was banned from the presence of God as a physical being, but timeless spiritual separation from God was not the purpose of his creation. The spiritual authority of the angels separated him from any possibility of making death a permanent curse. He received the knowledge of God pertaining to good and evil by his personal act of disobedience to God's commands; but he could not return to a state of peace with God by physical means.

Verse 22 identifies this curse to be the plan of God for physical man, but the way of returning to God was not disclosed within the curse. God's plan for this generation of man

(Adam to Noah) to regain spiritual life could only be revealed to individual people by their personal experience of discovering God's grace to care for them in the stress of their physical lives. This was God's revelation to them to produce a living faith for their daily lives. This was revealed by the obedience of Abel to make a sacrifice that was pleasing to God and the faith expressed by those who called upon the Lord for their salvation.

DEATH'S CURSE ON THE FIRST GENERATION OF MAN FROM ADAM TO NOAH

GENESIS 4:1-6:7

The central revelation of God throughout the whole Bible is His rule of life. God has given every generation of man the revelation that He rules all physical and spiritual life by the authority of His Kingdom of Life. No life in this world is more important than the spiritual life that comes from His throne of righteousness. Adam was God's key witness to the blessing of this life; he was created with it, but he lost it. He lived his whole life as a mortal being under the authority of a kingdom power that brought terrible pain and suffering through his own life and the lives of his children. Adam knew from experience that nothing is more important than obedience to God. It is evident from Cain and Abel that Adam was diligent to teach his children to worship God with a blood sacrifice.

CAIN

Genesis 4:1-12
"Now the _man_ (Adam) had _relations_ [Yâda'– sexual intercourse] ...with his wife Eve, and she conceived and gave birth to Cain, and she said, 'I have gotten a _man-child_ [`Îysh – human man, maleness; distinct from God or animal] ...with the help of the Lord`. And again, she gave birth to his _brother_ [`Âch – a masc. noun for two similar things bound together by strong affections: a twin] ...Abel. And Abel was a keeper of flocks, but Cain was a tiller of the ground. So, it came about in the course of time that Cain brought an _offering_ [Minchâh – a bloodless tribute; a cereal offering] ...to the Lord of the fruit of the ground. And Abel, on his part also brought of the firstlings of his flock and of their fat portions. And the Lord had regard (approval) for Abel and for his offering; but for Cain and for his offering he had no regard. So, Cain became very _angry_ [Chârâh – to glow with anger, to be incensed with rage;] ...and his _countenance_ fell [Pânîym – face. Cain turned his face away from God; meaning he had no regard for Him]. Then the Lord said to Cain, 'Why are you angry? And why has your countenance fallen? If you _do well_ [Yâṭab – of a mind to do good] ...will not your countenance be _lifted up_ [Seh-ayth` - face turned toward God to regard His righteousness] ...and if you do not do well, _sin_ [Chaṭṭâãh - habitual transgression] ...is couching at the door; and its _desire_ [Zûwd – be insolent, proud, self-sufficient] ...is for you, but you must _master_ it [Mâshal – to rule, to reign, to have dominance]`....And Cain told Abel his brother. And it came about when they were in the field that Cain rose up against Abel his brother and _killed_ him [Hârag – to murder; to slaughter by cutting the throat; to execute]. ...Then the Lord said to Cain, 'Where is Abel

your brother`? And he said, 'I do not know.  Am I my brother's _keeper_ [Shâmar–Godly mind to build a hedge of thorns around a garden so as to guard it] `? ...And He said, 'What have you done? The voice of your brother's blood is crying to Me from the ground. And now you are _cursed_ ['Ârar–human mind rendered powerless to resist the curse of death] ...from the _ground_ [`Ădâmâh – soil of the earth created to give life] ...which has opened its mouth to receive your brother's blood from your _hand_ [Yâd – power, strength]....When you cultivate the ground, it shall no longer yield its strength to you; you shall be a vagrant and wanderer on the earth`."

Genesis 4:25-26 reveals that Adam then had Seth; another son as an offspring in place of Abel (like Abel, the generations of Seth inspired people to trust God and call upon Him for life). Chapter 5:1-5, reveals that Adam was one hundred and thirty years old when Cain murdered Abel and he lived eight hundred years after the birth of Seth. The entire narrative indicates Adam had a large number of children and their generations continued to produce a large number of people in those nine hundred and thirty years.

Genesis 4:14-15
" Behold, thou hast driven me this day from the face of the ground; and from Thy face I shall be hidden, and I shall be a vagrant and a wanderer on the earth, and it will come about that whoever finds me will _kill_ [Hârag – murder] ...me. So, the Lord said to him, 'Therefore whoever kills {Hârag} Cain, _vengeance_ [Nâqam – to avenge oneself; to act as God] ...will be taken on him sevenfold`. And the Lord _appointed_ [Sûwm – to bring about a change; to set aside for special purposes] ...a _sign_ ['Ôwth – miraculous proof. Cain was transformed from the normal stature of a man to a _giant_ {Nephilim; people who dominated society by violence}] ...for Cain, lest anyone finding him should _slay_ him [Nâkâh – to strike or beat a person with the intent of taking his life. *(Context identifies the meaning of this word. It does not always infer the taking of a life; example: Moses _struck_ {Nâkâh}a rock]."

God took away Cain's ability to gain life from the earth and relegated him to live in cities where evil thrived. Cain's open rejection of God's counsel fueled the fire of open rebellion of men to reject God and live by the power of vengeance under satanic counsel (Genesis 4:23-24, Cain's descendant also committed murder).

Genesis 4:26
"And to Seth, to him also a son was born; and he called his name Enosh. Then men began to _call_ upon the name of the Lord [Qârâ` - the enunciation of a specific message to a specific recipient, intended to elicit a specific response; to call upon the person of God for His saving power]."

This verse reveals the movement of God upon the minds of those who would obey His counsel. God did not create the human race to perish, but to be saved. This verse is a clear revelation that God is primarily a saving God and reserves judgment for its proper time. God works through every generation to save every person who will be saved. God counseled Cain with instructions on how to live as a Godly person. He did not take his physical life when he turned away from Him because God's measurement of death's power is not upon the body, but the spirit.

Genesis 6:1-4

"Now it came about, when men began to multiply on the face of the land and daughters were born to them, that the sons of God (descendants of Adam) *saw* [Rââh – to view intellectually; to experience, to enjoy] …that the daughters of men were *beautiful* [Tôwb - desirable]; …and they took wives for themselves, whomever they *chose* [Bâchar– to be acceptable or judged the best after it has been tested. Men had no respect for women as a creation of God, but to lust after them as physical sex objects to be abused for their own pleasure.] …Then the Lord said, 'My Spirit [Rûwach – the breath of God; the Holy Spirit] …shall not*strive [Dîyn–a judicial word marking the act whereby an individual man's position and destiny is decided. It corresponds to its root word (Dûwn), meaning to make a legal judgment of guilt or innocence. God's Spirit was doing its work of convicting man of his evil; that by his repentance (mind)he would return to God. God withdrew His Spirit from men whose minds were completely under the darkness of death. This work of God will be repeated (II Thessalonians 2:6-7) at the time of the great apostasy to end the world – as it was in the day of Noah.] …with *man* [`Âdâm – generic mankind as physical beings] …*forever* [`Ôwlâm – what is hidden, concealed, the vanishing point of time whether past or future. Human life is not timeless.] …because he also is *flesh* [Bâsâr – the weakness of physical life designed to perish]; …nevertheless his *days* [Yôwm – the definitive judgment of God by chronological movement of time for physical beings to live. Because men were no longer responsive to God's Spirit; He reduced their longevity from a thousand years] …shall be one hundred and twenty years`.

The *Nephîyl* [N^{e}phîyl – giant, bully, tyrant, men of violence. The root word is (Nâphal); meaning to fail, to cause to fail, a violent circumstance or event] …were on the *earth* [`Erets – the inhabitation of man] …in those days, and also afterward when the sons of God (Adam) came into the daughters of men and they bore children to them. Those were the mighty men who were of *old* [`Ôwlâm – the most ancient past, antiquity, beginning with Cain] …*men* [`Ĕnowsh – individuals who were physically strong but spiritually weak, frail] …of renown."

These verses are a reference to Cain and his descendants. Satan did a deadly work in Adam but continued even more so in Cain. He lived almost a thousand years and was Satan's tool for totally corrupting humanity to the power of death. Every human being on this earth is born innocent but falls under this kingdom power of death and reveals it by their ungodly actions. Every generation has those people who stand out as prophets of Satan. The demonic tribulation the Nephilim brought upon the world was the main cause for God to shorten the life span of man. Men became completely immoral and mocked God when He directed Noah to build the ark. Moses had to deal with the Egyptian pharaoh who claimed to be a descendant of the "sun god". In Numbers 13, Moses encountered this same kind of demonic empowered men (Nephilim) possessing the land of Canaan. They were the Philistines whose every intention was to kill the Israelites.

God's revelation is that He is in control of this world. The power of evil has neither regard for God nor compassion for the life of man. The voice of death tries to drown out the voice of God, but it cannot. Genesis 5:21-23denotes that under God's judgment, one man with a strong faith would not be over-come by this awesome influence for evil. "And Enoch lived sixty-five years and became the father of Methuselah. Then Enoch walked with God three hundred years after he became the father of Methuselah and he had other sons and daughters. So, all the days of Enoch were three hundred and sixty-five years and Enoch walked with God; and he was not, for God took him."

This verse is a clear revelation that only the person who is under the spiritual rule of God has timeless life. God is about to pass judgment on the rebellious humanity of this generation for its history of glorifying death over His kingdom rule. It was not God's will that Enoch should suffer the same judgment as the unbelieving men of that day. God did not want physical death to be a witness against the authority of His Kingdom of Life; so, God took him (translated him to heaven as a spiritual being) as He also does for each of His Saints at their physical death.

Genesis 6:5-7, 17

"Then the Lord saw that the *wickedness* [Ra` - noxious moral deficiency] …of man was great on the earth, and that every intent of the thoughts of his heart was only evil *continually* [Yôwm – a none-ending sphere of time completely under the rule of darkness]. …And the Lord was *sorry* [Nâcham–to draw the breath forcibly; to grieve, to feel compassion] …that He had *made* ['Âsâh- to create something from nothing with the ethical obligation to design it with the God power of self-determination; "man's choice to be only evil continually"] …man on the earth, and He was grieved in His heart. And the Lord said, 'I will *blot out* [Mâchâh–to completely remove that segment of people who would not have a savior; it is the same word for God's power to forgive sin as if it had never existed] …man whom I have *created* [Bârâ- the Godly activity of bringing something into existence out of nothing] …from the face of the land, from man to animals to creeping things and to birds of the sky; for I am *sorry* (*grieved* by their ungodly character) that I made them. And behold, I, even I am bringing the flood of water upon the earth, to *destroy* [Shâchath – to bring to ruin; to cage the power of death as a lion on a rampage] …all flesh in which is the *breath of life* [RûwachChay – the intrinsic physical life which came from God] …from under heaven; and everything that is on the earth shall *perish* [Gâva` - death of the soul; physical death of the grave] `."

All unbelieving human beings were consigned to Hades to await the final great white throne judgment. All unbelievers (humanity ruled by death) from the beginning to the end of chronological time will suffer this fate. I Peter 3:18-20, in reference to the three days Christ was in the tomb says, "For Christ also died for sins once for all, the just for the unjust, in order that He might bring us to God, having been put to death in the flesh but made alive in the spirit; in which also He went and made proclamation to the spirits now in prison, who once were *disobedient* [Apeitheŏ– persuaded toward unbelief] …when the *patience* [Makrothumia – the person who has the power to avenge himself refrains from the exercise of this power] …of God kept waiting in the days of Noah, during the construction of the ark, in which a few, that is, eight persons were brought safely through the water."

This first generation (Dôwr) of man began with the creation of Adam as a Godly being. It ended with the destruction of all his descendants which had turned away from God to become evil beings controlled by the power of death. It reveals there were people in that generation who overcame death by a strong faith in God and they were energized by the throne of God with timeless spiritual life. The entire Bible is the revelation of God as the energizing power to transform believing individuals from death to His power of timeless life in His heavenly presence where death can never exist again.

God's judgment for cleansing the earth of human life which lived purely as physical beings, removed all but eight people. This is a clear revelation to all people at the time of God's judgment on this present generation; that it will once again be like the days of Noah. When only a small remnant of believers will exist, then the fury of God's judgment on death at the Apokalupsis of Christ will remove the earth, death, and the whole expanse created for the habitation of death into the Lake of Fire. *This will be God's permanent cleansing of all life that exists outside of Himself, so that death will never exist again.

Chapter 4

THE SECOND GENERATION OF MORTAL MAN

The significant difference of this generation from that of Adam; is the progressive revelation of God's intrusion into the world to reveal Himself as a saving God. Like the first generation of man, it began with a righteous man acceptable to God and it will end with the total depravity of unbelieving man that God will destroy with fire at the Apokalupsis of Christ's second coming; when only a remnant of believing people will survive the onslaught of death's power to consume human life. *The word mortal; means humanity under the curse of death.

NOAH

Genesis 5:28-29
"And Lamech lived one hundred and eighty-two years and became the father of a son. Now he called his name *Noah* [Nō'ah – rest] …saying, 'This one shall *give us rest* [Nâcham – comfort because of God's change of mind] …from our work and from the toil of our hands arising from the ground (the dry ground called out for judgment because of the blood of Abel) which the Lord had cursed`."

Genesis 6:9-10
"These are the records of the *generations* [Dôwr – the measure of a man's life from his birth to the birth of his children] …of Noah. Noah was a *righteous* [Tsaddîyq – one who has the just character of God; the standard of ethics and morality of God's throne of life] …*man* [`Îysh– masc. Heb. noun; male, a spiritual minded human being who reveals the identity of God] …*blameless* [Tâmîym – entirely whole, the pureness of a sacrifice, the divine standard which man must attain to meet all the requirements of God's Law; the holiness of God's throne of life] …in his *time* [Dôwr] Noah walked with God. And Noah became the father of three sons: Shem, Ham, and Japheth."

These verses establish the second generation of man to be subject to the saving work of God. The earth of the first generation of man was purified by water; the flood wherein God removed all the uncleanness of unbelieving man. The earth of this second generation of man will be purified by fire for God's complete removal of death. The theological purpose for the second generation of man; is that through man God will provide a savior for the human race. God's judgment of the flood and His deliverance of Noah by the ark is this truth: there is a blessed spiritual life for man beyond God's judgment on mortal flesh. God created man a spiritual heavenly being in His image and this image will not perish. The final end of man restored to spiritual life will not be earthly, but heavenly.

GOD'S COVENANT WITH MORTAL MAN

Genesis 8:20-9:7

"Then Noah built an altar to the Lord, and took of every *clean* animal [Tâhôwr – an animal that is not a mixed breed] …and of every clean bird and offered burnt offerings on the altar. And the Lord smelled the soothing aroma; and the Lord said, 'I will never again curse the ground on account of man, for the intent of man's heart is evil from his youth; and I will never again destroy every living thing as I have done. While the earth *remains* [Yôwm - chronological time] …seedtime and harvest, and cold and heat, and summer and winter, and day and night shall not cease`.

And God *blessed* [Bârak – greeted with reverence; a spiritual being with the promise of timeless life] …Noah and his *sons* [Bên – basically a reference to the male offspring of human parents; but also used idiomatically for "children" and "descendants"] …and said to them, 'Be fruitful and multiply and fill the earth. And the *fear* [Môwrâ`- a fearful dreaded thing] …of you and the terror of you shall be on every beast of the earth, on every bird of the sky, with everything that creeps on the ground and all the fish of the sea; into your hand they are given. Every moving thing that is alive shall be food for you, and I give it all to you as I gave the green plant. Only you shall not eat flesh with its life; that is, its blood. And surely, I will require your lifeblood; from every beast I will require it. And from every man, from every man's brother I will require the life of man. Whoever sheds man's blood, by man his blood shall be shed; for in the image of God He made man. And as for you, be fruitful and multiply; populate the earth abundantly and multiply in it`."

Like with Adam, God began the second generation of man empowered with spiritual life. Noah's first action upon leaving the ark was to worship God with a blood sacrifice. However, God's covenant is with man as a fleshly being which still has the unchanged sinful character of mortal man (under death's curse). God's covenant sealed the human mind to be in bondage to the kingdom power of death. Romans 5:12, "Therefore, just as through one-man sin entered into the world, and death through sin, and so death spread to all men, because all sinned."

God is patient in His judgments because He has a purpose for mortal mankind. By His foreordained judgment of grace, He will not allow man to be so violent that he could totally destroy the human race until it is His time to end it. God established a second covenant with mortal man to make it very clear that God made the earth for a purpose and only God can destroy it.

Genesis 9:11-17

"And I establish my covenant with you; and all flesh shall never again be *cut off* [kârath – cease to exist] …by the water of the flood, neither shall there again be a flood to *destroy* [Shâchath – the corruption which brought the earth to ruin] …the earth. And God said, 'This is the *sign*[`Ôwth – a supernatural appearance of God; an act that only God can do] …of the covenant which I am making between Me and you and every living creature that is with you, for all *successive* [`Ôwlâm – the hidden time that is beyond the vanishing point] …*generations* [Dôwr – the cycle of a man's life-time; beginning with the conception and birth of a man and the birth of his offspring]; …I set My *bow* [Qesheth – the visible strength of God to reveal Himself in the uncreated light of timeless life. Man says the rainbow is the natural reflection of sunlight off the water in the air and he makes up stupid stories of a leprechauns' pot of gold; but God says this revelation of heavenly light is visible only because He makes it visible] …in the *cloud* ['Ânân–the thunder-cloud that only exists for the purpose of bringing rain upon the earth; this was not existent before the flood], …and it shall be for a sign of a covenant between Me and the earth. And it shall come about when I bring a cloud over the earth, that the bow shall be seen in the cloud and I will remember My covenant which is between Me and you and every living creature of all flesh; and never again shall the water become a flood to destroy all flesh. When the bow is in the cloud, then I will look upon it to remember the everlasting covenant between God and every living creature of all flesh that is on the earth`. And God said to Noah, 'This is the sign of the covenant which I have established between Me and all flesh that is on the earth`."

This covenant established the state of God's mind toward mortal man. It is not His purpose that humanity should live in the fear of a catastrophic end of the world or lives without hope of having a savior. The rainbow is God's revelation of the truth of His timeless life that delivers sinful man from the curse of death and it is His will to do so for every person who will ever live. God is not a vengeful power as portrayed by the pantheon of Greek gods, or any self-serving god Satan creates in the human mind, or a figment of the imagination as presented by the atheist. He is the Living God of love who reveals Himself to all who will believe in Him.

THE FORMATION OF CIVILIZATIONS

The first thing Noah did when he left the ark was to make a blood sacrifice to God. His second recorded act (Genesis 9:20-21) was to plant a vineyard, drink of the wine, become drunk, and strip off his clothes. God's purpose for disclosing Noah's actions is to reveal the destructive power of death's rule over the natural man. Alcoholism destroyed Noah's family; and it was the controlling power which brought about the destruction of many civilizations.

The three sons of Noah established kingdoms according to their linage. The descendants of Ham and Japheth brought ruin to the world. Genesis 9:22, 24-27, Ham, Noah's second son, saw the nakedness of his father and told his two brothers. Ham was addicted to the sin of sexual immorality. Genesis 9:25-27; God cursed the entire linage of Ham (Canaanites) for this sin, with continual warfare with God's people. Ham became the founder of the land of Canaan (named after Ham's son Canaan, father of Nimrod, who formed the kingdoms of Babel, Assyria, Nineveh, and the cities of Sodom and Gomorrah in the land of the Philistines. Genesis 10:10-9. "And the beginning of his kingdom was Babel and Erech and Accad and Calneh, in the land of Shinar".

Genesis 11:1-9

"Now the whole earth used the same language and the same words. And it came about as they journeyed east that they found a plain in the land of Shinar and settled there. And they said to one another, 'Come, let us make bricks and burn them thoroughly`. And they used brick for stone, and they used tar for mortar. And they said, 'Come, let us build for ourselves, a city and a tower whose top will reach into heaven and let us make for ourselves a name; lest we be scattered abroad over the face of the whole earth`.

And the Lord came down to _see_ [Rââh` - to perceive intellectually] …the city and the tower which the sons of men had built. And the Lord said, 'Behold, they are one _people_ [`Am – the whole human race] …and they all have the same language. And this is what they began to do and now nothing which they purpose to do will be impossible for them. Let the authority of the heavens go down and there _confuse_ [Bâlal – this is a primary root word meaning to mix, to mingle oil into flour] …their language, that they may not understand one another's speech`. So, the Lord scattered them abroad from there over the face of the whole earth; and they stopped building the city. Therefore, its name was called _Babel_ [Babylon], because from there the Lord confused (mixed, mingled) the language of the whole earth; and scattered them abroad over the face of the whole earth."

The whole world (dry land) was created one single continent. God placed the descendants of Noah into ethnic groups over this whole world and created a language for each one. This occurred in the generation of Elishah and Tarshish, Kittim and Dodanim; the sons of Javan; the son of Japheth; the son of Noah.

Genesis 10:5

"From these the coastlands of the _nations_ [Gôwy–heathen people; a general word used particularly for Gentiles] …were separated into their _lands_ [`Erets – countries; territories of the earth] …everyone according to his language, according to their _families_ [Mishpâchâh – the anthropological category of race; nationalities] …into their nations."

Genesis 10:25

"And two sons were born to Eber; the name of the one was Peleg, for in his days the _earth_ [`Erets – physical planet, habitation of man] …was _divided_ [Pâlag – to split into parts; coast lands, continents]; …and his brother's name was Joktan."

Genesis 10:32

"These are the families of the sons of Noah according to their genealogies, by their nations; and out of these the nations were separated on the earth after the flood."

God makes it very clear that every person in the world is a descendant of Noah. God first separated Noah's unbelieving descendants by language and race. This placed the peoples of the world at specific locations by language and ethnicity. God's next separation of people was by breaking apart the one continent of the world into the Teutonic plates we have today (nations separated by the seas/coastlands). This took place in the generation of Shem in the day of Peleg (Genesis 10:21-25, and First Chronicles 1:19).

It is very clear that Columbus did not "discover" the American continent as if it was an unpopulated land. There is no such thing as the evolution of man, or a migration across an ice bridge, or a "lost tribe of Israel", or anything created by aliens from outer space.

James V. Holland

Chapter 5

CREATION OF SPIRITUAL ISREAL: THE PEOPLE OF GOD

ABRAHAM

Genesis 11:10-26 records the genealogy of Shem to Abram. Noah lived three hundred and fifty years after the flood. Abram was born in Ur of the Chaldeans three hundred and ninety-seven years after the flood. Shem lived six hundred and eighty years. He died five hundred and eighty years after the flood.

Nothing is revealed about Noah's descendants until Genesis 11: 27-12:4. These verses reveal Abram to be a descendant of Noah through his son Shem; through whom Abram was taught to walk with God by faith. God did not simply choose Abram at random. He (like Adam, Noah, Shem and Terah) talked with God and was blessed for their obedience to God's directions. His father (Terah) started a journey to Canaan from the land of the Chaldeans. Terah took Abram and his wife Sarai, Abram's brother Nahor and his wife Milcah and Abram's nephew Lot. They went as far as Haran and settled there until Abram was seventy-five years old.

Then it was time for God to call out Abram to create a *holy people* through whom He could accomplish His purpose for the redemption of humanity. God reveals Himself to all people by His Spirit; but all of His promises for spiritual life can be given only to those who will believe in Him and obey Him. His promises are not fulfilled in even one single person who claims a spiritual identity to God merely as a physical descendant of Abram.

Genesis 12:1-7
"Now the Lord said to Abram, 'Go forth from your *country* [`Erets – relinquish the piece of earth you hold as personal property.] …and from your relatives and from your father's *house* [Bayith – an earthly dwelling place built by the hands of man] …to the *land*{`Erets – the whole earth is the dwelling place of physical man] …which I will *show* [Rââh – to intellectually perceive, to give understanding, to ascertain by faith] …you; and I will *make* ['Âsâh – to labor with the ethical obligation to create something from its beginning and refine it to accomplish its purpose] …you a great *nation* [Gôwy – a general word referring to the entire populace of the gentile (heathen) world. This is God's revelation that all of Abram's *spiritual descendants* would come from the populace of the whole world under the curse of death.] …and I will *bless* [Bârak – to humble oneself and kneel before God to receive His blessing] …you and make your name great; and so, you shall be a *blessing* [Bᵉrâkâh – a gift to benefit a person with peace]; …And I will bless those who bless you and the one who *curses* [Qâlal – to be despised, to be little, to be insignificant and of small worth] …you, I will *curse* [`Ârar – to render powerless to resist God].

And in you all the *families* [Mishpâchâh – an ever-burgeoning circle of relatives with strong blood ties] …of the *earth* [`Ădâmâh – the entire earth created as arable land to produce growth. The body of Adam was created from this "earth". God cultivates the physical human race to produce a unique holy spiritual people] …shall be *blessed* [Bârak – To humble oneself and kneel before God to receive His gift of life.].

So, Abram went forth as the Lord had spoken to him and Lot went with him. Now Abram was seventy-five years old when he departed from Haran. And Abram took Sarai his wife and Lot his nephew, and all their possessions which they had accumulated and the *persons* [Nephesh – slaves] …which they had *acquired* [`Âsâh – to work, to labor, to toil, to procure] …in Haran, and they set out for the *land* [`Erets – the earth at large; the temporal scene of mortal human activity] …of Canaan (Genesis 9:5; the people God cursed); thus, they came to the land of Canaan. And Abram passed through the land as far as the site of Shechem, to the oak of Moreh. Now the Canaanite was *then* [`Âz – a temporal adverb referring to either the past or the present; it expresses a strict logical sequence] …in the land. And the Lord *appeared* [Rââh – to reveal oneself; to cause to ascertain] …to Abram and said, 'To your *descendants* [Zera` - to sow seed{singular} – the entire *spiritual line* of descendants from Abram and Sarah would be treated as a single unit] …I will give this *land* [`Erets– the earth at large; all humanity cursed by Death]. ` …So he built an altar there to the Lord who had appeared to him."

God began His revelation of salvation to Abram by telling him to leave his familiar home because the physical earth is not his permanent home. God would provide a physical life for him in the world of unbelieving man, but the earth is not the permanent home of any human being.

In Abram, God began to establish faith as the only response that is acceptable to Him because it is the acknowledgement that what God says is the only truth that sets man free from the curse of death. God's promise to Abram was to bring redemption to the *unbelieving humanity of the whole world.* He repeats the promise four times; twice to Abram (Genesis 17:6-8 and 22:16-18), once to Isaac (Genesis 26:3-4), and once to Jacob / Israel (Genesis 28:13-14).

God appeared to Abram; this is His signature that seals His progressive revelation of salvation for humanity. His appearance is the revelation of His Kingdom of Life in heaven creating His kingdom rule of spiritual life on earth. Abram's unbelieving physical descendants (as did the Canaanites) would possess the land (the whole earth) as their home and will perish with it in God's judgment; but Abram's spiritual descendants will be saved from the curse of death. They will be God's people through whom He will complete His work of spiritual redemption on the whole earth. God began this work of creating man with spiritual life with the first Adam, and He completed it with the second Adam (the Messiah; a true Israelite from heaven).

Hebrews 11:1-2; 8-10

"Now *faith* [Pistis – God's persuasion of the mind to know truth; the reality of what is intangible and unknowable by the physical senses; the ability to know the true identity of God] …is the *assurance* [Hupostasis – the basis or foundation for existence] …of things hoped for, the *conviction* [Elegchos – the revelation of truth] …of things not seen. For by it the *men of old* [Presbus – ancestors] …gained approval. By faith Abraham, when he was called, obeyed by going out to a place which he was to receive for an inheritance; and he went out not knowing where he was going. By faith he lived as an alien (having heavenly spiritual life restored by

God) in the land of promise as in a *foreign* [Allotrios – belonging to another, not one's own] …land, dwelling in tents with Isaac and Jacob, fellow heirs of the same promise; for he was *looking for* [Ekdechomai- to wait for with expectation] …the city which has foundations, whose architect and builder is God."

The holy people of God's making are built on the bedrock foundation of faith in the timeless presence of the Deity of Heaven to restore man to spiritual life. Unbelieving mans' affinity to the earth is to own it as their own possession and their treasure. Spiritual Israelites (Spiritual descendants of Jacob – Israel) affinity is toward heaven; not because they own it, but because God owns them as His own possession; His treasure. *There is no difference in the names "Spiritual Israelites" and "Christians". Both have the Timeless Spiritual Life of heaven as a free gift from `Ĕlôhîym – the One Single Deity's Throne of Life. Both have been cleansed by the blood of Jesus Christ – God's Messiah. God's gift of salvation is for every person of the whole world who will accept it by faith.

Genesis 13:12-18
"Abram settled in the land of Canaan while Lot settled in the cities of the valley and moved his tents as far as Sodom. Now the men of Sodom were exceedingly wicked and sinners against the Lord. And the Lord said to Abram after Lot had separated from him, 'Now lift up your eyes and look from the place where you are, northward and southward and eastward and westward; for all the *land* [`Erets – the whole physical earth and its human inhabitants] …which you see I will give it to you and to your {*spiritual*}descendants forever. And I will make your {*spiritual*} descendants as the dust of the earth; so that if anyone can number the dust of the earth then your descendants can also be numbered. Arise, walk about the land through its length and breadth; for I will give it to you`. Then Abram moved his tent and came and dwelt by the oaks of Mamre which are in Hebron, and there he built an altar to the Lord."

God made a covenant with Abram that He would establish a nation of people with the spiritual life given to every human being by their faith. This was a vision for Abram to see himself as a spiritual being empowered with spiritual life. God's promise was that a delivered people (people ruled by God's kingdom of Life) would inhabit the earth. Abram had physical limitations on how far he could see. This established God's assurance that Abram's personal life would be His holy temple; His dwelling place on earth is in His people. God's vision also extended on to the future and His dwelling place in the lives of Abram's spiritual descendants.

Abram was a man of God taken out of the heathen world. All of his spiritual descendants would be from the heathen world and the whole world would be the possession of God's people. It was God who determined where He would place the pagan people of this world and it was God who determined where He would place His people to do His redemptive work.

In 1959, the Spirit of God moved upon the inhabitants of the state of Nagaland, India. God converted eight hundred thousand headhunters to be fearless evangelists of the gospel of Christ; to reach India and all of the surrounding countries. God created the Garden of Eden for Adam to enjoy the purity of His presence. God's creation of a holy nation to possess the whole world would be established with the same spiritual power of life that identified Adam; created in the image of God. Every member of this spiritual nation is under the authority of God's blood and will be the presence of God to bring great blessings to the whole world. The force of death working in the pagan people of this world (the Canaanites possessed the land) is the temporary power of the flesh, but it has no power over the spiritually empowered people of God.

Galatians 3:26-29

"For you are all [<u>Huios</u> – the identity of the Father and the Christ are one and the same Deity revealed by the same sinless moral character. Every person given spiritual birth are sons of God through faith in Christ Jesus.] ... For all of you who were *baptized* [<u>Baptizō</u> – to immerse in water in token of purification from sin and spiritual pollution; the general significance is to be totally identified with the perfect life of Christ] ...into Christ have clothed yourselves with Christ. There is neither Jew nor Greek, there is neither slave nor free man and there is neither male nor female; for you are all One in Christ Jesus. And if you belong to Christ, then you are Abraham's *offspring* [<u>Sperma</u> – seed containing the germ of new fruit; used of living beings, meaning posterity or descendant; the sperma of God denotes God's power working the divine life in believers who thence derive the divine nature of life; God's children] ...*heirs* [<u>Klēronomos</u> – one who possesses power over what is given by lot; salvation is a gift] ...according to *promise* [<u>Epaggella</u> – a legal undertaking to do or give something; used primarily for the promises of God]."

Genesis 14:13

"Then a fugitive came and told Abram the *Hebrew* [<u>'Ibrîy</u> – This word is an early generic term for a variety of Semitic peoples and is somewhat akin to the word barbarian. It is an ethnic word to describe a diverse mixture of nomadic wanderers. This is the first time it is used in scripture to identify Abraham and his family with a humanistic term. The fugitive from battle told Abram that Lot had been taken prisoner.]. ...Now he was living by the oaks of Mamre the Amorite, brother of Eshcol and the brother of Aner, and these were *allies* [<u>Ba'al</u> –the main idea of this word is owner, master, lord, and thus identifies these men with the power of a Canaanite god. It is used here as very powerful partners or allies] ...with Abram."

The focal point of God's message to Abram in Haran is that God is forever moving upon the heathen world to claim lost humanity and Abram will forever be identified with them. He commanded Abram to take the initial step of faith; to get started. He was commanded to leave everything immediately. Abram recognized his personal responsibility; God was talking to him, not someone else. He had to obey Him right there where he lived and continue obeying Him wherever he lived.

This required a decision, a commitment and a submissive obedient spirit to a greater authority than one's self. God is the supreme authority to be obeyed. It is contrary to human nature to do this.

In 1976, Kingston Mphofu was a belligerent sixteen-year-old boy living in Francistown, Botswana. His father was a Baptist minister, but Kingston would not listen to him. Kingston was rescued by his father from a witch doctor as he was about to be a human sacrifice to Satan. Kingston experienced a transformation of his mind from unbelief to a faith that would lay hold of God. He was humbled before the Lord and expressed an urgent need to commit his life to

God Reveals His Glory [Doxa – True Identity]

Him. God delivered him from imminent physical death and now he had faith that God would deliver him from timeless death.

God gave Abram a vision of accountability for his future life of faith. God would direct him, bless him, protect him and enrich his life with the goodness of His heavenly kingdom. He learned that everything we have on earth is a gift of God's grace. He journeyed beyond Canaan, to Egypt. He encountered sinful people who were very bold in immorality and violence. It was the grace of God that delivered his wife Sarai out of their grasp. It was the grace of God that delivered Lot out of captivity from the hands of King Chedorlaomer; and caused Melchizedek, the king of Salem and priest of God the Highest, to bless Abram. It was by God's grace that He gave Abram a home in the homeland of the Canaanites as a temporary physical down payment in token of what Abram came to understand as a spiritual promise of timeless life in heaven. Abram did not own the land; thus, the land did not own him as it did these Canaanites.

Genesis 15:1
"After these things the *Word* [Dâbâr–a technical expression for prophetic revelation; a judgment from the throne of God] …of the Lord *came* [Hâyâh – to breath, to exist, the ever-present existence of "I Am Who I Am"] …to Abram in a vision, saying, 'Do not *fear* [yârê - the emotion and intellectual anticipation of harm; what one feels may go wrong for him] …Abram, I am a shield to you; your reward shall be very great`."

God revealed Himself to Abram so that he would not be led in his human mind to trust in earthly powers (pagan gods) for the spiritual life that can only come from heaven. What God offers man is His Kingdom power of timeless spiritual life. There is no evil power of death in Him. Satan causes us to fear; but God causes us to be at peace. All the blessings of Abram's life would not be by his natural means, but by the presence of God to do His kingdom work.

Genesis 15:2-6
"And Abram said, 'O Lord, what will You give me, since I am childless and the *heir* [Bên–first born son through which he receives social continuity] …of my house is Eliezer of Damascus`? And Abram said, 'Since Thou hast given no offspring to me, one born in my house is my heir`. Then behold, the word of the Lord came to him saying, 'This man will not be your heir; but one who shall come forth from your own *body* [Mê 'âh – internal organs of the body], …he shall be your heir`. And He took him outside and said, 'Now look toward the heavens and count the stars, if you are able to count them`. And He said to him, 'So shall your descendants be`. Then he *believed* [`Âman – to trust in with absolute conviction] …in the Lord; and He *reckoned* [Châshab- to impute, to make a judgment] …it to him as *righteousness* [Ts^{e}dâqâh – justified; a creation of heavenly life that cannot die, having the same holy character and authority as the Throne of God; timeless life.]."

God's revelation to Abram is that His nation of the whole earth (God's objective is to restore spiritual life to every human being who will ever live upon the earth from the day of Noah to the Apokalupsis of the Christ) is established upon a legitimate sonship relationship to the living God by right of spiritual birth. A child does not have any ability to create itself, nor can the people of God create itself a holy nation. The legitimate heir of Abram would be purely the work of God's grace. Abram placed his faith in God for the revelation that his rightful heir would be one individual person born by legitimate sonship (the life is in the blood); and that through this righteous relationship of birth, more people than Abram could count would also have a righteous relationship to God (their Father); and be the legal heirs to His kingdom of life.

This promise of an heir to Abram was the *Anti-Type* of God's promise to the whole world. The promise to Abram was fulfilled physically when Isaac was born. Through Isaac, a people of faith were led by God to bless the world. It was through this people that God's promise of *The Type* was also fulfilled physically when the legitimate heir to God's kingdom of Life was brought forth, The Messiah, Jesus the Christ. Only through Him can the whole world be blessed by the righteousness of God, Who by His grace gives timeless life to every single person who will believe in Him.

Romans 4:1-9

"What then shall we say that Abraham, our *forefather* [Patēr – a first author or beginner of anything] …according to the *flesh* [Sarx – the human body; physical life] …has found? For if Abraham was *justified* [Dikaioō – to bring out the fact that a person is righteous, or if he is not, to make him righteous] …by *works* [Ergon–performance to obtain any beneficial matter or thing] …he has something to boast about, but not before God.

For what does the Scripture say? 'Abraham *believed* [Pisteuō – to have a mental persuasion to the truth] …God, and it was *reckoned* [Logizomai–to decide what is good and what is evil. It is derived from (Logos – the mind of God spoken as an expression of intelligence); and (Legō – to speak by linking and knitting together in connected discourse the inward thought and feelings of the mind); a term technically applied to God's act of justification; His imputation of righteousness whose correlative is freedom from guilt] …to him as *righteousness* [Dikaiosunē – the standard of justice and holiness which identifies God as the kingdom power of life that cannot die] `. …Now to the one who works, his *wage* [Misthos – reward received in this life] …is not reckoned as a *favor* [Charis – grace: a favor done without expectation of return] …but as what is *due* [Opheilēma – debt; that which is strictly owed]. …But to the one who does not work but believes in Him who justifies the *ungodly* [Asebēs – Basically it means godless, without fear and reverence for God. It does not mean irreligious, but one who actively practices the opposite of what the fear of God demands.] …his faith is reckoned as righteousness, just as David also speaks of the blessing upon the man to whom God reckons righteousness apart from works: Psalm 32:1-2: 'Blessed Are Those Who's Lawless Deeds Have Been Forgiven, And Whose Sins Have Been Covered. Blessed Is The Man Whose Sin the Lord Will Not Take Into Account `.' "

Romans 4:13-18

"For the *promise* [Epaggelia – a legal term denoting an undertaking to do or to give something] …to Abraham or to his descendants that he would be heir of the *world* [Kosmos– the sum total of the universe; the sum total of the persons living in the world] …was not through the *Law* [Nomos – in general the assignment or distribution of a command], …but through the righteousness of faith. For if those who are of the Law are heirs, faith is made void and the promise is nullified; for the Law brings about wrath, but where there is no law, neither is there *violation* [Paidagôgos – an instructor or teacher]. …For this reason it is by faith, that it be in

God Reveals His Glory [Doxa – True Identity]

accordance with *grace* [Charis – the absolute freeness of the loving kindness of God to man] …in order that the promise may be *certain* [Bebaios - fixed, safe, trustworthy] …to all the descendants, not only to those who are of the Law, but also to those who are of the faith of Abraham, who is the father of us all, (as it is written, 'A Father Of Many Nations Have I Made You'[Tithēmi – to set or put in place]…in the sight of Him whom he believed, even God, who gives life to the dead and calls unto being that which does not exist. In hope against hope, he believed in order that he might become a father of many nations according to that which had been spoken 'So Shall Your Descendants Be'."

Hebrews 11:8-16

"By faith, Abraham when he was called, *obeyed* [Hupakouō – the revelation of faith as revealed in the humble acceptance of God's message] …by going out to a place which he was to receive for an *inheritance* [Klēronomia – an heir of Divine salvation, considered both as promised and as already bestowed]; …and he went out not knowing where he was going. By faith he *lived* [Paroikeō – to be a stranger in a foreign land for a short time] …as an alien in the land of promise, as in a *foreign* [Allotrios– land belonging to others; not one's own] …land, dwelling in tents with Isaac and Jacob, *fellow heirs* [Sugklēronomos – a personal equality based on an equality of possession] …of the same *promise* [Epaggelia – a legal term used only for the gifts of God with the emphasis on the gift fulfilled]; …for he was *looking for* [Ekdechomai – to wait on something with the full expectation of receiving it] …the city which has foundations, whose architect and *builder* [Dēmiourgos – one who works for the public; this word refers to God as the creator] …is *God* [Theos – the name of the one true God]. …By faith even Sarah herself received ability to conceive even beyond the proper time of life, since she considered Him faithful who had promised; therefore, also, there was born of one man, and him as good as dead at that, as many descendants as the stars of heaven in number, and innumerable as the sand which is by the seashore. All these died in faith, without receiving the promises, but having seen them and having welcomed them from a distance and having confessed that they were strangers and exiles on the earth. For those who say such things make it clear that they are seeking a country of their own. And indeed, if they had been thinking of that country from which they went out, they would have had opportunity to return. But as it is, they desire a better country that is a heavenly one. Therefore, God is not ashamed to be called their God; for He has prepared a city for them."

Genesis 15:12-16

"Now when the sun was going down, a deep sleep fell upon Abram; and behold, terror and great darkness fell upon him. And God said to Abram, 'Know for certain that your descendants will be strangers in a land that is not theirs, where they will be enslaved and oppressed four hundred years. But I will also judge the nation whom they will serve; and afterward they will come out with many possessions. And as for you, you shall go to your fathers in peace; you shall be buried at a good old age. Then in the fourth generation they shall return here, for the iniquity of the Amorite is not yet complete.'"

God began the first generation of man with Adam; created with the power of spiritual life. God began the second generation of man with Noah; a man who possessed the power of spiritual life because of his faith in God to deliver him from God's righteous judgment. Abram was a descendant of Noah and was also a man of faith. Through this man, endued with God's gift of spiritual life; God began the creation of a unique people which would be the spiritual descendants of Adam. This people would be born out of great pain and suffering and they would struggle against the kingdom powers of this world for the duration of their existence.

God's heir to His throne of heaven (Messiah) would come out of this people. He would bear the pain and suffering of God's judgment upon the sins of the whole world. This vision put Abram in terror and darkness; but he was given the assurance that the end work of God in the life of His people is the timeless peace of His deliverance from the curse of death which brings man nothing but pain and suffering.

SARAI AND HAGAR

Genesis 16:1-2
"Now Sarai, Abram's wife had borne him no children and she had an Egyptian maid named Hagar. So, Sarai said to Abram, 'Now behold, the Lord has prevented me from bearing children. Please go into my maid: perhaps I shall obtain children through her'. And Abram _listened_ [Shâma – to give undivided attention and obedience] …to the voice of Sarai."

God's progressive revelation given to Abram was interrupted in the same manner as Satan's appearance to the woman in the Garden of Eden. The result was that Abram made the same mistake as Adam. Both placed the desires of the flesh above the constraining wisdom of God. This story is the revelation of God that sin (rebellion, lawlessness of the flesh) is the permanent and continuing source of evil's controlling power of death over the physical life of man. Both Adam and Abram turned away from the voice of timeless spiritual life to listen to the satanic lie; the idea that man can usurp the authority of God and live by his own power of the flesh. Man establishes his own law as the determining factor of what is right and what is wrong. This lie is the power Satan holds upon the human mind to instigate the creation of every religion in the world.

Sarai (like Eve) spoke evil of God and transgressed against her purpose of creation. She blamed God for what she perceived as the permanent loss of her right to bear children. She was correct in that it was God who prevented her from having children; but it was not permanent, and it was for His glory, not hers. She despaired of waiting on God so she circumvented His righteousness so that her husband could have an heir by her authority. She would have the glory shine upon herself as a woman and remove the glory God intended for Abram's legitimate heir.

God did not stop the progression of human life because of Sarai's selfish, faithless unbelief. Hagar committed adultery by giving birth to an illegitimate heir to Abraham. Ishmael was born by right of the law of the flesh (Satan's rule) and not by the law of God's Kingdom of Life. God's command was that (Genesis 16:12) Ishmael and his descendants would live to the east of his brothers and forever be a lawless people at war with God's promised heir to His kingdom of Life. Ishmael's descendants still claim Abraham to be their father and the Moslem religion to be the true heir of [Allah – al (the) ilāh (god); Allah is not the true God, but an idol]. This is why this people have such a passionate hatred for the Jewish and American people (what they call the great Satan).

God Reveals His Glory [Doxa – True Identity]

GOD'S COVENANT OF CIRCUMCISION

Genesis 17:1-22

"Now when Abram was ninety-nine years old, the Lord appeared [Rââh] to Abram and said to him, 'I am *God Almighty* [`ÊlShadday – `Êl is a masc. Heb. noun which emphasizes might, strength, power; hence it was commonly used by men for the name of pagan gods. Shadday is a pl. masc. Heb. noun (like `Ĕlôhîym) meaning majesty, the Powerful One, the unchanging one. This title indicates the fullness and riches of God's grace and would remind the Hebrew reader that from God comes every good and perfect gift. He is never weary of pouring forth His mercies on His people and He is more ready to give than they are to receive."

This is the first appearance of this name in the scriptures. In Ex. 3:15; 6:3, El Shadday was the covenant name for God to the Patriarchs until the time of Moses. His covenant defined His moral and ethical character; thus, it was the divine title to address the royal God of Heaven.

The Hebrews, unwilling to use such a holy name changed it to the epithet of Jehovah (Yahweh; YHWH)]; …walk before Me, and be *blameless* [Tâmîyn – the holiness of Spiritual life, entire, whole, complete, perfect, sound (free from blemishes), faultless, innocent, honest; the divine standard of God's law of righteousness].

"And I will establish My *covenant* [B^{e}rîyth–the ancient custom of ratifying solemn agreements by passing between the divided parts of victims. Circumcision of the foreskin ratifies God's covenant for the multiplication of heirs to the throne of God; God passes between the body and the foreskin] …between Me and you and I will multiply you exceedingly`. And Abram fell on his face and God (`Êl) talked with him, saying, 'As for Me, behold, My covenant is with you, and you shall be the *father* [`Âb - begetter, forefather, originator, a strong bond of continuity between generations] …of a multitude of *nations* [Gôwy - person, inhabitant, people, tribe, a general word referring particularly to Gentiles, uncircumcised, wicked, (Isa. 2:2ff, people God redeems to spiritual life through the Messiah)]. …No longer shall your name be *called* [Qârâ - verb; to cry out, proclaim, to summon, the act of naming is an assertion of sovereignty over what is being named] …Abram (exalted father), but your name shall be Abraham (father of a multitude), for I will make you the father of a multitude of nations. And I will make you exceedingly fruitful and I will make nations of you and Kings shall come forth from you.   And I will establish My covenant between Me and you and your descendants after you throughout their generations for an everlasting covenant to be God to you and to your descendants after you. And I will give to you and to your descendants after you, the *land* [`Erets – The whole physical planet of earth as opposed to heaven. The earth was created for the habitation of man; and God dwells in all of it by the authority of spiritual life imparted to man. The earth will never stop its productivity, whether it be seeds for harvest or the seed of God producing a harvest of spiritual man (Isa. 45:22, "Turn to Me and be saved, all the ends of the earth")] … of your *sojournings* [Mâgûwr – a temporary dwelling that is not one's home],… all the land(`Erets) of *Canaan* [K$^e$na`an – humiliated; from the root word (kâna`– to be humbled before God in repentance, to subdue, to vanquish). The land of Canaan means all of the people of the earth God has cursed as enemies because they defile themselves by religious and moral perversions of every kind and they teach other people to do the same. Not only are they resistant to the word of God, but they are also wicked in character.] ...for an everlasting *possession* ['Ăchuzzâh – property seized, grasped, held fast, to pass to one's heirs for an indiscriminate future. God has decreed that He will take the righteous people who glorify Him, from all the land of the world that is possessed by people under His curse. This earth was created as a temporary dwelling place for God to bless the lives of believing people and God will not allow unbelieving people to physically or spiritually usurp a safe home as His dwelling place. Every redeemed person on this earth dwells in the timelessness of God and every lost person dwells in Hades] ...and I will be their God.

God said further to Abraham, 'Now as for you, you shall *keep* [Shâmar– to build a hedge of thorns around something to guard it; to be a watchman as a prophet; to keep safe; to observe a covenant as a command of God] ...My covenant, you and your descendants after you throughout their generations.

This is My covenant which you shall keep, between Me and you and your descendants after you: every *male* [Zâkâr– Adam was created a Spiritual power of life in a physical body with the God given purpose of reproducing spiritual life in every person born of woman] ... among you shall be circumcised. And you shall be circumcised in the flesh of your *foreskin* ['Oriâh – the uncleanness of the flesh, insensibility; from the root word ('Ârêl) meaning exposed, projecting loosely, unconsecrated]; ... and it shall be the sign of the covenant between me and you. And every male among you who is eight days old shall be circumcised throughout your generations, a servant who is born in the house or who is bought with money from any foreigner who is not of your descendants. But an uncircumcised male who will not be circumcised in the flesh of his foreskin, that person shall be *cut off* [Kârath – killed; one who is pledged to the judgment of death if he breaks the pledge of the covenant] ...from his *people* ['Am – a unit of people belonging to God]; ...he has *broken* [Pârar – to break in pieces, to dissolve, to violate, to annul, to annihilate] ...My covenant'."

God initiated this covenant to identify Himself as the authority of righteousness to faithfully fulfill His predetermined plan for restoring every lost person on earth to His image of timeless spiritual life. God upon His throne in Heaven is our exalted Father, who reveals Himself on earth as the Spiritual Father of every person born to be joint heirs with Christ in the timeless Kingdom of Righteousness. God commanded Abraham to ratify this covenant as the first man subject to its promise and its provisions. Every male of Abraham's family who would submit to this covenant in the flesh, did so as a faith agreement with God to be a member of His holy family by spiritual birth.

The provision of this covenant is that Abraham and every male of his family was to submit their bodies to God for a sacrificial cleansing of the flesh, which is under the curse of death. The human male is the holy representative of the person of God because of his created power for the propagation of the human race (life giver; the life is in the blood). The purpose of this covenant is for God to propagate a holy people in human bodies submissive to His authority and the character of His throne of righteousness. God's will be for His people on earth; to validate the holiness of spiritual life as God's presence in control of this world as He is in heaven.

This covenant was ratified by God passing between the man and the uncleanness (foreskin) of his flesh. This temporary(anti-type) covenant was fulfilled permanently by God's cleansing unholy man by the sacrifice of Himself in the flesh of a human body (the Messiah -

God Reveals His Glory [Doxa – True Identity]

the type). The authority of God's presence on this earth – Christ, transforms sinful man to a new creation of righteousness under the authority of His throne in heaven. He confirmed this covenant with His Passover; the sacrifice of His blood (the power of God's kingdom of Life) spilled out on the earth and placed on the altar in heaven.

I John 5:4-12

"For whatever is *born* [Gennaō – used to identify human life as a spiritual creation of God] …overcomes the world; and this is the victory that has overcome the world --- our faith. And who is the one who overcomes the world, but he who believes that Jesus is the *Christ* [Huios – one and the same Deity of Heaven revealed by His sinless character] …of *God* [Theos – the name of the one true God; the Greek name that is the same as `Ĕlôhîym]? …This is the one who came by water and blood, Jesus Christ; not with water only, but with the water and the *blood* [Haima – the substantial basis for life. {Lev.17:11, 'For the life of the flesh is in the blood.`}]. …And it is the Spirit who bears witness, because the Spirit is the truth. For there are three that *bear witness* [Martureō – to give confirmation] …the Spirit and the water and the blood; and the three are in agreement. If we receive the witness of men, the witness of God is greater; for the witness of God is this, that He has borne witness concerning His Huios - His presence on earth. The one who believes in the Huios - Christ of God has the witness in himself; the one who does not believe God has made Him a liar, because he has not believed in the witness that God has borne concerning His Huios - Jesus. And the witness is this; that God has given us timeless life and this life is in His Huios - Christ. He who has *Christ* [Huios – Heavenly Deity] has the life; he who does not have *Christ* [Huios- Deity of God] does not have the life."

Romans 4:9-12

"Is this blessing then upon the circumcised or upon the uncircumcised also? For we say, 'Faith Was Reckoned To Abraham As Righteousness`. How then was it reckoned to him? While he was circumcised, or uncircumcised? Not while circumcised, but while uncircumcised, and he received the *sign* [Sēmeion – finger posts of God; valuable not so much as for what they are but for what they indicate of the grace and power of the doer and his immediate connection with a higher spiritual world] …of circumcision, a seal of the righteousness of the faith which he had while uncircumcised, that he might be the father of all who believe without being circumcised, that righteousness might be reckoned to them, and the father of circumcision to those who not only are of the circumcision, but all those who also follow in the steps of the faith of our father Abraham which he had while uncircumcised."

THE PROMISED BIRTH OF ISAAC

Genesis 17:15-19

"Then God said to Abraham, 'As for *Sarai* [Sâray – a female name with the dominative relation of a man's wife ruling over all other females in her husband's house (servants, slaves)] …your wife, you shall not call her name Sarai, but *Sarah* [Sârâh – a queen, a noble lady of a royal court] …shall be her name. And I will bless her and indeed I will give you a son by her. Then I will bless her, and she shall be a mother of nations; kings of peoples shall come from her`. Then Abraham fell on his face and *laughed* [Tsâchaq – to laugh outright in merriment or unbelief] … and said in his heart, 'Will a child be born to a man one hundred years old? And will Sarah, who is ninety years old, bear a child'? And Abraham said to God, 'Oh that Ishmael might live before Thee`'! But God said, 'No, but Sarah your wife shall bear you a son and you shall call his name *Isaac* [Yitschâq – laughter; from the root word (tsâchaq)] …and I will establish My covenant with him for an everlasting covenant for his descendants after him`'."

Genesis 21:1-8

"Then the Lord *took note* [Pâqad – to visit; the Lord intervened on behalf of Sarah in a miraculous way so that she could conceive at an advanced age] …of Sarah as He had said, and the Lord did for Sarah as He had promised. So, Sarah conceived and bore a son to Abraham in his old age at the appointed time of which God had spoken to him. And Abraham called the name of his son who was born to him, whom Sarah bore to him, Isaac. Then Abraham circumcised his son Isaac when he was eight days old as God had commanded him. Now Abraham was one hundred years old when his son Isaac was born to him. And Sarah said, 'God has made laughter for me; everyone who hears will laugh with me`. And she said, 'Who would have said to Abraham that Sarah would nurse children? Yet I have borne him a son in his old age`. And the child grew and was weaned, and Abraham made a great feast on the day that Isaac was weaned."

God made Sarai barren so she could not give birth to a child by natural human means. God protected her and kept her morally clean until she was ninety years old and past time for childbearing. This was God's designated time to elevate her status for her child to be born of a queen, the ruler of her husband's royal court. Isaac could only be born by the movement of God upon his mother so he would be recognized and be acquainted with God's royal court of heaven. In this respect, Isaac was the anti-type to the Messiah (the type); Jesus came from His royal court of heaven to be placed in the womb of a woman by the Holy Spirit.

The idea that God can work His will in human life by the spiritual power of heaven was ludicrous to the people who believed physical man is the true authority in this world. If a child could not be born from the bodies of their youth, it could not be born at all. God by His power brought laughter to Abraham and Sarah in their old age; but at God's designated time He brought rejoicing to heaven and earth by the miraculous birth of the Messiah, the Christ, who would take away the sins of the world. God's [Huios–Jesus; Deity from heaven] brings the greater joy to the world than Hagar's son Ishmael.

God Reveals His Glory [Doxa – True Identity]

THE SACRIFICE OF ISAAC

Genesis 22:1-2, 4, 6-18

"Now it came about after these things, that God *tested* [Nâçâh–to put truth to the proof through the demonstration of stress. The KJV incorrectly translated this to be "tempt" (entice to do wrong). God did not tempt Abraham to do wrong, but He refined or revealed His own character to govern Abraham's mind to be the righteousness of God. Abraham's belief that God has the power to give life to the dead was proven by his faith.] …Abraham, and said to him, 'Abraham`! and he said, 'Here am I`. And He said, 'Take now your son, your *only* [Yâchîyd – Heb. adj. meaning alone, forsaken, an only child. In John 3:16, this word "only" is (Monogenēs – one of a kind; the only one of the family born to this father), but the Septuagint uses the Greek word (agapētos – beloved, dear, precious one)]…son, whom you love, Isaac, and go to the *land* [`Erets– the whole earth created for the domain of man as a spiritual being] … of *Moriah* [Môrîyâh - a combination of (Rââh – to perceive) (Yâhh – the sacred name) and (Yᵉhôvâh – the self-existent or timeless God). II Chronicles 3:1, 'Then Solomon began to build the house of the Lord in Jerusalem on Mount Moriah, where the Lord had appeared to his father David, at the place that David had prepared on the threshing floor of Ornan the Jebusite`. Abraham was to recognize the hill Moriah as the sacred place where God reveals Himself.]; …and *offer* [`Âlâh – to rise up, to lift up, to exalt. The idea of this word is the emotion of love for God that you commit yourself and all that is dear to you to be His possession; to do with as He pleases.] …him there as a *burnt offering* [`Ôlâh – to go up in smoke; an offering that was completely consumed by fire] …on one of the mountains of which I tell you."

"On the third day Abraham raised his eyes and *saw* [Rââh – to perceive; to see with understanding] …the place from a distance."

"And Abraham took the wood of the burnt offering and *laid* [Sûwm – to establish a new relationship; to set aside for special purposes. God placed the wooden cross of crucifixion upon the back of Jesus, {His Huios – Deity} to carry it to His place of execution] …it on Isaac his son and he took in his hand the fire and the knife. So, the two of them walked on together and Isaac spoke to Abraham his father and said, 'My father`! And he said, 'Here I am, my son`. And he said, 'Behold, the fire and the wood, but where is the lamb for the burnt offering`? And Abraham said, 'God will *provide* [Rââh – to see intellectually, to reveal oneself, to cause to see, to be fully aware of, to predetermine] …for Himself the lamb for the burnt offering, my son`.

So, the two of them walked on together. Then they came to the place of which God had told him; and Abraham built the *altar* [Mizbêach – from (Zâbach) – to slaughter, the place for individuals to act with the authority of God to ratify an agreement between heaven and earth by taking the life of innocent blood] …there and arranged the wood and bound his son Isaac and laid him on the altar on top of the wood. And Abraham stretched out his hand and took the knife to *slay* his son [Shâchat – to completely butcher an animal for total consumption by the sacrificial fire. *Jesus was scourged by the Roman army to be almost unrecognizable as a man and was nailed to a cross, but they did not have the power to kill Him.]. …But the angel of the Lord called to him from *heaven* [Shâmayim – the holy abode of God] …and said, 'Abraham, Abraham`! And he said, 'Here I am`. And he said, 'Do not stretch out your hand against the lad and do nothing to him; for now, I *know* [Yâda` - the confirmation of God's knowledge of man] …that you *fear* [Yârê` - a very positive feeling of awe or reverence for God which motivates or affects godly living] …God, since you have not withheld your son, your only son, from Me`.

Then Abraham raised his eyes and looked and behold, behind him a ram caught in the thicket by his horn; and Abraham went and took the ram and offered him up for a burnt offering in the place of his son. And Abraham called the name of that place *The Lord Will Provide* [Yᵉhôvâh-yireh – God will be seen; God will see to it. God unveiled His Deity with the sacrifice of the Christ to redeem the whole human race.] …as it is said to *this day* [Yôwm – The revelation of God is connected to His timeless Sovereign Being. What God reveals about Himself as a saving God is unchangeable and binding upon every human being past, present, or future.]. … 'In the mount of the Lord it will be provided`.

Then the angel of the Lord called to Abraham a second time from heaven and said, 'By Myself I have *sworn* [Shâba' – to confirm or bind by an oath] …declares the Lord, because you have done this thing and have not withheld your son, your only son, indeed I will greatly bless you and I will greatly multiply your *seed* [Zera' – people of the whole world related to God by the Abrahamic covenant] …as the stars of the heavens and as the sand which is on the seashore; and your seed shall *possess* [Yârêsh – to occupy by driving out previous tenants] … the *gate* [Shaᶜar – an opening to what is confined by an enclosure] …of their *enemies* [`ôwyêb – act. part. hating an adversary; those who have an attitude of hatred for you]. … And in your seed, all the *nations* [Gôwy – gentile people under the curse of death] … of the earth shall be blessed because you have obeyed My voice`."

Hebrews 11:17-19
"By faith Abraham, when he was *tested* [Peirazō- to try, to prove in a good sense what is good or evil in us] …offered up Isaac; and he who had received the promises was offering up his only *begotten* son [Monogenēs – the only son of a unique family]; …it was he to whom it was said, 'In Isaac Your Descendants Shall Be Called`. He considered that God is able to raise men even from the dead; from whom he also received him back as a *type* [Parabolē – a visible type of emblem representing something different from and beyond itself. Isaac was God's emblem of the death and resurrection of the Christ, through whom He laid claim to the lost human race.]"

God's test of faith for Abraham was to prove his powerful, emotional commitment of love for God. Abraham was faithful to obey God's command because he trusted God to take Isaac unto Himself as His rightful father. This test of faith was a two-way street. It was also a very emotional commitment on God's part to love Abraham so much that He revealed He would provide His [Own-Self - Christ] as the sacrifice to redeem him.

The purpose for the sacrifice of Isaac was that he was the anti-type of the Messiah to be sacrificed for the whole world. This was His pre-ordained plan to redeem all people to be His heavenly children. John 3:16, "For *God* [Theos – Greek word used to identify Elohiym as one single Deity as opposed to Greek mythology of a multiplicity of gods.] …so loved the world that He gave His *only begotten* [Monogenēs – morph of God to man] [Huios – Christ; the *Deity of Heaven* was not born as is a human being.] … that whoever believes in Him should not perish but has timeless life."

God's provision of a ram to take Isaac's place was a new revelation of God to accomplish His plan of redemption. What God had to do cannot be done by mortal flesh. The only power sufficient to destroy death is the Living Deity ruling from His Throne of Life. He had to submit His Own Sinless Deity to the death of the grave so that He could destroy death's power to separate life from His kingdom rule. God revealed His foreknowledge that He would provide the only sacrifice which would of necessity be raised from the death of the grave.

God promised Abraham that because of his obedience to His commands, his descendants (*Spiritual descendants of Jacob - Israel*) would inhabit the whole world. This would be possible by the actions of redeemed humanity endowed with the Spirit of God to love humanity as God loves them. God's love for man is the open door to the heart to tear down the barrier of hatred and redeem the spirit to timeless life. God's love is the power that changes the attitude of the mind to make a friend of an enemy.

II Corinthians 5:14-21

"For the love of Christ controls us, having concluded this, that one died for all, therefore all died; and He died for all, that they who live should no longer live for themselves, but for Him who died and rose again on their behalf. Therefore, from now on we recognize no man according to the flesh; even though we have known Christ according to the flesh, yet now we know Him thus no longer. Therefore, if any man is in Christ, he is a *new* [Kainos – consecrated into a qualitatively new use] ...*creature* [Ktisis– the sum total of the human race with life that God has created]; ...the old things passed away; behold, new things have come. Now all these things are from God, who reconciled us to Himself through Christ, and gave us the ministry of reconciliation, namely, that God was Christ reconciling the world to Him, not counting their trespasses against them, and He has committed to us the word of reconciliation. Therefore, we are ambassadors for Christ, as though God were entreating through us; we beg you on behalf of Christ, be reconciled to God. He made Him who knew no sin to be sin on our behalf that we might become the righteousness of God in Him."

THE DEATH OF SARAH AND ABRAHAM

Genesis 25

"Now Sarah lived one hundred and twenty-seven years; these were the years of the life of Sarah. And Sarah died in Kiriath-arba (that is, Hebron) in the land of Canaan; and Abraham went in to mourn for Sarah and to weep for her. Then Abraham rose from before his dead, and spoke to the sons of Heth, saying, 'I am a *stranger* [Gêr–foreigner, alien, pilgrim, sojourner, temporary guest, and visitor] ...and a *sojourner* [Tôwshâb – a squatter who could not possess land. He was an emigrant in a foreign country where he was not naturalized] ...among you; give me a burial site among you, that I may bury my dead out of my sight'.

And the sons of Heth answered Abraham, saying to him, 'Hear us, my *lord* [`Âdôwn – master, lord; a term of respect (the Jews used Lord as a reverent substitute instead of using the actual name of God], ...you are a mighty *prince* [Nâsîy – a person who is lifted up publicly, an exalted leader of families, a government figure, a king] ...among us; bury your dead in the choicest of our graves; none of us will refuse you his grave for burying your dead.

So, Abraham rose and bowed to the people of the land, the sons of Heth. And he spoke with them, saying, 'if it is your _wish_ [Nephesh – to live by drawing breath; the function of the soul (the life of the physical body) which acts in accordance to the thoughts of the mind] …for me to bury my dead out of my sight, hear me, and approach Ephron the son of Zohar for me, that he may give me the cave of Machpelah which he owns, which is at the end of his field; for the full price let him give it to me in your presence for a burial site.`

Now Ephron was sitting among the sons of Heth; and Ephron the Hittite answered Abraham in the hearing of the sons of Heth; even of all who went in at the gate of his city, saying, "No my lord, hear me; I give you the field and I give you the grave that is in it. In the presence of the sons of my people I give it to you; bury your dead`.

And Abraham bowed before the people of the land. And he spoke to Ephron in the hearing of the people of the land, saying, 'If you will only please listen to me; I will give the price of the field, accept it from me, that I may bury my dead there`.

Then Ephron answered Abraham saying to him, 'My lord, listen to me, a piece of land worth four hundred shekels of silver, what is that between me and you? So, bury your dead`.

And Abraham listened to Ephron; and Abraham weighed out for Ephron the silver which he had named in the hearing of the sons of Heth, four hundred shekels of silver, commercial standard. So, Ephron's field which was in Machpelah, which faced Mamre, the field and cave which was in it and all the trees which were in the field that were within all the confines of its border, were deeded over to Abraham for a possession in the presence of the sons of Heth, before all who went in at the gate of his city.

And after this, Abraham buried Sarah his wife in the cave of the field at Machpelah facing Mamre (that is, Hebron) in the land of Canaan. So, the field and the cave that is in it were deeded over to Abraham for a burial site by the sons of Heth."

Genesis 25:1-2; 5-11

"Now Abraham took another wife, whose name was Keturah. And she bore to him Zimran and Jokshan and Medan and Midian and Ishbak and Shuah."

"Now Abraham gave all that he had to Isaac; but to the sons of his concubines, Abraham gave gifts while he was still living and sent them away from his son Isaac eastward, to the land of the east. And these are all the years of Abraham's life that he lived, one hundred and seventy-five years. And Abraham breathed his last and died in a ripe old age, an old man and satisfied with life; and he was gathered to his people. Then his sons Isaac and Ishmael buried him in the cave of Machpelah, in the field of Ephron the son of Zohar the Hittite, facing Mamre, and the field which Abraham purchased from the sons of Heth; there Abraham was buried with Sarah his wife. And it came about after the death of Abraham that God blessed his son, Isaac; and Isaac lived by Beer-lahai-roi."

The death of Sarah and Abraham reveal God's message that the only permanent piece of this world that belongs to the children of God is that which can be purchased for the burial of the fleshly body. The only part of our lives that belongs to the earth is our dead bodies. This earth (land - `Erets) is the domain of death. It was not created to be the permanent home of God's spiritual people ruled by His Kingdom of Life.

God's command to Abraham was to leave the place of his birth and sojourn (live as a temporary visitor) in the habitat of the Canaanites (ungodly people who own the earth as their permanent home). God did not use him to create an earthly nationalistic religion to rule over people by the power of the flesh. Abraham and Isaac did not stake out and fight for a piece of land to be the permanent home of their descendants. They only fought to protect themselves from the evil of the world. God's purpose was to recreate Holy, Spiritual Man (Adam)with the spiritual power of life that cannot die; whose physical domain is the whole world ruled by the Throne of God's authority of timeless life.

The lives of both Abraham and Isaac were God's witness to the world for the power of the spiritual life to be at peace with God and man. They did not live by the power of the flesh but by the authority of God's righteousness. Nationalistic Israel will never cease to be at war because it is flesh under the rule of death. Their kingdom rule is a piece of land named – Israel.

ISAAC

Genesis 26:1-6
"Now there was a famine in the land, besides the previous famine that had occurred in the days of Abraham. So, Isaac went to Gerar, to Abimelech king of the Philistines. And the Lord appeared to him and said, 'Do not go down to Egypt; stay in the land of which I shall tell you. Sojourn in this land and I will be with you and bless you, for to you and to your descendants I will give all these lands and I will establish the oath which I swore to your father Abraham. And I will multiply your descendants as the stars of heaven and will give your descendants all these lands; and by your descendants all the nations of the earth shall be blessed; because Abraham obeyed Me and kept My charge, My commandments, My statutes, and My laws`. So, Isaac lived in Gerar."

Genesis 26:11-14
"So, Abimelech charged all the people, saying, 'He who touches this man, or his wife shall surely be put to death.' Now Isaac sowed in that land and reaped in the same year a hundredfold. And the Lord blessed him, and the man became rich and continued to grow richer until he became very wealthy; for he had possessions of flocks and herds and a great household, so that the Philistines envied him."

Genesis 35:28-29
"Now the days of Isaac were one hundred and eighty years. And Isaac breathed his last and died and was gathered to his people an old man of ripe age; and his sons Esau and Jacob buried him."

God has revealed the blessing and power of the spiritual life He gives to man by His grace. Abraham and Isaac were the beginning of God's creation of a people which would be identified by their obedience to His Will. God's revelation through Isaac's life of obedience is the peace the spiritual person has with the pagan people who do not know the Person of God.

ISAAC'S DESCENDANTS

Genesis 19: 1- 27
"Now these are the records of the *generations* [Tôwl^edah – fem. Heb. noun, this word is always used in the plural form and in the construct state. It refers to what is produced or brought into being by someone, and sometimes the results. It does not include the birth of the individual who started the life of descendants.] …of Isaac, Abraham's son: Abraham became the father of Isaac; and Isaac was forty years old when he took Rebekah, the daughter of Bethuel the Aramean of Paddanaram, the sister of Laban the Aramean, to be his wife. And Isaac prayed to the Lord on behalf of his wife because she was *barren* ['Âqâr – sterile; an abnormal shell around each egg so that no sperm could penetrate it]; …and the Lord answered him and Rebekah his wife conceived. But the children struggled together within her; and she said, 'If it is so, why then am I this way`? So, she went to inquire of the Lord. And the Lord said to her, 'Two *nations* [Gôwy – heathen peoples] …are in your womb; and two *peoples* [L^eôm – a community of people held together by a common bond to form a definable group] …shall be separated from your body; and one people shall be stronger than the other; and the older shall *serve* ['Âbad – to be enslaved] …the younger`.

When her days to be delivered were fulfilled, behold, there were twins in her womb. Now the first came forth red all over like a hairy garment; and they named him *Esau* ['Êsâv – to handle roughly; a derivative of ('Âsâh–all aspects of divine acts and actions to create or fashion something as a work in progress)] …and afterward his brother came forth with his hand holding on to Esau's heel, so his name was called *Jacob* [Ya'ăqôb – heel-catcher; supplanter (treacherous schemer); from the primary root ('âqab–to seize by the heel; to circumvent as if tripping up or seizing the heels)]; …and Isaac was sixty years old when she gave birth to them.

When the boys grew up, Esau became a skillful hunter, a *man* [`Îysh– a possessor of manliness] …of the field; but Jacob was a *peaceful* [Tâm – upright in a moral sense; wholesome, quiet] …man, living in tents. Now Isaac loved Esau because he had a taste for game; but Rebekah loved Jacob."

Isaac could not have children until God chose to make it possible. God gave Isaac two sons which demonstrated before birth just how violent their lives would be. The wickedness of each one is God's witness of the power of the sin nature that controls human life. Jacob is God's witness of what is required for Him to transform a person from death to life. He is a witness of what God has to do for every person ever born in this world. Only God can make the people of the whole world to be Abraham's spiritual descendants.

The Bible from this point on is the revelation of God to create a holy nation by restoring men individually to the spiritual life that was lost to the curse of death. The birth of Esau and Jacob was God's witness that He alone gives life to humanity as children of the flesh and He alone can give people the spiritual life of His heavenly throne. {Jacob is God's witness to the whole world every person's need to personally experience a transformation in his life by the conversion of his mind; to be redeemed by his personal faith in God.}

Before the children were born, God revealed they would live as normal fleshly beings empowered by the kingdom of death. Esau would despise his birthright and would lose the blessings of his father. He established people groups which lived by the might of the sword. Whatever Esau wanted; he would take it by brute force. The world will perish under the burden of such people as Cain and Esau which never cease their warfare with God. The sinful character of Esau was revealed when he could not get the blessing of his birthright.

Genesis 27:38-41

"And Esau said to his father, 'Do you have only one blessing, my father? Bless me, even me also, O my father`. So, Esau lifted his voice and wept. Then Isaac his father answered and said to him, 'Behold, away from the fertility of the earth shall be your _dwelling_ [Môwshab– from root word (Yâshab – to sit down, a place to exist] …and away from the dew of heaven from above. And by your sword you shall live and your brother you shall serve; but it shall come about when you become _restless_ [Rûwd – to have dominion over your own life (a wild animal which has broken its yoke and is on the loose; people in an unbridled moral state] …that you shall break his yoke from your neck'. So, Esau _bore a grudge_ [Sâṭam – to lurk for; to persecute] …against Jacob because of the blessing with which his father had blessed him; and Esau said to _himself_ [Lêb – the heart; the totality of mans' inner emotional being], … 'The days of mourning for my father are near; then I will _kill_ [Hârag– murder; the connotation of violence, especially in war or intrigue] …my _brother_ [`Âch – A general relationship whether by blood or affinity; fellow-man] …Jacob`."

The Edomites were the descendants of Esau (Genesis 36). They are said to have been shrewd; proud, self-confident, strong, cruel, and idolatrous. Though they were implacable enemies of Israel, it was forbidden to hate them (Deut. 23:7). Spiritual Israelites (descendants of Israel) have the mind of God which is perfect love. God has revealed that His spiritual people of this world will forever face the cruel onslaught of Ishmael and Esau (all the people of this world who despise the kingdom of God and are slaves to the kingdom of death). The ruling Herodians at the birth of Jesus were descendants of Esau.

God's revelation from the story of Jacob begins before his birth while he is still in the womb. He is God's witness that every human being will sin (as Adam did) and fall short of the glory of God. One unborn child (Esau) was born first because he was physically the strongest. Jacob was physically weaker, but he was stronger than Esau because he was a strong man of the mind. He was a fighter with a determined will to win, but his mind could become submissive to God to become the righteousness of God's throne of life.

Genesis 25:30-34 is the first record of the continuing struggle between the two brothers. Jacob devised a plan to get Esau to sell him the birthright of the first born. For Esau to get food for the body that was tantalizingly placed before him, he had to _swear_ an oath [Shâba–to complete, bind, confirm by oath one's unbreakable commitment to faithfully do what is promised (from the root word Sheba' or shib`âh, the sacred number seven; the number for God). To swear an oath to man was just as sacred and binding as swearing an oath to God.]. Esau's oath was to reject his birth identity with his father. In all practicality Jacob _killed_ Esau (Hârag – murder by intrigue). As a result, Esau determined to _kill_ Jacob (Hârag– murder by physical violence).

JACOB'S SPIRITUAL BIRTHRIGHT

Genesis 28-49 is God's revelation of His redemption of Jacob; from his violent nature under the curse of death to the renewing of his mind to become a person empowered by the righteousness of God's kingdom of life. Every human being is born with the spiritual life given to Adam. But every human being is also born with a sin nature and is guilty of bringing about his own spiritual death. Every person murders his own spirit and becomes a slave to sin by choice. Esau's oath sealed his mind to the power of darkness by committing the same sin as Cain. He turned his face away from God with a mind that was completely under the power of death.

Jacob (a sinner like every person of the whole world) had also killed his spirit. But he was a person who could respond to the light of God's revelation and voluntarily swear an oath of faith which would seal his mind to the higher power of life. God is the only authority in heaven and earth who can restore man to spiritual life, and He gives every human being the birthright to be saved from death. This birthright to be children of God is His gift of Love. He provides it purely by the love and grace of His own Deity, the Messiah, the Christ. `Ĕlôhîym, the God of Heaven Who cannot die, took upon Himself the flesh of man (Jesus, the Christ; the Messiah) and voluntarily died the death of the grave (the death of the Soul; the life of the body). He was resurrected from physical death by the authority of His Kingdom of Life (His Spirit which identified Him as the glory of heaven) and was restored to His rightful place on His Throne in heaven. By the action of His death and resurrection, He destroyed death's power to permanently keep human life separate from His rule. A person redeemed from the curse of death is one who is restored by spiritual birth to a new, timeless life. This is every person's God given birthright. God reveals this treasure of spiritual life to every person who will receive it (the action of the mind to believe the truth and grasp hold of the glory of God by the power of faith that will not let go). Before Jacob was born, God identified him as a man who would be delivered from death to become a true descendant of Abraham, a Spiritual Israelite.

Genesis 27:46-28:3

"And Rebekah said to Isaac, 'I am *tired* [Qûwts – the primary idea of this word is vomiting; a deep emotional reaction of revulsion] …of living because of the daughters of Heth; if Jacob takes a wife from the daughters of Heth, like these from the daughters of the *land* [`Erets – people of the earth] …what good will my life be to me'? So, Isaac called Jacob and blessed him and *charged* [Tsâvâh – to appoint someone over something; the picture of a superior giving a verbal communication to a subordinate (when God commands, it happens)] …him, 'You shall not take a wife from the daughters of Canaan. Arise, go to Paddan-aram, to the house of Bethuel your mother's father, and from there take to yourself a wife from the daughters of Laban your mother's brother. And may God Almighty (`ÊlShadday) bless you and make you fruitful and multiply you, that you may become a *company* [Qâhâl – community; an assembly of nations; the whole assembly of Spiritual Israel] …of *peoples* [`Am – the multitude of God's people] `.'"

Genesis 28:8-9

"So, Esau saw that the daughters of Canaan *displeased* [Ra '– inferior quality) …his father Isaac; and Esau went to Ishmael, and married besides the wives that he had, Mahalath the daughter of Ishmael, the sister of Nebaioth."

Esau was so entrenched in the physical world that he could not comprehend the concept of spiritual life. Jesus said many times that people have physical ears to hear, but they cannot understand what they hear because they do not have a mind to comprehend the validly of spiritual life. Jacob left his father Isaac with his blessings on his physical life (he would become very rich in the same manner of Esau). But he would return a different person with a greater wealth than Esau. He would have a new name and the blessings of God upon his timeless life.

JACOB'S DREAM

Genesis 28:10-22

"Then Jacob departed from Beersheba and went toward Haran. And he came to a certain place and spent the night there because the sun had set; and he took one of the stones of the place and put it under his head and lay down in that place. And he had a dream; and behold, a [çullâm–staircase] …was set *on* [Nâtsab– a position of authority] …the earth with its *top* [Rô`sh – the head person; the chief leader] …reaching heaven; and behold, the Angels were ascending and descending on it.,

And the Lord *stood* (Nâtsab – position of authority) …above it and said, 'I am the Lord, the God of your father Abraham and the God of Isaac; the *land* [`Êrets – whole earth as the dwelling place of man] …on which you lie, I will give it to you and to your descendants.

Your descendants shall also be like the dust of the earth and you shall spread out to the west and to the east and to the north and to the south; and in you and in your descendants shall all the *families* [Mishpâchâh – a subdivision of the larger tribe of all nationalities; a specific people set apart from all others] …of the earth be blessed.

And behold, I am with you and will keep you wherever you go and will bring you back to this land; for I will not leave you until I have done what I have promised you`.

Then Jacob awoke from his sleep and said, 'Surely the Lord is in this place and I did not know it`. And he was afraid and said, 'How awesome is this place! This is none other than the house of God and this is the gate of heaven`.

So, Jacob rose early in the morning and took the stone that he had put under his head and set it up as a pillar; and poured oil on its top. And he called the name of that place Bethel, however, previously the name of the city had been Luz.

Then Jacob made a vow, saying 'If God will be with me and will keep me on this journey that I take, and will give me food to eat and garments to wear, and I return to my father's house in safety; then the Lord will be my God. And this stone which I have set up as a pillar, will be God's house; and of all that Thou dost give me I will surely give a tenth to thee`."

Jacob awoke from sleep and was true to his character of a pagan person. He was overwhelmed by the idea of God talking to him, but he did not have any understanding of what God was revealing to him. Everything Jacob said in response to the dream is purely from the perspective of a fleshly mind to get the earthly treasure he wanted and not the treasure God offered him as a free gift.

The staircase was firmly secured at the top in heaven and at the bottom on earth. Both the Lord visible at the top of the staircase and the *angels* [Malᵓâk – to dispatch as a messenger] …ascending and descending on the staircase, reveal God is accomplishing the work of His throne on earth as He is in heaven. Nothing can destroy God's ability to make Himself known to man and to communicate His will to him. God's message to Jacob is the simple fact that He works His will to bless those who believe in Him. God would be present with Jacob so that he would become the current person in the line of Abraham through which God would establish a spiritually empowered people on earth. To accomplish this, Jacob had to stop moving away from God and start moving toward Him. God decreed by an oath that He would always be present with him and would not fail to bless him.

Jacobs first fleshly minded response was to put God in one place (he used a stone to be his idol), and secondly; to bargain with God with lying promises to get the things that God already provided. Jacob was such a liar and deceiver that he could not discern between good and evil. He continued on his journey unchanged by the vision except that he conceived of God as some kind of protector. As a result, God made him a slave for twenty years to other people as deceptive as himself. Through this whole sordid scene, he had twelve sons and one daughter by four women as contentious as the women of Canaan. From his twelve sons only one, Joseph, could be used by God to continue His work of creating a spiritual nation.

Nothing is said of Jacob's effort to move away from his fighting with his in-laws until Genesis 30:25, when Rachel gave birth to Joseph. Before he could leave, he manipulated the mating of the animals so as to increase his own flocks and herds while reducing those of Laban. In Chapter 31, he told Rachel and Leah that Laban had cheated him numerous times, but God would not allow Laban to hurt him. Then he lied about the animals and blamed his manipulation on a vision from God (Who can do no evil).

This lie is a revelation from God to the reader of this book of how easy it is for Satan to control the human mind to vindicate one's self from the guilt of sin by lying about it. Satan is the father of lies and he produces this same power in the human mind enslaved to the darkness of death, so people will not believe God. Because of Jacob's lie, Rachel and Leah believed that their father would also cheat them out of their inheritance as well. Rachel stole her father's house-hold idols in her own act of vengeance. Then they loaded up their children and drove their animals across the Euphrates River in secret.

It took ten days for Laban and his sons to catch up with Jacob. In Genesis 31:24, God gave Laban some good advice. "Be careful that you do not speak to Jacob either *good* [Tôwb – moral goodness as contrasted with moral evil] …or bad." This word to Laban is the revelation that only the God of perfect holiness can reveal guilt to a person's mind. One sinner cannot be the judge of another sinner.

Laban lied to Jacob in a manner to exert himself as a superior power over Jacob and accused him of stealing his gods. Jacob's answer was typical of his mind; he made up excuses that were none confrontational because he believed himself innocent of the charge. Jacob did not know that Rachel was the guilty one. Jacob permitted Laban to search the camp to prove his innocence. Rachel successfully hid the idols by sitting on them, so that Laban's charge seemed unfounded.

God Reveals His Glory [Doxa – True Identity]

Genesis 31:36-43, Jacob reveals the suppressed anger in his mind for his mistreatment he suffered from Laban. Laban responded with his own lying spirit to justify himself. Coming to the conclusion that neither one of them could get the best of the other, Laban proposed a covenant of truce. This covenant is very significant in Jacob's life because it is the first time, he is bound by an oath to God to be genuinely innocent in his actions. It is the first time he expresses a reverent fear of God's justice for his sins.

Genesis 31:44-55

"So now come, let us *make* [Kârath–to cut off a part of the body; to pledge one's own death (like the sacrificial animal) if the pact is broken] …a *covenant* [Bᵉrîyth – an agreement ratified by a sign] …you and I, and let it be a witness between you and me. Then Jacob said to his kinsmen, 'Gather stones`. So, they took stones and made a heap, and they ate there by the heap.

Now Laban called it *Jegar-sahaduth* [Yᵉgar` Shădûwthă` - to gather a heap of stones for testimony] …but Jacob *called* [Qârâ- to proclaim with a loud voice, to vocalize a specific message with authority] …it *Galeed* [Gal 'êd – a memorial] …. And Laban said, 'This heap is a witness between you and me this day`. Therefore, it was named *Galeed* and *Mizpah* [Miz`pah – the name of a city that would be at this location in the land of Gad] …for he said, 'May the Lord watch between you and me when we are absent one from another. If you mistreat my daughters, or if you take wives besides my daughters, although no man is with us, see, God is witness between you and me`.

And Laban said to Jacob, 'Behold this heap and behold the pillar which I have set between you and me. This heap is a *witness* ['êd – a perpetual record] …and the pillar is a witness that I will not pass by this heap to you for harm and you will not pass by this heap and this pillar to me for harm. The God of Abraham and the God of Nahor, the God of their father, judge between us`. So, Jacob swore by the *fear* [Pachad – terror, dread] …of his father Isaac. Then Jacob offered a sacrifice on the mountain and called his kinsmen to the meal; and they ate the meal and spent the night on the mountain. And early in the morning Laban arose and kissed his sons and his daughters and blessed them. Then Laban departed and returned to his place."

Genesis 32:1-2

"Now as Jacob went on his way, the angels of God met him. And Jacob said when he saw them, 'This is God's *camp* [Machăneh – a temporary protective enclosure for a tribe or army; from the root word (Chânan – to stoop down or bend down in kindness to an inferior] `. …So, he named that place *Mahanaim* [Machânayim – double encampment (second time he encountered God)]."

Jacob left the camp where he made the covenant with Laban and continued on his way in great fear to meet Esau. He was soon met by an encampment of Angels. God first met Jacob on his way to Haran; and now Jacob was met by an army of God a second time as he was near Edom and a battle with a man who wanted to kill him. This was the second time God revealed the power of spiritual life to Jacob; but it would require a third time before Jacob would lay hold of it.

Genesis 32:3-23 reveals the cowardly manner that Jacob tried to appease Esau's wrath. What Jacob expected was a physical battle and his death by the sword. This was not a battle he was prepared to fight. In desperation and fear, he cried out to God for help.

Genesis 32:9-12
"And Jacob said, 'O God of my father Abraham and God of my father Isaac, O Lord, who didst say to me, "Return to your country and to your relatives and I will prosper you". I am unworthy of all the loving kindness and of all the faithfulness which Thou hast shown to Thy servant; for with my staff only I crossed this Jordan and now I have become two companies. Deliver me I pray, from the hand of my brother, from the hand of Esau; for I fear him, lest he come and attack me and the mothers with the children. For Thou didst say, 'I will surely prosper you, and make your descendants as the sand of the sea, which cannot be numbered for multitude`.'"

God brought Jacob to the place where he could no longer get what he wanted by his deceitful promises or his own power of the flesh. Jacob cried out in desperation for God to act in the power of His strength to intervene for him, so he would not have to face Esau. Jacob sent all he had across the river, but he remained alone in the darkness; that is when he had to fight the most monumental battle of his life.

JACOB WRESTLES WITH GOD

Genesis 32:24-30
"Then Jacob was left alone and a _man_ [`Îysh – a spiritual being possessing {manliness - the righteous power of spiritual life of heaven}] ...wrestled with him until daybreak. And when He saw that he had not prevailed against him, He _touched_ [Nâga – God's authoritative physical contact] ...the _socket_ [Kaph – the written symbol of the eleventh character in the Hebrew alphabet; a concave vessel; a hollow concave place] ...of his _thigh_ [Yērēk – a soft place (genital area; stood for the foundation of man as the source of life). The strongest possible oath was ratified by placing one's hand there, i.e., God's covenant of circumcision.]; ...so the socket of Jacob's thigh was dislocated while he wrestled with Him. Then He said, 'Let me go, for the dawn is breaking`. But Jacob said, 'I will not let you go unless you bless me`. So, He said to him, 'What is your name`? And he said, 'Jacob'. And He said, 'Your name shall no longer be Jacob, but _Israel_ [Yisrâ`êl – from root words (sârâh – to prevail; anything strong) and (`êl – almighty; deity) meaning "He will rule as God".] ...for you have striven with God and with men and have prevailed`. Then Jacob asked Him and said, 'Please tell me your name`. But He said, 'Why is it that you ask My name`? And He blessed him there. So, Jacob named the place _Peniel_ [P^eniy`êl – face of God] ...for he said, 'I have seen God face to face, yet my life has been _preserved_ [Nâtsal – to snatch away for good or bad; to deliver; to set free; _to experience spiritual conversion_]."

Jacob wrestled with God in the darkness of the night. The human mind in the darkness of death does not know God and is powerfully resistant to yield to Him. The rising of the sun put light on the Man so Jacob could see the truth; he was struggling against God. Jacob yielded himself to God for His blessing of a new spiritual life empowered by His righteousness; and immediately bowed down to God to worship Him.

The proof of Jacob's new spiritual life as a person with the mind of God is revealed in his encounter with Esau in Genesis 33. Jacob usually placed his maids out front with their children, Leah and her children were next in line, and Rachel with Joseph was last. But instead of hiding behind them as he had been doing; sacrificing their lives above his own, the consecrated Jacob passed ahead of all of his family and bowed down seven times before Esau in humble submission to him. Jacob demonstrated nothing but humility and generosity toward his brother and thus was welcomed by Esau with the same gracious spirit of humility.

Jacob journeyed on to Succoth and built a home for his family. He purchased the land from Hamor to erect an altar to worship God. He called that place, *El-Elohe-Israel* [`Êl `Êlôhêy-Yisrâ`êl – the mighty God of Israel (the title given to a consecrated spot); this name declared Jacob's faith that he would forever be in the timeless presence of God].

Jacob's desire was to live in peace with the inhabitants of Canaan {God demands that His righteousness rules the mind of His people to reveal the reality of their identity as sanctified spiritual life); but it was not the same with his sons {whose minds would always remain under the rule of death}. *This is the mental condition of every person under the curse of death.

Genesis 34, details the sexual violation of Jacob's daughter Dinah, by Hamor's son, Shechem. Before Jacob and Hamor could settle the situation, Jacob's sons arrived with nothing but vengeance on their minds (the curse of death). They devised a scheme to circumcise Shechem, Hamor and all the men of the city. On the third day, they killed every man and looted the city. They took all their wealth, the women and children and all their livestock by force of the sword.

Genesis 34:30
"Then Jacob said to Simeon and Levi, 'You have brought trouble on me by making me *odious* [Bâ`ash – to stink; loathsome; to be hateful, wicked, evil deeds which are rotten to God] ...among the inhabitants of the Canaanites and the Perizzites; and my men being few in number, they will gather together against me and attack me, and I shall be destroyed, I and my household'."

Genesis 34:31
"But they said, (their response justified their evil actions) 'Should he treat our sister as a *harlot* [Zânâh – fornicator, whore] `?"

Jacob reacted to the violation of Dinah and to the actions of his sons with a patient, practical mind of God. He did not take God's place to make himself the judge of other people. However, his sons were blinded by their righteous indignation. They considered the violation of their sister the same as a horrible crime against themselves; but they considered their criminal actions of mass murder and thievery to be justified and a minor thing without consequences. They did not care anything about the safety of their father, just their own self-righteous vengeance. This is the power of death controlling the mind of physically minded people. It was the same justification of the Sanhedrin which crucified the Messiah.

GOD MOVES JACOB TO BETHEL AND EPHRATH

Genesis 35:1-3

"Then God said to Jacob, 'Arise, go up to Bethel and live there; and make an altar there to God who appeared to you when you fled from your brother Esau`. So, Jacob said to his household and to all who were with him, 'Put away the foreign gods which are among you and purify yourselves and change your garments; and let us arise and go up to Bethel; and I will make an altar there to God, who answered me in the day of my distress and has been with me wherever I have gone`.""

Genesis 35:6-7

"So, Jacob came to Luz (that is, Bethel) which is in the land of Canaan, he and all the people who were with him. And he built an altar there and called the place `ElBêyth-`Êl (the God of Bethel), because their God had revealed Himself to him when he fled from his brother."

Genesis 35:9-13

"Then God _appeared_ [Rââh – to see intellectually; to perceive; to experience; the work of the Holy Spirit speaking to the human mind] …to Jacob again when he came from Paddan-aram, and He blessed him. And God said to him, 'your name is Jacob; you shall no longer be called Jacob, but _Israel_ [Yisrâ`êl – He will rule as God (a person restored to the spiritual life of God; a Spiritually born Israelite)] …shall be your name`. Thus, he called him Israel.

God also said to him, 'I am God Almighty; be fruitful and multiply; a _nation_ [Gôwy – People of the whole world under the curse of death which experience God's conversion from death to His timeless life as Jacob did] …and a _company of nations_ [Qâhâl– (a multiplier) an unspecified convocation, multitude, army] … shall come from you, and _kings_ [Melek – Officials of many levels were designated to establish peace in a chaotic world] … shall come forth from you.

And the _land_ [`Erets – the whole earth created for the domain of man as spiritual beings of God's making] … which I gave to Abraham and Isaac, I will give to you, and I will give the _land_(`Erets) to your descendants after you`. Then God went up from him in the place where He had spoken with him."

*Spiritually born descendants of Abraham, Isaac and Jacob/Israel is a holy people of God's creation. Spiritual Israelites / Christians are the descendants of Abraham, Isaac and Jacob/Israel that is blessed by God as His Heavenly Children and are citizens of the whole world.

In this book, God's Saints of His first Covenant are denoted as "Spiritual Israelites".

Israelites, (descendants of Jacob's eleven sons), is a nationalistic body of people which is always in conflict with the world. They are citizens only of a piece of land they call- Israel.

Genesis 35:16-22

"Then they journeyed from Bethel; and when there was still some distance to go to Ephrath, Rachel began to give birth and she suffered severe labor. And it came about when she was in severe labor that the midwife said to her, 'Do not fear for now you have another son`.

God Reveals His Glory [Doxa – True Identity]

And it came about as her soul was departing (for she died), that she named him Benoni (son of my sorrow); but his father called him Benjamin (son of the right hand). So, Rachel died and was buried on the way to Ephrath (that is, Bethlehem). And Jacob set up a pillar over her grave; that is the pillar of Rachel's grave to this day. Then Israel journeyed on and pitched his tent beyond the tower of Eder. And it came about while Israel was dwelling in that land, that Reuben went and lay with Bilhah, his father's concubine (I Chronicles 5:1) and Israel heard of it."

The first time God called Jacob "Israel" was when he had a conversion of his mind for God to give him a new identity of spiritual life; to give him a spiritual birth with God as his Father. He struggled with this decision because it is very difficult for the human being to yield the control of his physical being, to be controlled by the mind of God.

This second time God blessed him was for revealing it was God Who was in control of his life, to live as a heavenly spiritual being that was first given to Adam; and to recognize the peace and power of God's love. God recorded this event in human history to be His witness of what He wants every person to experience for themselves. God wants every human being to live a timeless life as His children in the pure holiness of heaven.

God's salvation is the birthright of all mankind (humanity was created for this purpose), but God's gift of salvation can only be given to each individual person who will believe in Him and commit his/her life to Him by faith. It makes no difference to God who a person's parents are, Jew or Gentile. Only God can be the Father of a person born into His Spiritual Kingdom of Life. This account of Jacob and Esau reveals that the Spirit of God could be mentally heard by only one of them. Genesis 49:1-28, Jacob reveals that only one of his twelve sons (Joseph) was converted to spiritual life.

The good news is God's revelation that His gift of salvation does not affiliate His redeemed people with any earthly identity; be it a nation or a religion. The true and only affiliation God's redeemed people have is to the heavenly rule of God's Throne of Life, the Deity of God. <u>Spiritual Israelites</u> are redeemed Jews and Gentiles from all the people of the whole earth. Both are under the curse of death and both have been redeemed by the Passover Lamb to be one Spiritual Israel: the born from above children of God, spiritual descendants of Jacob/Israel.

MOSES

God's revelation through the patriarchs established His creation of people empowered and identified individually by the name Ĕlôhîym. God established Abraham's descendants as the ruling power of Egypt by the Godly power He had given to Joseph (a true spiritual Israelite). God's revelation of His kingdom rule by this one spiritually minded civil ruler blessed the whole world with the goodness of heaven (Ex.20:1). This revelation of God's blessings upon civil governments ended with the death of Joseph and the transformation of the sons of Israel (sons and descendants of Jacob) into slavery to the ungodly Egyptian government that did not know Joseph.

God continued His progressive revelation of His identity with the birth of <u>*Moses*</u> [Môsheh – rescued; drawn out of the water]. He was born a Hebrew; but by God's providence he was raised to adulthood in the house of the ruling Pharaoh. He was removed from that governing power when he was banished from Egypt for killing an Egyptian in defense of a Hebrew slave.

Moses lived forty years in the land of Midian (a son of Abraham by Keturah), until God revealed Himself in a manner which identified His kingdom rule as the power over this world. Confronted with the glory of God (the burning bush was the heavenly light of His holiness), Moses was commanded to remove his shoes. God gave Adam and Eve animal skins for clothing outside of the Garden of Eden, but the blood of animals shed to make shoe leather is not sufficient to atone for sin. Only the sacrifice of God's own blood can cleanse man with His righteousness to stand before Him on holy ground; bare footed, free of judgment. *The reality of this is revealed in Rev. 21.

GOD COMMISSIONED MOSES TO DELIVER THE HEBREWS

In Exodus 3:6-10, God revealed that He was knowledgeable of all the suffering of the Hebrews and He was sending Moses to be His voice to deliver them. In Exodus 3:11-12, Moses made his first excuse for not going. He was not strong enough within himself; he needed a sign that God was present to go before him. God's answer was for Moses to obey Him by faith; and the sign would be the completion of the task when he had brought the people out of Egypt to worship Him in the wilderness. Until then, Moses was not a man who could live by faith in an unknown God.

In Exodus 3:13, Moses made his second excuse for not going. He was afraid the Hebrew people would not follow him because he did not know God's name. God wanted him to know that he was not the one doing the work so he should remove every thought of personal failure. God's answer was far more extensive than Moses' question.

Exodus 3:14-15
"And God said to Moses, '_I AM WHO I AM_ ` [Hâyâh – to breath, to exist; I am He who is the ever-present timelessness of life - the only true identity of living Deity.] ...and He said, 'Thus you shall say to the sons of Israel, I AM has sent me to you`. And God furthermore said to Moses, 'Thus you shall say to the _sons of Israel_ (physical descendants of Jacob). The Lord, the God of your fathers, the God of Abraham, the God of Isaac and the God of Jacob, has sent me to you. This is My name forever, and this is My _memorial-name_ [Zikrôwn – to record an event; from (Zâkar: to impress on the memory a memorial celebration); God's deliverance of the people from Egypt was a memorial event which recorded the presence of the only living God doing the work of His Throne on earth to destroy the kingdom of death. The memorial-name of God for the permanent deliverance of man is "The Christ"- the anointed of God; the Messiah`.] ...to all _generations_ [Dôwr – the extended lifetimes of all men in the world]."

Exodus 3:18-20
"And they will pay heed to what you say, and you with the elders of Israel will go to the king of Egypt and you will say to him, 'The Lord, the God of the Hebrews has met with us. So now, please let us go a three days journey into the wilderness that we may sacrifice to the Lord our God`. But I know that the king of Egypt will not permit you to go except under _compulsion_ [Châzâq – powerful and able to resist; unyielding; requiring the stronger hand of God to over-

power the resistance]. ...So, I will stretch out My hand and strike Egypt with all My _miracles_ [Pâlâ - to show oneself extraordinary; used primarily with God as the subject; things beyond human powers or expectations] ...which I shall _do_ ['Âsâh – to create; to fashion the created object from design to completion; an activity which only God can do] ...in the midst of it; and after that he will let you go."

In Exodus 4:1, Moses responded to God with a third reason why he could not go back to Egypt. "What if they will not believe me, or listen to what I say? For they may say, 'The Lord has not appeared to you`." In His infinite wisdom God knew that the Hebrew people (including Moses) lived in the darkness of death and had no more respect for Him than the Egyptians and were just as resistant to obey Him. With great patience, God responded to Moses with His own resilience.

Exodus 4:2-9
"And the Lord said to him, 'What is that in your hand'? And he said, 'A staff`. Then He said, 'Throw it on the ground`. So, he threw it on the ground, and it became a serpent; and Moses fled from it. But the Lord said to Moses, 'Stretch out your hand and grasp it by its tail`; so, he stretched out his hand and caught it and it became a staff in his hand; 'that they may believe that the Lord, the God of their fathers, the God of Abraham, the God of Isaac, and the God of Jacob, has appeared to you`. And the Lord furthermore said to him, 'Now put your hand into your bosom`. So, he put his hand into his bosom and when he took it out, behold, his hand was leprous like snow. Then He said, 'Put your hand into your bosom again`. So, he put his hand into his bosom again; and when he took it out, behold, it was restored like the rest of his flesh. 'And it shall come about that if they will not believe you or heed the witness of the first sign, they may believe the witness of the last sign. But it shall be that if they will not believe even these two signs or heed what you say, then you shall take some water from the Nile and pour it on the dry ground; and the water which you take from the Nile will become blood on the dry ground`."

The purpose for God's miracles demonstrated to Moses was for him to gain a faith relationship with Him by experience. No pagan god had ever responded to those who worshipped them. No one had ever even though it possible for a man to talk with God and reason with Him. The greater revelation found in these passages is God's ability to deal with the human mind; to bring all people of the world to experience His deliverance from death by their personal faith. This is a critical issue with the Hebrew people. They were not the spiritually empowered descendants of Abraham until they would individually believe God and obey Him {Exodus 19}.

God created man in His image (the righteousness/sinlessness of His glory) and animated him to life by the indwelling of His Spirit. Adam was created with the mind of God to be His decision maker on earth. He was sinless and gave Him unquestioned obedience. When Adam surrendered his mind to the kingdom of death, he would no longer obey God. He could only obey the kingdom power of death which rules over man purely as a fleshly being. Death transformed him from a spiritual being of heaven to a mortal (under death) physical being on earth.

God's purpose is to restore mortal man to his original spiritual creation by destroying death's power to rule over the human mind. Mans' Will (mind) must be the same as God's Will (mind). This is God's judgment revealed in Rev. 20-21: there will be only {one Mind – God's Mind in the permanent heaven created for sinless man}. This is God's assurance that death will never exist again.

God's physical deliverance of the Hebrew people was as easy as simply commanding it and it would be done. But His deliverance of people from the earthly kingdom of death that ruled their minds could only be done by their own volition to turn from that power and surrender their will to the superior power of God's kingdom of life. The Hebrew people had to look at the miracles performed by the God who identified Himself as the Living God of their fathers and accept Him as their God. The Egyptians had to feel the positive power of the Living God and also see the negative worthlessness of their own gods. The consequences for believing in the Living God or rejecting Him was the same for both the Hebrews and the Egyptians, as it is for every human being of the earth.

God told Moses and the Hebrews that it was His presence on earth to deliver His spiritually minded people from their captivity to death that would be marked in the memory of humanity for all generations. This event {Passover} was the anti-type to the second appearance of God on earth as the promised Messiah. God told Moses in Exodus 4:8 that if the Hebrews did not believe by His first sign of pouring water from the Nile onto the ground and turning it into blood, they would believe by His second sign of making Moses' hand leprous and then well again. This was not a satanic magician's trick that could be duplicated. It was proof that the God who would lead them out of bondage was the Living God of creation and only He has the power over death and life.

In Exodus 4:10-13, Moses responded to God with a fourth reason why he could not go back to Egypt; he was not an eloquent speaker but slow of speech and slow of tongue. Verses 4:14-15, this refusal angered the Lord. He burned [Chârâh – to be incensed; to grow indignant; it refers to the fire or heat of anger just after it has been ignited] … against Moses. God responded to Moses with sarcasm; "Is there not your brother? I know that he speaks fluently. I will speak to you and you will speak to Aaron, and he will speak to the people."

In Exodus 4:18, Moses knew he did not have any choice, but he was still not willing to make that choice for himself. He still feared the wrath of Pharaoh from his experience of coming under his judgment. He went to his father-in-law and lied to him about why he was compelled to go to Egypt. In verse 4:19, the Lord spoke to Moses again and gave him an outright command; "*Go back* [Shûwb – repentance of the mind] …to Egypt, for all the men who were seeking your life are dead."

Verse 4:20, says that Moses eventually obeyed God; but verses 4:21-26 reveal that Moses was still not convinced that Pharaoh would not kill him. In verse 4:23, God had to make a veiled threat to kill his firstborn son. In verses 4:24-26, God met Moses for the purpose of taking away from him his innocent son; but Moses' wife flew into a rage, circumcised her son and threw the foreskin at Moses. She said, "You are indeed a bridegroom of *blood* [Dâm – bloodshed, slaughter, the guilt of murder] …to me." She looked at Moses in the same way he looked at Pharaoh. God's immediate response to this…. "So, He *let* him *alone* [Râphâh – to leave off, to relax, to let down the hand]." God knew that it is one thing for Him to shed His own blood to destroy death, (*God's preordained plan for the salvation of man was for His own person – Messiah- to be put to death by man) but it is not possible for man to do the same thing.

Moses and Aaron went on to Egypt, assembled the elders, and they believed Moses when they realized the concern God had for them. This was the good part; the people began moving toward God. God's revelation of Himself in these verses is that He will go to the utmost measure to convince unbelievers to obey Him, but He cannot make that decision for them. Every person turns their mind away from God and every person must turn their mind back toward God with the conviction that He is God.

However, Exodus 5 records Moses' worst nightmare. He and Aaron said everything to Pharaoh that God had commanded; but verse 5:2, "Pharaoh said, 'Who is the Lord that I should obey His voice to let Israel go? I do not know the Lord, and besides, I will not let Israel go`." Then he ordered the people to work harder than before. They had to meet their same quota of bricks but also gather the straw. Pharaoh accused them of being lazy; they wanted to go worship the Lord because they did not want to work. The angry people met Moses and Aaron. In 5:21, "And they said to them, 'May the Lord look upon you and judge you for you have make us odious in Pharaoh's sight and in the sight of his servants, to put a sword in their hand to kill us.`"

THE REVELATION OF GOD AS LORD

Exodus 5:22-23
"Then Moses <u>returned</u> (Shûwb) to the *Lord* [Y^e hôvâh – *JEHOVAH* -the self-existent timeless God] ... and said, 'O *Lord* [Âdônây- (the proper name for God) Lord over all, sovereign controller] ...why have You brought harm to this people? Why did You ever send me? Ever since I came to Pharaoh to speak in Your name, he has done harm to this people; and You have not delivered Your people at all`."

This Moses, who was consistent in expressing his unbelief in the person of God before he went to Egypt, is still the same old-line Moses. He initiated a belligerent conversation with God to express his righteous indignation. These two questions reveal the very common reference point of human thinking. The driving power of man is the idea that all life revolves around his own life as a superior physical being. God did not meet Moses' expectations, so he passed his superior judgment on Him. Moses was expressing the same thinking as the unbelieving Pharaoh, and every other unbelieving person in the world.

Exodus 6-14 is God's full answer to Moses` questions. His purpose was to change the reference point of mans` thinking from his limited earthly knowledge of God; to believe in Him with a true understanding of His identity as the Living God of heaven. He is Ĕlôhîym– the supreme judge of all life. `Ĕlôhîym was the present power of Deity to deliver physical Hebrews from bondage to Egypt; and He was the same present power of Deity (the Messiah), who destroyed the power of death by the power of His own blood. The God who created man with spiritual life is the same God Who restores man to His timeless spiritual life—not by compulsion, but by faith.

Exodus 6:1

"Then the Lord said to Moses, 'Now you shall see what I will do to Pharaoh; for under compulsion, he shall let them go and under compulsion he shall drive them out of his land'."

Pharaoh was fully convinced he was a god. He ruled over men as a god and he dictated the words of the idol-gods by the power of fallen angels. The Lord knew this man would never bow down in submission to Him. Moses was about to witness what the true living God can do to reveal Himself to the mind of a man so deeply entrenched in the darkness of death; to become a man who would admit that the God of the Hebrews-- is God.

Exodus 6:2-13

"<u>God</u> [`Ĕlôhîym – supreme divine judge] …<u>spoke</u> [Dâbar– both mental and oral revelation is meant] …further to Moses and said to him, 'I am the <u>Lord</u> (<u>JEHOVAH</u>); and I appeared to Abraham, Isaac, and Jacob, as <u>God Almighty</u>. [`ÊlShadday – the almighty one] …but by My name <u>Lord</u> (<u>JEHOVAH</u>), I did not make myself known to them. And I also established My covenant with them, to give them the land of Canaan, the land in which they sojourned. * (The <u>land</u> [`Erets – the whole physical planet of earth is the domain of spiritual man outside of heaven. God's people sojourn in this world. The Canaanites are the pagan peoples of the whole world]."

*Spiritual Israelites are world citizens and cannot be captive or enslaved by any world power or be slaves to the physical earth. God physically removed the Hebrew people from Egypt and established them in the land of Canaan; not to own it, but for His purpose of calling out true spiritual descendants of Abraham, Isaac and Jacob.

At the time He designated in His plan for the redemption of man by His Passover; He revealed Himself to the whole world as the Messiah/Christ; the heavenly Spiritual Being of God in human form in this place of death to completely remove death from existence. Until He does this: He must first remove its power over each and every individual person He identifies as His heavenly family {Spiritual Israelites / Christians}.

"And furthermore, I have heard the groaning of the sons of Israel {Hebrews} because the Egyptians are holding them in bondage; and I have remembered my covenant. Say, therefore, to the sons of Israel (Jacob), 'I am the <u>Lord</u> (<u>JEHOVAH</u>), and I will bring them out from their bondage. I will also <u>redeem</u> [Gâ`al – to fulfill the duties of relationship, kinsman-helper. God would purchase {Spiritual Israel} from bondage to sin by His own blood.] …you with an outstretched arm and with great <u>judgments</u> [Shephet – divine judgments brought upon Egypt. God's greatest judgment was the institution of the Passover. The Israelites observed this Passover annually in the land of Canaan until it was literally fulfilled in the death, burial and resurrection of God's (<u>Huios, the Christ</u>] `.

So, Moses spoke thus to the sons of Israel, but they did not <u>listen</u> [Shâmâ - to give undivided listening attention so as to hear intelligently and give obedience] …to Moses on account of their despondency and cruel bondage. Now the Lord spoke to Moses, saying, 'Go, tell Pharaoh, <u>King</u> [Melek – a false god; an idol-king] …of Egypt to let the sons of Israel go out of his land`. But Moses spoke before the Lord, saying, 'Behold, the sons of Israel have not listened to me; how then will Pharaoh listen to me, for I am <u>unskilled</u> [`Ârêl– exposed, projecting loosely

God Reveals His Glory [Doxa – True Identity]

as uncircumcised foreskin] …in *speech* [Sâphâh – to open the lips so as to talk. Moses said he had a speech impediment and could not talk eloquently.] `. …Then the Lord spoke to Moses and to Aaron and gave them a *charge* [Tsâvâh – to make firm; to appoint someone over something] …to the sons of Israel and to Pharaoh King of Egypt, to bring the sons of Israel (Jacob) out of the land of Egypt."

Sometimes God has to deal with His people with a firm hand. The God of heaven let it be known that He was through talking. Moses' speech impediment was not an issue; Aaron would speak for him. The people of Israel organized themselves into family units for travel and Pharaoh's objections were dealt with by God's firm hand. God did everything He said He would do, and He fulfills every promise to bless His people despite their arrogant objections.

GOD'S JUDGMENTS

Exodus 7:1-2
"Then the Lord said to Moses, '*See*, [Rââh – to show oneself, to appear, to reveal oneself, to cause to see] …I make *you* as *God* [`Ĕlôhîym – the absolute, supreme judge of the throne of life] …to Pharaoh, and your brother Aaron shall be your *prophet* [Nâbîy – one who is actuated by a divine spirit to be the authorized spokesman for God. He does not speak his own words, but those which he had received from God]. …You shall speak all that I *command* you, [Tsâvâh – God is not to be questioned. His commands are unique, requiring an inner commitment, not mere external, superficial obedience. When God commands, it happens!] …and your brother Aaron shall speak to Pharaoh that he let the *sons of Israel* [BênYisrâ`êl– In general, it is used idiomatically for "children" and "descendants" of Jacob/Israel.] …go out of his land."

The adoption procedure at the time of Abraham and common in Nuzi law meant that Moses' adoption by the Pharaoh's daughter made him equal to all the children of the Pharaoh. If this pharaoh was a god as he believed himself to be, then Moses was also a god equal to him.

God's purpose was to separate Moses from the house of Pharaoh and identify him with the True God of heaven. Moses was born a Hebrew and would be identified as a true son of God by spiritual birth (God is the Father Who gives His children Spiritual Life). Yisrâ`êl means he will rule as God. Every person born with the authority of God's throne is a Spiritual Israelite and totally immune from the power of death; whereas the Egyptians could not hide from the curse of death because they did not have a deliverer.

Exodus 7:8-9, God put everything in motion. He directed Moses and Aaron to stand in His place before Pharaoh and act in His power. They were speaking for God and in His power; so, for this reason Pharaoh would demand a *miracle* [Môwphêth- mighty acts of God's heavenly power over the natural world. The Septuagint renders it with the Greek word (Terata – that which for its extraordinary character is apt to be observed and kept in the memory)].

God's purpose for His judgments on Egypt was to reveal to Satan that the God he could not remove from His throne in heaven, the God who cursed him in the Garden of Eden, is the God of the spiritual people He calls Israel. Satan is the god of this world, but his rule of death over humanity is not permanent. God's people in this world of flesh have a greater spiritual power than the death that rules this world, because they are raised from the dead in Christ for the entire world to see the authority of God's kingdom of Life.

Exodus 7; 9-13, records God's first judgment; Moses cast down his staff and it became a serpent. Pharaoh called upon his _wise men_ [Châkâm– clever men who gave practical advice based on the divine revelation of their gods] …and the _sorcerers_ [Kâshaph – to use witchcraft to whisper magical spells or incantations] …and they also, the _magicians_[Charṭôm – scribes; men who practiced the occult, sorcery, and incantations] …of Egypt, did the same with their _secret arts_ [Lahaṭ- flaming, burning, blazing, flashing swords which hid the cherubim when Adam and Eve were cast out of the Garden of Eden. The angels which fell from heaven with Lucifer were hidden from sight and they gave idols the appearance of being alive. This was the power given to Pharaoh's court which gave him the illusion in his mind of being a god.] …. The fallen angels also turned staffs into serpents, but they were swallowed up by the greater power of Moses' staff.

*Satan continues to use these same powers of evil to turn the mind of every person away from God; to worship him. The end times reveal that Satan and these fallen angels will empower death to rule the whole human race. At this designated time, God will completely remove Satan and Death from existence.

I John 4:1-3: God says:
"Beloved, do not believe every spirit, but test the spirits to see whether they are from God, because many false prophets have gone out into the world.

By this you know the Spirit of God; every spirit that confesses that Jesus Christ has come in the flesh is from God.

And every spirit that does not confess Jesus is not from God; and this is the spirit of the anti-Christ, of which you have heard that it is coming, and now is already in the world."

Exodus 7:14-24, records God's second judgment; the turning of water into blood. Moses stretched out his staff over the Nile River and all the water in Egypt; absolutely every drop of water turned into blood. {This was not a "red tide" as propagated by those who try to prove that all God's judgments were caused by natural means.} Once again, the fallen angels duplicated the judgment; so once again Pharaoh was not concerned with God's demand. The work of the fallen angels reinforced his belief that he himself was a god.

{Satan is an expert at deluding the human mind by appearing as an "angel of light". God said in Matthew 24:24, "For false Christs and false prophets will arise and will show great signs and wonders, so as to mislead, if possible, even the elect." Satan has convinced the minds of the whole human race to reject Christ and be their own god.}

Exodus 7:25-8:15, records God's third judgment; the multiplication of frogs to _cover_ [Kâçâh – to conceal, to hide] … the whole land of Egypt. Once again, the fallen angels duplicated the plague and caused frogs to appear on the land. However, they could not remove the frogs; Pharaoh had to ask Moses to entreat God for him. Moses simply said, "The honor is yours. When would you like for the frogs to be gone?" Pharaoh said, "Tomorrow". The next

God Reveals His Glory [Doxa – True Identity]

day God killed all the frogs except those in the Nile. Because there was relief in the land, Pharaoh again closed his ears to the Lord. He still had the demonic belief that he had the power to make the God of Israel bow to his wishes.

Exodus 8:16-32 records the plague of insects. God began the plague with gnats. Moses struck the dust of the earth and it turned into gnats that covered the earth and man and beast. The fallen angels could not duplicate this feat. They told Pharaoh it was "the finger of God"; a small matter for one who is as powerful as the living God. But God's greater work was to harden the Pharaoh's heart again so that he would not listen to Him. *God identifies every person He cannot save by revealing the power of death ruling their minds.

Exodus 8:20-32 continues the plague of insects, but at this point God set the land of Goshen apart so that the plague would only be upon Egypt. God made a distinction between His people and Pharaoh's people. This action pitted Pharaoh against his own people. He agreed to let the Hebrews worship the Lord, but only in Egypt. It was imperative that the people of Egypt still recognized Pharaoh as a god. *Satan keeps the human mind in the darkness of death with world religions.

Exodus 9:1-7, relates the movement of God to kill all the livestock of the Egyptians but all those of the Hebrews remained alive. God again made a distinction between the livestock of the Egyptians and those of the Hebrews. God made it very clear that He created all life for the benefit of His people. What belonged to His people belonged to Him and what belonged to the Egyptians also belonged to Him. Pharaoh had no such power.

Exodus 9:8-11, relates Moses taking a handful of soot from a kiln and throwing it into the sky, where it became fine *dust* [`Âbâq – very fine powder driven by the wind] ... that covered the whole land of Egypt. This dust produced boils breaking out with sores on all the men and beasts of Egypt, including the magicians of Pharaoh's court. God revealed all life outside of heaven is under the curse of death and is under His judgment; but God hardened Pharaoh's heart again. * God must reveal Himself to every individual person of the world because death is the god power over the mind that separates all men from the Kingdom of Life. Faith is the action of the mind of every individual to believe the truth of God and is the only way man can be restored to God's Kingdom Rule of Life.

Exodus 9:13-35 relates the movement of God to reveal Himself as the power to create the earth and the heavens. God sent Moses to tell Pharaoh that he and all of Egypt were alive only by the grace of God. Men see the movement of God in natural life, but they will not believe a final judgment will come. God sent a hailstorm of such power that no one had ever seen before. The hail and fire from heaven would kill every man and animal living that would not find shelter. Again, only the land of Goshen and the sons of Israel escaped this tribulation.

This time Pharaoh confessed to Moses that he had *sinned* [Châtâ - to incur guilt upon oneself]; ...the Lord is the *righteous* one [Tsaddîyq–Heb. adj. The highest standard of ethics and morality; the just judge of the entire world; the one who righteously fulfills His part of the covenant with Israel] ...and the Pharaoh and the people of Egypt are the *wicked* ones [Râshâ- Heb. adj. Morally wrong, unrighteous, lawless, vicious and godless, devoid of spiritual life]. ...He asked Moses to make supplication with the Lord to stop the plague and he would let the Hebrews go. *(He sought to Bargain with God on his own terms.) The plague ceased as soon as Moses spread out his hands to the heavens; that Pharaoh would know the earth is the LORD'S.

But Moses knew Pharaoh would not let the people go because he and his court did not yet *fear* [Yârê` - Heb. adj. being afraid, anxious, reverence] …the LORD GOD.

Exodus 10:1-20, God told Moses that He had hardened Pharaoh's heart in order for Him to be revealed as the true God over this natural world; and that all the Israelites would always know that He is the Lord. God's power over the natural world would have to be revealed over and over to the Israelites in the future because they have the same vanity as all other people. They would soon forget what God did for them in Egypt and only believe in Him for what He could do for them afresh each day. Yesterday is the past; today is the only reality that demands our attention. It is not WHO GOD IS; but what He can do for us today that matters.

Moses and Aaron went to Pharaoh and said to him, "Thus *says* [`Âmar – the uttering of spoken words. God is not a mute stone idol; but the living God] … the Lord, the God of the Hebrews, 'How long will you *refuse* [Mâ`ên – to be unwilling in the mind to obey or surrender control of the self to the authority of a superior power] …to humble yourself before Me? Let My people go that they may serve Me`.'"

Death is the ruling power of darkness over the human mind. It is the nature of man to love the darkness of this kingdom rule because it frees him to do as he wishes without guilt. Pharaoh knew the Hebrew people and he knew their God. What he would not submit to be the idea that he also had to serve the Lord. He was still unable to see the truth of God's kingdom of life and its freedom from evil. God knows the depth of death's power and He is infinitely patient in bringing man to the place where there is a conversion of the mind, to act freely of its own volition. This is the restoration of spiritual life that glorifies God; when men serve God because they are motivated by His righteous mind.

Pharaoh agreed to allow the Hebrew people to worship God; but only the men could go. This hardening of his heart to disobey the Lord brought about another plague for all Egypt to experience the true nature of Pharaoh's rule of death. God brought such a number of locusts upon Egypt that all the plant life was completely consumed. Pharaoh was brought to repentance for his sin, but he still continued to act in obstinate unbelief to let the people go. *This is an example of death that completely permeates the mind of Satan (and man). He will not let humanity go even to the point of his own extermination in the Lake of Fire.

Exodus 10:21-29 is the plague of darkness. Moses stretched out his hand toward the sky and *darkness* [Chôshek - the total absence of light; the power of the grave to remove from the mind even the imagination of light] …so *thick* [`Ăphêlâh – the total power of hopelessness, wretchedness] … that it could be felt, covered the land of Egypt. The people of Egypt were individually isolated (as if in a tomb) in the darkness of their homes for three days, but the Hebrews enjoyed the full light of God in their homes. This is a clear revelation of the hopeless condition of every person separated from God by the curse of death. They are permanently separated from the light of God while the people of God are firmly secure in the light (first revelation of creation.)

Pharaoh commanded Moses to go worship the Lord, but he could not do it with his livestock. Moses told him that worship of the Lord required sacrifices and burnt offerings. Therefore, for the Hebrews it was an all or nothing proposition. No human being can establish conditions for worshipping the living God. There is only one way for God to destroy death and that is through the sacrifice righteousness required; His own blood offered on God's altar in heaven but also poured out on the ground by scourging and the torture of crucifixion.

God Reveals His Glory [Doxa – True Identity]

God hardened Pharaoh's heart again so that his decision was the total rejection for the Hebrews to worship the Lord, and he pronounced a death sentence on Moses if he ever saw his face again. Moses said, "You are *right* [Dâbar – to speak absolute truth]; …I shall never see your face again!" Moses would experience timeless spiritual life with God, but Pharaoh would experience Hades and the lake of fire.

Exodus 11 is God's final revelation to Pharaoh. The Lord said to Moses, "One more *plague* [Naga '– punishment meted out by God for sins of unbelievers] …I will bring on Pharaoh and in Egypt; after that he will let you go. When he lets you go; he will surely drive you out from here completely."

God gave the Hebrews favor in his sight so that the Egyptian people gave them all their gold and silver. The wealth of this world belongs to God and He distributes it as it pleases Him. He is a good steward to bless His people. This is a lesson for every person in the world who covets the wealth of God's world as their own possession. People consider themselves rich because they possess an abundance of what they believe empowers them to be totally self-sufficient. They reject the truth that the wealth of this world is fleeting; it can disappear in an instant, while God's gift of life is timeless (cannot die).

Exodus 11:4-8

"And Moses said (to Pharaoh), 'Thus says the Lord, about midnight I am going out into the midst of Egypt and all the first-born in the land of Egypt shall die, from the first-born of the Pharaoh who sits on his throne, even to the first-born of the slave girl who is behind the millstones; all the first-born of the cattle as well. Moreover, there shall be a great cry in all the land of Egypt such as there has not been before, and such as shall never be again. But against any of the sons of Israel [the descendants of Jacob] … a dog shall not even bark, whether against man or beast that you may understand how the Lord makes a distinction between Egypt and Israel. And all these your servants will come down to me and bow themselves before me, saying, "Go out, you and all the people who follow you", and after that I will go out. And he went out from Pharaoh in hot anger'. But again, the Lord hardened the Pharaoh's heart so that he would not let the people go."

God has declared by His own voice that no human being on the face of this earth can worship Him except those He delivers from the curse of death. God's Word says in I Corinthians 15: 50, "Now I say this, brethren, that flesh and blood cannot inherit the kingdom of God; nor does the perishable (life under the curse of death) inherit the imperishable (life free from death)."

Every religion in the world is enslavement of the mind to the kingdom power of death, to worship Satan and false gods. Every individual person perishes in the darkness of death by the authority of sin. Before God would remove His people from Egypt, He required every Egyptian to experience the pain of death. Every single human being is responsible to God for the sin of personal rebellion to God's authority and it is God Himself who exacts His righteous decree of life or death for every individual person. Pharaoh spoke his judgment upon Moses; but it will be God who has the last word. The show will be over for the entire human race when God speaks His righteous indignation upon the kingdom of death and destroys it when He makes His appearance in the Apokalupsis of the Christ and His Kingdom Rule of Righteousness.

Sin is the action of the mind under the authority of death; demonstrated by Pharaoh. He is the perfect example of every unbelieving person in the world who is led by Satan to reject the voice of God. Satan has sealed the minds of millions of people to the worship of false gods; while God has sealed the minds of millions to worship Him in truth. This distinction must be clear in the minds of all the people of the world. No human being has a Savior except those God makes His Spiritual Children by a personal act of faith in Him for the forgiveness of their sins. These are the true descendants of Abraham, Isaac, and Jacob and they are the only ones who will ever be delivered to a timeless existence with God.

God demonstrated His Heavenly Kingdom Rule of Life to the Egyptians with the death of all the first-born of men and animals. All fleshly life (man and animals) was created holy; but it will all perish under the curse of death. No life on this earth can escape this judgment.

God instituted the Passover, which demonstrated His power to the Hebrews to save their lives by the blood of the lamb on their door posts. This Passover in Egypt is the revelation that where death has once entered a person's life to destroy it (all people die because of sin); it cannot overpower the blood of God to restore that life again. Every person covered by the sacrificial blood of the true Passover Lamb (Jesus the Messiah) has been restored to God's throne of Life. Every person God saves to His timeless life is secure from the curse of death. The Messiah spoke these words to the Jews at the Temple in Jerusalem:

John 10: 14-18
"I am the good shepherd; and I know My own, and My own know Me, even as the Deity in Heaven knows Me and We are One; and I lay down My life for the sheep. And I have other sheep (Gentiles); which are not of this fold. I must bring them also and they shall hear My voice; and they shall become one flock (the true children of God) with one shepherd. *[God's witness of Himself is for the salvation of the whole world.]. For this reason, the God of Heaven loves Me, because I lay down My life that I may take it again. No one has taken it away from Me, but I lay it down on My own initiative. I have authority to lay it down, and I have authority to take it up again. This commandment I received from My God."

God decided the criteria for who He will save and who He will not save. No man decides that criteria for himself. God identified who would be delivered from bondage and who would perish because of it. God's purpose for the exodus of the Hebrews was to produce a single, unique new people to the world that has God as its creator. From this physical nation would come people who would hear God's voice and separate themselves from the power of death to be a spiritual people, God's children. Spiritual children of God are all the individual persons from the entire world who will hear the voice of the Messiah (the Christ), by faith believe the truth of His words, repent for their sins and be restored to the spiritual rule of God's Throne in Heaven. That is why God created man in His image; that He would restore His Spirit of Life to all who will believe His truth.

These individuals are sanctified as holy unto the Lord because they are cleansed by the sacrificial blood of God on His alter in heaven. The true Passover was enacted in the Holy Person of the Messiah in Jerusalem where Abraham was commanded to sacrifice Isaac. The

Messiah (Jesus the Christ) is God's sacrificial lamb, Who resurrected Himself from the death of the grave to return to His rule on the throne of God in heaven.

By this act, He destroyed the power of death to permanently separate man from Gods' rule in heaven. Only God's personal presence in this world can destroy the power of death; and He revealed it by His permanent Passover that removed His judgment of death upon every person He restores to His timeless Spiritual Life.

The Passover and the exodus of the Hebrews from Egypt established the rule of `Ĕlôhîym on His Kingdom Throne of Life in heaven, to be the same ruler of all life on the _earth_ [`Erets– this physical planet; the domain of man under the curse of death]. It was the Deity of God who removed life from the first born of Egypt. It was the Deity of God who yielded up His own life on a cross and took it up again. It was the Deity of God who made the judgment that death would rule over all life that is separated from Him; and it was the Deity of God Who made the judgment that death would not have the power of a permanent separation for those who, by faith, return to the kingdom rule of God for the forgiveness of their sins. Those who are given spiritual life by the Deity of God are the true spiritual descendants of Abraham, Isaac, and Jacob. These are the only people on earth who can experience the true Passover to worship the Living God. The God of Abraham, Isaac, Jacob and every Spiritual Israelite -- *IS GOD* (`Ĕlôhîym).

THE FIRST PASSOVER – THE PHYSICAL ANTI - TYPE OF CHRIST

Exodus 12:1-2
"Now the Lord said to Moses and Aaron in the _land_ [`Erets – the world inhabited by pagan people] …of Egypt. This month shall be the _beginning_ [Rô`sh – commencement of time for the particular purpose of worshipping the living God] …of months for you; it is to be the _first_ [Rî`shown – refers to precedence over former things; the first Passover revealed God's salvation that is predestined by God to come] …month of the year to you."

God is the authority for creating time (see Genesis 1:1). He has declared that the purpose of chronological time is to mark His presence in the world for the redemption of man. The present world calendar is the Roman calendar based on solar months. God established the Jewish calendar based on lunar months; not to measure time, but to mark the reoccurrence of festivals-Holy days for the worship of God.

His calendar began with the Passover in Egypt as the first time Israel would worship Him as the heavenly power to destroy death and give life. It was used in all the years God was preparing the world for His true Passover (the sacrifice of the Messiah). The first month of God's calendar was called Abib (Ex.13:4) until the exile. Afterward it was called Nisan (Neh. 2:1, and Ester 3:7). It corresponds to the latter part of March and the first part of April on the modern solar calendar.

The lunar calendar projected a sense of confidence and faith in the human mind toward the superior authority of God; to worship Him with hope and reverent expectation that there would be a final Passover. It was God's Passover (Christ) that finalized His judgment to remove the curse of death on His Children. Since that day, God's Spiritually born Children {Gentiles and Jews} celebrate the Passover with reverence and joy for what God has for done them, personally. It is the actions of each one to stand before God as a heavenly being of His creation and worship Him for sanctifying their lives to be His light in the darkness of this world.

Exodus 12:3-6

"Speak to the entire _congregation_ ['Êdâh –household, family; every single person is a participant in the Passover – it is not just an activity of Priests] …of Israel, saying, 'On the tenth of this month they are each one to take a lamb (a flock animal) for themselves according to their _fathers_ [`Āb–a head, chief, ruler, lord, master] …_households_ [Bayith – dwelling place; it means one who is the authority over a family] …a lamb for each household. Now if the household is too small for a lamb, then he and his neighbor nearest to his house are to take one according to the number of persons in them; according to what each man should eat, you are to divide (slaughter) the lamb.

Your lamb shall be an _unblemished_ [Tâmîym – Heb. adj. means entirely whole (literally, figuratively, and morally pure; not a mixed breed); faultless toward God; the divine standard of life God gives to man]

…_male_ [Zikrôwn – this noun derives from Zâkar (Adam was created a _male_ *(_the spiritual image of God_); meaning he was given spiritual life to be a visible memorial to the presence of God on earth; a memorial God impresses in the memory. *The lamb is representative of God's Lamb - His Own Heavenly presence.].

…a year-old _son_ [Bên – Basically a reference to the male offspring of human parents; when used with a subject noun it functions as an adj. (a son of one year – no other offspring of this family in this timeframe] …You may take it from the sheep or the goats.   * This word is representative of the Christ (the Huios – the singular presence of God in human flesh).

And you shall _keep_ [Mishmereth–the act of custody; two main senses: (**1**) an obligation or service to be performed (obedience to God); (**2**) something which must be preserved (recognize the great value of the object guarded)]

…it until the fourteenth day of the same month, then the whole *_assembly_ [Qâhâl–Masc. Heb. Noun. It identified the Hebrew community as the only people in the whole world God authorized to deliberate the affairs of the one and only true God -`Ělôhîym. Every other act of worship in the world is the worship of idols].

…of the congregation of Israel/Jacob is to *_kill_ [Shâchat – (1) to slaughter animals for sacrifice; (2) to cleanse the land of idol worship by massacre.] …it at _twilight_ [Nesheph – dusk; when the evening breeze prevails; between the two evenings] `."

*The Greek Septuagint translates Qâhâl with [Ekklēsia– Church- the congregation of the people of Spiritual Israel; the called-out body of Christ that is distinct from all other people of the world; having been redeemed from the curse of death by the blood of the Messiah, God's Passover Lamb.]. The revelation of the Passover established in Exodus is the anti-type of God's prophesy for the selection of the type; His true Passover Lamb as recorded in His New Covenant.

Exodus 12:7-13

"Moreover, they shall take some of the blood and put it on the two doorposts and on the lintel of the houses in which they eat it. And they shall eat the _flesh_ [Bâsâr – a living creature of

God's creation] ... that same *night* [Lay^elâh – a twisting away of the light; when God delivered His people from slavery to the darkness of death.]

...roasted with fire (God's purpose is to purify humanity - to be holy), and they shall eat it with *unleavened bread* {Christ is the Living Bread from heaven} and *bitter herbs* {the price God paid to remove the curse of death.}. Do not eat any of it *raw* {do not eat or drink the blood of an animal} or *boiled at all with water* – {man was created from water; but God's sacrifice is not a created being}.

but rather roasted with fire, both its head and its legs along with its *entrails* [Qereb – the center, the life functions of the body which are to be brought near to God; all that is within the body which causes it to function (bowls, heart, mind); from root word Qârab (to approach, draw near, intimate proximity to God).] . *God's sacrifice of Himself purifies the totality of the human being to be holy as He is holy.

...And you shall not leave any of it *over* [Yâthar – the smallest part divided from the larger part] ...until morning, but whatever is left of it until morning, you shall burn with fire.

{Christ's crucifixion left His body in the grave, but He descended into the pit of Sheol/Hades/Hell to reveal Himself to every person there. Their end would be the Lake of Fire. On the morning of the third day, the glorified Christ was revealed to be the totality of the Deity of heaven. As Christ was glorified and arose from the grave, so it shall be for every human being sanctified by the blood of the heavenly lamb.}

Now you shall eat it in this manner: with your loins girded, your sandals on your feet, and your staff in your hand; and you shall eat it in haste --it is the Lord's *Passover* [Peçach – a sparing, an exemption, immunity from penalty and calamity. The totality of the physical and spiritual life of every Israelite was protected by the blood of the sacrificial lamb].

For I will *go* ['Âbar – to thoroughly penetrate a stationary object] ...through the land of Egypt on that night and will strike down all the **first-born* in the land of Egypt, both man and beast. *{The physical lives of man and beast were real; but also figurative for the creation of the first physical human and animal life created holy, without sin, without death; all of created life that came under the power of the kingdom of death by the disobedience of Adam}.

And against all the gods of Egypt I will *execute judgments* ['Âsâh Shephet - to give justice or equity.]. ...I will not let the *destroyer* [Shâchath – one who acts wickedly (Satan)] ...to come into your house to smite you."] --- *I am the Lord*.

And the blood shall be a *sign* ['Ôwth– miraculous proof of something that only God can do; visible evidence of God's covenant to remove the curse of death from human life] ...for you on the houses where you live.

and when I *see* [Rââh` - to intellectually perceive] ...the blood as proof of faith and obedience

...I will *pass over* [Peçach – to spare; an exemption, an immunity from penalty and calamity; death cannot enter into God's house twice nor hold humanity permanently in the grave]

...you, and no *plague* [Negeph – a blow from God which is fatal or disastrous] ...will befall you to *destroy* [Mashchîyth – the power of death that fell upon Egypt] ...you when I *strike* [Nâkâh – the root meaning is to literally or figuratively hit something; a person can be struck on the cheek or be struck dead] ...the land of Egypt."

Exodus 12:14

"Now this *day* [Yôwm – a point in time which designates the sovereignty of God] …will be a *memorial* [Zikrôwn – (from Zâkar – to pierce, to impress on the memory); an object reminder by which something is brought to mind. *The Passover* was the most important revelation of God's presence in this world;]

…to you, and you shall celebrate it as a *feast* [Chag – The main idea is the celebration of a holy day. The three main festivals of Israel required a pilgrimage: the Passover with the Feast of Unleavened Bread, the Feast of Weeks, and the Feast of Tabernacles. It was a season of religious joy.]

…to the Lord throughout your *generations* [Dôwr – The period of a man's life. The plural is the continuous cycle of man's existence.] …you are to celebrate it as a *permanent* ['Ôlâm – what is hidden, concealed (the vanishing point of chronological time)] …*ordinance* [Chôq – a statute, regulation, law established by God which must be strictly obeyed]."

God designed the specific times in human history in which He reveals His kingdom work of destroying death. He gave specific instructions to the Hebrews for their involvement in the preparation for the first Passover. The people were to completely consume the sacrificial lamb cooked strictly by fire (the fire would not consume the meat, but it would purify it of all earthly contaminations. It reveals the purity of the Christ from heaven that was given to purify the human mind) and were instructed to complete this sacrifice in an annual celebration of the Passover in expectation of its fulfillment by God's Messianic deliverance.

God fulfilled this deliverance with the true Passover in which He, Himself, was the sacrificial lamb. God has instructed His people to understand what He accomplished by the blood of the Lamb {He removed the curse of death on His heavenly people}, and every true Israelite is to live in the continual expectation of the final deliverance from death that God will accomplish by the return of the Messiah as the Lion of Judah.

Jesus said in John 6:47-58

"Truly, truly, I say to you, 'He who believes in Me has timeless life. I am the bread of life". Your fathers ate the manna in the wilderness, and they died. This is the bread which comes down out of heaven, so that one may eat of it and not die. I am the living bread that came down out of heaven; if anyone eats of this bread, he shall have timeless life; and the bread also which I shall give for the life of the world is My flesh. Truly, truly, I say to you, unless you eat the flesh of *The Christ* and drink His blood (let God indwell you as His holy Temple.). Let God totally identify you as His Holy, heavenly creation, for you have no life in yourselves. He who eats My flesh and drinks My blood has timeless life and I will raise him up on the last day. For My flesh is true food and My blood is true drink. He who eats My flesh and drinks My blood abides in Me and I in him (restored to God's timeless Spiritual Life). As the living Deity sent Me and I live because the Deity of heaven is One; so, he who eats Me, he also shall live because of Me. I am the Living Bread which came down out of heaven; not as the fathers ate and died, he who eats this bread shall have timeless life.'."

God fulfills all His promises by His own holy presence in this world. God came into this world at Mt. Sinai (Exodus 19) and personally fulfilled the decrees of His Kingdom Rule of life by consecrating every believing Hebrew to His Holiness. He fulfilled His promise of the Passover by the coming of the Christ to cleanse (consecrate) every believing person by the cleansing of His Blood and continues to be the presence of the Living God Who fills every believer with the Holy Spirit of Life.

THE EXODUS FROM EGYPT

The exodus of the Hebrews from Egypt is God's affirmation that He fulfills His covenants with humanity to create a heavenly people by delivering them from bondage to death. This revelation is important to God because it reveals His true identity as the God of Life. Every human being is God's creation in His image, and He will pay the price to restore every person to the holiness of His Throne of Life.

God began the revelation of His salvation of His holy people on earth with the covenants He established with Noah, Abraham, Isaac and Jacob. In Genesis 9:1-17, God made a covenant with the human race that He would not again destroy the earth universally by a flood of water. Instead, God holds every human being individually responsible to obey His rule of righteousness. Thus, every individual person is responsible for his own death ("the wages of sin is death") and transversally, for his salvation by returning to God as Lord by a personal act of faith in the person of God ("but the gift of God is Life"). God began this revelation of personal responsibility with Abram.

God's covenant with Abraham, Isaac and Jacob seemed impossible to fulfill when God sent Joseph into Egypt as His ambassador to the pagan world government. Joseph remained true to Abraham's covenant to live in obedience to God's character of holiness and God blessed him. God then created a great famine which displaced Jacob's family of seventy people to live in Egypt. God's promise to Jacob was fulfilled. The Egyptians embalmed his body, and it was taken by his people at the exodus to be buried in the cave purchased by Abraham for his burial site.

Genesis 50:22-26

"Now Joseph stayed in Egypt, he and his father's household, and Joseph lived one hundred and ten years. And Joseph saw the third generation of Ephraim's sons; also, the sons of Machir, the son of Manasseh, were born on Joseph's knees. And Joseph said to his brothers, 'I am about to die, but God will surely *take care of* [Pâqad – to be in charge of as an overseer] …you and bring you up from this land to the land which He *promised on oath* [Shāba` - to strongly affirm a promise; to guarantee fulfillment by swearing an oath] …to Abraham, to Isaac and to Jacob`. Then Joseph made the sons of Israel (Jacob) swear {Shāba`}, saying, 'God will surely take care of you and you shall carry my bones up from here`. (*Belief and faith in God produce an enduring commitment to obey Him.) So, Joseph died at the age of one hundred and ten years; and he was embalmed and placed in a coffin in Egypt."

Exodus 12:29-41

29.Now it came about at midnight that the Lord struck all the first-born in the land of Egypt, from the first-born of Pharaoh who sat on his *throne* [Kiççêh – this word is figurative for the human act of honoring themselves to be equal with God.] ...to the first-born of the captive who was in the dungeon and all the first-born of the cattle.

30. And Pharaoh arose in the _night_ [Lay^{e}lâh – to twist away from authority (the night of darkness twists away from the light of day). Satan twisted his mind away from God, as does every person on earth. Pharaoh arose in the darkness of his mind.] ...he and all his _servants_ [`Ebed – Egyptians were true slaves of Pharaoh; to worship him and be treated as he pleased. God killed them because they were ruled by the kingdom of death. In Exodus 20:2, this word is not applied to the Israelites. They were not servants or slaves of Pharaoh, but ambassadors of God to reveal that His people are not in bondage to death but are sanctified as a spiritual people of His heavenly kingdom.] ...and all the Egyptians; and there was a great cry in Egypt, for there was no home where there was not someone dead.

31-32. Then Pharaoh called for Moses and Aaron at night and said, 'Rise up, get out from among my people, both you and the sons of Israel; and go worship the Lord as you have said. Take both your flocks and your herds as you have said and go and _bless_ [Bârak – to kneel down in worship; to pray for someone. Pharaoh wanted Moses to act as a priest and put him in a favorable position with God. He would not humble himself to do such a thing, but he still knew in his mind that it was the right thing to do.] ...me also`.

33. And the Egyptians _urged_ [Châzaq – This word is used twelve times to describe the condition of Pharaoh's heart as an obstinate sinner who acted negatively to God's decree. But for the Egyptian people it is a strong encouragement of support for the Hebrews to prove themselves courageous; a commitment the Egyptians could not make under penalty of death.] ...the people to send them out of the land in haste, for they said, 'We shall all be dead`. *If the Hebrews did not leave, they would remain under the curse of death as were the Egyptians.

34. So the people took their dough before it was leavened, with their kneading bowls bound up in the clothes on their shoulders.

35. Now the Hebrews had done according to the word of Moses, for they had _requested_ [Shâ`ēl – to ask for something that is to be expected. It was customary at the parting of a servant to give a gift. The Egyptians were willing to give them what they asked for if they would leave and do so quickly.] ...from the Egyptians articles of silver and articles of gold, and clothing.

36. And the Lord had given the people favor in the sight of the Egyptians, so that they let them have their request. Thus, they plundered the Egyptians. It is the nature of lost people to value physical wealth above the treasures of God.

37. Now the _sons_ [Taph – toddlers to adolescents; little children; this word describes humanity as God's own innocent little children who are dear to His heart.] ...of the Hebrews journeyed from Rameses to Succoth; about six hundred thousand _men_ [Geber – human males at the peak of their natural strength; valiant; strong in heart and physical strength. This word also describes the character of God's people to move steadfastly toward Him.] ...on foot, aside from the children.

38. And a _mixed_ [`Ereb – This masc. Hebrew word derived from `Ârab; meaning a mixed multitude, a promiscuous mass of foreigners, strangers, and wanderers.] ...multitude also went up with them along with flocks and herds, a very large number of livestock. *(Anthropologists report finding a large number of artifacts in Egypt which reveals a lot more people were prisoners in Egypt that just the Hebrews. They also report the existence of caves in the area of Athens which give an account of the exodus in exact detail as recorded in the Bible.)

God Reveals His Glory [Doxa – True Identity]

This verse reveals God's purpose is to deliver every human being from the curse of death who has the courage to follow Him. This was not blind faith, but a response to the witness God gave of Himself as the One and Only Living God Who rules heaven and earth.

39. And they baked the dough which they had brought out of Egypt into cakes of unleavened bread; for it had not become leavened, since they were driven out of Egypt and could not delay, nor had they prepared any provisions for themselves.

40. Now the time that the _sons_ [Môshâb – From the root word Yâshab; the inhabitants of a particular place for a set time.] ...of Israel/Jacob (Hebrews) lived in Egypt was four hundred and thirty years.

41. And it came about at the end of four hundred and thirty years, to the very day; that all the _hosts_ [Ts^{e}bâ`âh - a mass of people of many ethnic identities assembled to go forth to war; God created all men by His power and stands ready to preserve their existence] ...of the Lord went out of the land of Egypt.

God delivers the human race from its bondage to death to become servants of His Kingdom. It was many more years to come before the Hebrews became the physical nation of Israel and still many more years before Abraham's spiritual descendants (Jacob/Israel) became God's people of the whole world through the Christ. God knows the future, but humanity knows it only by hindsight.

God's salvation plan for His redeemed people is a limited time under the earthly rule of death {death has a limited time to serve God's purpose}. God created time for Him to reveal Himself by His actions in this world of death. The Messiah came at God's appointed time; and at God's appointed time every person is given the opportunity to turn to Him for their redemption. Spiritual Israelites (Jews converted from death to life as was Jacob) have a heavenly identity {Image of God} but they still exist in this physical world that suffers under the curse of death with all its tribulations. God wants His family to live as His holy people in this world; strengthened by the knowledge that it is God who controls the limited time for this world's existence as the place of death.

Exodus 13:17-14:31

17. Now it came about when Pharaoh had let the people go that God did not _lead_ [Nâchâh– this verb is used thirty-nine times to emphasize the truth that in God's kingdom rule, He is the single power that governs all life; be it spiritual or physical. The Israelites quickly discovered that God's rule of life was exceedingly more powerful than the kingdom of death that leads all the pharaohs of the world.] ...them by the _way_ [Derek – This noun means a physical passageway or trade route. It is used more often to designate the actions and behavior of wicked men.] ...of the land of the Philistines, even though it was near; for God said, 'lest the people change their minds when they _see_ [Rââh – to fully comprehend something by personal involvement] ...war, and they _return_ [Shûwb – to turn oneself around to go in an opposite direction. Spiritually it is to repent {to turn away from the way of death by turning to the Person of God}. In this verse it means a change of the mind; to turn away from following God by returning to the rule of slavery.] ...to Egypt`.

18. Hence God led the people around by the way of the wilderness to the _Red Sea_ [Sea of Reeds that is north of the (Red Sea -currently called the Gulf of Suez)]; ... and the sons of Israel _went up_ [`Âlâh – to ascend to a higher elevation; it is used in this verse in the figurative

sense of exalting oneself with a new identity; to rise up to take pride in oneself] …in martial {military} array from the land of Egypt. *A collective mindset encourages mental strength and commitment much more so than an individual facing the possibility of death, alone.

    19. And Moses took the bones of Joseph with him, for he had made the sons of Israel solemnly swear, saying, 'God shall surely *take care of* [Pâqad - a positive action by a superior in relation to his subordinates; the action of God to be an overseer to produce a beneficial result. Joseph used this word to make a contrast between the physical Egyptian overseers and God as a heavenly overseer.] …you; and you shall *carry* [`Âlâh – this verb is used in this verse as it was in the previous verse. God led Jacob to become a spiritual Israelite by a salvation experience by conversion; and He sent Joseph to Egypt as a slave. This verse is Joseph's witness that God would lift him up from his bondage to death and that he would have the same spiritual identity as his father, Jacob. God's witness is that all spiritual descendants of Abraham are His holy family under His timeless care.] …my bones from here with you`.

    20. Then they set out from Succoth and camped in Etham on the edge of the wilderness. *This area is north of the Red Sea {sea of reeds}. Etham would be on the Egyptian side of what is now the Suez Canal.

    21. And the Lord was going before them in a pillar of *cloud* [`Ânân – The specific shape of this cloud; its visibility in the daytime and its movement was a commanding and comforting heavenly witness that nothing could separate God from His people.] …by day to lead them on the way and in a pillar of fire by *night* [Lay^elâh – This noun means a twisting away of the light. It is common for the darkness to produce fear of what is unseen. The pillar of fire is God's light to give comfort to the mind. Night and day are the same to God; for He does not sleep like physical life. It was in the night that God killed the Egyptians and kept His people safe. Whether we are in a wilderness or the valley of the shadow of death, God commands us to trust in Him and fear no evil.] …to give them light that they might travel by day and by night. He did not take away the pillar of cloud by day or the pillar of fire by night, from before the people.

    God's commanding presence was a revelation to the Hebrews that His salvation is His deliverance from the darkness of death. God does not lead us to live in the darkness in this present form of physical life. Our salvation is to live in the light of His presence as sanctified, holy people. God was teaching the Hebrews to follow Him by faith; to keep their eyes on Him. Once you pick up the plow, you cannot turn away from it to go your own way.

Exodus14
    1. Now the Lord spoke to Moses, saying,
    2. 'Tell the sons of Israel/Jacob to turn back (go south) and camp before Pi-hahiroth, between Migdol and the sea (north end of the Red Sea- currently called the Gulf of Suez); you shall camp in front of Baal-zephon, opposite it, by the sea.
    3. For Pharaoh will say of the sons of Israel, "They are wandering aimlessly in the *land* [`Erets– physical earth as opposed to heaven]; … the wilderness has shut them in". *God led Moses to Succoth to retrieve the bones of Joseph (the sea of reeds is near here); then back north to the trade route along the Mediterranean Sea; then south again to the wilderness of Etham (Etham would be on the Egyptian side of what is now the Suez Canal; then farther south to the north most extension of the Red Sea that is currently called the Sea of Suez. This is where God

parted the Red Sea. God's purpose in this was two-fold. He was building spiritual character in the Hebrews (trust in God by faith); and at the same time was keeping them within striking distance of Pharaoh's army. God's deliverance through the Red Sea taught them to live for the future blessings of God and not to fear the powers of this world that enslaved them in the past.

    4. Thus I will harden Pharaoh's heart and he will chase after them; and I will be honored through Pharaoh and all his army; and the Egyptians will *know* [Yâdâ` - to learn from experience that Jehovah is God] …that I am the Lord. And they *did so*. [`Âsâh – Pharaoh set out with the determination to finish the job of annihilating the Hebrews. This is a very good illustration of the power of death over the human mind. The brutality of death was the only way this man could think. This is in stark contrast to the Hebrews whose minds were controlled by their fear. God was teaching them that the will to live by faith in Him is more powerful than anything they could understand. They would soon learn that God's judgment on Pharaoh would be fulfilled just as He said, and all God's promises to deliver His people are just as sure as if they have already been fulfilled.].

    *Revelation 20 – Satan will be released from the pit for his final effort to murder every person who will not *forsake* (activity of the Mind) the worship of Jesus. God instantly kills by fire, every one of those who turn away from Him like the angels did in heaven and casts them into Hades for the Great White Throne Judgment. Satan will be thrown into the Lake of Fire to be consumed as if he never existed. This is a fact that God will fulfill at His designated time.

    5. When the *king* [Melek – a false god; an idol-king] …of Egypt was told that the people had fled, Pharaoh and his servants had a change of heart toward the people, and they said, 'What is this we have done, that we have let Israel go from serving us`?
    6. So he made his chariot ready and took his people with him.
    7. and he took six hundred select chariots and all the other chariots of Egypt with officers over all of them.
    8. And the Lord hardened the heart of Pharaoh; king of Egypt. And he chased after the Hebrews as they were going out *boldly* [Lēstēs – openly and by violence; a noble person avenging a righteous cause by human wrath.]
    9. Then the Egyptians chased after them with all the horses and chariots of Pharaoh, his horsemen and his army, and they overtook them camping by the sea, beside Pi-hahiroth, in front of Baal-zephon.
    10. And as Pharaoh drew near, the Hebrews *looked* [Nâsâ or Nâçâh – gave their full attention to what they were seeing. They diverted their attention from God to the force that was bearing down upon them.] …and behold, the Egyptians were marching after them and they became very *frightened* [Yârê'- The meaning of this root word is to be controlled by fear of God; to give Him reverence (a God-fearer). After four hundred and thirty years in Egypt, they looked upon Pharaoh and his army with the same sense of fear/terror as if they were gods.]; …so the Hebrews cried out to the Lord.
    11. Then they said to Moses, 'Is it because there were no graves in Egypt that you have taken us away to die in the wilderness? Why have you dealt with us in this way, bringing us out of Egypt?

12. Is this not the word that we spoke to you in Egypt, saying, "Leave us alone that we may serve the Egyptians". For it would have been *better* [Tôwb – Hebrew adj. meaning good, pleasant, beautiful, excellent, lovely, delightful, cheerful, virtuous, moral goodness.] …for us to serve the Egyptians than to die in the wilderness`. *The Hebrews cried out to God; but they made Moses their scapegoat. They would not accept any responsibility for their own actions; and they reversed the blessings God gives to them and the death Pharaoh gives them.

13. But Moses said to the people, 'Do not *fear* [Yârê' – give reverence to Pharaoh]! …Stand by and *see* [Rââh' – gain a full understanding] …the *salvation* [Yᵉshûw'âh–The act of God to give aid to the distressed, produces deliverance and safety. The source of this salvation comes from outside the situation of oppression (heaven) and is greater than the oppressor.] …of the Lord which He will accomplish for you today; for the Egyptians whom you have seen today, you will never see them again forever.

14. The Lord (Jehovah) will fight for you while you keep silent`.

15. Then the Lord said to Moses, 'Why are you crying out to Me? Tell the sons of Israel to go forward.

16. And as for you, lift up your *staff* [Maṭṭâh–a tree branch, a rod signified correction in the sense of chastisement, a scepter connoted ruling, a staff was a symbol of one with authority leading a tribe of people] …and stretch out your hand over the sea and divide it; and the Hebrews shall go through the midst of the sea on *dry* land [Yabbâshâh– from root word (Yâbêsh–the earth became dry; completely without moisture as it did at creation). God separated the waters at creation and made the earth as solid footing for all life to walk on. God again created solid footing in the middle of the Red Sea and later, the Jordan River].

17. And as for Me, behold, I will harden the hearts of the Egyptians so that they will go in after them; and I will be honored through Pharaoh and all his army, through his chariots and his horsemen.

18. Then the Egyptians will know that I am the Lord, when I am honored through Pharaoh, through his chariots and his horsemen'.

19. And the angel of *God* ['Ĕlôhîym] …who had been going before the *camp* [Machăneh – a temporary protective enclosure for an army.] …of Israel, moved and went behind them; and the pillar of cloud moved from before them and stood behind them.

20. So it came between the camp of Egypt and the camp of Israel; and there was the cloud along with the darkness, yet it gave light at night. Thus, the one did not come near the other at night. *There is no darkness of death that can over-power the presence of God.

21. Then Moses stretched out his hand over the sea; and the Lord swept the sea back by a strong east *wind* [Rûwach – the Spirit of God; air put in motion by the breath of God] …all night and turned the sea into *dry land* [Chârâbâh – a desert] …so the waters were divided.

22. And the Hebrews went through the midst of the sea on the dry land and the waters were like a wall to them on their right hand and on their left.

23. Then the Egyptians took up the pursuit and all Pharaoh's horses, his chariots and his horsemen went in after them into the midst of the sea.

24. And it came about at the morning watch that the Lord looked down on the army of the Egyptians through the pillar of fire and cloud and brought the army of the Egyptians into confusion. *The mind of humanity under the power of death is always in confusion.

God Reveals His Glory [Doxa – True Identity]

25. And He caused their chariot wheels to swerve and He made them drive with difficulty; so, the Egyptians said, 'Let us flee from the Hebrews, for the Lord is fighting for them against the Egyptians'.

26. Then the Lord said to Moses, 'Stretch out your hand over the sea so that the waters may come back over the Egyptians, over their chariots and their horsemen'.

27. So Moses stretched out his hand over the sea and the sea returned to its normal state at daybreak, while the Egyptians were fleeing right into it; then the Lord overthrew the Egyptians in the midst of the sea.

28. And the waters returned and covered the chariots and the horsemen, even Pharaoh's entire army that had gone into the sea after them; not even one of them remained.

29. But the Hebrews walked on dry land through the midst of the sea and the waters were like a wall to them on their right hand and on their left. * Impossible in the sea of reeds.

30. Thus the Lord saved the descendants of Israel/Jacob that _day_ [Yôwm – the sovereignty of God revealed by the morning light] …from the hands of the Egyptians and they saw the Egyptians dead on the _seashore_ [Sâphâh – the boundary God established between the land and the sea. In this verse it designates the extent of God's judgment. Death cannot enter into God's holy dwelling by unsanctified people.].

31. And when the Hebrews saw the great _power_ [Yâd–authority of God's hand to deliver them from death.] …which the Lord had used against the Egyptians, the people _feared_ [Yârê' – gave reverence to God] …the Lord and they _believed_ [`Âman – an Aramaic word; a transitive confirmation of enduring trust; a new relationship with God that produces the power of His throne of life within the human being.] …in the Lord and in His servant Moses."

This revelation of God to deliver His people from the curse of death that ruled the Egyptian people is not a myth. It is God's revelation of Himself as the only power which can fulfill His covenant to deliver the spiritual descendants of Abraham, Isaac and Jacob/Israel; they alone are God's covenant people. This is of critical importance to God because it reveals His personal relationship with every human being in the history of the whole world. Human beings are not piecing on a chess board; God is not playing a game with Satan to win some and lose some. God created the human race in His image with spiritual life. Each and everyone have the same value of God's righteousness; because it is His will to restore every person to His timeless spiritual life that was given to Adam.

Exodus 15-18 reveals that God did not just deliver these people from Egypt and the kingdom of death that rules this world and then just dump them in the wilderness. He moved them through personal physical trials that prepared the hearts of those who would live with an enduring faith; a faith relationship with God that He alone can create. This commitment of trust in the minds of His children is God's revelation to every person He delivers from death. Every person without a personal faith relationship will remain in the domain of death. These were the people Moses led for three months of constant rebellion.

James V. Holland

Chapter 6

GOD IDENTIFIES SPIRITUAL ISRAEL AS HIS HEAVENLY PEOPLE

GODS SANCTIFICATION OF HIS PEOPLE

EXODUS 19

1. "In the third month after the _sons_ [Bên – It is believed that this word derives from Bânâh; meaning to build or manufacture. It is the same word used for the creation of Eve. It is basically a reference to the male offspring of human parents. Idiomatically, a son of Israel is a reference to the spiritually empowered person made (manufactured) holy by God as was Adam at his creation] …of Israel/Jacob had gone out of the land of Egypt, on that very day they came into the wilderness of Sinai.

2. When they set out from Rephidim, they came to the wilderness of Sinai, and camped in the wilderness; and there Israel camped in front of the mountain.

3. And Moses _went up_ ['Âlâh–to travel from a lower elevation to a higher one; the temple sanctuary was located on a mountain. God did not get there by climbing the mountain, but by descending to it from above. Physical man cannot ascend to God in heaven; He must come down to earth.] …to _God_ ['Ĕlôhîym – the divine judge of heaven and earth.] …and the Lord _called_ [Qârâ- not a random cry; to be called by name; to be summoned to court; God is to be obeyed without the slightest hesitation] … to him from the mountain, saying, 'Thus you shall say to the _house_ [Bayith – dwelling place; temple; from (Bâmâh- to build)] …of Jacob (a spiritual Israelite; a dwelling place God had built) and _tell_ [Nâgad – to bring forward to the light; to reveal something one could not possibly know otherwise] … the sons of Israel:

4. 'You yourselves have seen what I did to the Egyptians and how I _bore_ [Nâsâ or Nâçâh – to lift up; to be free; to forgive sins; to lift the eyes from the rule of the gods of the earth to the rule of the God of heaven] …you on eagles wings and brought you to Myself.

5. Now then if you will _indeed obey_ [Shâma' – to hear intelligently; to give undivided attention; to understand a message directly from God that cannot be disobeyed] …My voice and _keep_ [Shâmar – to guard or protect something as a great treasure; to keep alive the ways of the Lord]…My _covenant_ [Berîyth – divine oath; determination of the will; an agreement (treaty) between people and nations; a contract by individuals who are friends; a marriage oath between husband and wife; a constitution for God in heaven to govern his obedient children on earth] …then you shall be My _own possession_ [Çegullâh – a personal possession (of great wealth)one has acquired and carefully preserved as his most valuable private property. Spiritual Israel is God's personal property on this earth because He chose them, delivered them from bondage to death, and shaped them into a heavenly identity that can never be changed]…among all the _peoples,_ ['Am – the entire human race] …for all the _earth_ ['Erets – the physical planet created to be the habitation of man] …is Mine; *God created the human race for all to be saved, but He

is God only of a self-determining people in agreement with His Will. Human free-will is the character of God revealed by a commitment of faith to die to self-will; to live in obedience to His will. This power of free-will is the power of God to sacrificially love the entire human race.

  6. and you shall be to Me a *kingdom* [Mamiâkâh – dominion, reign, realm, royal rule, sovereignty] …of *priests* [Kôhên – God's ordained mediators to act as ministers of His spiritual rule; all of God's Israelites are priests of the Lord for His personal heavenly kingdom rule on the earth] …and a *holy* [Qâdôwsh – sacred, ceremonially and morally pure, sanctified as a holy sanctuary (Saints)] …*nation* [Gôwy – a large segment of a given body which is defined by context; the people of God surrounded by the pagan world, but is not part of that world.]. …These are the *words* [Dâbâr – the essential content of God's prophetic revelation which defines Him as God {The Messiah was God's WORD – the revelation of God's Mind}; an uncovering of heavenly unknown truth to the human mind; declarations or statements which define His rule over a unique, holy people; a heavenly constitution which identifies God's people on earth as the same people He rules in heaven] …that you shall *speak* [Dâbar – mental and oral communication of a singular thought or idea; Moses could not hear God's words and then repeat it from the thinking of his own mind; God's words cannot be expressed by the self-righteousness of the human mind as Eve did in the Garden of Eden, nor changed by godless men in pulpits and government offices.] …to the sons of Israel. `

  7. So Moses came and called the *elders* [Zâqên – the older men who were proven to be wise leaders; *(not *presbuteros*- ruling body as in the Septuagint)] …of the people, and set before them all these words which the Lord had *commanded* him [Tsâvâh–to delegate something to someone with orders; the picture of a superior giving orders to a subordinate; God is never to be questioned by anyone regarding His superior rule (Exodus 1:1, God's name means absolute supreme ruler); man was created a spiritual power with an inner, mental commitment to obey as an immediate response, never even entertain the thought of disobeying; however, man under the curse of death can make only an external, superficial commitment which he can disavow at his own discretion].

  8. And all the people answered together and said, 'All that the lord has *spoken* [Dâbar – there is no confusion to the oral sound of words to produce a mental confusion as to their exact meaning] …we will *do*`! ['Âsâh–this word conveys the authority of God to accomplish the Will of His Throne. What God commands will be instantly accomplished to perfect completion] …And Moses *brought back* [Shûwb – to turn oneself around; a spiritual return to God; to repent (turn from evil and turn to righteousness] …the words of the people to the Lord. *Every person must make a personal commitment to believe in God's supreme authority and demonstrate His character of obedience by repentance.

  9. And the Lord said to Moses, 'Behold, I shall come to you in a thick *cloud* ['Ânâm – the pillar of smoke which revealed the presence of God, which led the people through the desert] … in order that the people may hear when I speak with you and may also *believe* ['Âman – to have a firm, enduring trust] …in you *forever*. ['Ôwlâm – this word is used for the duration of man in the past and the future. The end of man is concealed, hidden, an indefinite continuance into the very near future. Every person for the endurance of the human race must know that God's words are from heaven and not the manufactured ideas of man; every person who hears the words of God spoken by man must hear the Holy Spirit validate their truth, or the man cannot

God Reveals His Glory [Doxa – True Identity]

be trusted. Moses had a relationship with God that was secure into His timeless rule.] `. ...Then Moses told the words of the people to the Lord.

10. The Lord also said to Moses, 'Go to the people and *consecrate* [Qâdâsh –declare God's holy covenant that His people are to be pure, holy, sacred to Him] ...them *today* [Yôwm – immediate and without end] ...and tomorrow, and let them *wash* [Kâbaç – to bleach, to purify] ...their garments.

11. and let them be *ready* [Kûwn – to stand firm, to be established, to be steadfast, faithful, reliable, certain] ...for the third day, for on the third day the Lord will come down on Mount Sinai in the sight of all the people`. * The Messiah – The Christ – The True Word of God – was raised from the grave and revealed Himself to man on the third day. He is the Living Temple of God inhabiting the mind of man; no human being can worship God except through Him.

12. And you shall set bounds for the people all around, saying, '*Beware* [Shâmar– the careful attention which was paid to the obligations of a covenant, to laws, to statutes] ...that you do not go up on the mountain or *touch* [Nâga'– God's touch is always authoritative to bring about the goodness of His Kingdom; for man to touch something holy is an evil act of emotional intent for death to rule over God (Satan's intent when he tore himself away from the rule of God's throne – only it was he who died and not God.)] ...the border of it; whoever touches the mountain shall surely be put to death.

13. No *hand* [Yâd – no physical hand is given the authority or responsibility to do evil in service to God] ...shall touch him, but he shall surely be stoned or *shot* [Yârâh –killed with arrows] ...through; whether beast or man, he shall not live. When the ram's horn sounds a long blast, they shall come up to the mountain`. *Gods final appearance to humanity living on this earth will be revealed by the trumpets of heaven (Revelation 19) to proclaim Him Lord of Lords and King of Kings, and He will bring the fury of His final judgment on the world as the place where death rules.

14. So Moses went down from the mountain to the people and *consecrated* (verse 10) the people, and they washed their garments.

15. And he said to the people, 'Be ready for the *third day; do not *go* [Nâgash – to be in proximity of something to touch it; in this context it means sexual contact; to be a slave to the physical rule of the mind (*Eve persuaded Adam to disobey God)] ...near a woman`.

This third day for the appearance of God on earth to adopt sanctified Israel as His holy people was the anti-type for God's promised appearance on earth as the living, resurrected Christ; to be worshipped as the only true God. God brought darkness and lightening upon the whole universe, shook the earth and opened the graves when Christ yielded His body as God's sacrifice to the rule of the grave. But on the third day, Christ appeared to His disciples and sanctified them with the Holy Spirit.

God sanctifies His people by His own blood upon His altar in heaven. His gift of timeless life is His covenant with every individual person who will receive it by faith in His true identity of the Living God. No one was consecrated to God by the action of human beings merely washing their clothes. This was a physical, symbolic testimony that the person had been saved by God's work of sanctification. God clothes the believer in His righteousness by His inward cleansing of the spirit. There is not even one single ritualistic practice that can accomplish what only God can do.

16. So it came about on the third day when it was morning (God's presence and revelation of truth dispels the darkness for people to live in His light), that there were *thunder and lightning flashes and a thick cloud upon the mountain and a very loud trumpet sound, so that all the people who were in the camp _trembled_ [Chârad – the mountain shook, and the people shook because of fear].

God's power over the forces of nature is at this point a reminder of His revelation that He is the superior power of creation for the existence of both spiritual and physical life and He was the power which destroyed the gods of Egypt. It is folly for a human being to perceive in his mind that he is a fleshly or spiritual being equal to or superior to God. The entire human race and all the angels will experience this revelation of God when the Apokalupsis of the Christ from heaven brings God's fierce judgment on death.

17. And Moses brought the people out of the camp to meet God, and they stood at the foot of the mountain.

18. Now Mount Sinai was all in _smoke_ ['Âshan – to burn, to be angry; the term is used metaphorically to describe God's anger toward the curse of death. Death rules everywhere man exists, but purity and holiness of Life rules where God reveals Himself.] ...because the Lord descended upon it in *fire; and its smoke ascended like the smoke of a furnace, and the whole mountain quaked violently.

*It is of great importance to comprehend this word as God's ability to so completely destroy all things physical and spiritual as if they never existed. God's consecration of His people is the absolute rule of His Kingdom throne of Life that cannot die; to completely remove the previous rule of death which enslaves humanity. God's final revelation of His supreme rule over everything outside of Himself is the lake of fire in Revelation 20:14-15, "And death and Hades were thrown into the lake of fire. This is the second death, the lake of fire. And if anyone's name was not found written in the book of life, he was thrown into the lake of fire." This is God's final work to destroy death and everything it killed. He will so utterly destroy it that it can never exist again and will not even be a memory in the human mind.

19. When the sound of the trumpet _grew louder_ [Châzêq – this word occurs only in this verse and II Samuel 3:1; it is an adjective of {Châzâq}, meaning God's strong hand. The connotation is something so powerfully strong that it is impossible for anything to resist it.] ...and louder. Moses spoke and God answered him with thunder.

Satan and the whole of creation will experience this same sovereignty of God at the Apokalupsis of Jesus when He destroys this world of death and creates a new kind of existence for man that is as pure and holy as God.

20. And the Lord came down on Mount Sinai, to the _top_ [Rô`sh – whatever is highest and supreme, that part which is not the dwelling place of man] ...of the mountain; and the Lord called Moses to the top of the mountain, and Moses went up.

God Reveals His Glory [Doxa – True Identity]

21. Then the Lord spoke to Moses, 'Go down, warn the people lest they break through to the Lord to *gaze* [Rââh – to perceive God by the physical sense of hearing. We cannot know God by the deceptive physical senses but by the Spirit of God speaking to the inner working of the mind. Thankfully, it has been revealed many times that insane and deaf people can recognize the truth of God spoken by the Holy Spirit and be saved.] …and many of them *perish* [Nâphal– the violent circumstance of being made to fall face down, prostrate before God's judgment of death.].

22. And also let the *priests* [Kôhên– one who acts as a priest; a chief ruler, principal officer or head of a family] …who come near to the Lord; consecrate themselves, lest the Lord break out against them'.

It is God's purpose that *no man* places himself above any other person as to claim a superior relationship to God and rule over men. *No human religion* can take or assume the place of God's sovereign rule; this is nothing but a ruling pagan hierarchy.

23. And Moses said to the Lord, 'The people cannot come up to Mount Sinai, for Thou did warn us, saying, "Set bounds about the mountain and consecrate it" '.
24. Then the Lord said to him, 'Go down and come up again, you and Aaron with you; but do not let the priests and the people break through to come up to the Lord, lest He break forth upon them'.
25. So Moses went down to the people and told them."

The God of heaven was merciful to sinful man to reveal Himself in all His holiness. Corrupted humanity must see God in all His sovereignty and acknowledge His *glory* (true identity – the purpose of the Bible). Humanity with minds and hearts ruled by the god of this world {Satan and the power of death} can only know God by the revelation of His wrath on sin and death (Jesus revealed this in His parable of the rich man in Hades and Lazarus in the bosom of Abraham). There is no thunder of God's wrath in the holiness of heaven; only on the earth wherein is the object of His wrath. Every person who would trespass upon the mountain in an effort to approach God without His sanctification would feel His wrath and perish. God calls man to Him by the work of His Spirit, not by man's own volition.

Jeremiah 10:1-16
1. "*Hear* [Shâma – hear with intelligence to give attention to obedience] …the *word* [Dâbâr – the essential content of God's prophetic revelation. It is used over 1400 times in the Old Testament and is translated by eighty-five English words in the King James Version.] …which the Lord speaks to you, O *house* [Bayith – temple, earthly dwelling place of God] …of Israel.
2. Thus says the Lord, 'Do not learn the way of the nations. And do not be terrified by the signs of the heavens. Although the nations are terrified by them.
3. For the customs of the peoples are delusion; because it is wood cut from the forest, the work of the hands of a craftsman with a cutting tool.
4. They decorate it with silver and with gold; they fasten it with nails and with hammers so that it will not totter.

5. Like a scarecrow in a cucumber field are they, and they cannot speak; they must be carried because they cannot walk! Do not fear them, for they can do no harm, nor can they do any good`.

6. There is none like Thee, O Lord; Thou are great and great is Thy name in might.

7. Who would not fear Thee, O King of the nations? Indeed, it is Thy due! For among all the wise men of the nations and in all their kingdoms, there is none like Thee.

8. But they are altogether stupid and foolish in their discipline of delusion – their idol is wood. *Also crosses worshipped as if they had the power of God.

9. Beaten silver is brought from Tarshish and gold from Uphaz, the work of a craftsman and the hands of a goldsmith; violet and purple are their clothing; they are all the work of skilled men. *The more lavish, and gaudy, the more people believe they are holy.

10. But the Lord is the *true* [`Emeth – firmness, stability, faithfulness] ...*God* [`Ělôhîym – sovereign ruler, judge]; ...He is the *living* God [Chay–the holy power for spiritual existence] ... and the everlasting King. At His wrath the earthquakes and the nations cannot endure His *indignation* [Za'am–the rage which ensues from the mind of pure holiness caused by the intrusion of anything unholy].

11. Thus you shall say to them, 'The *gods* [`Ělâhh – this Aramaic word corresponds to the Hebrew word `Ělôwahh, meaning pagan gods] ...that did not make the heavens and the earth shall perish from under the heavens`.

12. It is He who made the earth by His power, who established the world by His wisdom; and by His understanding He has stretched out the heavens.

13. When He utters His voice there is a tumult of waters in the heavens. And He causes the clouds to ascend from the end of the earth; He makes lightning for the rain and brings out the wind from His storehouses.

14. Every man is stupid, devoid of knowledge; every goldsmith is put to shame by his idols; for his molten images are deceitful and there is no breath in them.

15. They are worthless, a work of *mockery* [Ta'tûa – a fraud, the delusion of mindless men]; ...in the time of their *punishment* [Pᵉquddâh – the intervention of the superior power of God to bring about a permanent change] ...they will perish.

16. The portion of Jacob (Spiritual Israel) is not like these; for the *Maker* [Yâtsar – creator] ...of all is He, and Israel is the *tribe* [Shêbet– a stick for punishing; a ruler's staff; a scepter for ruling; a symbol of authority in the hands of a king. Psalm 45:6, 'Thy throne, O God, is forever and ever; a scepter of uprightness is the scepter of Thy kingdom`.] ...of His inheritance; the Lord of hosts is His name."

These verses of Jeremiah are God's revelation that everybody of men under the delusion that it is a ruling power of God is idolatry; it is self-worship. They rule over people with their beautiful robes and their symbols of spiritual authority; and people with minds deluded by death bow down and worship them. True Spiritual Israel is all people of this world who reveal their relationship to the living God by their acknowledgement of His truth by faith in Him alone. This relationship is revealed by a life of obedience to His rule of righteousness. They alone are God's symbol of authority for the timeless rule of His Throne of Life. The living God lives only in that person which He has made spiritually alive; transformed from death to life- demonstrated by the character of God (Be holy as God is holy).

Genesis 12:1-3 is the beginning of God's revelation that He would create a holy people from the human race. Abram was selected by God for this purpose because he was the last person in the lineage of Noah through Shem who remained faithful to God. He was sent out from the security of his home to dwell in the land of Canaan to be a blessing to the lost world. In Genesis 13:12-18, God revealed that Abram's spiritual descendants would come from all the lost people of the entire world. But God made no promise what-so-ever that He would bless the physical descendants of Abraham; for these people are still under the curse of death and will forever be perpetually at war with God and the world.

Exodus 19 is God's progressive revelation that Abram's legitimate heirs would be separated from his physical heirs by God's demand for them to be consecrated by His holiness. Salvation is the submission of the will to the sovereignty of the only true power for existence. Because of the nature of God this relationship produces peace in the mind so that it is no longer at war with Him and we joyfully give servitude of the flesh to the holiness of spiritual life. God's salvation is also revealed to be the indwelling power of God's heavenly throne to speak to the deaf ears of the unbelieving world. God's people are His messengers; they speak the irrefutable truth revealed by the Holy Spirit. God's message reveals the power of His love for man – but it also reveals His intense wrath toward every human being who rejects His gift of timeless life.

GOD'S HEAVENLY CONSTITUTION TO GOVERN SPIRITUAL ISRAEL

Exodus 20 is God's progressive revelation that His appearance to the Hebrews was a clear message to all of humanity, that He blesses all men who will submit their lives to His rule of righteousness. He is the Rule of His Throne of Life that is at work in this world to destroy the kingdom power of death. God's Word (revelation of His judgments for saved people) was given to those who would voluntarily submit to His sanctification. It is the revelation of His sovereign rule of righteousness on the earth as it is in heaven. His sovereignty is revealed in ten articles of a heavenly constitution which governs the lives of humanity that has been freed from the tyrannical rule of death and its total destruction of their lives.

Matthew 22:31-32
"Jesus said, 'Regarding the resurrection of the dead; have you not read that which was spoken to you by God, saying, I am the God of Abraham, and The God of Isaac, and the God of Jacob. I am not the God of the dead, but of the living`.'"

Matthew 22:35-40
"And one of the Pharisees, a _lawyer_ [Nomikos – a teacher of the law] …asked Him a question, _testing_ [Peirazō – the intention of proving that one has been evil or to make him evil. Satan is called Peirastês – a tempter to do evil.] …Him. 'Teacher, which is the great commandment in the Law'? And Jesus said to him, 'You shall love the Lord your God with all your heart, and with all your soul, and with your entire mind. This is the great and foremost commandment. *{This is the first four articles of the constitution}. The second is _like_ [Homoios - The two commandments which form the sum of the Law are on a par with each other] …it, you shall love your _neighbor_ [Piēsion – fellow man; all the people we interact with should be the object of our

loving concern] …as yourself. *{Articles six through ten} On these two commandments depend the whole Law and the Prophets`."

This constitution, the decree from God's heavenly throne is unchangeable and timeless. Obedience to God's righteous rule produces peace and love in this world as it is in God's heavenly realm. It was the only Word of God placed in the Ark of the Covenant; was fulfilled by God's presence on earth as the Messiah and continues to be fulfilled in the lives of God's Saints.

EXODUS 20:1-22

1. "Then God spoke all these *words*, [Dâbâr – Hebrew noun from {Dâbar}, meaning a declaration or statement; the essential content of God's revelation. "The word of the Lord" or "God spoke", was a technical expression for prophetic revelation (what God is doing in human life). God's prophetic words are still being spoken because He governs sanctified man for holy living on this earth.] … saying,

2. 'I am the Lord your God who brought you out of the *land* [`Erets – the physical planet of earth governed by the kingdom of death; as opposed to the spiritual life of heaven] …of Egypt, out of the *house* [Bayith – dwelling place; temple of idols] …of *slavery* [`Ebed – Hebrew noun derived from (`Âbad – meaning to work as a slave). `Ebed means an ambassador of a king. God sent Joseph and then Jacob to Egypt as His ambassadors to be temporary suffering servants to the earthly power of death. God's purpose was to reveal to them that every human being is a slave to the power of death. God's final revelation to the descendants of Joseph and Jacob is that death can only be destroyed by His indwelling/ruling presence in His people. God is continuing His work in this world of death through Abraham's legitimate spiritual heirs to be His suffering ambassadors; indwelt by God to be the light of the world].

FIRST ARTICLE

3. You shall have no other *gods* [`Ĕlôhîym – when this word is used as plural mas. noun as in Genesis 1:1, it is the all-encompassing sovereign rule of the singular, timeless existing Person of God; a self-existing spiritual being that cannot be created. When it is used as a singular noun as in this verse; it means a pagan god which is one of many created by man.] …before Me (in my place).

This revelation of God spotlights the rebellion of Lucifer before the throne of God in heaven and the curse of death that enslaves the mind of every human being. The human race was created in one single person. Adam had only one God; one Lord. That master is the righteous rule of God's kingdom power of Life that cannot die. However, servitude to God cannot be forced on man; it is purely voluntary. Like Lucifer, Adam and every single person on this earth acts as his own god. Every person who denies the sovereignty of the One True God truly is, however, in real bondage to a kingdom power (`Âbad – the Hebrews suffered from the reality of deaths rule over themselves and the Egyptians). Every person's slavery is real because it is empowered by the kingdom of death. But the "gods" they worship are merely extensions of their deluded minds to believe they are real. Actually, they do not exist; they have no power, no life, and no future. The greatest example of a fool is the person who says there is no God. This person is blind to the kingdom of death which rules over him and the truth of God's Word to free him from its curse.

SECOND ARTICLE

4. You shall not *make* ['Âsâh – to create something and refine it to completion.] ...for yourself an *idol* [Peçel – Hebrew noun derived from {Pâçal – which means to carve, hew, engrave wood or stone. Peçel refers to an object of adoration that has been made by human hands}.] ...or any *likeness* [Tᵉmûwnâh or Tᵉmûnâh – fem. Heb. noun meaning to give form, shape, physical appearance to something; to give a godly identity to anything] ...of what is in heaven above or on the earth beneath or in the water under the earth.

The critical issue of this revelation is God's identity as the sovereignty of spiritual life. His judgment is the revelation that: it is impossible for His Holy identity and spiritual power of Life to exist in anything outside of Him. Humanity under the curse of death has taken this power upon itself to deify men, women, angels and idols crafted by their own hands. Jesus died on a wooden cross because it was a Roman instrument for torture. But people will worship the cross instead of the Christ. People wear ornate crosses as jewelry, or vestments to designate holy religious authority. Many hang every design possible on their walls to indicate they are Christians. Crosses are designed in a specific way to represent and give credence to a particular religion and even in a manner to represent Satan as the victor over Christ. Some use it as their power to cast out evil spirits, and many manufacture pieces of wood and worship it as a "holy relic". They kiss it and bless people with it as if it is as sacred as God Himself. They sing hymns which magnify the cross as if it makes them holy. A real commitment to Christ is to bear the burden of the cross; but this is rejected and replaced with "sacraments" and ritual worship with every form of holy clothing. The Jews have made an idol of the laws of Moses and venerate themselves by worshipping their god at the temple wall; but they will not worship the God who wrote the laws.

People speak by their own authority to *"sanctify"* certain deceased human beings and worship them as "Saints" in heaven (they might be there, or they might not); who they can beseech in prayer for their particular blessings. People worship angels and deify Mary as a superior power over Jesus and make statues of her. Muslims glorify a martyr's death as the assurance for entering heaven. Many glorify the "tithe" or their "good works" to purchase their immortality. Some proclaim the true God in heaven was once a man and they can be God's of their own worlds in a future life (that is what this writer would call a real "alien). There seems to be no end to the imaginations of the human mind to replace the only true God.

5. You shall not *worship* [Shâchâh–this is not used in the general sense of worship. It is a reference to the mode of worship by bowing down, to prostrate oneself on the ground, to bow down on the knees and touch the forehead to the ground, to genuflect before an object of worship, or cross oneself to be blessed, or in any way show submission to what is believed to be a superior spiritual power.] ...them or serve them; for I, the Lord your God, am a *jealous* [Qannâ– to unequivocally permit no rivals. It is equivalent to (Qinâh – ardent zeal to be the sole object

of human worship).] ...God, *visiting* [Pâqad – God is the person in absolute charge. He is the overseer of His people. The strong under-current meaning is a positive action by a superior in relation to His subordinates. It is used for David to "take a census". It does not mean he counted the Israelites. It means God had him organize troops for battle; it was God's visible force to destroy evil. It is used for the Lord to intervene on behalf of Sarah in a miraculous way (Genesis 21:1). The true meaning is an action on the part of God which produces a beneficial result for His people. It is the revelation of God that He is in control of His people that they may not perish under the burden of death.] ...the *iniquity* ['Âvôn or 'Âvôwn – a depraved action. It is derived from {'Âvâh – to deviate from the proper path}] ...of the *fathers* [`Âb – parents, forefathers, ancestors, may be rendered "family"; any person who stands under God's authority to care for others. God holds every person responsible to Him for their own sins] ... on the *children* [Bên – son, grandson, descendants] ...on the third and the fourth generations of those who hate Me.

The English language gives this verse a negative inflection; meaning God punishes children for the sins of their fathers. The opposite is true; God will not permit the sins of the fathers to damage the lives of their children who choose to love God. Not all their children will love God; these are responsible for their own unbelief. But God will not allow men of flesh to perpetuate unbelief in their children as it was in the generation of Cain to Noah.

6. But *showing* [`Âsâh – to work, to create from beginning to completion; the connotation of an ethical obligation to perfect righteousness in what is created] ...*loving-kindness* [Checed – the attitude of love which contains mercy (forgiveness of sin); the unfailing grace which is the nature of God] ...to *thousands* [`Aleph - the name of the first letter of the Hebrew alphabet. It is used as a multiplier to indicate an indefinite or innumerable number; in context with God the basic idea of this noun represents an extreme number that is inclusive of the totality of the human race *(not the limitations of the English number thousand: see introduction)]...to those who *love* [`Âhab – an ardent and vehement inclination of the mind and a tenderness of affection at the same time (Agapē in Greek)] ...Me and *keep* [Shâmar – the careful attention which was paid to the obligations of a covenant.] ... my *commandments* [Mitsvâhs – the righteous judgments of God's throne that cannot be changed or disobeyed; from (Tsâvâh – to make firm the rule of God which requires an inner commitment to obey without question. It is opposite of statuary laws that are obeyed from fear of punishment for disobeying)].

These judgments reveal God's presence (His kingdom is within us) to empower holy living on earth as it is in heaven. Jesus revealed the holiness of God by His sinless life, because He obeyed and fulfilled all of God's Words in His mind and physical body as the *Only God* (Gk. Huios – one and the same person revealed by one and the same perfect character). The character of His life identified Him with the only true God. Our obedience reveals us to be children of God (people made holy by the person of the Christ). God's revelations of His heavenly character were not written for the unbelieving world but for all the people of the world whom He justifies and sanctifies by the authority of His Kingdom Throne of Life. People who love and obey God's Words for holy living are His shining lights in the darkness of this world of death. The power of His Words changes their lives from within the heart and mind so that they are a people of righteous behavior.

The truth of God's Words (Revelations)for holy living has suffered serious distortion from legalistic human judgments. God's Words do not have the concept of human law makers who define the boundaries for physical human beings, thoughts and/or actions in society which carry with them the authority to punish anyone who breaks a civil law. In this concept a person considers he is a righteous person if he does not break the law. He may not murder a person because of the fear of getting caught; but he relishes murdering a person in his heart. He has no fear of breaking "a law" because he does not believe that he will be found guilty of doing it; or he can plea bargain for no punishment. A government diplomat from another country can murder an American citizen, but by law cannot be tried for it (government immunity). A person with the legalistic mind of the flesh has no fear of God and lives without any governing authority but himself (Article One). The actions of people who will not obey this second revelation can only produce a world in chaos.

THIRD ARTICLE

7. You shall not *take* [Nâsâ` or Nâçâh – to speak a name; to lift up one's spirit to be entirely dependent on an object or power to be worshipped other than the one true living God, to call something God that is not the one true God] …the name of the Lord your God in *vain* [Shâv or Shav – nothingness, emptiness, anything which disappoints the hope which rests upon it, false hood, worthless], …for the Lord will not leave him unpunished who takes His name in vain."

It is an insult to negate the identity of `Ĕlôhîym to be a false god and to elevate a false god in His place; to give an idol or a religious belief the identity of the one true Living God.

Exodus 23:13
"Now concerning everything which I have said to you, be on your *guard* [Shâmar – the careful attention which is paid to the obligation of a covenant] …and do not mention the name of other gods {God's identity given to anything other than Him} nor let them be *heard* [Shâma` - to hear intelligently so as to give attention or obedience to what is said] …from your *mouth* [Peh – to speak with the authority of God]."

Matthew 15:7-9
"You hypocrites, rightly did (Isaiah 29:13) *prophesy* [Prophēteuō – foretell things to come] …of you, saying, 'This people honor Me with their lips, but their heart is far away from Me. But in *vain* [Matēn – folly, invalid, useless, futile, untrue, worthlessness] …do they worship Me, teaching as *doctrines* [Didaskalia – truth that only God can reveal] …the *precepts* [Entaima – a commandment which stresses the authority of the one commanding] …of men, for the Lord will not leave him unpunished who takes His name in vain`."

Generations of men have fostered the precept that cursing is the meaning of this revelation of God. Exodus 21-23 reveals Gods *ordinances* [Mishpât – a verdict pronounced judicially as a judgment against the actions of man which transgress God's justice.]. ...God governed the fleshly lives of Israel in these chapters to promote a peaceful society which is representative of His character to an unbelieving world. As it is with human laws, breaking these ordinances had consequences. In Exodus 22:28, God says, "You shall not *curse God* [Qâlal – to be despised, to be insignificant, to be of small worth] ... nor *curse a ruler* [Nâsîy- an exalted person who serves as a religious or civil leader] ...of your people."

"Cursing" {Qâlal} is the reality of the power of death that defiles the mind to berate God and people as to make them less important than ones-self. It took the legalistic minds of the Puritans to interpret cursing as "profanity". This sin was defined in infinitesimal detail and they devised an appropriate punishment for each case. However, lost humanity considers the filthiness that comes out of their mouths not to be sin at all. A man can publicly espouse filthy language and justify it with the inane expression "excuse my French". The youth of every generation are continually changing the concept of cursing/profanity in their common language to express the emotions of their defiled minds.

Jesus concluded His teachings to the legalistic Pharisees in Matthew 15, with these words of admonition: Matthew 15:10-11, "And after He called the multitude to Him, He said to them, 'Hear, and understand. Not what enters into the mouth *defiles* [Koinoō – to make unclean, to pollute] ...the man, but what proceeds out of the mouth, this defiles the man`.'" "Cursing" and "profanity" are the actions of a depraved mind which reveal a person's character; but **"vain"** in this revelation reveals - the rejection of the true identify of God. It declares God's judgment upon every single religion in the world.

FOURTH ARTICLE

8. Remember the *Sabbath* [Shabbâth – noun meaning intermission: (seventh day, seventh year)] ...*day* [Yôwm –When connected with the sovereignty of God; it is time of worship that is under His control for the revelation of Himself] ...to *keep* [Shâmar–to tend, to watch over, to observe, to guard, to protect, to fulfill a responsibility] ... it *holy* [Qâdâsh - morally clean, pure, sacred. It is God's time; so, honor Him with it].

Our days on earth are valuable to God; and we must learn that one day we spend in worship and fellowship with Him is more valuable than the six days He has given us to satisfy the needs of the flesh. We need God more than we need food for the body, or a ball game.

9. Six days you shall *labor* ['Âbad – kept in bondage, to be enslaved (stewards to God for physical work to take care of daily living)] ... and *do* ['Âsâh – our ethical obligation to be good stewards of our time to care for the needs of the body] ...all your *work* [Mᵉlâkâh–fem. Heb. noun; meaning deputyship (ambassador), ministry, the practice of skills to produce fruit of the spirit (the concept of living as a Godly person caring for the needs of ourselves and our fellow man). This word is opposite of (âmâl or yâg` - meaning manual and servile labor)].

This verse is God's revelation that the spiritual life of His people is His creation of man in His image. This verse emphasizes the identity of man (Adam) created a spiritual being in a fleshly body to take care of his environment. Adam was responsible to live by God's authority as a holy being and not a slave to his flesh. We are to be good stewards of our physical lives. Adam was God's authority on earth and was charged with the responsibility to be His overseer for the good of all living things. But never did God command him to exalt the needs of the flesh above the needs of the spirit. For us to do so declares physical man to be more important than God.

10. But the seventh day is a Sabbath of the Lord your God; in it{literally: in your gates; what you do for the care of your physical life}you shall not *do* ('Âsâh) any *work* (M^elâkâh), you or your son or your daughter, your male or your female *servant*['Ebed – an Israelite in indentured servitude to another Israelite for six years] …or your cattle or your *sojourner* [Gêr – a person who enjoys certain civil rights but not property rights. This word is a reference to a fellow Israelite who is a guest in your home. It denotes Abraham and all his spiritual descendants are to be sojourners in this world because it is not our permanent home and we are not to live as it is.]

This verse is a revelation of God to His own people, not to the unbelieving world. It is God's promise that He will always be present with His people to guide them in this present time of His redemptive activity. To remember the Sabbath day is to glorify God every day by the actions of sanctified man for the good of all mankind and to periodically focus a demonstration of faith in the glory of God as His assurance of timeless life. A day of worship and fellowship with God is a healing balm for the weariness of physical life; and a potent reminder that God is preparing a timeless Sabbath rest for all the true Israelites of the world. The seventh revelation of creation reveals God's purpose for creating His sanctified people is to worship Him in His timeless rule when death and the flesh cease to exist. (Revelation 21-22)

Isaiah 58:13-14
"If because of the *Sabbath* [Shabbâth – an intermission in regular activities; a time of rest from the activity of providing for the flesh; a sacred time for ministering to the spirit in the worship of God] …you *turn* [Shûwb – to turn oneself around from the activities of the flesh to return toward the Lord; repent] …your foot from *doing* ['Âsâh – an ethical obligation of obedience to continue or complete a work] …your own pleasure on My *holy day* [Qôdesh – something that is set apart as sacred] …and call the Sabbath a delight, the holy day of the Lord *honorable* [Kâbêd – to be heavy, weighted: to be esteemed; heavy with glory, awesome in might and joy], …and shall honor it, desisting from your own ways, from seeking your own pleasure, and speaking your own *word* [Dâbâr – God's word of revelation; do not replace God's words with your own words {I do not need church; I worship God my way}], …then you will take delight in the Lord, and I will make you ride on the *heights* [Bâmâh – the high places where God forbid the pagans and the Israelites to worship false gods] …of the *earth* ['Erets – the physical planet that is the habitation of man (God will bless his people with His own presence as if it were the heights of heaven)]; …and I will feed you with the *heritage*['Uzzîyâ - strength of God] …of Jacob (God converted him from the power of death to the power of spiritual life) your father, for the *mouth*[Peh – direct communication; speaking person to person] …of the Lord has *spoken* [Dâbar – mental or oral communication]."

This revelation of God for the Sabbath cannot in anyway be a legalistic law as is taught by the precepts of mankind. Jesus revealed this to be so in Matthew 15. Legalistic law (traditions) perpetuated by nationalistic Israel in the time of the Christ was the actions of the Jews to supersede the authority of God by their own authority. This revealed their worship of Jehovah was in vain.

11. For in six days the Lord made the heavens and the earth, the sea and all that is in them, and rested on the seventh day; therefore, the Lord blessed the Sabbath day and made it holy.

This verse was first given as God's seventh revelation of creation (see Genesis 2:1-3). It is repeated in God's heavenly constitution as His admonition for His people to be Holy as He is Holy and not to make our temporary physical lives more important than our worship of Him. We are to know that His throne of Life is a constant, guarding presence in our earthly temple (heart and mind), and we will glorify Him in our earthly worship as we will in our timeless spiritual worship in a new heaven where we will be completely sanctified as holy, as God is Holy.

God says in Hebrews 10:23-25, "Let us hold fast the confession of our hope without wavering, for He who promised is faithful; and let us consider how to stimulate one another to love and good deeds, not forsaking our own assembling together as is the habit of some but encouraging one another and all the more as you see the day drawing near." (In the last days Satan will be empowered to desecrate the temple of God – the heart and mind of man – to worship him and live by the power of death. It will be as it was in the day of Noah when only a small remnant of humanity will remain true to worship God.)

Every revelation of the Sabbath was progressively taught to the Israelites in their personal experience of living. In Exodus 16, God fed the Hebrews with manna each day of the week. The manna was perfect food for all life in heaven and on earth. The Hebrews gathered only what they needed for each individual day and it satisfied their physical hunger. On the sixth day they gathered what they needed for that day and enough for the seventh day. The holiness of God was revealed in the manna for the seventh day because it was a faith gift; it would not rot. He gave them what they needed to sustain both their physical and spiritual lives. God's blessing for physical life was a gift; they did not have to work for it. God's blessing of timeless life is also a faith gift from God; it cannot be achieved by human effort. Redeemed humanity continually celebrates the completed seventh revelation of creation (God's gift of timeless life in His presence) by having a designated day set aside for worship. Our worship of God gives recognition to the world that His kingdom of life is more important than all the physical world has to offer.

In these verses of Exodus 20:8-11, God taught the Hebrews that the Sabbath is holy because it belongs to God and not to man. God's heavenly constitution, (erroneously called the Ten Commandments), taught them that He is the single ruling power of life and the law of heaven is sinlessness. God's purpose is to bless man with His holiness. The Sabbath is spent in worship of God in recognition of the fact that the life God gives us belongs to Him and is His timeless holiness.

In Exodus 31:12-18, God taught the Hebrews that the seventh revelation of creation is His gathering to Himself all who belong to Him. They were to celebrate the Sabbath as a sign of the perpetual covenant of their timeless relationship with God. If they profaned the seventh day, they were to be cut off from among His people by being put to death. They could not have life on earth if they did not want God's timeless life.

In Exodus 35-40, God taught the Hebrews that the seventh revelation of creation was achieved by His holy sacrifice which transforms man from death to life. The people were commanded to make every sacrifice necessary to build a dwelling for God to demonstrate His holy presence. When the tabernacle was completed; Exodus 40:34-38, "Then the cloud covered the tent of meeting and the glory of the Lord filled the tabernacle. And Moses was not able to enter the tent of meeting because the cloud had settled on it and the glory of the Lord filled the tabernacle. And throughout all their journeys whenever the cloud was taken up from over the tabernacle the sons of Israel would set out; but if the cloud was not taken up, then they did not set out until the day when it was taken up. For throughout all their journeys, the cloud of the Lord was on the tabernacle by day and there was fire in it by night, in the sight of all the house of Israel." Redeemed mankind (bought with a priceless sacrifice) celebrates the seventh revelation in recognition that God is present with absolute control to save human life from the curse of death and He is the permanent light unceasingly leading spiritual mankind to their future life in heaven.

God kept the holiness of the seventh revelation before Israel throughout the Old Testament (Leviticus, Numbers, Deuteronomy, II Kings, I Chronicles, II Chronicles, Nehemiah, Psalms, Isaiah, Jeremiah, Ezekiel, and Amos). However, the New Testament reveals that national Israel had profaned the glory of the Sabbath with the glory of man:

Mark 2:23-28
"And it came about that Jesus was passing through the grain fields on the Sabbath and His disciples began to make their way along while picking the heads of grain. And the Pharisees were saying to Him, 'See here, why are they doing what is not lawful on the Sabbath'? And He said to them, 'Have you never read what David did when he was in need and *became hungry* [Peinaō – to be famished from lack of food; from Penēs (to toil for daily substance; to be so poor one earns his bread by daily labor). Jesus identified Himself with David and all His saints in speaking of Himself as suffering with them in every respect as a human being], …he and his companions: how he entered the house of God in the time of Abiathar the high priest and ate the *consecrated bread* [Prothesis – to set forth fresh bread (the sustenance of life) before the Lord for open view or daily display], …which is not lawful for anyone to eat except the priests, and he gave it also to those who were with him?' And He was saying to them, 'The *Sabbath* [Sabbatōn (Greek)] was made for *man* [Anthrōpos – a generic name for humanity created in the image of God] …and not man for the Sabbath. Consequently, *The Christ* [Huios Anthrōpos – The holy character of God demonstrated in man so as to make the identity of the two indiscernible. Jesus is God's High Priest of heaven and God's people are His earthly priests.] …is Lord even of the Sabbath."

Jesus made it clear that the seventh revelation of creation (the timeless Sabbath) is God's blessing man with the same holy character as His own. Obedience to this fourth article of God's constitution does not qualify man to be saved; but on the contrary, it is the expression of love God's children have for their heavenly Father and their desire to be near to him. They are blessed to eat of that spiritual food which God provides for His priests.

FIFTH ARTICLE

12. *Honor* [Y^{e}rêmay – elevated; from Rûwm (to be held high with respect, exalted)] …your *father* [`Ab -father, grandfather, forefather, ancestor. When used with {Em} it re-presents your male parent as the one who gave you spiritual life.] …and your *mother* [Em- mother, grandmother, and ancestors. When used with {`Ab} it represents your female parent in whose body our own bodies develop for physical life.] …that your days may be *prolonged* [`Ârak – to make longer, to lengthen your life] …in the *land* [`Ădâmâh –the planet earth, soil which grows food, habitation of physical man; God owns this land, and He owns every man He gives both physical and Spiritual life] … which the Lord your God gives you.

God delivered the Hebrews from their bondage to Egypt. He delivered them into His own presence to sanctify them as a heavenly spiritual people, free from the earthly bondage to the flesh. God's governing rule in heaven is absolute obedience to the authority of Ĕlôhîym. God's rule over His sanctified children on earth requires the same obedience to His righteousness. Obedience is the judgment of His Throne of Life for Him to bring about the salvation of the world. God empowers every member of His family to be obedient to His righteousness, to be a "light to the nations". People who will not worship the living God have no spiritual life and have no hope of His timeless presence. People who worship God honors their parents as a holy creation of God for the perpetuity of the human race created in His Image.

Jesus said in Matthew 18:1-6, and again in Matthew 19:13-15
"At that time the disciples came to Jesus, saying, 'Who then is greatest in the kingdom of heaven'? And He called a child to Himself and set him before them, and said, 'Truly I say to you, unless you are converted and become like children, you shall not enter the kingdom of heaven. Whoever then humbles himself as this child, he is the greatest in the kingdom of heaven. And whoever receives one such child in My name, receives Me; but whoever causes one of these little ones who believe in Me to stumble, it is better for him that a heavy millstone be hung around his neck and that he be drowned in the depth the sea`. Then some children were brought to Jesus so that He might lay His hands on them and pray; and the disciples rebuked them. But Jesus said, 'Let the children alone and do not hinder them from coming to Me; for the kingdom of heaven belongs to such as these`.'"

The holiness of God's people begins when they are children. All people are born with Spiritual Life. It is this identity of God in children which He empowers to obey their parents. God said again in Ephesians 6:1-3, "Children, obey your parents in the Lord, for this is right. Honor your father and mother (which is the first commandment with a promise), that it may go well with you and that you may live long on the earth."

The idea of exalting our human parents has the strong connotation of establishing an order of rule for the purpose of protection and care (God's commissioned overseers of the innocent). The rule of children over their parents is rebellion and chaos. It is the same thing as the earthly kingdom of death ruling over the heavenly kingdom of righteousness. The consequence is the child will rule the family with a legalistic mind that challenges all authorities throughout their lives ("that is not fair"; "you are mean to me"; "you are too strict"; "I never get my way"). Legalism always rejects obedience to authority because it is the tyranny of slavery to sin. Disobedient children shame their parents, as we shame our Father in heaven by our disregard for His authority.

Psalms 127:3-5
"Behold, children are a gift of the Lord; the fruit of the womb is a reward. Like arrows in the hand of a warrior, so are the children of one's youth. How blessed is the man whose quiver is full of them; they shall not be ashamed when they speak with their enemies in the gate."

Proverbs 22:6
"Train up a child in the way he should go; even when he is old, he will not depart from it."

Proverbs 23:12-14, training a child involves self-discipline of the body so that it is not the slave of a wicked mind. "Apply your heart to discipline and your ears to words of knowledge. Do not hold back discipline from the child; although you strike him with the rod, he will not die. You shall strike him with the rod and deliver his soul from Sheol (Hades)."

This article of God's constitution reveals the depth of His love as a heavenly Father for those who would be obedient to Him as spiritual children. His promise is an earthly life sustained by the One Who is the master over death. Obedience to God's righteousness produces righteousness. God said again:

Proverbs 3:1-8
"My sons do not forget my teaching but let your heart keep my commandments; for length of days and years of life, and peace they will add to you. Do not let kindness and truths leave you; bind them around your neck, write them on the tablet of your heart. So, you will find favor and good repute in the sight of God and man. Trust in the Lord with all your heart and do not lean on your own understanding. In all your ways acknowledge Him, and He will make your paths straight. Do not be wise in your own eyes; fear the Lord and turn away from evil. It will be healing to your body, and refreshment to your bones."

God has defined the difficult; but most important task of training the mind of a child is to be submissive to the power of infinite goodness. God is not telling us to beat our children to submission. He is telling us to be disciplined by the power of His love to minister to our children, to create within them the discipline of perfect love. People who are disciplined to love God with all the heart and mind and love others as themselves reveal this discipline of love as children by loving their father and mother.

This fifth revelation of God declares that He will accept nothing less in His people than the discipline of His own character of love. There is no greater blessing upon the human family than the relationship of parents and their children as a living testimony of their love for one-another.

SIXTH ARTICLE

13. You shall not *murder* [Râtsach – the unlawful killing of a human being with malice aforethought, either expressed or implied; to dash in pieces; to slay; to destroy by an intentional action; to massacre helpless victims. Murder identifies the human mind that is completely under the kingdom rule of death.].

Genesis 9:6,
"Whoever *sheds* {Shâphak – to slaughter; pour out the lifeblood} …*mans'* [`Âdâm– generic man created in God's Image] …blood, by man his lifeblood shall be shed. In this state of mind, Lucifer and every human would murder God if it were possible. This was the Sanhedrin's state of mind to murder Jesus.]."

There are four Hebrew words in the Old Testament for murder: *Râtsach, Hârag* [to strike with deadly intent; Esau sought to murder Jacob], *Nâkâh*– [to strike something lightly or severely. This is an ambiguous word used five hundred times for a nonfatal blow, i.e.: Moses struck the river and a rock; God struck the people with blindness. However, it is used ninety times for a person to strike a person with the intent to murder (Genesis 4:14-15, people strike Cain to murder him)]; and *Nâga`* - [to touch, strike, kill, to punish, divine chastisement. Genesis 3:3, Eve said to touch the tree of Good and Evil would place you under God's judgment of death]. It is unfortunate that all of these words are translated in the KJV by the English word "kill".

Exodus 21:12-36 gives us numerous examples of the ingenuity of the human mind to destroy human life for personal gain.

Numbers 35:30, 33-34
"Whosoever *murders* [Râtsach – KJV says kills] … any person, the murderer shall be put to death at the evidence of the mouth of witnesses, but no person shall be put to death on the testimony of one witness. So, you shall not *pollute* [Chânêph – make profane with wickedness. {Juarez is the murder capital of Mexico and the Middle East has become the murder capital of the world}.] …the land in which you are for blood pollutes the land and no *expiation* [Kâphar – to cover, to make an atonement, to cleanse, to appease, to be merciful] …can be made for the land for the blood that is *shed* [Shâphak – to slaughter people] …on it, except by the blood of him who shed it. *(In Romans 13, God mandates that governments act in His authority to control evil from the destruction of society by putting convicted murderers to death). And you shall not *defile* [Tâmê` - to desecrate what is holy] …the land in which you live, in the midst of which I *dwell* [Shâkan – the pillar of fire and the cloud] …for I the Lord am dwelling in the midst of the sons of Israel."

Hosea 4:1-2

God Reveals His Glory [Doxa – True Identity]

"There is no faithfulness, or kindness or knowledge of God in the Land. There is swearing, deception, murder, stealing and adultery. They employ violence so that *bloodshed* [Dâm – blood given to man for the sanctity of life ("the life is in the blood"); God heard the blood of Able crying out from the earth.] …follows bloodshed." *Today women demand their right to murder their own babies. The Supreme Court has removed it as the law of the land.

In Numbers 35:6-28, God differentiates between murder and killing. God instructed Israel to designate forty-eight cities as places of refuge for a person who murders someone or unintentionally kills someone. Both the manslayer (murderer) and the one who kills accidentally are considered guilty of murder until they stand trial and proven guilty or innocent. The city of refuge protected the innocent from someone trying to be an avenger. If a person is found innocent of murder, he is to remain in the city until the death of the High Priest. If he leaves the city before the death of his divine protector, the avenger can *kill* (English) him [Nâkâh – strike, beat, or take his life].

The concept of *killing* is [Mûwth – to die; simply "to lose one's life"]. A person grows old and "dies". An executed person "is caused to die". A person "killed" in war is caused to die. To kill an animal for a sacrifice is [Shâchat – to slaughter. Abraham took his knife to *slay* {to slaughter his son for a sacrifice}. Animals can be killed {slaughtered for food}. In Judges 12:1-6, Jephthah was the judge of Israel who *slew* {slaughtered/caused to die} forty-two thousand men of Ephraim in battle, in response to Ephraim initiating a war against Israel.

God's admonition for His people to be of a sound and holy mind that they shall not murder identifies them with the holy life in heaven and separates them from humanity that hates righteousness and loves evil. God's love for man is His power to "touch" us that we should not die for shedding blood but be saved by His blood poured out as a sacrifice for us.

Mathew 5:21
"Jesus said, 'You have heard that the ancients were told, You Shall Not Commit *Murder* [Phŏnĕuō – to intentionally take a person's life; one who takes a person's life is a {Phoneus – murderer}] …and whoever commits murder shall be liable to the court`.'"

John 8:44
"You are of your father, the devil, and you want to do the desires of your father. He was a *murderer* [Anthrōpŏktŏnŏs – manslayer] …from the beginning."

I John 3:15
"Everyone who hates his brother is a *murderer* (Anthrōpŏktŏnŏs); …and you know that no murderer has timeless life abiding in him."

Acts 21:38
"Then you (the Apostle Paul) are not the Egyptian who some time ago stirred up a revolt and led four thousand men of the *assassins* [Sikariŏs– an assassin; dagger-man; derived from the Latin (sica; a short dagger)] …out into the wilderness."

Mark 14:1

"Now the Passover and Unleavened Bread was two days off; and the chief priests and the scribes were seeking how to seize Him (Jesus) by stealth and *kill* (English) Him [Apŏktĕino – to murder; slay; to destroy; to slaughter as a sacrifice for the nation]."

I John 3:12
"Not as Cain who was of the evil one, and *slew* [Sphazō – to butcher] …his brother."

Acts 8:32, Isaiah 53:7
"He (Jesus) was led as a sheep to *slaughter* [Sphagē – butcher an animal for sacrifice]"

Murder has been the rule of man since Cain turned his face away from God. This author has been a witness to six bloody civil wars in a span of only eight years. Murder has become such a rampant power of evil that people commit this crime against the righteousness of God just for the fun of it. Religious groups are chopping people's heads off so the world will fear them. Hundreds of thousands of unborn children have been murdered in the womb.

The highest numbers of shows on television are murder mysteries and gory horror shows. The world has become intoxicated with the satanic desire to inflict as much pain and mayhem upon the human race as possible. Mans` laws to govern murder separate it by intent; first, second and third degree and punishes the offender with jail time or probation. Ungodly people reject God's words of Romans 13:1-5 for the government to execute murderers. They consider it to be "inhumane" and murderers are released from confinement to murder again.

There are countries around the world where the streets run red with blood. This is the judgment of God proclaimed (Matthew 24) as the rule of Satan over human life in the last days (desolation of abomination to destroy the temple of God/human heart). How can God possibly bless any people when the world is under the rule of God's enemy?

SEVENTH ARTICLE

14. You shall not commit *adultery* [Nâ`aph – to apostatize God's creation of marriage.]"

This word labels a person with the stigma of one who lusts for the flesh, whether male or female. Death began when Eve convinced Adam that the power of human life was in the flesh, not the Spirit of God. This human precept completely rejects the authority of God to create everything that is good for man; and replaces it with the authority of man to satisfy every desire with the knowledge of good and evil (the rule of death). This rampant sin has been one of the most destructive powers in the world and will be one of the most visible signs of Satan's rule before the Apokalupsis of the Christ. Sexual perversion and the destruction of marriage has become a ruling power of people as a "human right". Infidelity rules the minds of lost humanity, but God's people are responsible to Him to honor their marriage vows.

EIGHTH ARTICLE

15. You shall not *steal* [Gânab – this is the primitive root word for 'to thieve`.].

Thievery labels a person with the stigma of one who has no respect for God or man. This person has no respect for property rights; and gives himself the right to take what he wants to please his carnal nature. God outlines numerous examples of thievery in Exodus 22:1-14.

NINETH ARTICLE

16. You shall not bear *false* witness [Sheqer – an untruth; a sham; a lie; deceitfulness; perjury; the stigma of being a completely worthless person who destroys the character of others] …against your *neighbor* [Rêa` or Rêya` - These words define a personal friend].

Every human being is created in the image of God and is to be loved as a spiritual being. To give a false witness against what God loves is the same as giving a false witness against God. This is illustrated in Exodus 23:1-9. To defame the character of an honest person is an affront to God, Himself. God especially detests liars calling Him a liar.

TENTH ARTICLE

17. You shall not *covet* [Châmad–this word describes the forbidden tree in the Garden of Eden; to have an inordinate, ungoverned, selfish desire for what pleases the eye; to desire the physical things which delights the soul.] …your neighbor's *house* [Bayith – to take pride in having a dwelling place you did not build for yourself. Jesus said He would build His people a dwelling place in the perfect environment of God's presence. God used this word to reveal the ungodly power of envy that we would make (God's temple: the human mind – the decision-making power of man to be nothing more than the weakness of the flesh) a den of robbers]; …you shall not covet your neighbor's *wife* [`Ishshâh – God created Eve from Adam's body to make them one body. God says you cannot break asunder what God put together. To destroy a marriage relationship is a sin against creation and a personal affront to God.] …or his male or female servant or his ox or his donkey or anything that belongs to your neighbor.

Thievery, false witness and coveting in any form are acts of the character of death, which reveals death is the master of that person's mind to hurt people without any regard for them. This is Satan's attack upon God in His creation; that he could not do in God's heavenly presence.

Mark 7:18-23
"And He (Jesus) said to them, 'Are you so lacking in understanding also? Do you not *understand* [Noeō - to perceive with thought coming into consciousness as distinct from the perception of the physical senses?] …that whatever goes into the man from outside cannot defile him; because it does not go into his heart, but into his stomach, and is eliminated?` (Thus He declared all foods clean.) And He was saying, 'That which proceeds out of the mind; that is what defiles the man. For from within, out of the heart of men, proceed the *evil thoughts* [Dial-ogismos–this word has only a negative meaning (from *Dialogizomai* – to reason within oneself); to dispute with objectionable thoughts and act in a negative direction], …fornications, thefts,

murders, adulteries, deeds of coveting and wickedness, as well as deceit, sensuality, envy, slander, pride and foolishness. All these evil things proceed from within and defile the man`."

Exodus 20:18-19, is the peoples' response to God's spoken Words {His articles of His governing power for holiness}:

"And all the *people* [`Am – a congregation of God's people separated from the human race; the tribe of spiritual Israel] …*perceived* [Râ`âh – comprehend the mind of God by the capacity of the human mind {I Corinthians 2:1-13, the Holy Spirit reveals God's mind to the mind of man}.] …the thunder and lightning flashes and the sound of the trumpet and the mountain smoking; and when the people *saw* {Râ`âh} it, they trembled and stood at a distance. Then they said to Moses, *speak* [Dâbar – speak for God] …to us yourself and we will *listen* [Shâma` - to hear intelligently; give attention and obedience] … but let not God speak to us, lest we die."

This body of people revealed the character of the whole human race under the curse of death. John 3: 19 – 20, "This is the verdict: Light has come into the world, but men love darkness instead of light because their deeds are evil. Everyone who does evil hates the light and will not come to the light for fear that their deeds will be exposed." They do not want to hear God's word because they feared that awesome power revealed on that mountain would always be with them to judge the actions of their daily lives.

Exodus 20:20, is Moses' response to the people:

"And Moses said to the people, 'Do not be *afraid* [Yârê'–a primitive root word meaning caused to be frightened; when used in reference to the exalted person of God it means to revere Him and render Him proper respect of submission and trust] …for *God* [`Ĕlôhîym – (plural) the supreme power over all life; divine majesty] …has come in order to *test* you [Nâgâh – to reveal the reality of the human mind that can only be known by expressing a positive or negative response to Him] …and in order that the *fear*{Yârê` - reverence] …of Him may remain with you so that you may not *sin* [Châtâ` - a primitive root word meaning failure to be the spiritual person of God's image]; …to *prove* {Nâçâh– to refine His holy, heavenly character of life in the weakness of human flesh; to walk more closely with Him as the angels do in heaven. God's saints are to be holy as He is holy and live saintly lives that our sinfulness will not be exposed and make us shameful and reproached in the eyes of unredeemed mankind} `] …So the people stood at a distance while Moses *approached* [Nâgash – to draw near to God with an intimate relationship] …the *thick cloud* [`Ărâphel – a thick darkness that shuts out all-natural light] …where God was."

Moses revealed to them that their fears were not grounded in the Divine Majesty of God, but in the reality of their ungodliness. These people would be the first to gain a trust in God by worshipping Him in the familiarity of a temple that was alive with His presence. In this temple they found that God deals with the sinfulness of His people by His love and forgiveness.

God Reveals His Glory [Doxa – True Identity]

GOD'S TEMPLE

Exodus 20:22-26
"Then the Lord said to Moses, 'Thus you shall say to the sons of Israel; you yourselves have <u>seen</u> [Râ`âh – understood spiritual truth] …that I have <u>spoken</u> [Dâbar – spiritual truth spoken by word of mouth] … to you from heaven. You shall not make other <u>gods</u> [`Ĕlôwahh – deity created by man] …besides Me; gods of silver or gold you shall not make for ourselves. You shall make an <u>altar</u> [Mizbêach – direct revelation of the centrality of a sacrificial system for the atonement of sin. The first use of this word is in Gen. 8:20; when after the flood, Noah built an altar to worship God. This same word is central to God's continuing development of Spiritual Israel.] …of <u>earth</u> [`Ădâmâh – The soil God created to give life to physical man] …for Me, and you shall <u>sacrifice</u> [Zâbach – to slaughter a living animal (blood offering)] … on it; your <u>burnt offerings</u> [`Ôwlâh – an offering purified by fire ascends upward from earth to heaven. The man must put his hand on the animal's head and God will accept his burnt offering to make atonement for him (personal relationship with God)] …and your <u>peace offering</u> [Shelem – a voluntary offering to acknowledge God's goodness] …your sheep and your oxen; in every place where I cause My Name to be remembered, I will come to you and bless you. And if you make an altar of stone for Me, you shall not build it of <u>cut</u> stones [Gâzîyth – dressed, hewn stone (the work of man's mind as to what is acceptable)],… for if you <u>wield</u> [Nûwph – to quiver, vibrate, sprinkle, rubbing, sawing, shaking] …your <u>tool</u> [Chereb – any cutting instrument that has a destructive effect (the same word is used of a sword for war and the swords God placed East of the Garden of Eden] …on it, you will profane it. And you shall not go up by steps to My altar, (it did not have steps) that your <u>nakedness</u> [`Ervâh – shame, uncleanness of the mind; to offer a sacrifice with the superior attitude that it is inconsequential to its purpose. Man cannot hide the evil of his mind; it will always be exposed by his evil actions.] …may not be <u>exposed</u> [Gâlâh – to be disgraced because the glory of God has departed from you; God will not accept your sacrifice.] …on it`."

Exodus 20:22-26 is God's continuing revelation to His people. Humanity had long been worshiping gods of their own creation and continually does so with a multitude of religions. God is worshipped in His heavenly temple by the angels {Isaiah 6:1-7}; but now He has [Nâgash} approached man to have an intimate relationship with Him on earth; that man would love Him and not fear Him. He would accomplish this by the construction of a Temple.

This temple is the initial movement of God to reveal His authority to cleanse His people by the blood sacrifice of animals (the innocence of God's creation that cannot sin). It would be constructed in the wilderness (the human race completely devoid of the knowledge of God; there is no spiritual life in them). The earthly temple is powerfully alive; it is the holy living presence of the God of heaven, the voice of the Living God to (1) bring sinful man into His presence for sanctification, and (2) to provide a way to create a powerful trust relationship that man will speak to Him and hear with understanding when God speaks intimately to man.

Exodus 24-31, these chapters reveal a very unique revelation of God's familiarity with His people. Such a thing is absolutely impossible for all the people of the world who worship idols or any other false concept of relating to a created god.

Exodus 24:1-8, God began the revelation of His Temple by inviting Moses, Aaron and his two sons and seventy of the _elders_ [Zâqên – this word recognized people for their experience with gifts of leadership, wisdom and justice. They were counselors to kings and city officials; but they were never burdened or charged with the responsibility of ruling over anyone.] …to worship Him on Mt. Sinai until the people accepted God's covenant.

Exodus 24:9-11
"Then Moses went up with Aaron, Nadab and Abihu and seventy of the elders of Israel; and they _saw_ [Râ'âh – to observe, get acquainted with, examine, gain understanding of truth] …the _God_ [`Ĕlôhîym] …of Israel; and under His feet there appeared to be a pavement of sapphire, as _clear_ [Tôhar – from the root word {tâhêr'}, meaning to be so pure as to radiate a bright light. This word reveals Gods purification of His people (under His feet) to be holy as He is holy] …as the _sky_ [Shâmeh – the expanse in which God placed the stars and planets is so clear that man can see everything in it; but most important is the awesome truth that man on earth can touch God in His heavenly abode] …itself. Yet He did not stretch out His _Hand_ [Yâd – the open hand; indicating the utmost power to protect, instead of to destroy.] …against the _Nobles_ [`Âtsîyl – This word designates something that is separated from all other things; having a sense of the greatest value] …of the sons of Israel; and they _beheld_ [Châzâh – to contemplate with great pleasure; to select something of great value for themselves] …God; *and they ate and drank with Him."

Moses, Aaron and his sons and the elders experienced the close fellowship with The Living God that He yearns to have with the human race. The New Testament disciples ate and drank with Jesus, but they did not comprehend the truth of His identity until He ascended back to heaven. The church eats and drinks with God in its observance of the Lord's Supper. It is the personal celebration by each individual to thank God for His atonement of their sins.

Exodus 24:12-13
"Now the Lord said to Moses, 'Come up to Me on the mountain and remain there, and I will give you the stone tablets with the _law_ [Tôwrâh– instruction, doctrine {only God can reveal His doctrines}; the essential meaning is Teachings.]…and the _commandments_ [Mitsvâh – God's teachings to His people which described the particular conditions of His heavenly covenant with Spiritual Israel]…which I have written for their _instruction_ [Yârâh– to lay a foundation to build on; the connotation of controlling the basis for the identity of a people. This is the first time God wrote His spoken word on stone tablets that humanity cannot alter with their own precepts`] …So Moses arose with Joshua his _servant_ [Shârath – to do service as a priest for the worship of God.] …and Moses went up to the mountain of God."

God Reveals His Glory [Doxa – True Identity]

Exodus 24:15-18

"Then Moses went up to the top of the mountain and the *cloud* ['Ânân – This word is used eighty times and three-fourths of these refer to the pillar of cloud that led the Israelites and later covered the temple of Solomon. In this verse it reveals the over-whelming holy presence of God covering His meeting place with His redeemed humanity.] ...*covered* [Kâçâh – to conceal, to hide, to clothe, to cover sin; God's covering or hiding sins is forgiveness; His righteous judgment which reveals the magnitude of God's love and grace and is His commandment for the Godly character that identifies His people.] ...the mountain.

And the *glory* [Kâbôwd – from {Kâbêd}; the awesome heavy weight of the visible revelation of the appearance of God is the greatest treasure man can possess. God revealed Himself in a way that man could comprehend His true identity as the single authority for life to exist.] ...of the Lord *rested* [Shâkan–to reside permanently with humanity made in His image; to inhabit man with timeless life.] ...on Mt. Sinai, and the cloud covered it for *six days* [Shishshâh – Six is the number for man made in God's image; one number short of Seven, the number for God. This word is the revelation of God crowning created man as His decision maker on earth which returns to Him by obedient faith as His heavenly children.]; ...and on the *seventh day* [Sh^ebîy 'îy – from {Shib 'îym}; the cardinal number "one" multiplied to infinity; the revelation of the fullness/sacredness of the only living Deity, who is to be permanently worshipped by spiritual life of His creation.] ...He *called* [Qârâ- to summon a specific person by name to a specific response; the word Ekklesia/Church means "the called-out ones". The Holy Spirit calls man out by name and each man's response is to call upon the name of God.] ...to Moses from the midst of the cloud. To the minds of the sons of Israel (physical descendants of Jacob) the appearance of the glory of the Lord was like a consuming fire on the mountain *top* [Rô'sh - the head of a man's body; the ruling mind of God which is master over all life; the person of God is the supreme ruler of all spiritual life and all created life is responsible to Him. This revelation of the Glory of God gave rise to the idea that it was impossible for Moses to come back down the mountain. In verse 14, Moses left Aaron and Hur in charge of their legal matters; and the people believing Moses was dead, turned their minds to make their own "god" they would not fear.] ...And Moses entered the midst of the cloud as he went up to the mountain top; and Moses was on the mountain *forty* days and *forty* nights ['Arbâ 'îym– foursquare; multiple of the cardinal number four from the root word {Reba '–to be prostate before God in worship}.]"

God's revelation of the position of man before the supremacy of God is absolute reverence of the mind without even the minutest thought of self. The words days/nights did not mean human time; but God's revelations of His identity to destroy the power of death in human life. The darkness of death is completely removed by the light of God. This is the way it will be when redeemed humanity will worship God in His timeless presence where there is no death.

When Moses came down from the mountain, he had the mind of God to abhor sin (His face shone with the glory of God). Revelation 21-22 reveals God's perfect heaven is such holiness that His mind is the only mind (there is no death in God). This is God's assurance that death can never exist again. God revealed through Moses that every human being who will respond to His call to come to Him; will be transformed from death to life where death can never exist again and will not even be remembered in the mind of man.

Exodus 25-31 is God's full instructions to Moses for constructing a physical temple which reveals God's heavenly presence has been brought to man; that each individual can (like Moses) personally worship Him in His presence. Everything about this temple is *ALIVE*; it is God's revelation of His living presence to sanctify every individual person on earth who will return to Him (Jews and Gentiles are all the same to God; all people are sinners.). The temple was God's way for mankind to personally/individually experience God's sanctification that was revealed in Moses on Mt. Sinai; as His requirement to be His holy people {Spiritual Israel}. God's salvation is not in the faithfulness of man going to the temple; it is in the Person of God who makes His temple alive in the one who worships Him.

I Corinthians 3:16-17

"Do you not know that you are a <u>temple</u> [Naos – habitation of God; the Holy of Holies] …of <u>God</u> [Theos – the name of the one true God] …and that the <u>Spirit</u> [Pneuma – the invisible, immaterial and powerful breath of God which gives life to man] …of God <u>dwells</u> [Oikeō - inhabits] …in you? If any man destroys the temple of God, God will destroy him, for the temple of God is <u>holy</u> [Hagnismos – consecrated, purified by expiation (atonement)] …and that is what you are."

***** God woke this writer in the night and initiated a conversation. What transpired can only be revealed in the first person. God asked me a question; where were the people who wrote your English Bible when Moses met Me on the mountain? You have done a good job of translating spiritual truth from what I wrote, but now I will be your Teacher to reveal the fullness of what occurred on that mountain.

To do so, I must remove every concept of physical thinking from your mind that I may speak to you as My Spiritual Image. You measure your physical life by the beating of your heart. As a human being you can only think of Me and spiritual life in the same confines of time as yourself (eternity is a measurement of time). I do not measure your spiritual life as a physical creation.

I first revealed Myself to Moses by a burning bush, which was My Holiness revealing My presence. It was the same fiery image of the Seraphim (Isaiah 6) around My Throne, the revelation of My Holiness. The fire on the mountain was My Holiness. Moses asked Me My name. I said, *I AM THAT I AM*. I tell you now; *I AM –TIMELESS LIFE*. I made you in *MY IMAGE* – a Spiritual Being of timeless life.

So, who was this Moses prostrate before Me? He was the same Image of Life {My Holiness} that you will be when I summon you. Because *I AM …YOU ARE*! Now to reveal My Image in you, I will open up your life to show you how I made you. I have implanted Myself in the memory of every human being's mind I restore to My Image.

At the age of five, demonic spirits would call you in the night to go with them. You went with them twice. The third time I commanded you not to go with them. You recognized My voice and obeyed Me. At the age of six you began to search for Me. You discovered you could not find me in a building. At the age of fourteen you could not find me in other people. At the age of nineteen I put you in the very heart of the French/Algerian civil war. I did not put you on an Air Force base; I put you in the midst of the people suffering the trauma of imminent death. You experienced their fears with them. I put you on the street to witness an assassination

God Reveals His Glory [Doxa – True Identity]

attempt on the life of General Charles DeGaul. I gave you a live TV broadcast so that you could see the assassin's bullet miss his head and hit the ground beside him. *(See the movie Day of the Jackal.) I saved you from a court-martial when you were accused of someone else's crime. I taught you that you do not control the unseen forces that could take your life. I do!

I put you in the best Baptist College to teach you that I cannot be found simply in the study of the Bible as a literary assignment. I put you in Uganda, Africa. From your experience with Idi Amin, I taught you the depth of degradation that death produces in the human mind. Then I put you on a street in Dallas to teach you the overwhelming joy that comes when you realized that you cannot find Me, but I can find you.

I put you in the pastorate of two churches in which the people had turned a deaf ear to the Holy Spirit. I put you there for My Spirit to be the life of the churches. Then I put you in Angola, Africa. I put you there to witness My authority to speak to a people who would hear Me. You saw the courage required of My people in the midst of great suffering; and the fearless courage of My missionary family which walked with Me. You sought that courage for yourself because you envisioned doing great things for Me. I told you NO! –Because you do not have the ability to suffer as they do. You will never accomplish anything by your own strength. You asked Me to do with you whatever I could. I said, I will be the strength to carry you through every assignment I give you. But I warn you; there's really not much I can do with you. You humbled yourself and said the crumbs off My table would suffice.

The occasion arose that you had to drive your Land Rover through hostile country at night. The missionary with you was able to get you through several roadblocks, but you did not know you had to cross a bridge where soldiers were throwing people into the river and taking their vehicles. When you got near to the bridge I said, "look for the open door" and that was your only concern. Heavily armed soldiers surrounded you for a while; then the leader told you to get out of the vehicle at the same moment when I moved the men which were Infront of your vehicle. To create confusion, you yelled out for all to hear, obrigado! (Thank you in Portuguese). Then without any hesitation you drove through that open door. You had no fear for your life.

One night in Luanda, I directed you to jump out of your vehicle and pour out My righteous indignation upon a people who thought they could start a riot by throwing themselves under the wheels of your vehicle. You physically jerked the man out from underneath your vehicle; stood him up and with a very authoritative voice ordered him and the crowd to clear the street and do not do that again. They obeyed you.

I gave Bert and Jenny Sutton My strength on many occasions to fearlessly serve Me in Angola, Botswana and Brazil (which I believe to be the truth because I read their book and was absolutely amazed at what God did to bless their work).

I gave you and Harrison Pike the courage to enter an African village at night to rescue a Pastor and his family from the raging battle that could take their lives – and yours. He can remember the many other times I led him through perilous situations in Brazil and Angola. At the town of Sá da Bandeira, I gave June Pike the courage to run across an intersection in the crossfire of a gun battle.

At the first roadblock you encountered when you left Sáda Bandeira, I instructed you to tell the communist backed soldiers what I was doing in northern Angola. It was a tense moment for the others with you, but you took it as My message to reveal Myself to them.

Your mission party drove four vehicles over one thousand miles without gas stations. I stopped all your gas gauges at the one-half mark. When you crossed the Namibia border you discovered every tank was bone dry. Your mission party wept and gave Me the glory for your deliverance. (*See Appendix)

Some months later the Angola Mission was disbanded, and your family was left in Johannesburg. I sent you into Soweto, the suburb of Johannesburg that was involved in a bloody battle. You walked the streets; you went into the bombed and burning buildings preaching the good news that I am the Living God who can establish the only peace of the heart and mind that comforts them. You told them to give their lives to Me and I would produce a life that is worth living. They listened to you; and you brought a quietness that settled over the area.

In Botswana, I sent you to speak to Savimbi, the most feared and powerful witchdoctor in the country. You calmly engaged him in a conversation for him to tell you where he gets his power. He said the book of Revelation. You complemented him for trusting in the Bible; then you introduced him to the books that reveal Me to be the real God he should follow. He was literally shocked by what you told him. He said you were the only person in the world who had no fear of him and spoke non-threatening words of truth that did not condemn him. Then the demons rose up and physically threw you out of his house. I gave the news to you later through Horace Burns that Savimbi read those books and gave his life to Me.

On another occasion in Botswana, you were asked to take three very large African women to the hospital. When you got there, you discovered one was having a baby while wedged in the floorboard between the front and back seats. The two other women were struggling to get her out but could not move her. I gave you Samson strength and without even thinking about it, you quickly picked her up and put her on a gurney. I found it humorous that you were walking on very shaky legs when you got home. You find it humorous as well now that you remember it; *which I do, but not without thanking God for being there; and for not allowing the woman to name the baby after me. It is a common thing with the Tswana people to name their children from the people and events of their birth. These people have some really humorous names.

I put you in Mexico, to be a witness to the total lawlessness of another country governed by a State religion. For two hours I put you on national television with President Jimmy Carter. I opened the door for you to be recognized and welcomed by the people and government officials. I pulled your family out when they started killing every non-Catholic they could find (including the Presidents sister and My servant, Jim Philpot. I made you a witness to his murder and his family terrorized by the police. *A Catholic priest tried to kill me as well. It did not bother me, but it sure scared the Mexican pastor with me.). Your family suffered through two years of very painful arsenic treatments to kill the diseases eating your insides out; but I made sure you survived the diseases and the cure.

Then for eight years, I made you Pastor of a church in the most unchurched place in America. I used you to destroy the demonic powers that ruled without any opposition. You were the only person in this State who walked with me to do this. Finally, the intensity of this spiritual battle brought you to utter despair. I destroyed the demonic powers by the power of My presence. You accomplished your work there, so I moved you on to three more churches to destroy the power of well-organized groups that boasted of how easy it was to destroy My churches. I put you – *MY IMAGE* - there to teach them to sing a different tune.

God Reveals His Glory [Doxa – True Identity]

You remember these things and a whole lot more. You remember these things because; *I AM... YOU ARE.* Now I teach you these heavenly things so that every single one of My Heavenly Children will understand the value of their lives as My redeemed people. Every single one is my image with My mind – My presence to destroy the power of death that works unceasingly to destroy you.

I revealed every detail of My Living Temple to Moses while he was before Me because every redeemed life is My Temple in which I dwell. I put My Spirit of Life in every single human being at their conception and every single human being is responsible to Me to be My decision makers on earth. All people have free will and are responsible for their own fate. Now you know why I revealed the whole truth of who this man Moses was prostrate before Me; and most importantly, who you are. Now, you obey Me and write what I reveal to be the truth from My written Word; and let people decide for themselves whether they believe it or not.

OFFERINGS FOR THE SANCTUARY

Exodus 25:1-2,
"Then the Lord spoke to Moses, saying, "Tell the *sons of Israel* [Bên – sanctified descendants of Jacob; Spiritual Israel]...to raise a *contribution* [Terûwmâh – an obligatory tax from every male who was older than twenty/self-dependent] ...for Me; from every man whose *heart* [Lêb– the totality of a man's inner or immaterial nature; the deepest, innermost feelings/free-will given to all of God's created life] ...*moves* him [Nâdab– to incite, to impel to do freely, the free movement of the will for divine service or sacrifice] ...you shall raise My contribution."

The only people in the world God authorized to build a place of worship were those who were consecrated (made holy by spiritual birth) by God's movement upon them in the heart and mind to worship only Him, as the one true God. The temple was holy as God and His people are holy. All other people build temples to worship false gods and build their own little kingdoms.

God instructed Moses to build a tabernacle - temporary earthly temple (constructed by man from materials that only God can create/make), but Spiritual Israel/Spiritual descendants of Abraham were given the full responsibility to pay the price for the materials {Sinful man must pay the price for his redemption. That is why God came into this world in human flesh: to pay that price}. These people were to follow God's detailed instructions on how to build the temple and how they were to worship in it. God made this demand for a purpose: man, cannot worship God by his own will or ways. It is God's way – or no way. Solomon built a magnificent temple in a later generation; but it was still temporary. Herod built another; but it was still temporary.

The New Testament is God's progressive revelation that no human being can worship God except through the permanent Holy Temple God builds. The good news is that God not only provides the temple, but most importantly, paid the price of redemption for us. This temple was God's revelation that the sanctification of sinful humanity cannot be accomplished in heaven, but only by His presence in His creation. The true heavenly temple that would be revealed in God's proper time; would be the Messiah; who would be the presence of God incarnate to enact {be} the only/onetime, acceptable sacrifice for reconciling humanity under God's judgment of death. All of humanity can and must respond to God's call to come to Him for their salvation; by calling upon the name of God- Jesus. God's Salvation is now or never. It is God's way-or no way!

II Corinthians 5:14-21,
"For the love of Christ *controls* [Sunechō – confines the mind to be under the authority of God] ... us, having *concluded* [Krino – to form a mental judgment or opinion; to come to a decision] ...this, that *one died* for all [Apothnēskô - to die the death of the grave; the curse of death on all humanity;] ... therefore all died; and He died for all that they who live (sanctified/restored to Spiritual Life) should no longer live for themselves, but for Him who died and rose again on their behalf. Therefore, from now on we recognize no man according to the flesh {viewpoint of the human mind that he is only flesh}; even though we have known Christ according to the flesh (the Epiphaneia/incarnation of Christ), yet now we know Him thus no longer. Therefore, if any man is in Christ, he is a *new* [Kainos – consecrated into a qualitatively new identity] ...*creature* [Ktisis – God's creation of an entirely different kind of man – Spiritual Adam}]; ... the old things passed away, behold, new things have come. Now all these things are from God, Who *reconciled* [Kataliassô- the divine work of redemption}] ...us to Himself through Christ. God Himself, by taking upon Himself our sin and becoming an atonement by His blood, established a relationship of peace with mankind which the demands of His justice have hitherto prevented (God's Passover has laid aside / withdrawn His wrath upon all mankind that submits to His purification of the human spirit).]."

God's Spirit must lead each individual person to go to God through Jesus – the Christ – God's Living Temple; the only sacrifice empowered for the remission of sin. It does not make any difference if you are a Jew or a Gentile; for every human being – God's way is forever the only way to timeless spiritual life and no demonic lie or human precept can change it.

Exodus 25:3-9,
"And this is the contribution which you are to raise from them: *gold* [Zâhâb – this element is representative of the wealth of the world, i.e., the Person of God; (1) because it covers everything in the temple (everything is God made and is as pure and holy as He is); (2) because God is the only power which can create gold, and thus, (3) no person can create his own God. Nothing on earth is more valuable to humanity than God and nothing is more valuable to God than to possess the human heart.] ...*silver* [Keçeph – pale in color; pale in the sense of pining to pay any price to obtain abundant wealth. Silver is an abundant element and is a reminder that there is nothing more valuable than God's gift (abundant life of heaven). Only God can create spiritual life –wealth more precious than anything on this earth and that is what we are to pine for.] ...and *bronze (brass)* [N^{e}chosôseth – something that is made from copper as its primary base. Copper is an abundant ore but unlike gold it cannot be found in its pure form. The ore must be smelted and mixed with zinc to give it strength. Brass is a good example of human life; it has great value to God because only He can purify it and only, He can infuse it with His Spirit to make it strong.] ...*Blue* [T^{e}kêleth – violet colored *dye* {Tâbal – to dip; plunge; immerse; anoint; all the material is anointed as the consecrated, holy presence of God; Exodus 28:31 'and you shall make the robe of the ephod all (completely) of blue'}.] ...*purple* ['Argâmân–purple colored *dye*] ...and *scarlet* ['Arg^{e}vân – a deep reddish purple *dye*] ...material (the covering of

God Reveals His Glory [Doxa – True Identity]

natural man must be dipped in the God made coloring that marks them with the permanent identify of His Royal Throne), _fine linen_ [Sh^eshiy – natural silk cloth; silk is not made by man; which made the covering Jesus wore so valuable that the Roman soldiers gambled to possess it.], …and _goat hair_ [Êz– the hair of a female goat used to make strong cloth for covering the top of the temple], …_rams' skins_ [`Ôwr – naked hide (tanned without hair)] …dyed red, _porpoise skins_ (water proof covering over the tanned goat hides), _acacia_ [Shittîym– sticks of wood having the properties of {shôtêt– to pierce/flog/goad/scourging thorns}] …_wood_ [`Êts – all trees created to bear fruit for food/to give life; wood cannot be made by man, but is used as the basic construction material of the earthly temple and as the fuel for the sacrifices.] …_oil_ [Shemen – perfumed olive oil] …for _lighting_ [Mâ`ôwr – a luminous body. The perfumed oil is burned to acknowledge the unseen presence of God Who gives light (life) to the world in the darkness of death.] …spices [Bôsem – sweet fragrance of the balsam plant] …for the _anointing_ oil [Mishchâh–to consecrate a vow by rubbing with oil] …and for the fragrant _incense_ [Q^etûret – from {qâtar}; to fumigate a tight place to drive out the spiritual occupants. The temple of God cannot be the habitation of both death and life. Anointing the temple with oil and incense commemorates the presence of God on earth to make man holy as He is holy.] …_onyx stones_ [Shôham – something blanched/bleached; the natural pale green color of beryl] …and _setting stones_ [`eben – construction material; twelve onyx stones were engraved with the twelve tribes of Israel and were set in the shoulder straps of the _ephod_ [Ephod is a transliteration of the Hebrew word {`Êphôwd}; the vest of the high priest worn only for worship.] …and for the _breastplate_ [Chôshen – a visible pocket or container attached to the outside of the ephod.] … The breast plate covered the heart of the High Priest. It contained twelve onyx stones and the _urim_ [`Ûwrîym – plural of {`ûwr}; a flame, {source of light/truth] …and _thummin_ [Tummîym – perfection; the emblem of complete, absolute truth God speaks to the human race]."

Urim and Thummin are two words that reveal the source and person of absolute truth is the God of heaven. He communicates/speaks to man by the Holy Spirit. It is unknown what the emblems were; only that the breast plate was worn only by the High Priest and only when in the presence of God for worship. They revealed the High Priest as the only person through whom God spoke truth to the people.

The fallen angels were the source of power for Pharaoh and God warns us in I John 4:1, "Beloved, do not believe every spirit, but test the spirits to see whether they are from God, because many false prophets have gone out into the world".

`Ĕlôhîym is not only the One True God; He is the only spiritual power Who speaks to man and enables man to speak to Him. God speaks truth by _His Word_ [Logos – the intelligence of God's mind revealed in the person of God's High Priest – Jesus the Christ – God's Living Temple for the salvation of man.] God's Spirit reveals Jesus to be "_the Light of the World – the Truth that sets us free from the rule of death_". The Holy Spirit speaks to the mind and not to the ear. He reveals God's heavenly truth to the mind of every man who will hear it. He inspires our minds to speak to God through worship and prayer.

Exodus 25:8-9
 "Let them _construct_ [`Âsâh – the ethical obligation to fashion an object as the creative activity of God] …a _sanctuary_ [Miqdâsh – a consecrated (holy) thing or place where God dwells

among His people on earth.] …for Me, that I may *dwell* [Shâkan – permanently reside by causing His name to be fixed upon it. Nothing on earth is holy unless God is in it; He is what makes it holy] …among them. According to all that I am going to *show* you [Râah – to intellectually understand by experience. The human being in the darkness of death must experience God in the mind {faith/belief} to know Him.] …as the *pattern* [Tabnîyth – a model for building. A model airplane can be a thing of great beauty, but its power is in a real airplane. The temple was visible to man on earth as a beautiful creation of God, but its power was the presence of the Throne of Heaven to inhabit man and produce the true image of God.]…of the *tabernacle* [Mishkân – the basic meaning is residence; a temporary dwelling place designated as the only physical meeting place on earth that is a sanctuary of God.]…and the pattern of all its furniture, just so you shall *construct* it [`Âsâh – the ethical obligation for Israel to take what God provides and refine it to completion. What God refines to completion in redeemed humanity (His temple) is His Holiness of life that destroys death and changes the entire character of the human race.]"

God moved Moses from Egypt to build His temple in the wilderness {humanity completely devoid of knowledge of God}. The temple of Solomon and Herod were more permanent, but eventually by God's purpose, were replaced by Jesus/Messiah - God's revelation of His true, permanent temple; the thirty-three-year embodiment of God's tabernacle in human flesh to destroy the power of death to hold the human Spirit in the grave. Until it is time for Christ to return and complete His work of permanently destroying the power of death; the power of God's tabernacle resides in the heart of every human being who is in Christ and Christ in him. Every Spiritual Israelite / Christian is God's meeting place.]

THE ARK OF THE COVENANT

Exodus 25:10-22
"And they shall construct an *ark* [`Ârôwn – The basic meaning is a container; a receptacle for God's sacred objects that He created; the tablets of God's constitution/testimony are the witness of His spoken Word; a pot of manna and Aaron's rod that budded] …of acacia *wood* [`êts - trees that bear fruit. In Genesis 2:9, every tree in the Garden of Eden was a fruit tree, but God's tree of life was one of a kind; it bore its fruit from heaven and is the same trees that are on both sides of the street of Gold that comes from the Throne of God. In Deuteronomy 16, God forbids any kind of tree to be planted anywhere near His temple and forbids man from destroying orchards] …. *Acacia wood* [Shittâh–from the root word shôṭêṭ - to pierce; flog; to goad; to scourge with thorns. This particular wood is used to denote man as a creation suffering under the burden of death. The specific reason for building everything in the temple of acacia wood is to emphasize man's inability to make anything that is spiritually alive; only God can produce wood and only God can make something that reproduces itself (Aaron's rod that budded). All of the wood is overlaid with pure gold. This is God's revelation that He is the only power which can produce spiritual life of heaven – in something that is dead.] …The ark is to be two and a half cubits *long* [`Ôrek – from the root word {`Ârak – to make long, to prolong, long suffering, slow to anger. Deuteronomy 4:40, "to live long on the land".}; `Ôrek is used as a measurement of the Ark to designate the Person of God and the spiritual life given to man as a protracted, timeless existence. Psalm 21:4, "He asked *life* {Chay – life that is intrinsically

God Reveals His Glory [Doxa – True Identity]

good; that which comes from God is timeless.} ...of Thee, thou didst give to him, *length*{'Ôrek) of *days* {Yôwm – the sovereignty of God to exist as timeless Deity; and man, to be created a non-eschatological being} ...*forever* {'Ôlâm –timeless} ...and *ever* {'Ad – the Hebrew language did not have a special or general term for the past, present, future. 'Ad is used to designate the identity of God s timelessness}] ...and one and a half cubits wide, and one and a half cubits high {The power of God is inside the Ark. Revelation 21 reveals the city of God as a perfect cube}. And you shall overlay it with *pure* [Tâhôwr – clear, purified] ...gold, *inside* [Bayith – life God puts inside His house is untouchable by anything outside of His house {impervious to death}] ...and outside you shall overlay it (sealed by the holiness of God and is untouchable by sinful man under the penalty of death), and you shall make a gold molding around it." *Only God can make pure gold. Man cannot create his own God any more than he can create pure gold, and he can obtain spiritual life only from the Living God.

Exodus 25:12-15; these verses identify the Ark as untouchable by men. They are to *carry* [Nâgâh – to lift up, to be extolled and exalted to take way sin; God transports the burden of sin on His own shoulders to remove the burden of guilt from man. Sinful man is never without the presence of God for cleansing the Spirit.].

Exodus 25:16
"And you shall put into the ark the *testimony* ['Êdûwth – this word is always used with reference to the revelation of God; His spoken word He wrote on stone tablets. The testimony is the heart and life of the temple; it is the revelation of God's mind.] ...which I shall give you."

The Messiah was the true testimony of God's spoken word and He ascended back to heaven where He is identified as "Elohiym". The Holy Spirit is His presence to speak His truth to man.

Exodus 25:17
"And you shall make a *Mercy Seat* [Kappôreth – a cover, propitiation, atonement. The Mercy Seat was God's covering for the Ark. The High Priest once a year on the Day of Atonement went behind the curtain which led to the Holy of Holies, carrying the blood of the sin offering which he sprinkled on the Mercy Seat. God initiated the Mercy Seat; perfected in His own Person {Jesus the Messiah}. When the Christ was crucified in Jerusalem; God ripped down the curtain to the Holy of Holies and destroyed the earthly temple built by men. Every method of atonement created by man is all in vain. Only God can put the sins of man behind His back as if they never existed, and that only by covering the mercy seat with His Own Blood.] ...of pure gold, two and a half cubits *long* ['Ôrek] and two and a half cubits wide."

Exodus 25:18-22
"And you shall make two *Cherubim* [K^erûwb – a singular, specific kind of angel which ministers God's watch care for His people. {Hebrews 13:2 'Do not neglect to show hospitality to strangers, for by this some have entertained angels without knowing it. '}. Their significance on the Mercy Seat was to cause man "to bless/worship God; to address God with praise and adoration.] ...of gold, make them of hammered work at the two ends of the mercy seat. And

make one cherub at one end and one cherub at the other end; you shall make the cherubim of one piece with the Mercy Seat at its two ends. And the cherubim shall have their wings spread upward, covering the Mercy Seat with their wings and facing one another; the faces of the cherubim are to be turned toward the Mercy Seat. And you shall put the Mercy Seat on top of the ark, and in the ark, you shall put the testimony which I shall give to you. And there I will meet with you; and from above the Mercy Seat, from between the two cherubim which are upon the ark of the testimony I will _speak_ [Dâbar – this verb focuses not only on the content of the spoken verbal communication but also and especially on the time and circumstances of what is said.] …to you about all that I will _give_ [N^{e}than- to bestow as a gift of honor] …you in _commandment_ [Tsâvâh – to constitute, make firm, establish, to ordain, to commission, to delegate with superior authority {God's word is not to be questioned –it is to be obeyed}] …for the sons of Israel."

The temple God established on this earth is His Living Presence that rules heaven and earth. The ark (Naos of God) speaks His message of salvation. The angels over the mercy seat are still ministering to men to worship God. Genesis 3:24, Cherubim guarded against Adam and Eve's reentry into the physical Garden of Eden. The angels will continue to serve God in this world until The Christ returns. Hebrews 1:7, "And of the angels He says, 'Who makes His angels _spirits_ [Pneuma – divine ministers] …and His _ministers_ [Lĕitŏurgŏs – public servant functionary in the temple of God] …a _flame of fire_ [Phiŏx – God's holiness that is as active and powerful as aflame of fire to purify] `.''

THE TABLE OF SHOWBREAD

Exodus 25: 23-30,
"And you shall make a _table_ [Shulchân – a meal spread out for all to eat, from the root word {Shâlach–to be sent out; to send someone or something as a messenger}] … of acacia-wood, two cubits long and one cubit wide and one and a half cubits high. And you shall overlay it with pure gold and make a gold border around it. And you shall make for it a rim of a handbreadth around it; and you shall make a gold border for the rim around it. And you shall make four gold rings for it and put rings on the four corners which are on its four feet. The rings shall be close to the rim as holders for the poles to carry the table. And you shall make the poles of acacia wood and overlay them with gold, so that with them the table may be carried. And you shall make its _platters_ [Q^e'ârâh – a flat piece of gold with a shallow cut out hollow; from the root word {Qâra' - to rend; to tear}] …and its _bowls_ [Kaph – palm of the hand; kaph is the eleventh character in the Hebrew alphabet and is written like a round hollow of the hand; thus, the bowl is a small concave vessel turned upward to expose the palm of the hand.] …and its _pitchers_ [Qashvâh – to be round; a jug or pitcher] …and its _basins_ [M^{e}naqqîyth – containers for sacrificial blood] …with which to pour _libations_ [Nâçak– drink offerings to anoint a king]; …and you shall make them of pure gold. And you shall set the _bread_ [Lechem – food for man or beast; especially bread from grain] …of the _Presence_ [Pânch–showbread: {the body of Christ before the face of God}; God's action of turning His face to look upon something to show His favor] …on the table before Me at _all times_ [Tâmîyd – continuously without interruption]."

The table of showbread, as was the ark; was made of acacia wood {what God provides from the earth; not trees that bear fruit but trees that produce suffering;} covered with pure gold

God Reveals His Glory [Doxa – True Identity]

{what God makes that has its value from heaven}; and the utensils were made completely of pure gold. This within itself reveals the priceless value of God's holy temple. But of greater importance to God is the revelation of the purpose for creating man. The revelation that the earth was created for man as a physical habitat included the revelation that the earth was the first planet God created in the universe and is the only planet in all of God's creation that provides an inexhaustible supply of food and water to support physical life. The man created from the earth was also given spiritual life to make him the image of God. God created man to be a heavenly being in the timeless presence of His throne of Life.

In the center of the Garden of Eden was the Tree of Spiritual Life that maintained a timeless identity with God. Man was given God's controlling power over all created life on the earth. To act as a spiritual being not under death, he was instructed to eat of this tree because it was the only food that nourished the mind for righteous (sinless) living.

The table of showbread was maintained daily, without fail; in recognition of God's unfailing, timeless provision of spiritual life in His own body that would be destroyed by death but restored to life. Humanity that eats this living bread is restored to timeless life.

In Exodus 12:20, God commanded unleavened bread to be eaten at the Passover meal. In Exodus 16:4, God told Moses that He would rain bread from heaven and the people were to gather a day's portion every day, which God could test them to see whether or not they would obey His instructions.

In Exodus 23:25, God said to Moses, "You shall *serve* ['Âbad – to be enslaved to hard labor: to serve God as subjects to a king] …the Lord your God, and He will *bless* [Bârak–to bend the knee; to worship; to make something subservient to a greater power] …your bread and your water; and I will remove sickness from your midst."

God created bread and water to meet the need for a healthy human body. But it is only the "living bread" –the Showbread in God's temple that heals the human spirit.

THE GOLDEN LAMPSTAND

Exodus 25:31-40
(31) "Then you *shall make* ['Âsâh – to fashion something to completion] …a *lampstand* [Mᵉnôrâh – chandelier; fem. of (mânôwr– a yoke for plowing; the frame of a loom); Menorah is a descriptive word for the entire lamp which reveals the distinctive work of God)] …of pure gold.

The lampstand *base* [Yᵉrêkâh - fem. of (yärėk – to be soft as the generative parts of the human body. *The base (*foundation*) of God's light from heaven was a baby brought forth from a woman to suffer the curse of death that rules all human life. The basis of God's salvation covenant is to create new life in man by a spiritual birth from above. This is not accomplished by force but by the gentleness of God's love.)]

and its *shaft* [Qâneh – erect/straight as a rod; unbending; unchanging; unalterable truth. The power of the entire menorah is the Person of God. It is from the root word {Qânâh – to erect; create; purchase; possess; recover.} Qâneh – {the shaft} – is God's revelation that He is God, the progenitor, who creates all life. To create His spiritual children, He had to purchase them to sanctify them.]

is to be made of *hammered* work [Miqsheh– to twist, turn, bend; from root word (Qâshâh- dense, tough, severe; this word marks the restlessness, impatience, petulance, and irritability with which Pharaoh's course of action was characterized while he was resisting Moses and God; and the work of Satan and the Jewish Sanhedrin to snuff out the light of the Messiah.].

…its *cups* [Gᵉbîya'– calyx (base leaves of a flower)] …its *bulbs* [Kaphtôwr – decorative wreath shaped disk; to encircle. A bulb was carved in the shaft directly underneath each of the three branches on both sides of the shaft to indicate that *the* six branches are supported; empowered; encircled by the authority of God.

and its *blossoms* [Pirchach – young buds beginning to open from the calyx; new life has its source from God; the creator.] …*shall be* [Hâyâh – to exist, become, come to pass, accomplished. This verb makes a strong statement about the being or presence of a person or thing is by the one who has divine control of all things. Only God can give Spiritual Life to man.] …of *one piece* [`Echâd – united as one singular identity] …with it.

And *six branches* [Shishshâh – primitive number meaning more than five (fingers of the hand); from the primitive root word {Sîye – to be bright; cheerful; glad}. The six branches are God's revelation that light does not come from man; it is the light of God shining on man that makes him glad.]

shall go *out from* ['Ålâh – to ascend up or be raised up from a lower place to a higher place. All six branches come from the shaft and are curved upward in shape; are equal in height and importance to reveal God to be the supreme power for giving revelation of truth to the world through two separate covenants for the resurrection of man.]

its sides [Tsad – to sidle off as another of the same. The six branches have the same identity as the base and shaft.]; …*three* branches [Shᵉlôshâh – a primitive number having the meaning of something permanent. It is used as the base number as a multiplier to get one-third, thirteen, thirty. Man was created in God's image to multiply his children through both covenants; to be His permanent heavenly children. All of God's children will ascend up to Him by the authority of His light.]

of the lampstand from its *one side* [`Echâd – united as one; alike; alone.] …and three branches of the lampstand from its *other side* [`Echâd – united as one; alike; alone. *The three branches on one side and the three branches on the other side had diversity in their purpose, yet both are united as one people of God {Old Testament and New Testament}. God's heavenly temple {three branches} was first revealed in the wilderness of Mt. Sinai. This temple worship established God's covenant to redeem man from the curse of death; to worship Him by personally offering a blood sacrifice. The second revelation of God's temple {three branches} was in the wilderness of the Gentile world. God established a new covenant; man is redeemed by the sacrifice of Gods' own blood {Messiah}. By this, God purchased all His people {the six branches} from the curse of death to hold them in the grave. They all ascend to God.].

Three cups (calyx) shall be shaped like *almond blossoms* [Shâqad – the first tree to bloom in the Spring; its meaning is "be alert, sleepless, on the lookout for God's presence".]; …in the one branch, a bulb and a flower, and three cups shaped like almond blossoms in the other branch, a bulb and a flower –so for six branches going out from the lampstand.

and in the lampstand *four* cups ['Arbâ 'âh - the number four as a multiplier; foursquare; from the root word {Râbâ - to sprawl on all fours (lie prostrate face down).}. This word was

God Reveals His Glory [Doxa – True Identity]

used of Moses prostrate before God and joined to God. The three cups on each side bow down to the central cup {fourth cup}] …shaped like almond blossoms, its bulbs and its flowers.

And a bulb (God's stamp of authority and empowerment) shall be under the first pair of branches coming out of it, and a bulb under the second pair of branches coming out of it, and a bulb under the third pair of branches coming out of it, for the six branches coming out of the lampstand. Everything God does in human life is undergirded by the power of His Kingdom of Timeless Life.

Their bulbs and their branches shall be of one piece with it; all of it shall be one piece of hammered work of pure gold.

Then you shall make its *lamps* [Nêrâh – to glisten with the light of a candle; from the root word {Nâkar – to scrutinize; to look intently; to recognize.} The darkness of death makes recognition of God impossible. The flickering candlelight is God's revelation that His truth of salvation is revealed to humanity in the weakness of the flesh; therefore, man must be diligent to pay attention; give recognition; have an intellectual knowledge of what God reveals in the darkness. *The Messiah was the "Light of the World", but very few recognized Him.]

*s*even in number [Shib 'âh – the sacred full One; infinity; from the root word {Shâb – complete}; the seventh light is in the center of the shaft; the seven lights are recognized as one single light]

and they shall mount its lamps so as to shed light on its *face* [Pânel – the part that turns toward something to show favor. God spoke to the High Priest from above the Ark of the Covenant. This was placed in the Holy of Holies; separated from the Holy Place by a veil. The Holy of Holies always opened to the East. The Table of Showbread was placed on the north side of the Holy Place, the lampstand was placed on the South side of the Holy Place and the Bronze Alter was at the East entrance.

Anthropomorphically, God's face was upon the Showbread to signify that it was always in His presence. This entire phrase for placing the lampstand in the Holy Place is from the word {'Âlâh – to ascend up in sacrificial smoke}. It has many usages, but in this case, it is God's purpose for the lampstand to be placed in the position to shed its light upon the Showbread; signifying it is a burnt offering {Passover Lamb} ascending up to God.]."

The Holy of Holies and the Holy Place are one single revelation that GOD is the light of His throne shining upon man to destroy the power of death that enslaves him. His first revelation was given on Mt Sinai to establish His Covenant of Salvation through Physical Tabernacle worship. This revealed that it was easy for God to come down to man to free him from his enslavement to death's power, but it is very difficult for sinful man to approach a Holy God.

His second revelation was to establish His Covenant of Salvation through His Own Person – The Living Temple of Heaven brought down to man as God's sacrifice of atonement. This revealed two things: (**1**) the Life, Death and Resurrection of the Messiah took place on this earth where death was given its power; (**2**) the Christ was brought forth as a baby in Bethlehem {the Incarnation of God revealed He gives a heavenly, spiritual birth to His Children to recreate them as One with Himself}. This covenant revealed His salvation to be His free gift of timeless life by regeneration; spiritual birth from heaven enacted by every person's personal commitment (*faith*) to give their life to God; trusting in <u>**HIS SACRIFICE - SHOWBREAD**</u> for their salvation.

James V. Holland

Chapter 7

GOD REVEALS HIMSELF BY PROPHESY

Prophesy [N^{e}bûw'âh – Heb; A spoken or written disclosure of spiritual teaching; from root word {Nâbâ' – to prophesy; to speak or sing spiritual truth by inspiration of the mind}. True prophets speak God's message by the power of the mind under the influence of the Divine Spirit. The message will be understood only by those who hear with a believing mind.]. Amos 3:8, "The Lord God has spoken, who can but prophesy?" "The word of the Lord came to the prophet" is literally used hundreds of times in the Old Testament. Ezekiel 13:2-3, "Prophesy against the prophets of Israel that prophesy, and say thou unto them that they prophesy out of their own hearts, 'Hear ye the word of the Lord`; woe unto the foolish prophets that follow their own spirit and have seen nothing`."

Prophesy [Prophêtĕis – Gk. The declaration of that which cannot be known by natural means; it emanates from God and is the forthtelling of the will of God, whether with reference to the past, present or future. It signifies the speaking forth of the mind and counsel of God to the mind of spiritual man to know truth that is fulfilled.]

Genesis 1:26-28
    The entire Bible is the prophetic Word of God which establishes His mind to be the supreme authority of His Kingdom Rule of Life in heaven and on this earth. The sole Rule of God's mind to the human being is His purpose for recreating human life with His authority of Righteousness that cannot die. This Rule was first revealed by His authority to create human life in His Image (pure holiness). Adam was created with this spiritual life empowered by his mind to be totally obedient to the authority of God's Will; and by this authority he was charged to rule over his physical world. The finality of God's purpose for this prophesy will be accomplished in Revelation 21-22; when He establishes redeemed humanity in the presence of His throne where death can never exist again, because His mind is the only mind in the timelessness of His perfect heavenly rule.
    God's prophesy to achieve this end of man is fulfilled by the authority of His Kingdom Rule of Life; revealed first by His personal presence in this world as The Christ Who destroyed the power of death to hold redeemed humanity in the grave. Secondly, the Deity of The Christ will return to remove this habitation of death and every person under its power and will place death in obedience to His Rule. Revelation 20 reveals God's final actions to completely abolish death and every vestige of life under its control by throwing it all into the Lake of Fire. Not only will it be impossible for death to exist again, but God completely erases it from the human mind as if it never existed.

Genesis 2:7-17

These verses reveal Gods prophecy that the decision-making power of God's mind was given to all of humanity to act by the sole authority of free will. Satan acted by the power of his mind to resist God's authority and he became the instrument of death. He deceived Eve to believe she also could be equal to God by rejecting His authority. When Adam surrendered his mind to this power, he condemned the entire human race to be of the same mind. Now every human being lives a purely physical life oriented to obey the rule of death which empowers one's self to be his own god. The human mind under the darkness of death is secure in the belief that all is well. Then without any warning, in a single heartbeat, they are in the darkness of the grave and there is no escape.

God prophesied that beginning with Abraham, He reveals His redemption of the human race is by the restoration of a proper relationship between Himself and man by the authority of the mind to believe truth (faith); which (like Adam at his creation) again depends on the obedience of man to the Word of God. God fulfilled this prophesy through the sinlessness of the second Adam; the Deity of heaven revealed in human flesh - Jesus Christ.

Romans 10:8-13

"But what does God say? The Word is near you, in your mouth and in your heart– that is the word of faith which we are preaching, that if you confess with your mouth Jesus as your Lord and believe in your heart that God raised Him from the dead, you shall be saved; for with the heart man believes, resulting in righteousness; and with the mouth he confesses, resulting in salvation. For the Scripture (the revelation of God's Mind) says, 'Whoever believes in Him will not be disappointed.' For there is no distinction between Jew and Greek; for the same Lord is Lord of all, abounding in riches for every person of the human race who calls upon Him; for whoever will call upon the name of the Lord will be saved (restored to timeless Spiritual Life)."

Ephesians 1:3-11

"Blessed be the Deity of Heaven and our Lord Jesus Christ, who has blessed us with every spiritual blessing in the heavenly places in Christ, just as He chose us in Him before the foundation (creation) of the world that we should be holy and blameless before Him. In love He predestined us to adoption as sons through Jesus Christ to Himself, according to the kind intention of His will to the praise of the glory of His grace, which He freely bestowed on us in the Beloved. In Him we have redemption through His blood, the forgiveness of our trespasses according to the riches of His grace which He lavished upon us. In all wisdom and insight, He made known to us the mystery of His will, according to His kind intention which He purposed in Him with a view to an administration suitable to the fullness of the times, that is, the summing up of all things in Christ, things in the heavens and things on earth. In Him also we have obtained an inheritance, having been predestined according to His purpose who works all things after the counsel of His will."

Hebrews 1:1-4

"God (Thĕŏs/'Ĕlôhîym), after He spoke long ago to the fathers in the prophets in many times and in many ways, in these _last days_ [Eschatos – that which concludes ever thing; the

God Reveals His Glory [Doxa – True Identity]

development of God's plan of salvation comes to the final and decisive judgment] …has spoken to us in His [Huios-Christ] …whom He *appointed* [Tithēmi–to set in place as a gift, the predetermined will and testament of God] …heir of all things, through whom also He *made* [Poieō – the final producing and bringing forth something which has an independent existence of its own.] …the *ages* [Aiōn –Christ's timeless rule that is to come has a purpose; to permanently separate regenerated man from all humanity under the curse of death.]. …And He is the *radiance* [Apaugasma – shining splendor of the holiness of God] …of His *glory* [Doxa – Jesus gives recognition to the true identity of God] …and the exact *representation* [Charaktēr – the express image of God's holiness]…of His *essence* [Hupostasis – a distinct identity of timeless spiritual life emanating from the throne of God {you see Jesus, you see God}] …and *upholds* [aphĕrōŏiŏĕngkō – to bear or carry a heavy burden]…all things by the *word* [Rhēma – the operative or all-powerful command of God] …of His *power* [Dunamis – the inherent will of God's throne revealing His salvation in Christ]. …When He had made *purification* [Katharismos-the sacrifice of cleansing; the sacrificial death of Jesus for God to Passover – remove His judgment on His sanctified people] …of sins, He sat down at the *right hand* [Dexios–equal honor and dignity of God] …of the Majesty on high; having become so much *better* [Krima – superior] …than the angels, as He has inherited a more excellent *name* [Onoma – the superior character identified by the name – Christ.] …than they."

Hebrews 1:8-12

"But of the Huios (Christ) He says, 'Thy Throne, O God, Is *Forever* [Aiōn – timeless] …and ever, And the *Righteous* [Ĕuthus– True and permanent governing power that cannot die.] …*Scepter* [Rhabdŏs – Baton of royalty] …is The Scepter Of His *Kingdom* [Basileia – The royal dominion of heaven – timeless Spiritual Life], …Thou Hast *Loved* [Agapaō – a direction of the will (mind) and finding one's joy in it] …*Righteousness* [Dikaiosunē – the stated command of God's justice for the salvation of man, which man accepts by faith as his own standard of living as a spiritual being (Romans 3:21-23, 'The righteousness of God has been revealed, being witnessed by the Law and the Prophets, even the righteousness of God through faith in Jesus Christ for all those who believe; for there is no distinction; for all have sinned and fall short of the glory of God.')] …and hated *Lawlessness* [Anomia – iniquity; not having, knowing or accepting the rule of God]. …Therefore, God, Thy God, Hath *Anointed* [Chriō – to cover over with oil or an ointment for a sacred or religious identity] …Therewith the Oil of Gladness above Thy Companions {all life in heaven and earth}."

Romans 5:6

"For while we were still *helpless* [Asthĕnēs – weak, strengthless, moral sickness], …at the *right time* [Kairos – that which time gives an opportunity; the appropriate time at which foreordained events take place or is necessarily accomplished] …Christ died for the *ungodly* [Azeglio – without fear and without reverence of God]."

Romans 5:8-9

"But God *demonstrates* [Prŏïstēmi – to stand before (in rank), to preside, to rule] …His own love toward us, in that while we were yet sinners, Christ died for us. Much more then, having now been *justified* [Dikaloō – the action of revealing the fact that he is righteous] …by

His blood, we shall be _saved_ [Sōzō – spiritual and timeless salvation in regard to deliverance from death] …from the _wrath_ [Orgē– anger as a state of mind] …of God through Him."

The first generation of man began with Adam as a creation of Heaven. It did not take long before the darkness of death ruled the minds of the whole human race. God had to intervene and destroy that generation. There were only eight people left through which God originated this present generation. Jesus, the Deity of heaven, reveals that this present human race will again come to an end just as it did in the time of Noah and only a remnant of God's people will be saved. The difference is the human race and the world itself will come to the end of its existence. Jesus answered His disciple's question; "how will this world come to an end?"

Matthew 24-25, and II Peter 3, warns us that the _Apokalupsis_ [the unveiling of Jesus from heaven with interpretation of being known as the complete judgment of God's throne of Life on the power of death] …will be preceded by a tremendous tribulation in which God unleashes the power of death upon the world to rule the mind of every person who will not be saved. This is what brings the created order to the fulfillment of its purpose. This tribulation is the _Môw`êd of Satan_. The time God created for Satan to be worshipped by humanity enslaved to the power of death.

Matthew 24:1-2

"And Jesus came out from the _temple_ [Hieron– refers to the outer buildings and courts of the sacred enclosure] …and was going away when His disciples came up to point out the temple buildings to Him. And He answered and said to them, 'Do you not see all these things? Truly I say to you, not one stone here shall _be left_ [Aphiemi – to emit forth as a voice; to be the tabernacle of God] …upon another, which will not be _torn down_ [Kataluo –to unloose or release from the burden; that which it was bound for] `.'"

God created the Old Testament temple worship and He destroyed it at the proper time to reveal a new and permanent, **_living temple._** Jesus told his disciples that God's judgment had begun with the removal of the Old Testament sacrificial worship. It would be replaced with God's own one-time sacrifice. God destroyed the Old Testament _Holy of Holies_ when Christ was crucified and completed the destruction of the temple in 70 A.D. by the Roman army.

Matthew 24:3

"And as He was sitting on the Mount of Olives, the disciples came to Him privately, saying, 'Tell us, when will these things be and what will be the sign of Your coming and of the _end_ [Sunteleia – not the actual end but the fulfillment of events leading to the end…of the age`?'"

Matthew 24:4

"And Jesus answered and said to them, '_See to it_ [Blepo – mental vision, take heed of the precepts of men] …that no one misleads you`.'"

God's disciples must not be led to their destruction by apostate teachings that will rule the world. Only believers who are strong in their faith in the true identity of the Christ can

God Reveals His Glory [Doxa – True Identity]

survive this warning; because God will unleash the full power of death to lay claim to every person who will not believe in the Christ. This satanic power will be a roaring lion to destroy every witness to the truth of Christ.

I Peter 4:17

"For it is *time* [Kairos – that which time gives an opportunity to do, the necessity of a task at hand whether good or bad] …for *judgment* [Krima – a judicial sentence for punishment] …to begin with the *household* of God [Oikos – the body of God's Saints, all who belong to Him. God will reveal His sheep from the goats.]; …and if it begins with us first, what will be the *outcome* [Telos – the limit, the end at which a person or thing ceases to be] …for those who *do not obey* [Apeitheo – the inward attitude of unbelief expressed outwardly by negative actions; wolves in sheep's clothing.] …the *gospel* of God [Euaggelion – revelation from God which results in salvation]."

The rule of death over the human mind will identify the pseudo believers from the believers. Both the saved and the lost of this world reveal their identity by their physical character and the words that come out of their mouth, whether they have the mind of Satan or God.

I Thessalonians 5:1-4

"Now as to the *times* [Chronos – the succession or measurement of the passing of time] …and the *epochs* [Kairos – that which time gives an opportunity to do] …brethren, you have no need of anything to be written to you. For you yourselves know full well that the *Day of the Lord* [Hemera – the work or labor of God to separate spiritual light and spiritual darkness; the time of judgment; the sovereignty of Elohiym which gives history its meaning] …will come just like a thief in the night. While they are saying, 'Peace and Safety`, then *destruction* [Olethros – corruption; an injurious force which the subject cannot hinder. The apostasy of satanic origin will be unleashed for the destruction of the human race as it was in the day of Noah. It will come upon them suddenly like *birth pangs* [Odin – sorrow; distress; the actual sharp pains that come at the time of childbirth.] …upon a woman with child; and they shall not escape. But you, brethren, are not in *darkness* [Skotos – spiritual darkness implying ignorance or error] …that the day should *overtake* [Katalambano – come upon] …you like a thief."

The true believer lives in the light of God and recognizes His movement upon the earth to identify the sheep from the goats as the Sunteleia, not the Telos. True believers cannot be deceived by the works of Satan. Physically, we can easily tell if it is day or night. But the death covering the world is an invisible power. It can only be recognized by its destruction of human life, the rampant killing of human beings by human beings on a world-wide scale. The Sunteleia will increase to the point that God must stop it by the Telos – the Apokalupsis of Christ; or there will not be any saved people left on the earth.

Matthew 24:5-14

"And many will come in My name, saying 'I am the Christ` and will mislead many. {False prophets clothed in the name of Christ will gain a large following}. And you will be hearing of wars and rumors of wars, see that you are not frightened for those things must take place, but that is not yet the end. For nation will rise against nation, and kingdom against kingdom, and in various places there will be famine and earthquakes. But all those things are merely the beginning of birth pains. Then they will deliver you to tribulation and will kill you and you will be hated by all nations on account of My name. And at that time many will fall away and will deliver up one another and hate one another. And because lawlessness is increased most people's love will grow cold. But the one who endures to the end, he shall be saved. And this gospel of the kingdom shall be preached in the whole world for a witness to all the nations, and then the end shall come." *This world will not end until the last person is saved, who will be saved.

Matthew 24:15
 "Therefore, when you see the *abomination* of desolation [Bdelugma – anything that loosens the connection of man from God by sinful actions of sinful men] …which was spoken of through Daniel the prophet; standing in the *holy* place [Hagios – that which is consecrated to the service of deity, sharing in God's purity and abstaining from earth's defilement; the spirit of the human being that is God's holy temple. Every saved person is God's temple, but there are many wolves wearing sheep's clothing with false teachings, denying the identity of Christ.]. … Let the reader understand."

In Daniel 9:24-27, the angel Gabriel gave Daniel a vision of the destruction of temple worship which would occur before the first coming of the Messiah. It was fulfilled by the occupation of Israel by the Roman army which desecrated Israel as the unique people of God's making. The desecration of the minds of nationalistic Jews was so powerful that the religious leadership of that people (the Sanhedrin) looked upon God's message of His kingdom rule with such a passion of hatred for Jesus that they had Him put to death. The abomination of desolation will be the satanic desecration of the human mind as the place of God's dwelling, so that people will cease to believe in God for their salvation and will kill those who do.

II Thessalonians 2:1-4
 "Now we request you, brethren, with regard to the *coming* [Parousia – to be present] …of our Lord Jesus Christ, and our *gathering together* [Espisunagōgē – an assembling together in one place] …to Him, that you may not be quickly shaken from your *composure* [Nous – in this verse – a sound mind.] …or be disturbed either by a spirit or a message, or a letter as if from us, to the effect that the *day* [Hēmera – a division of time; daytime or nighttime; the time of timeless spiritual life or spiritual darkness; the division of time which reveals the appearance of the Christ] …of the Lord *has come* [Enistēmi – this instant of present time.]…Let no one in any way deceive you, for it will not come unless the *apostasy* [Apostasia – to forsake, to make a choice not to believe, to separate oneself from God, the movement of one's belief in Christ to be placed in Satan] …*comes first* [Erchomai – reference to the movement of time; a future event with reference to priority.], … and the *man* [Anthropos – a generic name for the human race in distinction from God or animals. It denotes the mind of man under the curse of death whose conduct or way of nature is completely opposed to God. It does not denote one single person (Satan), but unbelieving man in totality (666).] …of *lawlessness* [Anomia –one whose total

character is identified with death {goats/tares}]...is revealed, the _son of destruction_ [Huios Apoleia – one whose total character is death, excluded from salvation;] ...who opposes and exalts himself above every so-called god or _object of worship_ [Sebasma – an object to be venerated], ...so that he takes his seat in the _temple of God_ [Naos – habitation of God, the Holy of Holies; the human being was created to be the holy temple of God, but only by regeneration. Satan is allowed to take control of the mind of every unregenerate person and God is rejected.] ...displaying himself as being _God_ [Theos – used by the Greek philosophers as the name of the true God; as opposed to the pantheon of Greek gods.]"

Jesus never entered the Naos in Jerusalem, only the temple grounds. He did not identify Himself as God's High Priest, or the earthly stone temple as the Naos of Heaven. The right of entry to this temple was reserved only for the Jewish priests who hated God so much that they destroyed the Messiah, the true Naos of God. The apostasy is the power God gives to Satan and the fallen angels {sea beasts and land beasts} to destroy the human mind; to reveal every person who will not believe in God for their salvation. Satan's warfare with God will continue to intensify until the Coming of Christ {the Telos}.

II Thessalonians 2:7-12

"For the _mystery of lawlessness_ [Musterion Anomia – secretly rejecting the law of God in the mind] ...is already at work; only He who now restrains will do so until He is taken out of the way. And then that lawless one will be revealed whom the Lord will slay with the breath of His mouth and bring to an end by the _appearance_ [Epiphaneia – The visible presence of God]; ...of His _coming_ [Parousia – presence of God; The Apokalupsis of the Christ; Revelation 19]; ...that is the one whose coming is in accord with the activity of Satan, with all power and signs and false wonders and with all the deception of wickedness for those who perish, because they did not receive the love of the truth so as to be saved. And for this reason, God will send upon them a deluding influence so that they might believe what is false, in order that they all may be judged who did not believe the truth but took pleasure in wickedness."

The apostle Paul wrote a warning to Timothy (I Timothy) that people with the power of apostasy will bring the church to destruction. He faced leaders of the church whose minds were filled with human precepts contrary to the identity of Christ, teachings contrary to the law of God for holiness.

II Timothy 3:1-5

The abomination of desolation will destroy the totality of human society. "But realize this, that in the last days difficult times will come. For men will be lovers of self, lovers of money, boastful, arrogant, revilers, disobedient to parents, ungrateful, unholy, unloving, irreconcilable, malicious gossip, without self-control, brutal, haters of good, treacherous, reckless, conceited, lovers of pleasure rather than God, holding to a form of godliness, although they have denied its power."

The abomination of desolation is not the act of one person in a temple building in Jerusalem, but the power given to death to rule the human mind; to destroy the Naos of Christ ruling the mind of redeemed humanity. Revelation 13:1-10; the *sea* [Thalassa – the wild and turbulent people controlled by death; empowered by the Satanic lie] ...*beast* [Thēriŏn– fallen angels empowered by the Satanic lie to control the affairs of the nations to remove any knowledge of God.] ... and Revelation 13:11-18; the *earth* [Ge – the lost population of the whole world] ...*beast* [Thēriŏn - fallen angels empowered to raise up false prophets to lead the entire lost world to worship Satan] ... will completely capture the human race that will not be saved. The temple of the human mind (the rightful dwelling place of God) will be completely controlled by the forces of death. The spirit of apostasy is given power to mark (reveal the identity of every person who will not be saved by the total character of death); 666 is the number for the totality of humanity completely devoid of spiritual life. The realities of Jesus' words are revealed in the ungodly people ruling the whole world who have no respect for human life and hatred for God.

The time of desolation is also the work of God to save every person who will be saved (wheat and sheep). It is the work of God's grace that none of the wheat should be damaged. The passion of God is that He will not yield even one human being to timeless death if He can possibly save it. Jesus' last word before His ascension was His Great Commission to save every person who will be saved.

Matthew 28:16-20

"But the eleven disciples proceeded to Galilee, to the mountain which Jesus *had designated* [Tassō – to set in order or its proper category; every act of God through His people is designated as the high and holy presence of God.]. ...And when they saw Him, they worshiped Him; but some were *doubtful* [Gĕ– humanistic -not yet qualified in their mind].

...And Jesus came up and spoke to them, saying, 'All *authority* [Exousia – The executive power which a supreme ruler grants to enable someone to act with equality, right, liberty, and permission of the granting ruler.] ...has been given to Me in heaven and on earth. Go therefore and *make disciples* [Mathēteuō – This word is used only four times in scripture because it applies only to God. It means a disciple of God is one who not only learns but becomes attached to one's teacher and becomes his follower in doctrine and conduct of life.] ...of all the *nations* [Ethnos – The entire race of mankind considered in a noble or enlarged view as one single nation.] ...*baptizing* [Baptizō– the physical action of a person having been redeemed by the atonement of God's Passover Lamb; to be submerged in water as a symbolic identity with the reality of Christ in His death, burial and resurrection.] ...them in the *name* [Onoma–to be baptized into the name means to convert your mind to the mind of that name; to the faith, character, purpose and delegated power and authority of that name which identifies the person] ...of the *Heavenly Deity* ['Ĕlôhîym-Jehovah- the progenitor of life; the progenitor of all life is God's personal name related to sanctified humanity] ...and the [Huios – The identity given to Jesus as one and the same Deity of heaven. The name Jesus identifies human life recreated in God's image by a spiritual birth issued as a command from the throne of God, to be children of God!] ...and the *Holy Spirit* [Hagios – consecrated devotion to the service of God – Pneuma–the immaterial, invisible force of God which reveals the mind and activities of God to the mind of man.], ...*teaching* [Didaskō - instructing by word of mouth, information calculated to influence the understanding of the person who is taught.] ...them to observe all that I commanded you; and lo, I am with you always, even to the *end of the age* [Sunteleiatouaiōnes – action of God to complete, accomplish, terminate the duration of His redemption of human life.]."

*This age of redemption (God's purpose for creating humanity) does not end until God has claimed the very last person who will be saved. At that point it will be as it was in Genesis when only eight people were righteous, and God destroyed the world with water. The time will come when this world has completed its purpose; then God will dispose of everything He created that is the habitation of death: fallen angels, the earth, man and Satan.

Matthew 24:29-31
"But immediately after the tribulation of those days the sun will be darkened, and the moon will not give its light, and the stars will fall from the sky and the powers of the heavens will be shaken, and then the sign of the Deity of Heaven will appear in the sky, and then all the tribes of the earth will mourn, and they will see the Christ coming on the clouds of the sky with power and great glory. And He will send forth His angels with a great trumpet and they will gather together His elect from the four winds, from one end of the sky to the other."

The imagery of these verses clearly defines the truth that the God Who created the universe will totally remove it as if it never was because it is the habitation of death that was first removed from heaven (death began at the throne of God and will be destroyed by the Rule of Christ). Lost humanity living on the earth at the time of the Apokalupsis (Jews and Gentiles) will stand before Christ for His judgment. They will be identified as the goats / tares and will descend into Hades. All the believers of the ages will come with Christ from Paradise and all the believers left on earth (Jews and Gentiles) will also be raised {I Corinthians 15: no longer under the power of death} to meet the Lord in the air for the Rule of Christ's final judgment on death. All of the angels and every human being that will ever live on the earth will be a witness to Christ's appearance for His final judgment on death and the creation of a purified heaven for His purified people.

Matthew 24:35-39
"Heaven and earth will pass away, but My words shall not pass away. But of that day and hour no one knows, not even the angels of heaven, nor the Christ, but the Creator alone. For the _coming_ [Parousia – the second presence of Christ; the Apokalupsis] …will be just like the days of Noah. For as in those days which were before the flood they were eating and drinking, they were marrying and giving in marriage, until the day that Noah entered the ark, and they did not understand until the flood came and took them all away; so, shall be the coming of the Christ, the King of Kings."

These verses are a clear warning that the darkness of death will so pervade the minds of unbelieving man that none of them will believe any of the warnings that God gives them. The appearance of Christ will be a shock to their senses because of the severity of His judgment and the fact that it is too late for repentance. This present time of God's redemption will end and will never exist again because Christ will complete His work of destroying the kingdom power of death and every life it claims by throwing it all into the lake of fire (Revelation 20).

Isaiah 2:1-4

"The _word_ [Dabar - n. matter or thing, an account of God's actions; a prophetic revelation of God;] ...which Isaiah the son of Amos _saw_ [Chazah– a vision; the real sight of the divine presence through the mind of His prophet] ...concerning Judah and Jerusalem.

Now it will come about that in the _last_ [`achărîyth - the ultimate outcome, the remotest and most distant part] ..._days_ [Yowm – the revelation of God's sovereignty which gives history its meaning] ...the _mountain_ [Hôr – This word has the implication of the high and holy dwelling of God. (*The rule of Christ). His word carries the strength of heaven] ... of the _house_ [Bayith– the uplifted dwelling place of God which He builds] ...of the Lord will be _established_ [Kuwn – stand firm, fixed, be ready, be prepared, be determined, be brought into an incontrovertible existence] ...as the _chief_ [Rosh – supreme leader] ...of the mountains, and will be raised above the hill; and all the _nations_ [Gowry– a group of people defined by context; i.e.: all the saints of God from the beginning of the world to its end.] ...will stream to it. And many _peoples_ [Am– a group which has certain unified, sustained relationships within itself; Spiritual Israel, the people of God] ...will come and say, 'Come, let us go up to the mountain of the Lord, to the house of the God of Jacob; that He may teach us concerning His _ways_ [Derek – the actions and behavior of men empowered by the mind of God (the only Mind in heaven)], ...and that we may walk in His _paths_ [Orach – a figurative word describing the way to Life that is not under the curse of death.]'... For the _law_ [Torah– instructions] ...will go forth from Zion, and the word of the Lord from Jerusalem. And He will _judge_ [Shaphat – give justice or equity {the sheep to heaven and the goats to Hades}] ...between the nations, and He will _render decisions_ [Yakach – be the only decision maker for what is right and wrong] ...for many peoples; and they will hammer their swords into plowshares, and their spears into pruning hooks. Nation will not lift up sword against nation, and never again will they _learn_ [Lamad – to learn and to teach; to be the source of knowledge] ...war."

These verses prophesied the universal reign of God (Revelation 20 – Prophesy of Christ's Rule) that is the absolute power of peace. It is a time when men are taught only the wisdom of God's law of rightness and commit no sin against one-another. Resurrected humanity will live as the true spiritual beings of rightness which was created in the beginning (Adam in the image of God). This kind of peace is not possible in this present world where the human mind is ruled by the power of death. It will be possible only in the Rule of Christ because it has a security from the power of death that only God can give. His final judgment on death will be on those who turn their minds away from worshipping Him (Gog and Magog). It is only after this revelation of the rule of God's Throne of Life that He can create a perfect heaven where death can never exist again and will never be a memory in the minds of humanity (Revelation 21-22).

This prophecy will be fulfilled in Revelation 20-22. After God has finished the total destruction of death so that it ceases to exist (Revelation 20), then He will create a perfect heaven (where death can never exist again) for every human being He has restored to spiritual life (His Holy Image).

Hebrews 12:1-8
"Therefore, since we have so great a cloud of witnesses surrounding us, let us also lay aside every encumbrance and the sin which so easily entangles us and let us run with endurance

the race that is before us, fixing our eyes on Jesus, the author and perfecter of faith. Who for the joy set before Him endured the cross, despising the shame and has sat down at the right hand of the throne of God? For consider Him who has endured such hostility by sinners against Himself, so that you may not grow weary and lose heart. You have not yet resisted to the point of shedding blood in your striving against sin; and you have forgotten the exhortation which is addressed to you as sons. My son does not regard lightly the discipline of the Lord, nor faint when you are reproved by Him; for those whom the Lord loves He disciplines, and He scourges every son whom He receives. It is for discipline that you endure; God deals with you as with sons; for what son is there whom his father does not discipline? But if you are without discipline, of which all have become partakers, then you are illegitimate children and not sons."

Romans 8:5-11

"Those who live according to the sinful nature have their minds set on what that nature desires, but those who live in accordance with the Spirit have their minds set on what the Spirit desires. The mind of sinful man is death, but the mind controlled by the Spirit is life and peace; the sinful mind is hostile to God. It does not submit to God's law, nor can it do so. Those controlled by the sinful nature cannot please God. You however are controlled not by the sinful nature but by the Spirit, if the Spirit of God lives in you. And if anyone does not have the Spirit of Christ, he does not belong to Christ. But if Christ is in you, your body is dead because of sin, yet your spirit is alive because of righteousness. And if the Spirit of Him Who raised Jesus from the dead is living in you, He Who raised Christ from the dead will also give life to your mortal {under the judgment of death) bodies through His Spirit, who lives in you."

James V. Holland

Chapter 8

GOD DESTROYS DEATH BY HIS PRESENCE

EPIPHANEIA – THE SACRIFICIAL LAMB OF GOD

A NEW COVENANT: JESUS OUR HIGH PRIEST

Hebrews 3:1-4
"Therefore, holy brethren, partakers of a heavenly calling, *consider* [Katanŏĕō– fully understand] ...Jesus, the *Apostle* [Apŏstŏlŏs – one sent forth from God as His ambassador to officially reveal His message of salvation from the kingdom rule of death.] ...and *High Priest* [Archiĕrĕus – the chief ruling spiritual power; higher than all others] ...of our *confession* [Hŏmŏlŏgia - acknowledgement of the truth that God is Life; there is no death in Him.]. ...He was faithful to Him who appointed Him, as Moses also was in all His house. For He has been counted worthy of more *glory* [Dŏxa – revelation of the true identity of God] ...than Moses, by just so much as the builder of the house has more honor than the house. For every house is built by someone, but the builder of all things is God."

Hebrews 8:1-2, 6-13, 10:9-14
"Now the main point in what has been said is this: we have such a high priest who has taken His seat at the right hand of the throne of the Majesty in the heavens, a minister in the sanctuary and in the true tabernacle which the Lord pitched; not man"....."Now He has obtained a more excellent ministry by as much as He is also the *mediator* [Měsitēs – Jesus possessed both the sinlessness of deity and the form (identity of flesh; sinful man without sin] ...of a better covenant, which had been enacted on better promises. For if that first covenant had been faultless, there would have been no occasion sough for a second. He says, 'Behold, days are coming says the Lord when I will effect a *new covenant* {Testament – His Will designating His inheritance given to man upon His death.} with the house of Israel and with the house of Judah; for this is the covenant that I will make with the house of Israel: I will put My Laws into their minds, and I will write them upon their hearts and I will be their God, and they shall be My people. And they shall not teach everyone his fellow citizen and everyone his brothers, saying know the Lord; for all shall know Me from the least to the greatest of them. I will be merciful to their iniquities and I will remember their sins no more`.

When He said, 'A new covenant; He has made the first obsolete, but whatever is become obsolete and growing old is ready to disappear." ... "Then He said, 'Behold, I have come to do Thy Will– Testament. {Jesus is the testator of God's Will that is valid upon His death. The children of God are the beneficiaries of God's Will} `. He takes away the first Testament in order to establish the second. By this *Will,* we have been sanctified through the offering of the body and blood of Jesus Christ once for all. And every priest stands daily ministering and offering time after time the same sacrifices which can never take away sins; but He, having offered one sacrifice for sins for all time, sat down at the right hand of God, waiting from that time onward until His enemies be made a footstool for His feet. For by one offering He has _perfected_ [Tĕlĕiŏō – accomplished the removal of God's judgment on the human race] …for all time those who are sanctified."

Daniel 9:20-27
"Now while I was speaking and praying and confessing my sin and the sin of my people Israel and presenting my supplication before the Lord my God on behalf of the holy mountain of my God, while I was still speaking in prayer, then the _male Gabriel_ [Gabrîy`ēl – Radiance of Holiness; Male identifies Gabriel as an angelic being whose mind is completely ruled by the power of God's mind.] …whom I had seen in the vision previously, came to me in my extreme weariness about the time of the evening offering.

And he gave me instruction and talked with me, and said, 'O Daniel, I have now come forth to give you _insight_ [Sâkal – ability to act wisely; Genesis 3:6, the forbidden fruit was to be desired to make one wise, but it was very unwise to eat it] …with _understanding_ [Bîynâh – intelligence of God and not one's own understanding]. …At the beginning of your supplications (prayers) the command was issued, and I have come to tell you, for you are highly esteemed; so, give heed to the message and gain understanding of the vision.

Seventy [Shib'îym – multiple of sheba' - the cardinal number seven - the sacred full-one] …_weeks_ [Sh^ebû'ah–a special feast in Israel's lunar calendar. Seventy weeks is an indefinite number known only to God for man to worship Him as their redeemer.] …have been decreed for your people and your holy city, to finish the _transgression_ [Pesha' - willful deviation from; and therefore rebellion against the path of Godly living], …to make an end of sin, to _make atonement_ [Kâphar – to cover over, propitiate, ransom, atone, expiate] …for _iniquity_ ['Âvôwn – perversity of moral evil; perversion of life (rejection of holiness); perversion of truth (rejection of God); perversion of intent (willful disobedience);beginning with Adam the entire human race turned away from the holiness of God.], …to bring in _timeless_ ['Ôwlâm or Ôlâm – concealed; i.e., the vanishing point; the timeless presence of God that was before, during and after His use of time] …_righteousness_ [Tsedeq –The standard of holiness that makes it impossible for God to die. This masculine word has a two-fold significance. It has a relational meaning; Genesis 15:6, 'Abraham believed in the Lord and He counted it to him for righteousness.'. And it has a legal significance of justice in conformity to the Throne of God. Psalms 35:24, 28, 'Judge me, O Lord my God, according to thy righteousness; and let them not rejoice over me. And my tongue shall speak to thy righteousness and of thy praise all day long.''

Cohesively, this word embodies all that God requires of His redeemed people to identify them as His Heavenly Image with His authority of timeless life.] …to seal up vision and prophecy, and to _anoint_ [Mâshach - consecrate] …the _most holy_ [Qôdesh – person that is set apart for the work of God is sacred, holy. The most holy is the Christ of God. This verse is a reference which identifies Jesus; the coming Messiah.]. …So, you are to know and discern that from the issuing of a decree to _restore_ [Shûwb- to move back to the point of departure; the point when Adam turned his face away from God.] …and _rebuild_ [Bânâh – to build something to perfection from what already exists. In this verse it has the metaphysical meaning of God rebuilding His people as His dwelling place.] …_Jerusalem_ [Y^erûwshâlaim – this is an ancient spelling of a city for God's people. It has the duel meaning of (1) created by God, and (2) the power of peace that only God can establish. This ancient word designates God's creation of a holy people who God creates to be at perfect peace with Him.] … until *Messiah* [Mâshîyach–the anointed One for a special function. The Greek word "Christ" emphasizes the special anointing of Jesus of Nazareth as the visible Deity of God Who restores man to His image as Adam was in the beginning.] …the *Prince* [Nâgîyd–chief leader; king; ruler]. …Seven weeks and sixty-two weeks; it will be built again, and the *width* [Rechôwb – an avenue or broad area; a flat expanse, {Genesis 13:7, "Arise, walk through the land in the length of it and in the breadth of it, for I will give it unto thee."} Length and breadth encompass an entire territory. God's redemptive work encompasses the entire domain of man.] …and *wall* [Chârûwts – from root word {Chârats – (lit) to wound; (fig.) to be alert, decisive.}. Chârûwts brings us to the focal point of this prophecy. The strength of Jerusalem is the incisive Will of God to remove His judgment on sin by the wounding of the Messiah; and the incisive will of the people is to identify themselves with the Messiah as a new creation of God. *The action of the Messiah is God's protective wall around His people.] …even in *times* ['Êth – Basically, this is a concept of time that only God knows and predestines to reveal Himself (Epiphaneia) in human life. The Messiah came at God's appointed time. It was the appropriate time for His divine judgment.] …of *distress* [Tsûwqâh – oppression, affliction, anguish. The Jewish people were under the boot of the Roman occupation and murder of their people. This was God's appointed time for the Messiah to be His sacrificial lamb for His Passover. He was selected by the Jewish Sanhedrin and crucified by the Romans outside the city. The action of the Messiah is inclusive for the redemption of the entire human race under the curse of death.]. …Then after the sixty-two weeks the Messiah will be *cut off* [Kârath – This word is used by God to seal His covenant with man for the extermination of death by the covenant of circumcision given to Abraham; {the action of God walking between man and the power of death}. This is accomplished by the death, burial, resurrection and ascension of the Messiah back into the ruling heavenly Throne of 'Ĕlôhîym.]

But this is not for himself; or the people of the *prince* [Nâgîyd – one who reveals himself a chief leader over a portion of all the people {Satan revealed himself a ruler of the fallen angels in heaven and the people of earth}.] …who is to come will *destroy* [Shâchath – a primitive root word meaning to decay; it is the dissolution or total corruption of the entire human race.] …the *city* ['Îyr – a quarter of a village without walls] …and the *sanctuary* [Qôdesh- a sacred place; the human heart that God sanctified as His Holy Naos.]. …And its end will come with a *flood* [Stêṭeph–overwhelmed, inundated, conquered] …even to the end there will be war; desolations are determined. And he will make a firm covenant with the many for one week {God limits the time Satan is given to rule}, but in the middle of the week he will *put a stop to* [Shâbath – desist from exertion; cease from being] …*sacrifice* [Zebach – the slaughter of an animal by the head of a family; a communal meal of a sacrifice shared by the priest and the family providing the animal (Passover) …and grain offering; and on the *wing* [Kanâph – an edge or extremity, the demonic lie that extends to the four corners of the earth] …of *abominations* [Shiqqûwts or Shiqqûts- God's hatred for the whole system of idolatry] …will come one who makes *desolate* [Shâmên – stupefy, astonished, devastated, desolate] …even until a complete *destruction* [Kâlâh – complete annihilation], …of one that is decreed, is poured out on the one who makes desolate{the Apokalupsis of Christ puts an end to the rule of death and its destruction of the human race}|."

This vision given to Daniel by the angel Gabriel reveals the _coming_ (Parousia) of the Messiah as the _Epiphaneia_ [the personal revelation of God by His visible presence – the Christ] to establish God's covenant for the removal of the curse of death on humanity that originated with Adam. This is God's revelation of His Deity to remove the power of death to hold God's people in the grave. It also reveals the release of death to swallow up the whole human race and His coming (Parousia) by the Apokalupsis of the Christ (Epiphaneia) from heaven to abolish the earth as the place of death, the fallen angels who are instruments of death, Satan the progenitor of death, every human being under the curse of death, and death itself. The whole purpose for the creation of physical life is for God to destroy death so that it can never exist again. He is the only power who can do that. This prophecy reveals the totality of God's work He designed in Genesis 1:1-2, is fulfilled by the power of His presence in creation from the beginning to the end of the existence of man.

Matthew 1:1
"The _book_ [Biblos – God's revelation of His true identity.] …of the _genealogy_ [Genesis – the origin of existence of a family line] …of Jesus Christ, the God of David, the God of Abraham."

Matthew 1:17
"Therefore, all the generations from Abraham to David are fourteen generations; and from David to the deportation to Babylon fourteen generations; and from the deportation to Babylon to the time of Christ fourteen generations."

Every detail of God's personal movement upon the earth for the creation of His Spiritual Children was revealed by His prophets spoken in His first Covenant. This covenant revealed His purpose to cleanse sinful man by the power of His presence through temple worship {the Temple built by Moses was the Presence of the Living God in a physical structure}. His second covenant revealed His sanctification of sinful man would be fulfilled by regeneration; restoring the Naos of His Temple in the human heart as it was in the creation of Adam; the Presence of God's Holiness in a physical body. The Messiah was the second Adam, the Presence of the Living God in a physical body. The first Adam was created in a natural body; the sinless second Adam (Christ) was raised a spiritual body.

I Corinthians 15:44-49
"If there is a natural body, there is also a spiritual body. So, it is written: The first man Adam became a living being the last Adam, a life-giving Spirit. The Spiritual did not come first, but the natural and after that, the Spiritual. The first man was of the dust of the earth, the second man from heaven. As was the earthly man, so are those who are of the earth; and as is the man from heaven, so also are those who are of heaven. And just as we have borne the likeness of the earthly man, so shall we bear the likeness of the Deity from heaven."

I Corinthians 15:54-57
"When the natural man has been clothed with the Spiritual, and death with the Throne

God Reveals His Glory [Doxa – True Identity]

of Timeless Life, then the saying that is written will come true: Death has been swallowed up in victory. Where O death, is your victory? Where O death is your sting? The sting of death is sin. But thanks be to God! He gives us the victory through our Lord Jesus Christ."

John 1:1-5
"In the *beginning* [Archē–To be the first and only timeless ruling power of life which creates every other form of life] …was the *Word* [Logos – revelation of intelligence, the articulate utterance of the mind of God. Jesus is the presence of God's mind to reveal His authority of Deity over death.] …and the Word was with *God* [Theos – the Greek name of the only true God. It is the same as the Hebrew word `Ĕlôhîym.] …and the Word was God. He was in the beginning [Archê] with God. *All things* [Pas – everything within the totality that comes into existence] … *came into being* [Ginomai–to be given life from the mind of God; from the throne of God] …by Him, and apart from Him nothing came into being. In Him was *Life* [Zōe – the spiritual life that is the essence of God's Holy identity and power. It is distinguished from bios; temporary physical life] …and the Life was the *light* of men [Phos – God's revelation of His holiness; it comes only from God and cannot be quenched. It was given to Adam to make him the image of God and is restored to redeemed humanity through the person of God – the Christ]. …. And the light *shines* [Phaneros- to make something phenomenally conspicuous; the identity of Jesus as the Christ cannot be denied because He did the works that only God can do.] … in the *darkness* [Skotia–the consequences of sin that makes the person under the power of death to be very unhappy], …and the darkness did not *comprehend* [Katalambanō–to take for one's self; to seize; to lay hold of; to mentally comprehend; to be something so foreign to human thought as to be impossible to be true.] …it."

John 1:9-14
"Christ was the true light which coming into the world, *enlightens* [Phōtizō – the power of God's Spirit to reveal truth to the human mind and it be received as truth. {I Corinthians 2}] …every man. He was in the *world* [Kosmos – the sum total of the material universe and the sum total of human life living in It.] …and the world was *made* [Ginomai – to be formed; to be created from nothing but the mind of God] …through Him, and the world did not know Him. He came to *His own* [tàidiōs –His private property; ones He is familiar with on an intimate basis] …and those who *were His own* [oi ïdoi–nationalistic Israel; those who were blessed by God but reject a familiar relationship with Him and deny His identity] …did not *receive* [Livyâh – to be attached to something; to be woven together like cloth; from {Lâvâh – to join as one}] …Him.

But as many as received Him, to them he gave the *right* [Exousia – Permission; authority; liberty; power (right and might)]…to *become* [Ginomai – given spiritual life from heaven]…*children* [Tekna–those who have the holy character of their Father] …of God, to those believing into His name, who were born not of *blood* {human parents} , nor of the *will* [Thelêma – the decree of the human mind to acquire by his own means what only God provides] …of the *flesh* [Sarx – the human body devoid of the Spirit of God] …but of God.

And the *Word* [Logos – the revealed intelligence of God] …*became* [Ginomai - God's revelation of Himself brought forth in human form] …flesh, and dwelt among us {Epiphaneia}, and we beheld His *glory* [Doxa – God's true identity as the saving God revealed through His Deity - Jesus, the Christ.] …as [Monogenēs – the only form [Huios-Christ} which reveals the

Deity of Heaven. The revelation of the Deity of God as One Spiritual Being Who reveals Himself as the life giving Deity; the Huios-Christ reveals man's relationship with God is by Sonship / God's children by a spiritual birth; and Holy Spirit for the purpose of destroying death's power of darkness over the human mind] ...from the {God – the creator of all life}, *full* [Pierēs – overflowing; nothing can limit God] ...of *grace* [Charis - rejoicing for God's favor that cannot be repaid] ...and *truth* [Alētheia– the unveiled reality of God's mind – Jesus: if you can see Jesus, you can see God]."

Philippians 2:5-13
"Have this mind in yourselves which was also in Christ Jesus, who, although He *existed* [Huparchō– {Hupo – the beginning from which something comes into being (Life)} and {Archō – the supreme ruler over all life}. These two words combined mean Jesus continues to be in the flesh of man what He has always been; the Deity of God can never change whether He is ruling in heaven or on the earth.] ...in the *form* [Morphē – the heavenly essence of God; what He really is and not the outward appearance of what the heavenly spiritual beings look like (the angels also glow with His holiness)] ...of God, did not regard *equality* [Tòēinaiisa – These words are used to emphatically express the identity of Jesus; I AM what I have always been in heaven and will continue to be I AM in the appearance {morphe} of man. These words are of great importance to redeemed humanity. Man was created a heavenly being in God's image and will continue to have the same identity whether on earth or in heaven.] ...with God a *thing to be grasped* [Harpagmos – This word appears only in this verse. It means Christ's identity of Deity in this world is not something that He can take by force. The Jewish Sanhedrin had Jesus crucified because of this issue; He said He is the Messiah - He and God are One. Christians are persecuted by atheists and ungodly false religions because we worship the One True Deity of Heaven.] ...but *emptied Himself* [Ekenōse–This word is of vital importance to Spiritual Israel. God put His Spirit of Life in man {Adam} which gave him the inward image {Morphē} of God. Man does not shine with the Holiness of God's heavenly light but is empowered to reveal the character of God as children of *light* (Phōs – the revelation of God's righteousness and holiness.) Jesus removed His heavenly shining glory of Deity to reveal Himself as the Christ; not by His heavenly identity but by what He does as Deity.] ...He is called the *Huios Theos* – [One and the same heavenly Deity revealed by the same holy character and power of Deity.] ... and the *Huios Anthropos* – [the holy character of Deity restored in man as a heavenly creation.]. ... Jesus said many times, "if you do not believe Me by My words, believe me by what I do. Only God can do these things."

We are commanded to walk as children of light (character of God) and not of darkness (death). Christ is the same Deity in heaven and on the earth and, so are the sanctified children of God, whether in the darkness of this world or the glorious light of heaven. He gave up His heavenly identity to become a human baby in Bethlehem {Morphē} but His light of Holiness was still shining upon Him to identify Him as Deity in human flesh. It was NOT A STAR, but His heavenly Glory that led the Wise Men (astrologers) to Him (they were the only ones God permitted to identify it).

He gave up His outward heavenly identity of God to be the light of the world that all men may see God. ...taking the *form* {Morphē} of a *bondservant* [Doulos – a slave; one who is in a permanent relation of servitude to another, His will altogether consumed in the will of the

God Reveals His Glory [Doxa – True Identity]

other.] Jesus was not half-God and half-man. He was the {Morphē – the pure essence of Deity who changed His outward appearance to that of man - the Deity of heaven without the shining glory of Deity}. Every human being transformed from death to life is subservient to the Throne of Life.]

To fulfill His plan to destroy death as devised in Genesis 1:1-2; He had to accomplish it on earth in the {Morphē of man – the spiritual life of God in the weakness of flesh.} Being wholly God, He had the power of God to destroy death. Being wholly spiritual man, He could destroy the power of death ruling the mind of man by the Godly actions of His own mind; to yield up His own life to death by means of His crucifixion and burial. And being wholly God, He resurrected Himself from the grip of death and thus, destroyed the power of death to hold spiritual man in the grave.

Every person under the curse of death who turns his mind away from living apart from God and returns his mind to God by faith is liberated from the curse of death. Only in Christ is spiritual man free indeed, because only God can do the works of God. And being found in *appearance* [Schēma – fashion; external form; Jesus was wholly a man. There was no difference between Him and every other man except His inner sinless form which was a servant to His kingdom of righteousness.] …as a man, *humbled himself* [Tapeinoō–He brought about the recognition of His humanity by demonstrating *His* dependence on the ruling power of His throne.] …by becoming *obedient* [Hupēkoos – a servant to the will of God, which is necessary to convert the mind to belief in Him alone for salvation] …to the point of *death* [Thanatos – natural death that is God's curse on unbelieving man is a permanent separation from God.] …even death on a *cross* [Stauaroō- a form of punishment that effected the most severe pain on the human body; God's sacrificial act of love for man to atone for his spiritual death.].

*Jesus experienced the pain of death when He surrendered His physical identity to the power of death. The first time was in the Mount of Olives when He sweated drops of blood in anguish to surrender His body to the power of death. The second time was yielding the life of His body to death on the cross and He cried out with mental anguish, "My God, why have you abandoned Me?"

Matthew 6:9-12, Jesus, knowing how difficult it is for the human being to face the death of the body, led His disciples to pray.

The Greek text: "Father {Creator} of us in the heavens let be sanctified the name of You, let come the kingdom of You, let be done the will of You in heaven and on the earth; the Showbread (*Jesus*) Your timeless presence; gives us living bread that gives spiritual life from heaven (John 6:43-58; John 17;), and the debts of us forgive as also the debtors of us we forgive. And not let us continue into temptation but rescue us from the evil one."

"Our Father Who is in heaven; Sanctifier is your Name. Your kingdom come; Your will be done on earth as it is in heaven. Your Living Bread gives us our spiritual life from heaven. Forgive us our debts as also we forgive our debtors; and do not let us continue into temptation but deliver us from the evil one."

The message of this prayer is: There is no death in God's Holy Kingdom of Timeless Life. He sanctifies us to identity us with Himself as the holy spiritual Deity in heaven. God's blessing is to free us from our bondage to death that rules our bodies of flesh. We are to live out our physical lives subservient to the Deity of heaven, who already lives within us.

JESUS' BIRTH IN BETHLEHEM

Luke 2: 1-38, records God's personal witness to the Epiphaneia of Christ.

"Now in the fifteenth year of the reign of Caesar Augustus, a *decree* [Dogma – a command with a conclusive result] …went out for all the *inhabitable world* [Oikoumenē–this word in the proper context can mean the entire earth; or the entire Roman Empire; or the country where the seven churches of Asia Minor were settled; or in this case the particular inhabited country of Syria. The English word "ecumenical" is derived from this word.] …to be registered. This was the first census taken while *Cyrenius* [Kurēniŏs - Quirinius is the Latin spelling.] …was governor of Syria.

And all were proceeding to register for the census; everyone to his own city. And Joseph also went up from Galilee; from the city of Nazareth to Judea, the city of David which is called Bethlehem, because he was of the household and family of David. He went to register along with Mary, who was engaged to him as his wife and was with child. (Matthew 1:24-25, says Joseph took Mary into his home as her caretaker to identify her as his wife and kept her a virgin until she gave birth to Jesus. The Interlinear Greek-English New Testament says, 'to be taxed with Mary his espoused wife').

And it came about that while they were there; the days were completed for her to give *birth* [Tiktō–to bring forth. God used this particular word to reveal this was not a natural human birth with a human father. This child was the timeless Deity of heaven appearing in human *form* {Morphē - Jesus did not change His identity; He changed His appearance from a Spiritual Being in heaven to a Spiritual Human Being {the second Adam; pure and holy as Adam at his creation. He was fully God and fully man.].

And she gave *birth* [Tiktō – brought forth] … her *first-born son* [Prōtokos–The first revelation of the whole human race to have the preeminence of being raised from the dead and not be subject to death. The Saints in Christ by spiritual birth have the rights of the second Adam to inherit His heavenly identity. When a Christian dies the dead physical body goes to the grave. But the spirit ascends to Paradise, the abode of Christ.].

And she wrapped Him in cloths and laid Him in a manger because there was no room for them in the inn. And in the same region there were some *shepherds* [Poimēn–this word is the metaphysical identity of God's presence as a Spiritual Pastor of His sheep. It is used in this verse to reveal the reality that it was God shepherding real people to go to Jesus and worship Him.]….staying in the fields *keeping* [Phuiassō – to preserve life from danger or harm] …*watch* [Phulakē– A division of time; the night divided into four watches.] …over their flocks by night.

*The entire Bible records the presence of Deity to shepherd humanity as His beloved children in this world (the darkness of death). Jesus said He is the Good Shepherd, and nothing can take His sheep from His providential care. Every person reading this book can rejoice for the many occasions God has ministered to your spirit; to shepherd your mind to know the

God Reveals His Glory [Doxa – True Identity]

identity of Christ and to obey Him

And an angel of the Lord suddenly stood before them and the _glory_ [Doxa– the true identity of God. The angel glowed with the holiness of God to reveal himself a messenger from God and everyone in that light was in the holiness of God.] ...of the Lord shone around them; and they were _terribly_ [Měgas – the intense outward revelation of the condition of the mind] ..._frightened_ [Phŏběō–a protracted (to lengthen in duration) state of fear]. ...And the angel said to them, 'Do not be _afraid_ [Phŏběō]; ...for behold, I bring you good news of a great _joy_ [Chara – the condition of the mind to be calmly happy; delighted; cheerful; peaceful.]...which shall be for all the _people_ [Laôs – the whole human race in general]; ...for today in the city of David there has been _born_ [Tiktō- the preexisting Christ was "brought forth" from the womb] ...for you a _Savior_ [Sōtēria–salvation of sinful man by the authority of Deity]...who is _Christ_ [Christŏs – Messiah; anointed one] ...the Lord. And this will be a _sign_ [Sěměiŏn – a miraculous revelation from God to reveal something hidden or secret] ...for you; you will find a _baby_ [Brěphŏs – an unborn child; the timeless Deity of God] ...wrapped in cloths and _lying_ [Kěimai– to lie outstretched; meaning to be appointed (set) for affliction.] ....in a _manger_ [Phatē –from {Pâtěōmai - to eat}; a crib for animal fodder] `."

*This revelation of the _coming_ [Parousia – presence of the Messiah] ...was God's sign that He will fulfill the Devine purpose for the removal of the curse of death on all created life. The English words "born, baby, lying, manger" have no spiritual meaning and go completely unnoticed. However, the Greek words are His sign to fully reveal the identity of Jesus as the Messiah. Tiktō and Brěphŏs reveal the Messiah is God in human appearance and He is to be worshipped as the Living God. Kěimai and Phatē are words of purpose. The Messiah would be brutally treated by humanity under the curse of death; but received by all animal life because it does not have a mind to sin.

"And suddenly there appeared with the angel a multitude of the _Heavenly_ [Ŏuraniŏs – the appellation (title, name) of God.] ..._Hosts_ [Stratia – army; *There appeared God's army of angels celebrating the most monumental event of human history.] ...praising God, and saying, 'Glory to God in the highest, and on earth _peace_ [Ěirēne – the harmonized relationship between God and man as a created spiritual being] ...among _men_ [Anthrōpŏs – human imperfection in contrast to God] ...with whom He is _pleased_ [Ěudŏkia – takes pleasure in] `. ...And it came about when the angels had gone away from them into heaven, that the shepherds began saying to one another 'Let us go straight to Bethlehem and see this _thing_ [Rhēma – the spoken word of God's instructions; God's revelation of His heavenly presence on earth.] ...that has happened which the Lord has made known [Gnōrizō – to come to know what was unknowable] ... to us'.

And they went in haste and _found_ [Aněuriskō – to find something by diligent searching] ... their way to Mary and Joseph, and the baby {Brěphŏs} as He lay {Kěimai} in the manger. And when they had seen this, they made known {Gnōrizō} the statement / thing {Rhēma} which had been told them about this Child. And all who heard it wondered at the things which were told them by the shepherds. But Mary treasured up all these things, pondering them in her heart. And the shepherds went back, _glorifying_ [Dŏxazō - magnifying the true identity of God] ...and praising God for all that they had heard and seen, just as had been told them."

Luke 2:21-38, two witnesses to the Epiphaneia of Christ:
"And when eight days were fulfilled before His circumcision, His name was then called Jesus; the name given by the angel before He was placed in the womb. And when the days for their purification according to the Law of Moses were completed, they brought Him up to Jerusalem to present Him to the Lord: as it is written in the Law of the Lord, 'Every first-born male that opens the womb shall be called Holy to the Lord and to offer a sacrifice according to what was said in the Law of the Lord; a pair of Turtledoves or two young Pigeons`.

And behold, there was a man in Jerusalem whose name was Simeon; and this man was righteous and devout, looking for the *consolation* [Paraklēsis – calling to one's side (waiting for the coming of the Messiah to give life to man).] ...of Israel; and the Holy Spirit was upon him. And it had been *revealed* [Chrēmatizō – to transact business; God's saints were publicly called Christians because it was their chief business; Simeon inquired of the Lord and He responded with a divine admonition or instructions] ...to him by the Holy Spirit that he would not see death before he had *seen* [Oida – perfect of (ĕidō); to perceive in the mind by divine knowledge] ...the Lord's Christ.

And he came in the Spirit unto the *temple* [Hiĕrŏn – a holy place; not the Naos (Holy of Holies) but the entire temple grounds and buildings surrounding the Naos.] ...and when the parents brought in the child Jesus, to carry out for Him the custom of the Law, then he took Him into his arms and *blessed* God [Ēulŏgŏĕ – to thank or invoke a benediction; to celebrate with praises addressed to God acknowledging His goodness and His glory (true identity).], ...and said, 'Now Lord, You have let Your bond-servant *depart* [Apŏluō – to be fully free; released; dismissed; (lit.) let die] ...in peace according to Your word; for my eyes have seen Your *salvation* [Sōtērĭŏn – (noun) virtually stands for the Deity of Christ as Savior.] ...which You have prepared in the *presence* [Prŏsōpŏn – outward appearance; face of the Lord revealed for all to see with their eyes; to be acknowledged for His identity of the Lord.] ...of all *peoples* [Laòs – plural word meaning the whole human race], ...a *Light* [Phōs – the luminous appearance of God in heaven which identifies Him as Holy Life. The Deity of Heaven reveals Himself in human appearance to the mind of men that they can know Him as the God of heaven.] ...of *Revelation* [Apōkalupsis – the intense expectation of absorption to the Deity of Christ.] ...to the Gentiles, and the *glory* [Doxa – true identity of the holy people of God] ... of Your people Israel`.

And Mary and Joseph were amazed at the *things* [Rhēma – God's spoken revelation of His heavenly presence on earth] ...which were being said about Him. And Simeon blessed them and said to Mary, 'Behold, this child is *appointed* [Kĕimai – same word used of Jesus in the manger; to be outstretched (set); predestined for afflictions] ...for the fall and *rise* [Anastasis – resurrection from death] ...of many in Israel, and for a *sign* [Sēmĕiŏn – a miraculous revelation from God to reveal something hidden or secret] ...to be opposed; and a sword will pierce even your own *soul* [Psuchĕ – the life given to the body of Adam; the life that animates the flesh to afflictions, aversions; moral activities and sinful activities.] ...to the end that *thoughts* [Dialŏgismŏs – discussions, debates, reasoning, deliberations] ...from many hearts may be *revealed* [Apŏkaluptō – something revealed directly to the mind is uncovered, exposed. God's revelation of the identity of Christ is believed to be truth.] `.

And there was a *prophetess* [Prŏphētis – a self-assumed title of the daughter of a prophet]

God Reveals His Glory [Doxa – True Identity]

...Anna, the daughter of Phanuel of the tribe of Asher. She was advanced in years, having lived with a husband seven years and then as a widow to the age of eight-four. And she never left the temple grounds, _serving_ [Latrĕuō – to give homage (worship) to God] ...night and day with fasting and prayer. And at that very moment she came up and began giving thanks to God and continued to speak of Him to all those who were looking for the _redemption_ [Lutrôsis – ransoming] ...of Jerusalem."

GOD'S WITNESS OF THE EPIPHANEIA TO THE CITY OF JERUSALEM

Matthew 2
"Now after Jesus was born in Bethlehem of Judea _in_ [Ēn – this word is a designation of time God created for the purpose of revealing His presence for a specific task.] ...the days of Herod the king, behold _magi_ [Magŏs–Persian astrologers; they were called Elymas, an Arabic word meaning "wise". Matthew used the word Magŏs; meaning Persian priests who were wise in their knowledge of the Jewish religion.] ...from the east arrived in Jerusalem, saying, 'Where is He who has been _born_ [Tiktō – brought forth] ..._King_ [Basilĕus – the sovereign foundation of power] ... of the Jews: For we _saw_ [Ĕidō- a verb used only in the past tense; to know by perception; to perceive something in the mind.] ..._His star_ [Astēr - lights strewn across the sky having movements by the rotation of the earth. This is not the word for a fixed star that is permanently in view, or a comet. The Magi reveal that it was _His_ (Jesus) _heavenly Holiness_– light that radiates from Him; was shepherding them to Jerusalem and thus they perceived by the Holy Spirit the true identity of the child to be the Deity of God.] ...in the east and have come to worship Him'.

And when Herod the king _heard_ [Akĕuō – a verb denoting to hear intransitively; meaning he fully grasped the situation that would spur him to react to the message.] ...it, he was troubled and all Jerusalem with him. And gathering together all the chief priests and scribes of the people, he began to inquire of them where the Christ was to be born. And they said to him, 'In Bethlehem of Judea, for so it has been written by the prophet.'

Micah 5:2.
"And you Bethlehem, _land_ [Gē – a particular region of arable soil {people who God cultivates to produce believers}] ...of Judah, are by no means _least_ [Ĕlachistŏs – less important] ... _among_ [Ēn – a primary preposition denoting a fixed position in place, time or state. This is a different word from that in the first verse.] ...the leaders of Judah; for out of you shall come forth One who will go forth for Me to be the _Ruler_ [Hēgĕŏmia – official authority of Deity to govern]. Who will shepherd My people Israel?"

Then Herod secretly called the magi and ascertained from them the _time_ [Chrŏnŏs – a space of time; or the date of an occurrence] ...the light _appeared_ [Phainō – to shine; to become evident. This information was disclosed to Herod as he revealed it in verse 16 to be close to two years.]. ...And he sent them to Bethlehem and said, 'Go and make careful search for the Child; and when you have found Him, report to me that I too may go and worship Him'.

And having heard the king they went their way; and lo, the light which they had seen in the east went on before them until it came and stood over where the Child was. And when they saw the light which identified Jesus as the presence of God, they rejoiced exceedingly with great joy. {The context of this revelation indicates that the Magi were the only ones who could see the light and identify the location of Jesus and their arrival would not bring in an unwanted crowd. God was safe-guarding Jesus from Herod.}

And they came into the <u>*house*</u> [Ŏikia – this word has the distinct meaning of a single dwelling place of a family. This word again raises the possibility that Jesus could have been close to two years of age.] …and saw the child (not a baby) with Mary His mother; and they <u>*fell down*</u> [Piptō – to prostrate oneself in humble homage and worship] …and worshiped Him; and opening their treasures they <u>*presented to Him gifts*</u> [Dōrŏn – this word specifically means to present a gift as an expression of honor for the support of the temple and the needs of the poor. This was God's providence to take care of His Living Temple and His family while in exile in Egypt] …of gold and frankincense and *myrrh* (a bitter resin that is an astringent, an antiseptic, a stimulant, an ingredient to make perfume, it is one of the ingredients to make the holy anointing oil for the priests, it was used for embalming and to make a tincture of myrrh (a narcotic to deaden pain). And having been warned by God in a dream not to return to Herod, they departed for their own country by another (different – unobserved by Herod) way.

Now when they had departed, behold, an angel of the Lord <u>*appeared*</u> [Phainō – the actual outward appearance of shinning with the holiness of God] …to Joseph in a dream, saying, 'Arise and take the Child and His mother, and flee to Egypt and remain there until I tell you; for Herod is going to search for the Child to <u>*destroy*</u> [Apŏllumi – to destroy to the point that there is no trace of Him] …Him`. And he arose and took the Child and His mother by night and departed for Egypt; and was there until the death of Herod, that what was spoken by the Lord through the prophet might be fulfilled, saying, 'Out of Egypt did I call <u>My Huios - Deity</u>`.

Then when Herod saw that he had been tricked by the magi, he became very enraged and sent soldiers and slay all the male children who were in Bethlehem and in all its environs, from two years old and under according to the time which he had ascertained from the magi. Then that which was spoken through Jeremiah the prophet was fulfilled, saying, 'A voice was heard in Ramah, weeping and great mourning, Rachel weeping for her children; and she refused to be comforted, because they were no more`.

But when Herod was dead, behold, an angel of the Lord appeared in a dream to Joseph in Egypt, saying, 'Arise and take the Child and His mother, and go into the land of Israel; for those who sought the Child's life are dead`. And he arose and took the Child and His mother and came into the land of Israel. But when he heard that Archelaus was reigning over Judea in place of his father Herod, he was afraid to go there. And being warned by God in a dream, he departed for the regions of Galilee and came and resided in a city called Nazareth, that what was spoken through the prophets might be fulfilled; 'He shall be called a Nazarene`."

GOD'S FIRST REVELATION OF JESUS – THE MESSIAH

Luke 2: 41-45, Jesus was taken to Jerusalem for the Passover celebration at the age of twelve. Following the Passover, Mary and Joseph discovered that Jesus was not in the caravan returning to Nazareth. Thus, they began a frantic search for Him.

God Reveals His Glory [Doxa – True Identity]

Luke 2:46-50,
"And it came about that after three days they found Him in the *temple* [Hiĕrŏn– The entire complex of the temple grounds. The only place Jesus never entered was the Naos – the inner sanctuary; because Jesus is the living naos of God's permanent temple.] …sitting in the midst of the *teachers* [Didaskalŏs – the teachers of the Jewish religion]; …both listening to them and asking them questions. And all who heard Him were amazed at His understanding and His *answers* [Apŏkruptō – truths God keeps secret from the wise; the mystery of the unsearchable riches of Christ revealed to those who have a mind to believe].

And when they (Mary and Joseph) saw Him, they were astonished; and His mother said to Him, '*Son* [Tĕknŏn – a human child brought forth from her womb] …why have You treated us this way? Behold, Your *father* [Patēr– one who stands in the place of a nourisher or protector of children.] …and I have been anxiously looking for You`. And He said to them, 'Why is it that you were looking for Me? Did you not *know* [Ĕidō– to know truths by perception that cannot otherwise be known] …that I must be busy in the affairs of *My Father* [Patēr – Jesus and the God of heaven are one Spiritual Deity. While in the morph of man, He was *subservient* {fulfill the purpose of the Christ} to the ruling authority of His throne in heaven. *This is a perfect living witness to our own subservient relationship we have to our heavenly Father.]. And they did not understand the [Rhēma –message spoken only by God] …which He had made."

Luke 2:51-52 is all that is recorded of Jesus' adolescence to adulthood.
"And He went down with them and came to Nazareth; and He continued in *subjection* [Hupŏtassō – to be subordinate and obey the parental role given to Mary and Joseph] …to them; and His mother treasured all these things in her heart, and Jesus kept increasing in wisdom and stature and in favor with God and men."

THE BEGINNING OF THE PUBLIC MINISTRY OF JOHN   C. A.D.25-27

Luke 3:1-3
"Now in the fifteenth year of the reign of Tiberius Caesar, when Pontius Pilate was governor of Judea, and Herod was tetrarch of Galilee, and his brother Philip was tetrarch of the region of Ituraea and Trachonitis, and Lysanias was tetrarch of Abilene, in the high priesthood of Annas and Caiaphas, the word of God came to John, the son of Zachariah, in the wilderness. And he came into the district around the Jordan, preaching repentance for the forgiveness of sins."

Matthew 3:1-3
"Now in those days John the *Baptist* [Baptistēs– baptizer; this word is used only of John as the only person who identified people with God by immersing themselves in God's forgiveness.] …came preaching in the wilderness of Judea, saying, 'Repent for the kingdom of heaven is at hand`. For this is the one referred to by Isaiah the prophet, saying, 'The voice of one crying in the wilderness; make ready the way of the Lord, make His paths straight`!"

John's message was both revolutionary and encouraging to the common people so that they flocked to him. But he also got the attention of the political and religious leaders.

Matthew 3:5-12

"Then Jerusalem was going out to him, and all Judea and the entire district around the Jordan; and they were being baptized by him in the Jordan River as they confessed their sins. But when he saw many of the Pharisees and Sadducees coming for baptism; he said to them, 'you brood of vipers, who warned you to flee from the *coming* [Měllō– The idea of expectation; to intend to act by compulsion or necessity. What the Jews feared might happen was about to be a reality.] … *wrath* [Ŏrgē– The original meaning of this word was unbridled desire, excitement of the mind, passion. It changed by virtue of passion to become anger (the strongest of all passions). Heated anger became "wrath" of men and governments.].

* The most effectual governing power is God. Hebrews 3:10-11, 4:3, expresses God's anger with Israel in the wilderness; I Thessalonians 2:14-16, expresses God's wrath upon Jews who killed His prophets, and kills God's people (Spiritual Israel). Romans 9:19-22, God expresses His wrath upon people who find fault in Him and tells Him what to do. In John 3:31-36, God pours out His wrath on every person who calls Him a liar and will not believe the truth of His salvation message spoken by the Messiah – Jesus, the Christ.

Therefore, bring forth fruit *in keeping with* [Axiŏs – deserving; worthy of; works which reveal the true character (identity) of a person] … r*epentance* [Marturia – evidence given in a court of law; repentance must be justifiably true, or it is a false witness.]; …and do not suppose that you can say to yourselves, 'We have Abraham for our father`; for I say to you, that God is able from these stones to raise up children to Abraham. *(Only God can make the spiritual descendants of Abraham). And the axe is *already laid* [Kĕimai– He is saying here that unbelieving minds are controlled by the power of death and these people are set for the same end as death – the Lake of Fire.] …at the root of the trees; every tree that does not bear good fruit is cut down and thrown into the fire. As for me, I baptize you with water for repentance; but He who is coming after me is mightier than I, and I am not fit to remove His sandals. He will baptize you with the Holy Spirit and fire. And His winnowing fork is in His hand and He will thoroughly clear His threshing floor; and He will gather His wheat into the barn, but He will burn up the chaff with unquenchable fire`."

These verses are God's affirmation to His decision that was made in Genesis 1:1-2. His salvation is to restore every person who comes to Him through Christ to a new identity of His heavenly creation of Timeless Spiritual Life. And every lost (unregenerate human being) is trash to be consumed in the Lake of Fire, along with death and Hades.

John 2:23-25, a group of people proclaimed to Jesus that they were His followers; but Jesus rejected them because He knew the truth of what was in their minds.

God Reveals His Glory [Doxa – True Identity]

BEGINNING OF JESUS' MINISTRY C.27 A.D.   (12 events)

JESUS` BAPTISM

Matthew 3: 13-17

"Then Jesus arrived from Galilee at the Jordan to be baptized by John. But John tried to prevent Him, saying, 'I have need to be baptized by You, and do You come to me'? But Jesus answering, said to him, 'Permit it at this time; for in this way it is fitting for us to *fulfill* [Plērŏō – to make replete; the action of restoring sinful man to the fullness of God by taking the sins of the world upon Himself. Jesus did not repent for Himself, but for the entire human race redeemed by His atonement.] …all *righteousness* [Dikaiŏsunē–The total character of the holiness of God that is required to identify His heavenly children. The sinless Jesus was baptized to identify Himself as the Deity of Heaven Who establishes His new creation of redeemed man as Spiritual Life that cannot die, because we are no longer under His judgment of death. God's righteousness is appointed to rule the mind of every person who, by faith, obeys His command to believe and obey His word revealed in His Deity, The Christ`.].

Then he permitted Him to be baptized. And after being baptized, Jesus *went up* [Anabainō – to spring straight up out of the water (Jesus revealed His authority over all creation to His disciples at a later time by walking on water; but He did it this time by standing above the water.)] …*immediately* [Ĕuthus–one swift motion that could not be seen by the human eye] …from the water; and behold, the heavens were opened and He saw the Spirit of God *descending* [Katabainō – for something to appear from a higher position to a lower position but not be seen until it is suddenly there] …as a dove, and coming upon Him, and behold, a *voice* [Phōnē – the articulate sound of a voice speaking from above so that those who heard it focused their attention upon Him] …out of the heavens, saying, 'This is My *beloved* [Agapētŏs – dearly loved; the highest emotional value of the heart which esteems the one loved above all others.] … [Huiŏs – a relational word; it defines the Deity of Heaven, the Deity of Christ and Deity of the Holy Spirit as one single, supreme Deity of heaven.] …in whom *I am well pleased* [Ĕudŏkĕō – this is a combination of two words which stresses the feelings of God's mind toward what He accomplishes to fulfill His purpose for creating the world. What He accomplishes through Christ is preeminent in His mind for fulfilling His plan for the total destruction of death and for the redemption of His beloved creation – man. What God accomplished through the Christ reveals the fullness of His glory (true identity) as the work that only God can do.] `."

John 1:32-34

"And John bore witness saying, 'I have beheld the Spirit descending as a dove out of heaven and He remained upon Him. And I did not recognize Him, but He who sent me to baptize in water said to me, 'He upon whom you see the Sprit descending and remaining upon Him, this is the one who baptizes in the Holy Spirit`. And I have seen and have borne witness that this is the [Huios – One and the same Deity] …of God."

Huios is used in Revelation 21:6-7, to reveal the relationship of God with redeemed man in His heavenly presence, "And He said to me, 'It is done. I am the Alpha and the Omega, the beginning and the end. I will give to the one who thirsts from the spring of the water of life without cost. He who overcomes shall inherit these things, and I will be his God and he will be My [Huios– one and the same spiritual life of God's righteousness that cannot die.] `."

JESUS WAS TEMPTED IN THE WILDERNESS

Matthew 4: 1-2

"Then Jesus was led up by His Spirit into the *wilderness* [Ěrěmŏs – solitude; a place totally devoid of the knowledge of God] ... to be *tempted* [Pěirazō – To prove the mind of Jesus: to maintain His identity and emerge from testing with His revelation of God's power of Life to destroy the kingdom of death that ruled Satan.]. ...by the devil. And after He had *fasted* [Něstěuō- English translation: to voluntarily abstain from food. This would be accurate if Jesus was just a man who could starve to death. Being the Deity of God, it means He devoted Himself to strengthen the purity and simplicity of His mind by placing earnest prayer above the needs of the flesh.] ...*forty* [Tessarakŏnta- The English translation of this word makes the same mistake as it did in translating the forty days and forty nights of Moses on Mt. Sinai. This present revelation concerns Jesus (the visible Deity of God) being led by the Holy Spirit to prepare Himself for His encounter with Satan.

The meaning in this context is the completeness of the Deity of Heaven for Jesus to overcome the insidious power of death. This is what God requires of man created in His image; to defeat the power of death with the spiritual authority of God's Kingdom Rule of Life.] ...*days* [Hēmēra – Metaphorically, the light of God revealed by the Word of God.

It is a time of judgment {enlightenment} that proves the reality of God's authority to govern the human mind by his faith in God.] ...and *nights* [Nux – Metaphorically, weakness of the mind to doubt God and suffer alienation from Him. Forty days and nights is the revelation of Jesus preparing His mind to speak the words to Satan which define His identity as the Deity of Heaven.]. ...He *afterward* [Hustěrēsis – subsequently] ...*hungered* [Pěinaō – The root word is {Pěnēs} – to work for one's food. Jesus anticipated and prepared Himself to overcome the deception of the kingdom of death that rules the human mind by Living Bread.]...This same word is used in Matthew 5:6, 'Blessed are those who hunger and thirst for *righteousness* [Dikaiŏsunē – the divine character or quality of being holy; to live by the authority of God and not be ruled by the power of death].`John 4:31, 34, in response to the disciple's efforts for Him to eat, He said, 'I have food to eat that you do not know about. My food is to do the will of Him who sent Me and to accomplish His work`."

Jesus had disciplined His mind to be tested. Now He hungered for the spiritual food - truth of God's word to counter the deceptive lies of Satan.

Matthew 4: 3-11

"And the tempter came and said to Him, 'If You are the *Huios* {Deity of God}, command that these stones become bread`. But He *answered* [Apŏkrimŏmai –to begin to speak in response to what was said previously] ...and said, 'It is written, Man shall not *live* [Zaō– to be alive by divine authority] ...on bread alone, but on every *word* [Rhēma – This word is different from Logos, which is God's revelation of His mind. Rhēma was used in the Book of Romans to mean the gospel message of salvation revealed in the person of Christ.

In Luke 2, God used it as four specific words which were His sign to man that the baby

(Jesus) is God in human form. It is used here to mean individual scripture verses which the Holy Spirit brings to remembrance for use in times of need. Jesus' answer revealed His identity as the Deity of God, which countered Satan's attempt to make Him nothing more than flesh and blood with the need for physical food.] ...that proceeds out of the mouth of God`.

Then the devil *took* [Paralambanō–to associate oneself in a familiar relationship; to assume to have equal authority. Satan makes the assumption that he is God and Jesus could receive everything he offered Him if Jesus would agree with this assumption.] ...Him into the holy city; and he had Him *stand* [Histēmi – to take a stand, to assert Himself as God's appointed Messiah] ...on the *pinnacle* [Ptĕrna – The New American Standard used this word "Pinnacle", and the King James used the word "Wing". These words are used to designate the basis Satan wanted Jesus to take as the platform for Him to lift His heel against God. In the Greek text, Ptĕrna means "to lift the heel against someone". Jesus used this word in John 13:18, concerning Judas. He quoted Psalms 41: 9, "Even my close friend in whom I trusted, who ate my bread, has lifted up his heel against me." For Jesus to take a stand that He is the Messiah and prove it (the pinnacle, the basis for proving His identity) by jumping off the temple with the assertion that the angels would be given the charge to see that He could not be injured. This would be the sin of lifting His heel against God. Jesus said, 'It is written (Deut. 6:16) you shall not put the Lord your God to the test`. This sin is repeated over and over again by people who will believe in God only if He will prove He is God by doing what they want Him to do. When it is pointed out to them the reality of God's providential care; their response is yes, but what has He done for me today?

Again, the devil *took* [Paralambanō] Him to a very high mountain and showed Him all the *kingdoms* [Basilĕia – This word is primarily an abstract noun denoting sovereignty, royal power, domination. This power is revealed by the vastness of the human race to create and dominate the world with every form of religion that is nothing more than the rule of death.] ...of the world and their *glory* [Dŏxa–This word primarily signifies an opinion and honor resulting from a good opinion of themselves. Satan used this word to assert his own opinion of himself as the power of God to rule over human life and honored himself by offering Jesus what he {himself}did not possess. Dŏxa is used in the scriptures for the nature and acts of God which reveals His true identity. He particularly glories in His identity of the Christ to destroy the works of Satan and restore His Spiritual Life to every person who will surrender the mind to God by faith.] ...and he said to Him, 'All these things will I give to You if You *fall down* [Piptō – to prostrate oneself in homage and worship] ...and worship me`. Then Jesus said to him, 'Be gone Satan! For it is written, (Deut.10:20, "you shall worship the Lord your God and serve Him only".) ` Then the devil left Him; and behold, angels came and began to *minister* [Diakŏnŏs- only God and the angels know their heavenly functions] ... to Him."

This same Satanic test is revealed to be a reality in the mind of every person whose assumption is that his form of worship (his kingdom rule) is superior to what God requires: which is simple faith in God that you can put your life in His hands with the assurance that He is the one who does the saving; not you. This is revealed when Jesus informed His disciples that He must go to Jerusalem to die. Peter objected,' no! You cannot do that`! Jesus responded with, 'Get behind me Satan! `

It would be a wonderful thing if every child of God would recognize Satan's deceptive testing our faith in God and our human assumption that we can govern our own lives by our mind {as he did with Eve} and stand with Jesus and proclaim – 'get behind me Satan`!

FIRST CONVERTS

John 1:35-51

"Again, the next day after the baptism of Jesus, John the Baptizer was standing with two of his disciples and he looked upon Jesus as He walked and said, 'Behold <u>the Lamb of God</u> [òAmnŏstoũθeou -the article {ò} designates the reality of the expected One who would personally fulfill God's sacrifice for deliverance from His divine judgment. (Genesis 22:8, "And Abraham said, 'My son, God will provide Himself a lamb for a burnt offering`."). The absence of the article stresses the nature and character of His sacrifice as only a symbolic act.] …Who <u>takes away</u> [Airō– to expiate sin by physically taking upon Himself this burden that is firmly attached to the human race] …the <u>sin</u> [Hamartia – the governing power of death over the human race] …of the world`.

And the two disciples heard him speak, and they followed Jesus. And Jesus turned and beheld them following and said to them, 'What do you seek`? And they said to Him, 'Rabbi (which translated means Teacher), where are You staying`? He said to them, 'Come and you will see`. They came therefore and saw where he was staying and they stayed with Him that day, for it was about the tenth hour.

One of the two men was Andrew, Simon's brother. He found first his own brother Simon, and said to him, 'We have found the Messiah, the Christ`. He brought him to Jesus. Jesus looked at him and said, 'You are Simon the son of John; you shall be called <u>Cephas</u>–a small stone; which is translated Peter`.

The next day Jesus purposed to go forth into Galilee; and He found Philip. And Jesus said to him, 'Follow Me'. Now Philip was from Bethsaida, of the city of Andrew and Peter. Philip found Nathanael and said to him, 'we have found Him of whom Moses in the Law and also the prophets wrote, Jesus of Nazareth, the son of Joseph`. And Nathanael said to him, 'Can any good thing come out of Nazareth`? Philip said to him, 'Come and see`. Jesus saw Nathanael coming to Him, and said of him, 'Behold, an Israelite indeed, in whom is no guile`! Nathanael said to Him, 'How do You know me`? Jesus answered and said to him, 'Before Philip called you, when you were under the fig tree, I saw you`. Nathanael answered Him, 'Rabbi, you are the Huios (Deity) of God; You are the King of Israel`. Jesus answered and said to him, 'Because I said to you that I saw you under the fig tree, do you believe? You shall see greater things than these`. And He said to him, 'Truly, truly, I say to you, you shall see the heavens opened, and the angels of God ascending and descending on the Huios of Man`.

JESUS` FIRST MIRACLE

John 2:1-11

"Three days after securing His first disciples; Jesus, His mother and His disciples were invited to a wedding in Cana of Galilee. When they ran out of wine, His mother told Him of the situation. The host had six stone water pots for the Jewish custom of purification, which would contain twenty to thirty gallons each. Jesus had the servants fill them to the brim with water. The headwaiter tasted the water which had become wine and declared it to be the good wine that was supposed to be served first, and the poorer wine served last. Verse 11, "This beginning of His *signs* [Sēmĕiŏn – the revelation of divine authority and power] ...Jesus did in Cana of Galilee, *revealed* [Phanĕrŏo – The movement of the Holy Spirit upon the mind to recognize God's revelation of His true character that is hidden; that can only be known by His actions.] ...His *glory* [Dŏxa – the exhibited character and acts of Deity in the flesh which declare His true identity.] ...and His disciples *believed* [Pistĕuō – faith which entrusts one's spiritual being in God's hands] ... in Him."

JESUS' FIRST CLEANSING OF THE TEMPLE

John 2:13-17

"And the *Passover* [Pascha – This is the Greek spelling of the Hebrew- pasach.] ...of the Jews was at hand and Jesus went up to Jerusalem. And He found in the *temple* [Hiĕrōn – sacred place; the entire building complex surrounding the central Naos. Jesus was in an outer court that was open to everyone.] ...those who were selling oxen and sheep and doves, and the moneychangers seated. And He made a *scourge* [Phragĕlliŏn – a whip used for public punishment; the whip itself was a sign of authority and judgment] ...of cords, and drove them all out of the temple with the sheep and oxen; and He poured out the coins of the moneychangers and overturned their tables; and to those who were selling the doves He said, 'Take these things away; stop making My *Father's* [Patēr – The metaphorical presence of Deity, the progenitor of both physical and spiritual life in every single human being.] ...house a house of merchandise'. His disciples remembered that it was written: Psalms 69:9, 'For *zeal* [Qin`âh - jealous; envy] ...for Your *house* [Bayith – a place of worship or sanctuary] ...has consumed me and the *reproaches* [Cherpâh – contemptuous hatred] ...of those who reproach You have fallen on me'."

Hebrews 13:15-16, God's house is a place of prayer.
"Through Him (Christ) then, let us continually offer up a *sacrifice* [Thusia – This word primarily denotes the act of offering yourself as a servant of God by doing good to others to meet their needs as Christ did for us to meet our needs. This is a spiritual sacrifice of the priesthood of believers and is metaphysically revealing Christ to the world.] ... of *praise* [Ainĕsis – to speak to God with your personal thanksgiving for all the mighty works He has done for you.] ... to God, that is, the fruit of lips that *give thanks* [Hŏmŏlŏgĕō – {Hŏmŏu- together at the same place and time (Peter and John arrived at the tomb at the same time)} and {Lŏgŏs {the expression of thought communicating the will of God as His revelation of truth}. These words together mean God's people are to meet together in the same place and time and confess our personal allegiance to Christ as the Master and Lord of our lives and acknowledge ourselves as faithful and loyal servants to His Kingdom of Life.] ...to His *name* [Ŏnŏma–give recognition to God's authority to identify Him with His children.] ... And do not neglect doing good and *sharing* [Kŏinŏnia – to have a common partnership with Godin the suffering of Christ with the realization of the Passover Meal, that God is passing over your personal sins; sharing in the work of the Holy Spirit to minister to the physical and spiritual needs of the church body. Fellowship with Jesus in your worship; talk and sing to Him personally. He is not a third person who is not here.] ...for with such sacrifices God is *pleased* [Ĕuarĕstĕō–to gratify entirely; to be in full agreement; God's personal word to each of His people to say, 'Thank you for a job well done.`].

*Judas was the only person who ate the Passover meal with Jesus who knowingly would betray Him. Do not eat the Passover meal if you are a Judas, an unbelieving person.

GOD'S RELATIONSHIP WITH SPIRITUAL ISRAEL IS: SONSHIP

Hebrews 1:1-6, these verses reveal the theological truth of what God accomplished in heaven to make man His spiritual children.

"God, after He *spoke* [Lalĕo – the articulated, distinct sound of the formed word in human language heard by the ear and understood by the mind] …*long ago* [Palai – ancient time from beginning of man] …to the *fathers* [Patēr – patriarchs; progenitors of Spiritual Israelites; Abraham, Isaac, Jacob, Joseph, David, and etc.] …in the *prophets* [Prŏphētēs – the proclaimer of divine secrets; one upon whom the Spirit of God rests] …in *many portions* [Pŏlumĕrōs – piece-meal; all of God's revelations have the One God as their source and were given progressively.] …and in *many ways* [Pŏlutrŏpōs – many methods or forms of communication {voice, signs, dreams, etc.}],

…in these *last days* [Ĕschatŏs – the close of the period of the testimony of the prophets; terminating with the presence of Christ for God to speak for Himself.]…has spoken to us in [Huiŏs – Jesus] the visible presence of Deity Who reveals His relationship with redeemed man is by *Sonship* – Spiritual Birth of God's Children recreated in His Image…whom He *appointed* [Tithēmi – to put in the place of service; God put Himself in the place {position of service - Epiphaneia} to accomplish what only He can do: release man from his bondage to death and give him free-will of his mind to return to God's Kingdom Rule of Spiritual Life.] …*heir* [Klērŏnŏmŏs – the secure title to an inheritance received as a gift] …of all things, through whom also He *made* [Pŏiĕō – to cause something to come into existence] …the world.

And He is the *radiance* [Apaugasma – a bright light coming from a luminous body; the Deity of God: the white light of holiness revealing the total absence of darkness; death] …of His *glory* [Dŏxa – the true identity of God exhibited by His character and the actions of His timeless Divinity] …and the *exact representation* [Charaktēr – a graver: the tool for engraving a perfect image; the seal or die which makes an impression that perfectly corresponds to the instrument producing it.]…of His *nature* [Hupŏstasis – the basic essence of God; the authority for the existence of life in which our confidence depends]…and *upholds* [Phĕrō – to carry a load, to be moved by the Holy Spirit, not by the will of man but by the mind of God. {II Peter1: 20-21, 'But know this first of all, that no prophecy of Scripture is a matter of one's own interpretation, for no prophecy was ever made by an act of human will, but men moved (Phĕrō) by the Holy Spirit spoke from God. '}] …all things by the *word* [Rhēma – the sword of the Spirit, which is the word of God. It is the individual scriptures which the Spirit brings to mind.] …of His *power* [Dunamis – supernatural power of God working in Spiritual man.]…. When He had made *purification* [Katharismŏs – the action and result of cleansing; expiation (purification of sin by atonement.) Jesus is the full authority of Deity on earth to cleanse man, to restore him to spiritual life] …of sins, He sat down at the *right hand* [Dĕxiŏs – right side; this word indicates the power of the throne which achieves the purpose of the throne] …of the Majesty on High.

having become as much *better* [Krĕittōn – stronger power in effecting the activities of God] …than the angels, as He has *inherited* [Klērŏnŏmĕō – to possess the gift of birthright by

God Reveals His Glory [Doxa – True Identity]

virtue of sonship; not because of a task accomplished (salvation of man)] …a *more excellent* [Diaphŏrŏs – a surpassing kind; different from all others] …*name* [Ŏnŏma – title; authority; attributes of God] …than they.

For to which of the angels did He ever say, 'You are My son, today I have *begotten* [Gĕnnaō – to be given the life of God] …you'? And again, 'I will be a Father to him, and He shall be a son to Me`?] *Through Christ alone; God is our Father, and we are His children.

And again, when He *brings* [Ĕisagō – to make Jesus known as the King of Kings when He brings with Him all the children of God from paradise] … the *first born* [Prōtŏtŏkŏs–this word was used of the Christ being the "proto-type" – the revelation of sinless God in human form to destroy the kingdom of death. He will finish this work when He brings the full wrath of God upon death for its final destruction. Revelation 19 records the exuberant joy in heaven by the angels and all God's children when the Apokalupsis is announced to them] … into the world, He says, 'And let all the Angels of God *worship Him* [Prŏskunĕō – This word means: to express reverence, give homage to Jesus with a kiss. This word reveals why Jesus questioned Judas for identifying Him with a kiss of death. "

* John 10:30, Jesus said, 'I and the Father (the ruling Deity of Heaven) …are *one* {Hĕis – one and the same Deity in number; and Hĕn– one and the same Deity in essence.} ` Jesus cleansed man with His own blood to make God's children holy as He is holy.}. John 10:32, Jesus said, 'I showed you many good works from the Father; for which of them are you stoning Me`? John 10:37-38, Jesus said, 'If I do not do the works of My *Father* {the ruling authority of the Throne of Life in Heaven}, do not believe Me; but if I do them, though you do not believe Me, believe the works, that you may know and understand that the Father is in Me, and I am in the Father`.].

Hebrews 2:10-11
"For it was fitting for Him, for whom are all things, and through whom are all things, in bringing many sons to glory, to *perfect* [Tĕlĕiŏō – to recreate man in the perfect image of God so as to be identified with Him as His heavenly children by birth.] …the *author* [Archēgŏs – the life Christ had in the flesh was His same life in heaven; {He gave His authority of Spiritual Life to man} which is His decree directly from the Throne of Life] … of their *salvation* [Sōtēria – to be delivered from the curse of death and preserved to God's identity of perfect holiness] … through Christ's sufferings. For both He who *sanctifies* [Hagiazŏ- to make holy by purification] … and those who are sanctified are all from one *Father* {the Deity of Heaven who creates all life}; for which reason He (the ruling Deity of Heaven) is not ashamed to call them *brethren* [Adĕlphŏs–a plural word meaning an entire community belonging to God based on its identity of the same origin of life – Christ.]."

John 3:1-7, Jesus simplified this revelation of sonship in His message to Nicodemus. He revealed the manner in which God gives spiritual life to His children.
"Now there was a man of the Pharisees named Nicodemus, a *ruler* [Archōn – the first or highest in rank or power for governing people] … of the Jews; this man came to Him by night and said to Him, 'Rabbi, we know that You have come from God as a teacher; for no one can

do these _signs_ [Sēmĕiŏn – miracles; a Godly action which reveals something hidden or secret] … that You do unless God is with Him.

Jesus answered and said to him, '_Truly_ [Amēn – a Hebrew word transliterated into Greek and English meaning "God is trustworthy; God is truth". This same word is translated as "verily" when God introduces new revelations of His mind.] …truly, I say to you, 'unless one is _born_ [Gĕnnaō – the procreation properties of the Deity of Heaven to give both physical and spiritual life to His children; in this verse it is the revelation of God creating new spiritual life in human beings still living on this earth.] … _again_ [Anōthĕn – "from above"; the Deity of God is our heavenly Father Who gives us Spiritual Life by the authority of His Throne of Life.] … he cannot _see_ [Ĕidō – to know the Deity of God by the limitations of the human mind. Oido is the perfect tense of Ĕidō, meaning absolute or divine knowledge. Every person who is given new spiritual life from the Throne of God has the power of God's mind {Oido} to know Him in truth]. … the _kingdom of God_ [Basilĕia – the realm of sovereign royalty, holiness unknown to physical man`].

Nicodemus said to Him, 'How can a man be born {the procreation of physical man} when he is old? He cannot enter a second time into his mother's womb and be born, can he`?

Jesus answered, 'Truly, truly, I say to you, unless one is _born of water_ {the divine power to create man a physical being from the water of the expanse. By the progenitive authority of God as the creator of all life; He created Adam a physical being and breathed spiritual life into him. God gave the human male His progenitive authority to have children with both physical and spiritual life. Deaths rule in this world destroys both the physical and spiritual life of every person. Through Jesus, God restores His timeless spiritual life to the physical human being as a new creation of God} … _and the Spirit_ [Pnĕuma–The breath of God. The Holy Spirit again breathes life into physical man to give him new birth as a timeless spiritual creation; a child of God made in His image.] … he cannot enter into the kingdom of God. That which is born of the flesh is flesh, and that which is born of the Spirit is Spirit. Do not marvel that I said to you, "You must be _born_ (given life) _again_ (from above; from your heavenly Father) `."

John 4:1-6, Jesus was reaching a large number of people in Judea which was disturbing to the Pharisees, so He returned to Galilee. He made it a point to go through Samaria, to a town called Sychar. He had an appointment to meet a woman at Jacob's well who could understand spiritual things. Jesus gave the revelation to this Samaritan woman that the One God is to be worshipped by all people as a Living Spiritual Being. Jesus revealed to her that He is the Deity all people are to worship.

John 4:7-26, Jesus used the human need for water to cross the barrier between the Jews and the Samarians. He told the woman to give Him a drink. Her response was "Jews have no dealings with Samaritans." Verse 10, "Jesus answered and said to her, 'If you knew the gift of God and who it is who says to you, give me a drink, you would have asked Him, and He would have given you _living_ [Zaō – a primary verb (action) meaning to make alive] … water." The woman wanted to know where she could get this water that she did not need to come back to the well. Verses 13-14, "Jesus answered and said to her, 'Everyone who drinks of this water (the well) shall thirst again; but whoever drinks of the water that I shall give him shall never thirst; but the water that I shall give him shall become in him a _well_ [Pēgē – a gushing fountain from

God Reveals His Glory [Doxa – True Identity]

within; a source of spiritual life] ...of water springing up to [Aiōniŏs– the {timeless existence} of God. The word {eternal}is the human measurement of time and has nothing to do with God] *life* [Zŏē – life force of God; God is *timeless spiritual life of Deity* and the creator of all life] `."

The woman still did not recognize Jesus' divine identity, nor did she comprehend the spiritual truth of God's salvation. He revealed His knowledge of her personal life and her accountability to God. Verse 16, "He said to her, 'Go, call your husband and come here`." Verses 17-18, "The woman said, 'I have no husband`. Jesus said to her, 'You have well said you have no husband; for you have had five husbands and the one whom you now have is not your husband; this you have said truly`."

Jesus' answer awakened the woman's mind to realize He was not an ordinary Jew. Verse 19, the woman said, 'Sir, I perceive that You are a prophet. Our fathers worshiped in this mountain and you people say that in Jerusalem is the place where men ought to worship`. The woman's theological statement opened the door for Jesus to reveal the true message of why He was talking to her.

In verses 21-24, Jesus said to her, "Woman, believe Me, an *hour* [Hōra – This word has many meanings in relationship to time. Jesus used it to designate the present time that God has fulfilled His Word for the coming of His Messiah.] ... is coming when neither in this mountain, nor in Jerusalem, shall you worship the Father. You worship that which you do not know; we worship that which we know, for *salvation* [Sōtēria–deliverance, preservation. The purpose of the Messiah is God's presence to deliver His people from the curse of death.] ...is from the Jews (Jesus was a Jew). But an hour is coming and now is, when the true worshipers shall worship the *Father* [Patēr – The ruling Deity of Heaven. Jesus used this word to enforce the truth that only God can create life; physical and spiritual] ... in spirit and truth; for such people the Father seeks to be His worshipers. *God* ['Ĕlôhîym] is spirit and those who worship Him must worship in spirit and truth." She said, 'I know that Messiah is coming (He who is called Christ); when that One comes, He will declare all things to us`. Jesus said to her, 'I who speaks to you am He`.

Jesus was interrupted at this point by His disciples; they were astonished that Jesus was talking to this woman. The woman fled the scene and returned to her city. She said to the men, 'come see a man who told me all the things that I have done; this is not the Christ is it`? She was seeking confirmation of God's presence. She did not want to appear foolish to them with a false message. A number of them believed the truth of her words. So, a large number started to the well to see for themselves if Jesus is the Messiah.

Meanwhile Jesus had to teach His disciples the simplicity of how to witness to people. The responsibility of man is to sow the seeds of the gospel and God will do the harvesting. Everyone involved in reaching people rejoice together. People are not of one mind with God if they pass judgment on the human race as unsavable.

The woman sowed the seed to the men of the city, and many believed because of her testimony. So, the Samaritans asked Jesus to stay with them (which He did for two day). Many of them believed Jesus and testified that this One is indeed the Savior of the world. Jesus had finished the purpose for going to Samaria. He had saved the lives of many people and He had taught His disciples that God's salvation is for the whole world. His people must sow the message to the world that is white for harvest. People sow the seed; but God does the harvesting.

Verses 35-38

"Do you not say, 'There are yet four months and then comes the harvest`. Behold I say to you, 'lift up your eyes and look at the fields; that they are white for harvest. Already He who reaps is receiving *wages* [Misthŏs – the reward for God's work in this present time] … and is gathering fruit for *life* [Zōē– the life God has in Himself - Aiōniŏs – the timelessness of God.] … that he who sows and He who reaps may rejoice together`. For in this case the saying is true, one sows and *another* [Allŏs – a different one of a kind Who creates a different kind of life; a spiritual existence is all life that is in God's heavenly presence.] … reaps`."

Jesus taught His disciples that His people must have the mind of God to do the work of God. They must see Him with spiritual eyes of faith and surrender the mind to obey Him. They must see every person in this world as spiritual beings Jesus died to save. He demonstrated this in Samaria and then He went on into Galilee.

GALILEAN MINISTRY   A.D. 27-29 (55 events)

John 4:46-54

"Jesus healed a *royal official's* son [Basilikŏs – he belonged to the royal court of either King Herod, Pilate, or the Chief Priests of the temple]….Jesus said to the man, 'Unless you people see *signs* [Sēmĕiŏn – hidden miracles that only God can do; things in heaven that appeals to understanding deity] …and *wonders* [Tĕras – a divine revelation causing man to marvel] … you simple will not *believe* [Pistĕuō – not be persuaded to place confidence in God.] `

Jesus said to him, 'Go your way; your son *lives* [Zaō– to be alive spiritually and physically;] `. The man believed the *word* [Lŏgŏs- the divine expression of God's mind that speaks to the mind of man.] … that Jesus spoke to him and he started home. His *slaves* [Dŏulŏs – One who is in a permanent relation of servitude] …met him saying his son was living. When given the time of healing was while Jesus spoke to him; he himself believed and his *whole household* [Ŏikia – the meaning of this word {when} spoken by Jesus, meant the whole estate of a dwelling place. Every person in this man's dwelling was converted to faith in God. The meaning of this word was lost in later Greek writings; to mean simply a physical house.]." *When Jesus speaks it is a heavenly command and has an immediate heavenly result. People's lives are changed from physical thinking to the spiritual authority of God's mind.

Mark 1:21-28 and Luke 4:31-37

"Jesus went into Galilee preaching the gospel of God, saying, 'The *time* [Kairŏs – the specific time for God to reveal Himself; the fulfillment of His prophecy] … is *fulfilled* [Plērŏō – to make replete; to identify the Deity of God in the days of His flesh – Messiah] … and the *kingdom* [Basilĕia – the sovereignty, royal power, dominion of heaven] …of God *is at hand* [Ĕggizō– to be near; it would not be completed until God's Passover]; … *repent* [Mĕtanŏĕō – to change one's mind or purpose; to think differently after the fact (the Passover). *Pronoeo* means to change the mind beforehand.] … and believe in the gospel {Jesus was telling people to believe in Him by virtue of His identity and not just His actions.}' And they (Simon, Andrew, and Jesus) went into Capernaum; and immediately on the Sabbath He entered the synagogue and began to teach. And they were amazed at His teaching; for He was teaching them as one having authority, and not as the _scribes_ [Grammatĕus- Pharisees who were teachers of the law]. ... And just then there was a man in the synagogue possessed by the spirit of an _unclean demon_ [Daimŏnizmaï- possessed with devils]. ... And he cried out with a loud voice, 'Ha! What do we have to do with You, Jesus of Nazareth? Have you come to destroy us? I know who You are– You are the _Holy One_ [Hagiŏs – separated from all other physical men; as Deity] ... of God`! And Jesus rebuked him, saying, 'Be quiet and come out of him`! And throwing him into convulsions, the unclean spirit cried out with a loud voice and came out of him. And they were all amazed so that they debated among themselves; saying, 'What is this? A _new_ [Kainŏs– a different language they had never heard before] ... teaching with authority! He _commands_ [Ĕpitassŏ– to be in charge of one as a duty] ... even the unclean spirits and they _obey_ [Hupakŏuō – to heed or conform as subordinates to an authority] ...Him`. And immediately the news about Him went out into all the surrounding district of Galilee."

****This author has been a witness many times to God's protection from demonic people. One memorable occasion was a demon possessed man living across the road from my church. I could visit the man and he would be a polite person. But when I said the name, Jesus, he would snarl like an animal and physically throw me out of the house.

The demons were beating this man to death and he was hospitalized with a pain that could not be removed. I went to see the man and as soon as I opened the door the demons knocked the man out of his bed. I went to a corner in the room and simply said, Come Lord Jesus, Come. Instantly the demons came out of the man with a stinking smell and screaming.

The man lay unconscious for a few minutes and then crawled to his bed. He cried out to God to save him. He told me he had invited Satan into his life to spite his mother. He had not been able to say the word Jesus for fifteen years. God did not take his pain away and he died in ten days – but he led eight people to Christ in that time.

Demons have no power over people who have the mind of Christ! This is a theological truth that I learned from experience. I pastored a church in the most unchurched city in the U.S. I was harassed constantly with threats to kill me and spiritually newborn church members were being driven from the church. The chairman of the deacons told me the church had all the people they wanted in it. I was distraught in the face of such spiritual power.

The Lord met my need one night when the oppression was at its peak. The physical sign of God was the pure holiness of His presence. Just for an instant I was in a white light. There was no voice; just an over-whelming power of His love for me. All the demonic oppression ceased immediately.

No human being can do what only God can do, and His presence is His unceasing power to reveal His true identity of 'Ĕlôhîym. He is Lord of heaven and earth.

Matthew 8:1-4
"And when he had come down from the mountain, great multitudes _followed_ [Akŏlŏuthĕō – metaphorically – disciples; people who live in union with Jesus so as to be identified with Him in His likeness.] ...Him. And behold, a leper came to Him and bowed down to Him, saying, 'Lord if you are _willing_ [Thĕlō – the will of the mind to establish the resolve and determination of one's identity.] ... You can _make me clean_` [Katharizō – to make clean by purging the disease from his body. Lepers carried the stigma of a contagious disease that made

other people die. He wanted to know if Jesus was willing to remove the defilement of death; to purify him with the holiness of His disciples.]

And He *stretched out* [Ěktěinō–to reach out to the man with a physical touch. No one but God would dare touch this man for fear of death. Jesus reached out to the man to draw him close to Him. This word expresses the love God has for sinners to draw them near to Him. This action would cause the Jews to curse Him as a demon and many of His disciples to withdraw from close contact with Him. It is the nature of death to cause self-righteous people to condemn other people but justify themselves].

... His hand and touched him, saying, 'I am willing; be *cleansed* [Katharizō – to remove the defilement of death so as to be pure and holy as a true disciple of God.] ... And immediately his leprosy was cleansed. ...And Jesus said to him, '*See* [Hŏraō – actions of the body to reveal intent] ...that you tell no one; but go show yourself to the priest and *present* [Prŏsphĕrō – to place the proper sacrifice before the alter as a witness of repentance] ...the *offering* [Dōrŏn – an offering to help people in need] ...that Moses *commanded* [Prŏstassō - this word is a mild prophetic revelation stressing that the one giving the command is actually the Deity of God]."

****Jesus' healing of a leper was a challenge to the will of His followers. The leper was healed but the intent of many of God's disciples was not of the same mind. Walking close to Jesus can be an unsettling experience for people who love this life and are not prepared to give it up. Jesus knew this when he called Peter to be a disciple; knowing he would deny Him in fear. He knew Judas loved money more than His Person and gave Him the "kiss of death" in the garden. All people who identify themselves as disciples of Jesus must know that their true identity will be exposed when they worship Jesus face to face in His coming Kingdom Rule. The leper was obligated to God to keep his mouth shut and demonstrate a public act of obedience that demonstrated his proper relationship to God. God is working at this present moment to separate the sheep from the goats. His sheep identify themselves by demonstrating the character of God and the goats identify themselves by demonstrating the character of death.

John 5:1-17, Jesus healed a man with a crippling illness. The background for this was God's miraculous healing of people at the pool of Bethesda. A multitude of people were *waiting* [Ekdechomai–expecting to be the one God would heal] ...for God to disturb the water. Jesus knew the man had been ill for thirty-eight years, so He simply asked him if he wanted to get well. The man said he was desperately trying to get in the water, but someone always got in before him. Jesus said, "Arise, take up your pallet and walk", and then disappeared in the crowd. Some Jews saw the man and confronted him for carrying his pallet on the Sabbath. The man said, "The man who healed me told me to pick up my pallet and walk." The man did not know Jesus and could not identify Him. Later Jesus found the man in the *temple* [Hieron –This word means the whole complex of the temple in Jerusalem]. ...Jesus said to him, "Behold, you have become *well* [Hugies – meaning a sound healthy body]; ...do not *sin* [Hamartanō – the act of continually missing the mark in having a relationship with the true God] ...anymore, so that nothing worse may befall you." The man then identified Jesus to the Jews as the man who healed him and told him to pick up his pallet and walk.

God Reveals His Glory [Doxa – True Identity]

Verse 5:16
"And for this reason, the Jews were persecuting Jesus, because He was doing these things on the Sabbath."

Verse 5:17
"He said, 'My Father is working until now, and I Myself am working`."

John 5:18-47, Jesus reveals the true identity of the living God. Read these verses with the reality that Jesus is talking to you, personally. Let Him cleanse your mind of all the theological garbage you have put in it that prevents Him from working in your life.

5:18
"For this cause therefore, the Jews were seeking all the more to *kill Him* [Apŏkuĕo – This is the combination of two words; (1) Apŏ- to move something away from you so that it ceases to exist. (2) Kuma – to swell something up with a billow to destroy it with force. As a verb the whole word means: to destroy an idea by destroying the person speaking.] … because He was not only *breaking* [Luō – to be unloosed from something that binds you; to declare a commandment of law to be of no effect.] …the Sabbath, but also was calling God, *His* [Idios – this word denotes the truth that Jesus possessed a heavenly familiar relationship with God as one Spiritual Being that is not possible for any other human being] …own Father, making Himself equal with God."

5:19, Jesus reveals the heavenly familiar relationship between Himself and God, the Father.
"Jesus therefore answered and was saying to them, '*Truly*, [Amĕn – trustworthy] …truly, I say to you, [Huios – The Deity of God revealing Himself in the form {morph} of man] …can do nothing of Himself, unless it is something He *sees* [Blĕpō – a verb meaning to take heed, behold, perceive, contemplate, to act circumspectly. Jesus uses this word to mean what man sees Him doing in the form of man is actually seeing the true Deity of God.] …the Father doing; for whatever the Father does, this thing the Huios {Deity of Christ} also does in like manner."

Jesus reveals the truth that all of the saving work of God is replete through Him. He is the Deity of God in human form to exact God's justice for His spiritually born children. The Father is creating new spiritual life in the human being only through the work of the Huios - Christ.

5:20
"For the Father *loves* [Philĕō – to love with the meaning of having a common interest with another to accomplish the same objective. The Father and the Christ accomplish the work of heaven by empowering the light of God to shine in the darkness of the human mind.] …the Christ and shows Him all things that He Himself is doing; and greater *works* [Ergon – the miracles Christ performed on earth reveal the love, grace, and majesty of the heavenly Father.] …than these will He show Him, that you may marvel."

*What is most important to God is the revelation of the mysteries of God that cannot be known by the finite mind of man. Only Jesus reveals the [*Doxa* – true identity of God.] *It is impossible for human beings to deify other human beings as Saints in heaven and be worshipped for answering the prayers of man.

5:21

"For just as the Father *raises* [Egeirō – to awaken those in the darkness of death; to become attentive to one's own dangerous spiritual position and the salvation of God's deliverance from it.] …the dead and *gives them life* [Zōopoieō – to restore the power of God's Throne of Life to spiritually dead humanity.] …even so, the Huios/Christ also gives life to whom He *wills* [Theiō – Jesus is the revelation of the mind of God to save lost humanity. This word means He personally, is the visible Deity of God to press into action what is decreed in heaven.]."

*Jesus said many times, you see Me you see God, and My actions of doing what only God can do prove the truth of my words.

Verses 22-23

"For the Father does not *judge* [Krino- to make a judicial distinction and pass sentence in a private manner unknown to man.] …anyone, but He *has given* [Didumŏs–the power of God to administer divine justice] …all *judgment* [Krisis - God made the judgment in heaven before creation that the wages of sin are death. He revealed His justice in the Huios/Christ, who took the sins of all humanity upon Himself (Passover) to nullify that judgment and declare His salvation to be "the gift of God is timeless life".] …to the Huios/Christ, in order that all may *honor* [Timaō – to fix a value upon a person.] …the Huios/Christ, even as they honor the Father. {God is one Deity in heaven and on the earth} He who does not honor the Huios/Christ does not honor the Father Who sent Him. The valuation of God the Father, God the Huios/Christ and God the Holy Spirit are due the same highest reverence for removing His judgment of death and replacing it with God's gift of His timeless Spiritual Life.

These verses emphasize the need of man to recognize the identity of God as One Single Spiritual Being Who created man a Spiritual Being in His image. He recreates His image of holiness by the power of His Mind {the Christ- Huios} to cleanse the mind of man {turn back to God by faith}; He restores man to His image by the authority of His Throne of Life {the Father} to give us a new spiritual identity as His own children; and the Holy Spirit {the breath of God} Who {1Corinthians 2:1-13} reveals the *Doxa* – true identity of both God and His regenerated children to be of One Mind.

John 5:24-27, Jesus reveals the power of God's salvation is to destroy the power of death that holds His children in the grave. This is the first resurrection revealed in this disclosure of God's Doxa.

"Truly, truly, I say to you, he who hears My word and *believes* [Pisteuō – to have a mental persuasion of what is truth] …Him Who sent Me, has [Aiōnios – the timeless life of God] …and does not come into judgment but has *passed out of death* [Metabainō Ek Thanatos- to moveout from under the earthly rule of death] ...*into life* [EisZōe – to move into the heavenly spiritual rule of God's Throne of Life]....Truly, truly, I say to you, *coming to you* [Ěrchōmai- a verb that designates present tense; God's kingdom rule of life has been moved to the earth to rule the mind of His redeemed children.]...*an hour* [Hōra–a Greek word that designates a definite point of time in human existence when an appointed action is to begin.] ...and now is, when the *dead* [Nĕkrŏs –the spiritual condition of unsaved humanity] ... shall hear the voice of the [Huios Theos – the Deity of God revealing His mind]; ...and those who *hear* [`Akŏuō - the sensational perception (understanding in the mind to believe what is said) that it is God's voice that is sounding] ...shall *live* [Zaō – to be spiritually alive; the same as the Deity of God is the living God.].

For just as the Father has life in Himself, even so He gave to the Huios/Christ also to have the timeless power of the Throne of Life in Himself; and He gave Him *authority* [Ěxŏusia – "it is lawful"; The Deity of God present in this world {the Christ}, has the legally endued power to reveal the identity of God in His heavenly rule.] ...to *execute* [Pŏiěō – 'to bring forth fruit`; *the power of Christ to regenerate the Spirit of God in human life originates from the Throne of God*] ...*judgment* [Krisis – the Divine act of distinguishing and separating holy spiritual life from physical life.] ...Jesus knows the mind of every human being because He is the Huios – Christ [Anthrōpŏs – Spiritual Deity of God ruling the mind of man; distinguishing him from animal life] ...Adam was created a physical being from the earth. He was given a Soul, which is the life of the body. This made him a living physical being. God breathed into him His Spirit, which made him a heavenly spiritual being {image of God} created for a timeless existence in God's presence as His children. Hebrews 1, The Christ is the Deity of God in His physical creation to regenerate unholy man to the holy image of God. The Spiritual Life from the Throne of God produces the holy character of God which is higher than the angels."

*To be given a spiritual birth from God is the first resurrection of God's children by His Holy Righteousness – the power of life that cannot die."

John 5:28-29, Jesus reveals the second resurrection will be the permanent separation of redeemed humanity from those who remain under the curse of death

"Do not marvel at this; for an *hour* [Hōra – the designated future time of the Apokalupsis of Christ to separate the sheep/wheat from the goats/tares] ...is coming in which all who are in the *tombs* [Mnēměiŏn– all of humanity is under the judgment of death; every human being will die] ...shall hear His voice and shall come forth; those who did the *good* [Agathŏs – something that *is* good; the good tree brings forth good fruit. God is called good because He is the only **Life** that is not under the rule of death; He brings forth good fruit {humanity restored to timeless life by the first resurrection}.] ... to a *resurrection of life* [Anastasis – The second resurrection is {Revelation 21-22} to permanently live with God in His heavenly presence and be of one mind with Him.]; ...those who *committed* [Prassō – to practice; to repeatedly, habitually act in a specific unchanging manner] ...*evil* [Phaulŏs – worthless, wicked; diametrically opposite of good] ... to a resurrection of *judgment* [Krisis – {Revelation 20:11-15} The Great White Throne judgment of God on spiritually dead humanity are thrown into the Lake of Fire.]."

John 5:30-47, Jesus reveals the fact that human beings deluded by the power of death will not believe God's revelation of His identity.

5:30-31, the witness of the Messiah:
"I can do nothing on My own *initiative* [Ĕmautŏu – to make one's self superior to all others. Jesus can do nothing apart from the total Deity of God.].

As I hear, I judge; My judgment {final judgment to pass sentence} is *just* [Dikaiosunē - the righteousness of God; the highest authority that can stand the test of life that cannot die] …because I do not seek My own *will [Thelêma - *This word requires a thorough explanation because it is expressing the mind of God. The (–ma) at the end of the word indicates that it is not the will of God, but the result of His will. The will of God is not a command, but the revelation that there is not even a trace of evil in Him (there is no death in God); there is only love for all life He creates. He finds great joy in what is done by His Deity {Creator, Huios/Christ, Holy Spirit} and in what should be done by all life created in His Image. Jesus is telling us that the God Who saves and the people who are saved are all one single unit in fulfilling the will of God.] …but the will of Him who sent Me. If I alone bear witness of Myself, my *testimony* [Marturia – that which anyone witnesses or states concerning a person or thing] …is not true."

The testimony of Jesus to reveal the [Doza –the true identity of God]; is that which He declares with the authority of the Deity Who knows the full truth and identity of God: The One Who sent Him into the world.

John 5:32-35, Jesus reveals to the Jews that God has revealed Himself to them through the prophets; but His word was rejected. He has revealed Himself through a spirit-filled prophet (John the Baptizer) and He is still rejected.

"There is another who bears witness of Me, and I know that the testimony which he bears of Me is true. You have sent to John, and he has borne witness to the truth. But the *witness* [Marturia–the testimony of God] …which I receive does not come from man, but I say these things that you may be *saved* [Sōzō – the spiritual and timeless salvation granted immediately by God to those who believe on Christ.]. …He (John) was the lamp that was burning and was *shining* [Phainomai- A message phenomenally presenting itself with no necessary assumption of any beholder at all; a light that is not visible to the mind because it is received only as a figment of the imagination; the truth of the message was not received as a reality. The Jews had created a Messiah in their minds that was not fulfilled by Jesus and He was not received as the true Messiah]. …and you were willing to *rejoice* [Ágailiaō - ecstatic joy and delight] …for a *while* [Hōra – a short time] …in his *light* [Phōsphŏrŏs – the illuminating truth John was preaching],"

John 5:36, Jesus' witness is not by words, but the works of God.
"But the *witness* [Marturia – the declarations of Jesus concerning Himself] …which I have is greater than that of John; for the *works* [Ergon – the miracles Christ demonstrated to reveal His identity of the true Messiah were actions that only God can do.] …which the Deity of Heaven has given Me to *accomplish* [Tekeuiō - actions stressing the actual accomplishment

God Reveals His Glory [Doxa – True Identity]

of the end in view] …the very works that I do; bear witness of Me, that the Deity of Heaven has sent Me."

Jesus raised Lazarus from the dead; but the Jews said He was not the Messiah because He could not save them from the Romans nor save Himself on the cross; and they did all they could to disprove His resurrection from the grave

John 5:37-38, the witness of the Heavenly Deity.
"And the Father who sent Me, He has borne witness of Me. You have neither *heard* [Akouō - to hearken, to understand, to hear with the ear of the mind to effectually perform or grant what is spoken] … His voice at any time, nor *seen* [Horaō – mental perception, pay attention, take heed of the presence of God; the Messiah.] …His form. And you do not have His *word* [Logos–intelligence, formulation of thoughtful expressions in the mind, what you hear with the ear has no meaning to you] …*abiding* [Menō - to remain, to endure, to persevere, to stand firm so as to remain alive] …in you for you do not believe Him whom He sent."

John 5:39-47, Witness of the Scripture.
"You search the Scriptures because you think that in them you have the timeless life of God; and it is these words that bear witness of Me; and you do not have the desire to come to Me that you may have *life* [Zōe – the identity of God Who is Spiritual Life and the creator of all life]….I do not receive *glory* [Doxa – recognition of the true identity of God] …from men; but I know you, that you do not have the *love* [Agapē – benevolence that belongs only to God. This love is given to God's children that they may reveal a true identity with Him.]. of God in yourselves. I have come in My Father's name and you do not receive Me; if another shall come in *his own name* [Idiōtēs – a person of power, i.e., priest, president, pope, teacher, rabbi, etc.] …you will receive him. How can you believe, when you receive *glory* [Doxa – recognition of true divinity] …from one another and you do not seek the *Doxa* [True identify of God] …that is from the one and only God? Do not think that I will *accuse* [Katēgoreō – to speak openly against] …you before the Father; the one who accuses you is Moses, in whom you have *set your hope* [Elpis – the expectation and confidence of future good fortune]. …For if you *believed* [Pisteuō – absolute mental persuasion] …Moses, you would believe in Me; for he wrote of Me. But if you do not believe his writings, how will you believe My words?"

*How many versions of the Bible have been written since the New Testament; that which was written by the disciples of Jesus? How many of them are true to God's inspired word? How many have been written in a multitude of languages simply to teach the precepts of men? These questions are immaterial! The real question is what Jesus revealed to the Jews. *Can you recognize the truth of God's Word by* **FAITH**? Do you believe the [Doxa – God's true identity] …. revealed in them? Do you believe what God reveals to you, personally?

Faith is a verb; your mental action to submit your mind and actions to Him to be converted to His living image in this world. Jesus revealed to the Jews that He is the Living Word of God in this world to speak to the minds of all humanity; and the Lord's Prayer reveals He is the Living Bread from heaven. He is the Temple of God that nourishes and sustains your Spirit to live in this material world to be Spiritual Children of God.

James V. Holland

The fifty-five events in Jesus' Galilean ministry reveal another challenge to the skeptical mind of man; do you believe what you see? Luke, chapter 7 reveals a variety of people's responses to Jesus' identity.

Luke 7:1-10

"When He had *completed* [Plēroō – (1) to fill the temple of God with incense to remove all spirits but the Spirit of God, (2) to fulfill a prophecy, (3) to fully explain the truth of God's identity, (4) to perform perfect obedience to the Law of God in His own person and fully enforce it as Doctrines of God.] …all His discourse in the hearing of the people, He went to Capernaum.

And a certain *centurion's* [Hěkatŏntarchŏs - the Roman captain of one hundred men] …*slave* [Doulos – one who is in a permanent relation of servitude to another] …who was highly regarded by him, was *sick* [Kakōs – at the point of death] …and about to die.

And when he heard about Jesus, he sent some Jewish *elders* [Presbus – respected representatives of Israel] …asking Him to come and save the life of his slave.

And when they had come to Jesus, they earnestly entreated Him, saying, 'He is worthy for You to grant this to him; for he *loves* [Agapaō– God's love toward man] …our *nation* [Ethnos – the people of God] …and it was he who built us our synagogue.'

Now Jesus started on His way with them; and when He was already not far from the house, the centurion sent friends, saying to Him, 'Lord, do not trouble Yourself further, for I am not worthy for You to come under my roof; for this reason, I did not even consider myself worthy to come to You, but just say the word and my servant will be healed.

For I, too, am a man under *authority* [Exousia – executive power which governs a nation], …with soldiers under me; and I say to this one, 'Go!' and he goes; and to another, "come!" and he comes; and to my slave, 'Do this!' and he does it.'

Now when Jesus heard this, he marveled at him, and turned and said to the multitude that was following Him, 'I say to you, not even in Israel have I found such great faith.' And when those who had been sent returned to the house, they found the slave in good health."

*This man's mind was governed by his insight of God's mind to love people. He had faith in God's authority to heal his servant simply by Jesus' commands.

Luke 7:11-23

"And it came about soon afterwards, that He went to a city called Nain; and His *disciples* [Mathētěs – an adherer; one who accepts instructions given to him and makes it his rule of conduct] …were going along with Him, accompanied by a large multitude.

Now as he approached the gate of the city, behold, a dead man was being carried out, the only son of his mother, and she was a widow; and a sizeable crowd from the city was with her.

And when the Lord saw her, He felt compassion for her, and said to her, 'Do not weep.' And He came up and touched the coffin; and the bearers came to halt. And He said, 'Young man, I say to you, arises!' And the dead man sat up and began to speak. And Jesus gave him back to his mother.

And *fear* [Phobos – reverence for God; yet with a sense of timidity] …gripped them all and they *began glorifying* [Doxazō – simply to recognize God's presence is brought to light] …God, saying, 'A great *prophet* [Prophētēs – this word was used of soothsayers who announced beforehand the will of the gods] …has arisen among us!' and 'God has *visited* [Episkeptomai –

God Reveals His Glory [Doxa – True Identity]

God is observing something; examining it closely] …His people!' And this *report* [Logos – to speak without saying anything intelligent or understanding] …concerning Him went out all over Judea, and in the entire surrounding district."

Luke 7:18-23

"And the disciples of John reported to him about all these things. And summoning two of his disciples, John sent them to the Lord, saying, 'Are You the *Coming One* [Erchomai – "He who is coming" is a title of the Messiah] …or do we look for someone else?'

And when the men had come to Him, they said, 'John the Baptist has sent us to You, saying, 'Are You the Coming One, or do we look for someone else?' At that very time He cured many people of diseases and afflictions and *evil* [Pŏnĕros – all the mischief in the world created by Satan] …spirits; and He *granted* [Charizomai – to be gracious to give a thing willingly as a gift] …sight to many who were blind.

And He answered and said to them, 'Go and *report* [Apaggellō – to carry word back] …to John what you have seen and heard: the blind receive sight, the lame walk, the lepers are cleansed, the deaf hear, the dead are raised up, the poor have the Gospel preached to them. And *blessed* [Makarios – possessing the characteristic of deity; the state of the believer in Christ] …is he who keeps from stumbling over Me."

Luke 7:24-35

"And when the messengers of John had left, He began to speak to the multitudes about John. 'What did you go out into the wilderness to look at? A reed shaken by the wind. But what did you go out to see? A man dressed in soft clothing. Behold, those who are splendidly clothed and live-in luxury are found in royal palaces.

But what did you go out to see? A *prophet* [Prophētēs – One who speaks openly before another and is the technical name for an interpreter of a divine message. The prophets in the pagan religions were called "soothsayers". Jesus revealed John was not a soothsayer, but one to whom God revealed His purpose for the Messiah was to reestablish man as a spiritual being of heaven with the full authority of life from the Throne of God.]? Yes, I say to you, and one who is *more* [Pĕrissŏtĕrŏs – superabundant in Godly character] …than a prophet. This is the one about whom it has been written:

Malachi 3:1

"Behold, I send My messenger before your face, who will prepare Your *way* [Hodos – the way of the Lord God, denoting the revealed will of God as the way leading to Him] …before You."

Luke 7:28-35

"I say to you, among those born of woman, there is no one greater than John (this phrase identifies John as a physical person serving God in this world of flesh); yet he who is least in the kingdom of God is greater than he (this phrase identifies every person who receives the Spirit of Life has the authority of the Lord God for His salvation; he/she is a spiritual being of heaven.).

And when all the people and the tax-gatherers heard this, they acknowledged God's *justice* [Dikaloō – this word means either to bring out the fact that a person is righteous, or if he is not, God will make him righteous.] …having been *baptized* [Baptizō –to be immersed in water to be identified with God by His purification of sin] …with the *baptism* [Baptisma- the result of having been baptized] …of John.

But the Pharisees and the *lawyers* [Nomikos – Pharisees and Scribes trained in the legal practice of law] …rejected God's *purpose* [Boulē–This word means to deliberate and reflect upon counsel given a person. The modern-day Greek Parliament is called Boulē.] …The Pharisees and Lawyers reflected upon God's *Will* [Thelêma – God's counsel to recognize His salvation and His urging to accept it; but would not.] …for themselves, not having been baptized by John.

"To what then shall I compare the men of this *generation* [Genea – a multitude of contemporaries in a particular space of time with reference to the spiritual state of society at that time.] …and what are they like?

They are like children who sit in the marketplace and call to one-another; and they say, 'We played the flute for you, and you did not dance; we sang a dirge, and you did not weep.'

For John the Baptist has come eating no bread and drinking no wine: and you say, 'He has a demon!' The Son of Man has come eating and drinking; and you say, 'Behold, a gluttonous man and a drunkard, a friend of tax-gatherers and sinners!'

Yet *wisdom* [Sophia–the knowledge of how to regulate one's relationship with God] …is *vindicated* [Dikaloō– God's justification of man to establish the righteousness of God (regeneration of the Spirit) by faith.]."

Luke 7:36-50

"Now one of the Pharisees was requesting Him to dine with him. And He entered the Pharisee's house and reclined at the table.

And behold, there was a woman in the city who was a *sinner* [Hamartōlos – a heinous and habitual sinner]; …and when she learned that He was reclining at the table in the Pharisee's house, she brought an alabaster vial of perfume. And standing behind Him at His feet, weeping she began to wet His feet with her tears and kept wiping them with the hair of her head, and kissing His feet and anointing them with the perfume.

Now when the Pharisee who had invited Him saw this, he said to himself, 'If this man were a prophet, He would know who and what sort of person this woman is who is touching Him that she is a sinner.'

And Jesus answered and said to him, 'Simon, I have something to say to you.' And he replied, 'Say it, Teacher.'

'A certain moneylender had two debtors: one owed five hundred denarii and the other fifty. When they were unable to repay, he graciously forgave them both. Which of them therefore will love him more?'

Simon answered and said, 'I assume the one whom he forgave more.' And He said to him, 'You have judged correctly.'

And turning toward the woman, He said to Simon, 'Do you see this woman? I entered your house; you gave Me no water for My feet, but she has wet My feet with her tears and wiped them with her hair. You gave Me no kiss. But she, since the time I came in has not ceased to kiss My feet. You did not anoint My head with oil, but she anointed My feet with perfume. For

God Reveals His Glory [Doxa – True Identity]

this reason, I say to you, her sins, which are many, have been forgiven; for she loved much. But he who is forgiven little, loves little.' And He said to her, 'Your sins have been forgiven.'

And those who were reclining at the table with Him began to say to themselves, 'Who is this man who even forgives sins?'

And He said to the woman, 'Your faith has saved you; go in peace.'"

***The scriptures reveal that even when people interact with the Deity of God, they cannot "see" Him; they cannot mentally believe in Him because of the darkness of death that rules the mind. At Bethsaida, Jesus fed five thousand people from two fish and five loaves of bread with twelve baskets left over. At Decapolis, He fed another four thousand people from seven loaves of bread and a few small fish; with seven baskets left over. But still people did not believe Him to be the Christ. All they wanted from Him was more free food.

Matthew 13:1-17

"On that day Jesus went out of the house and was sitting by the sea. And great multitudes gathered to Him so that He got into a boat and sat down, and the whole multitude was standing on the beach. And He spoke many things to them in _Parables_ [Parabolē - A comparison or simile in which spiritual things are compared to natural things. The spiritual things are concealed from the natural, carnal, inattentive minds of man because they are obscure in their heavenly nature.] …saying,

'Behold, the sower went out to sow; and as he sowed, some _seeds_ [Spŏrŏs – The revelation of God represented by the natural seed sown. Metaphorically, the gospel message of heaven is given to every human being]; …_fell_ [Piptō- came under judgment] …beside the _road_ [[Pâshat – a Hebrew word meaning 'to deploy in a hostile environment'.] The Greek text uses the word [Hŏdŏs - a natural path (made by man); a course of conduct; a way of thinking] …and it was trampled underfoot, and the birds of the air ate it up. {Luke 8:12, "And those beside the road are those who have heard; then the devil comes and takes away the word from their heart so that they may not believe and be saved."}

And other seed fell on _rocky places_ [Pĕtrōdĕs – hardened hearts, bitter minds] …where they did not have much soil; and immediately they sprang up because they had no depth of soil. But when the sun had risen, they were scorched; and because they had no root, they withered away. {Luke 8:13, "They believe for a while, and in time of temptation they fall away."}

And others fell among the _thorns_ [Akantha – a briar patch; something evil which inflicts pain] …and the thorns _came up_ [Anabainō – reasoning that troubles the mind /thoughts that are antagonistic towards God] … and _choked_ [Apŏpnigō – to stifle; prevent growth] …them out. {Luke 8:14: "they bring no fruit to maturity".}

And others fell on the good soil and yielded a crop, some a hundredfold, some sixty and some thirty. He who has ears, let him hear.'

And the disciples came and said to Him, 'Why do You speak to them in parables?'

And He answered and said to them, 'To you it has been granted to know the _mysteries_ [Mustēriōn – to shut the mouth; silence imposed by initiation into religious rites; knowledge outside the range of unassisted natural apprehension; which is known only by Divine revelation and known only in a manner and time appointed by God, and only to those who are illumined by His Spirit.] …of the *kingdom* [Basilĕia – an abstract noun denoting sovereignty, royal power and dominion of Deity] …of heaven, but to them it has not been granted.

For whoever has, to him shall more be given, and he shall have *abundance* [Pĕrissĕuō – to super abound in quality and quantity]; …but whoever does not have, even what he has shall be taken away from him.

Therefore, I speak to them in parables; because while *seeing* [Blĕpō – verb; to have bodily sight] …they do not *see* [Blĕpō - noun; perception] …and while *hearing* [Akŏē– verb; the act of hearing] …they do not *hear* [Akŏē– the sense of understanding what is heard] … nor do they understand. And in their case the *prophecy* [Prŏphēteia – prediction] …of Isaiah 6:9-10, is being *fulfilled* [Anapiĕrŏō – to completely occupy the mind. Thessalonians 2:10-16 fulfills this prophecy of Isaiah.].

You will keep on hearing but will not understand; and you will keep on seeing but will not perceive; for the heart of this people has become *dull* [Pachunō - stupefied; callous], …and with their ears they scarcely hear, and they have closed their eyes lest they should see with their eyes and hear with their ears and understand with their heart and *return* [Ĕpistrĕphō– revert; convert; turn about in a reverse direction – a deliberate and voluntary act of conviction in response to the presentation of truth.] …and I shall *heal* [Iaŏmai– to make whole; healing of the heart and mind to act as a spiritual being.] …them.

But *blessed* [Makariŏs – fortunate; happy] …are your eyes because they see; and your ears because you hear. For *truly* [Amēn – trustworthy; sure; absolute truth] …I say to you that many prophets and *righteous* [Dikaiŏsunē – justified equality of God's character] …men *desired* [Dŏulĕia – to make one-self a slave; to serve God as the Master over their lives] …to see what you see and did not see it; and to hear what you hear and did not hear it.'"

LAST JUDEAN AND PEREAN MINISTRY C. A.D. 29-30 (42 Events)

John 8:12-59, Jesus reveals He is the light of the world to unbelieving Jews.
"Again, therefore Jesus spoke to them (He had just forgiven a woman caught in adultery), saying, 'I am the *light* [Phōs – to shine, to reveal, to make evident; revelations to the mind to see spiritual things {Luke 16:9, believers who receive a spiritual revelation from God for a New Spiritual Birth and have the mental capacity to live as spiritual beings – are called "sons of light}. In this verse, Jesus is the light which illuminates the minds of men to see God.] …of the *world* [Thanatŏō - The impenetrable darkness of death. Jesus is the only light of heavenly truth that can penetrate this darkness.]; …he who *follows* [Akŏlŏuthĕō – verb; accompanies, joins in union with a group; metaphorically; discipleship, to be of the same mind] …Me shall not walk in the *darkness* [Skŏtia – immoral darkness of death; emblematic of sin or spiritual depravity], …but shall have the light of *life* [Zōē – the timeless life of God that cannot die].'

The Pharisees therefore said to Him, 'You are bearing witness of Yourself, Your *witness* [Marturia – noun; evidence, testimony, what is put on record] …is not true.'

Jesus answered and said to them, 'Even if I bear witness of Myself, my witness is true; for I know where I come from, and where I am going; but you do not know where I come from, nor where I am going. You people *judge* [Krinō – to subject to censure] …according to the *flesh* [Sarx – the carnal nature of the body]; …I am not judging anyone. But even if I do *judge* [Krisis – a decision of divine justice] …My judgment is true; for I am not alone in it, but I and He {the

God Reveals His Glory [Doxa – True Identity]

Deity in heaven} …Who sent Me. Even in your *law* [Nōmōs – Mosaic Law that governed the actions of natural man. {God is subject only to the rule of righteousness}.] …it has been written that the testimony {Marturia} of two men is true. I am He {Christ} who bears witness of Myself, and the Father {Deity ruling the Heavenly Throne of Life}, Who sent Me bears witness of Me.'

And so, they were saying to Him, 'Where is Your Father?' Jesus answered, 'You know neither Me, nor My Father; if you knew Me, you would know My Father also.'

These words He spoke in the treasury as He taught in the temple; and no one seized Him because His *hour* [Hōra– a point in chronological time when an appointed action is to begin.] …had not yet come.

He said therefore again to them, 'I go away, and you shall seek Me, and shall *die* [Apothlilō – the natural death of the physical body] …in your *sin* [Hamartia – all of humanity, Jews and Gentiles are under God's judgment that "all men are sinners"] … where I am going, you cannot come.'

Therefore, the Jews were saying, 'surely He will not kill Himself, will He, since He says, 'Where I am going, you cannot come.'

And He was saying to them, 'You are from below, I am from *above* [Anō– that which is above; the heavens]; …you are from below. I am from above {heaven}; you are of this *world* [Kŏsnŏs – the created earth; the place of death; the condition of human affairs in alienation from God.]. …I am not of this world. I said therefore to you, that you shall die in your sins; for unless you believe that I am He (the Christ – Messiah) you shall die in your sins.'

And so, they were saying to Him, 'Who are You?' Jesus said to them, 'What have I been saying to you from the beginning? I have many things to speak and to judge concerning you, but He who sent Meis *true* [Alēthēs–not hidden; true to fact] …and the things which I heard from Him, these I speak to the world.'

They did not realize that He had been speaking to them about the Deity of Heaven. Jesus therefore said, 'When you lift up the [Huios – Christ/Messiah on the cross], then you will know that I am He, and I do nothing on My own initiative, but I speak these things as the God of Heaven *taught Me* [Didaskō – caused to give instruction (teach earthly man heavenly things)] …And He who sent Me is with Me; He has not left Me alone, for I always do the things that are pleasing to Him.'

As He spoke these things, many came to *believe* [Pistĕuō – to have faith in Him; to entrust their spiritual life to the timeless care of God] …in Him. Jesus therefore was saying to those Jews, who had believed in Him,

'If you abide in My *word* [Lŏgŏs – Jesus is the spoken revelation of the mind of God and the visible reality of God's salvation by redemption. He reveals the will of God to save human life is to turn him back to God with a genuine repentant heart. God knows the mind of every human being so the commitment must endure for the entire lifetime(abide) of that person.] …then you are truly *disciples* [Mathētēs – a learner; one who reveals he is a believer by adhering to the Deity of God] …of Mine; and you shall know the *truth* [Alētheia – the reality lying at the basis of an appearance; *the truth of the gospel reveals the perversion of it*], …and the truth shall make you *free* [Ĕlĕuthĕrŏō – to be made free, delivered from bondage to death, sin, corruption and bondage to the Law].'

They answered Him, 'We are Abraham's *offspring* [Spĕrma – (Plural) natural born physical children (descendants) of Abraham] ` ...and have never yet been enslaved to anyone; how is it that You say, 'You shall become free'?

Jesus answered them, 'Truly, truly, I say to you, everyone who commits sin is the slave of sin. And the slave does not remain in the house forever {people die}; the Christ does remain forever. If therefore the Christ shall make you free, you shall be free indeed.

I know that you are Abraham's offspring; yet you seek to put Me to death because My word has no place in you.

I speak the things which I have seen with the Father in Heaven; therefore, you also do the things which you heard from your father.'

They answered and said to Him, 'Abraham is our father.' Jesus said to them, 'If you are Abraham's children, do the deeds of Abraham.

But as it is, you are seeking to put Me to death, the Christ who has told you the truth which I heard from the Deity of Heaven; this Abraham did not do.

You are doing the deeds of your father.' They said to Him, 'We were not born of fornication; we have one Father, even God.'

Jesus said to them, 'If God were your Father you would love Me; for I proceeded forth and have come from the Deity of Heaven; for I have not even come on My own initiative, but He sent Me.

Why do you not understand what I am saying? It is because you cannot hear My word.

You are of your father the devil and you want to do the desires of your father. He was a murderer from the beginning and does not stand in the truth because there is no truth in him. Whenever he speaks a lie he speaks from his own nature, for he is a liar and the father of lies.

But because I speak the truth, you do not believe Me. Which one of you convicts Me of sin? If I speak truth, why do you not believe Me?

He who is of God *hears* [Akŏē – understanding in the mine what is heard with the ears] ...the words of God; for this reason, you do not hear them, because you are not of God.'

The Jews answered and said to Him, 'Do we not say rightly that You are a Samaritan and have a demon?'

Jesus answered, 'I do not have a demon; but I honor the Deity of Heaven, and you dishonor Me. But I do not seek My *glory* [Dŏxa – the true identity of Jesus is the Deity come from heaven.]; ...there is One who seeks and judges. Truly, truly, I say to you, if anyone keeps My word, he shall never *see* death [Thĕōrĕō - (noun), to look on death as a spectator; it is used in this verse as a (verb), to experience death.].'

The Jews said to Him, 'Now we know that You have a demon. Abraham died and the prophets also; and you say, 'If anyone keeps My word, he shall never taste of death. `

'Surely You are not greater than our father Abraham, who died? The prophets died too; whom do You make Yourself out to be?'

Jesus answered, 'If I glorify Myself, my glory is nothing; it is the Deity of Heaven who glorifies Me, of whom you say, 'He is our God`.

And you have not come to know Him, but I know Him; and if I say that I do not know Him, I shall be a liar like you, but I do know Him, and keep His word.

Your father Abraham rejoiced to see My day, and he saw it and was glad.'

God Reveals His Glory [Doxa – True Identity]

The Jews therefore said to Him, 'You are not yet fifty years old, and have You seen Abraham?'

Jesus said to them, 'Truly, truly, I say to you, before Abraham was born, I Am.'

Therefore, they picked up stones to throw at Him; but Jesus hid Himself and went out of the temple."

John 9:1-41, Jesus continued to reveal His identity to the Jews when He healed a man born blind.

"And as He passed by, He saw a man blind from birth. And His disciples *asked* [Ĕrōtaō – To interrogate; to expect and answer.]….saying, 'Rabbi, who sinned, this man or his parents, that he should be born blind?'

*This word is important to the scriptures because there are two words used for asking a question. {1} Ĕrōtaō - the petitioner is on a footing of equality or familiarity that lends authority to the request. Jesus always used this word when speaking to the Heavenly Deity. (1a) A king making a request from another king. (1b) The Pharisee who desired Christ to eat with him; indicating the superior conception he had to Christ. {2} Aiteo- The attitude of one who is lesser in position; men asking something of God. Matthew 7:7, "Aiteo and it shall be given you." (2a) a child to a parent, (2b) a subject to a king, (2c) the High Priest to Pilate asking for the crucifixion of Christ, (2d) Martha speaking to Christ.

Jesus answered, 'It was neither that this man sinned, nor his parents; but it was in order that the works of God might be *displayed* [Phanĕrŏō– To render what is apparent; to reveal what is concealed and invisible.] …in him. * The Phaneroo is the work of the Holy Spirit to reveal to unbelievers the truth that Jesus is the Christ – Messiah, heavenly Deity.

We must *work* [Ĕrgazŏmai– to toil as an occupation; to have the effect of engaging the blind man is the occupation of God] …the works of Him who sent Me, as long as it is *day* [Hēmĕra – (noun) the light of God revealing His salvation to lost humanity]. *Night* [the darkness of death] …is coming when no man can work. While I am in the world, I am the *light* [Phos – the truth revealed by the Deity of Heaven] …of the world.'

*Christ is the only truth that can penetrate the darkness of spiritual death controlling the human mind and enables people to know Him. Christians / Spiritual Israelites; spiritual descendants of Abraham, Isaac and Jacob, continue to do this work of God; they carry God's message of salvation (His light bearers) until the end of this age of God's redemption.

When He had said this, He spat on the ground and made clay of the saliva and applied the clay to the eyes and said to him, 'Go, *wash* [Niptō – cleanse the eyes] …in the pool of *Siloam The meaning of this word is *Sent* [Apŏstĕllō – the combination of two words meaning "set apart". God directed Jesus to go to this appointed place. He was sent by the Father to; "set apart" a man born physically blind.] … And so, the man went away and cleansed the eyes and came back seeing – both physically and spiritually. *All people are born spiritually blind. Only God can enable people to "see" Him; to know His identity.

The neighbors, therefore, and those who previously saw him as a beggar, were saying, 'Is not this the one who used to sit and *beg* [Prŏsaitĕo – to earnestly and continuously plead for help]?' Others were saying, 'This is he,' still others were saying, 'No, but he is like him.'

He kept saying, 'I am the one.' Therefore, they were saying to him, 'How then were your eyes opened?' He answered, 'The man who is called Jesus made clay and anointed my eyes, and said to me, "Go to Siloam and cleanse your eyes"; so, I went away and cleansed my eyes and I *received sight* [Anablĕpō– verb; looked up to heaven; spiritual awareness of the presence of God. He was given both physical and spiritual sight].' And they said to him, 'Where is He?' and he said, 'I do not *know* [Ĕido – a primary verb used only in the past tense; to know by perception`].

They brought him who was formerly blind to the Pharisees.

Now it was a Sabbath on the day when Jesus made the clay and opened his eyes.

Again, therefore, the Pharisees also were asking (Ĕrōtaō) him how he received his sight. And he said to them, 'He applied clay to my eyes, and I cleansed them, and I see.'

Therefore, some of the Pharisees were saying, 'This man is not from God, because He does not *keep* [Tērĕō – to fulfill the commandments; to watch over, preserve the commandments; give heed to the commandments.] ...the Sabbath.' But others were saying, 'How can a man who is a *sinner* [Hamartōlŏs – an adjective denoting a heinous and habitual sinful character] ...perform such *signs* [Sēmĕiŏn – revelations of divine authority and power]?' ...And there was a division among them.

They said therefore to the blind man again, 'What do you say about Him, since He opened your eyes?' And he said, 'He is a *prophet* [Prŏphētēs – A proclaimer of a divine message. This would be impossible to the thinking of these Jews, so to them Jesus was nothing but a "sooth-sayer".].'

The Jews therefore did not believe it of him; that he had been blind and had received sight, until they called the parents of the very one who had received his sight. And they questioned (Ĕrōtaō) them, saying, 'Is this your son, who you say was born blind? Then how does he now see?'

His parents answered them and said, 'We know that this is our son and that he was born blind; but how he now sees, we do not know; or who opened his eyes, we do not know. Ask him; he is of age; he shall speak for himself.'

His parents said this because they were afraid of the Jews; for the Jews had already agreed that if anyone should *confess* [Hōmōlŏgĕō – to declare openly by way of speaking out freely the deep conviction of facts.] ...Him to be Christ, he should be put out of the synagogue [Apŏsunagōgŏs – excommunicated; expelled from attendance of the synagogue and from all fellowship with Israelites.] ...For this reason, his parents said, 'He is of age; ask him.'

So, a second time they called the man who had been blind and said to him, 'Give *glory* [Dŏxa– God's self-manifestation of His true identity] ...to God; we know that this man is a sinner.' He therefore answered, 'Whether He is a sinner, I do not know; one thing I do know, that whereas I was blind, now I see.'

They said therefore to him, 'What did He do to you? How did He open your eyes?' He answered them, 'I told you already and you did not listen; why do you want to hear it again? You do not want to become His disciples too, do you?'

God Reveals His Glory [Doxa – True Identity]

And they *reviled* [Lōidŏrĕō – to abuse, ranting slander] ...him and said, 'You are His disciple, but we are disciples of Moses. We know that God has spoken to Moses; but for this man we do not know where He is from.'

The man answered and said to them, 'Well, here is an amazing thing that you do not know where He is from, and yet He opened my eyes (both physically and spiritually). We know that God does not *hear* [Akŏuō – God hears and answers the prayers of repentant minds, but not the voices of belligerent sinners] ...sinners; but if anyone is God-fearing and does His will, He hears him. Since the beginning of time, it has never been heard that anyone opened the eyes of a person born blind. If this man were not from God, He could do nothing.'

*Jesus set this man apart to identify Himself as the potter Who molded Adam from the dust of the earth. He gave him a soul, the life of the body with physical sight. Then He breathed into him God's Spirit of life. He was made for this purpose; to not only see God, but to live as a heavenly creation.

They answered and said to him, 'You were born entirely in sins [this was the Jews way of saying he was born physically blind as God's judgment upon an illegitimate birth], and you are teaching us?' And they put him out [excommunicated him].

Jesus heard that they had put him out; and finding him, He said, 'Do you believe in the Deity of God -Theos?' *The New American Standard Bible changed the word – Theos; to Anthropos – "Deity of Man – the Christ".

He answered and said, 'And who is He, Lord, that I may believe in Him?'

Jesus said to him, 'You have both *seen* [Hŏrasis – noun; vision, to look upon in physical appearance] ...Him, and He is the One who is talking with you.' (Spiritual vision of God.)

And he said, 'Lord, I believe.' And he *worshiped* Him [Prŏskunĕō – prostrated himself in adoring reverence and continually kissed His hand – as the angels do in heaven].

And Jesus said, 'For *judgment* [Krima – noun; judicial decision for or against man's unbelief or his belief] ...I came into this world, that those who do not see (spiritual blindness – no knowledge of God)may see(eyes cleansed of the darkness of death to believe in God by faith – activity of the mind); and that those who see (self-justification; activity of the mind to deny the identity of Jesus)may become blind (spiritual darkness – unable to see the Doxa of God – under the judgment of death).'

Those of the Pharisees who were with Him heard these things and said to Him, 'We are not blind too, are we?' (Spiritual darkness - ignorant of the identity of Jesus)

Jesus said to them, 'If you were blind (spiritual darkness; no knowledge of God) you would have no *sin* [Hamartia – moral deviation; rejection of God]; ...but since you say, 'We see (the sin of self-justification and rejection of the Person of God), your sin *remains* [Mĕnō – to stay in a given place; an unchangeable relationship to God].'"

John 10:1-42, Jesus continued His heavenly work by revealing to these Jews that God's salvation is through Him; by His light of truth, they will not be spiritually blind. All their work of self-justification is in vain. He taught them with the parable of the Good Shepherd.

"Truly, truly, I say to you, he who does not enter by the door {Christ – the Messiah is the Deity of God Who gives man access to heaven. This door is open until the last person who will be redeemed; enters that door.} ... into the *fold of the sheep* [Aulē – an uncovered space around a palace; this is the illustration that the Throne of God is the permanent place of safe-keeping from the power of death that works in the night to do the work of Satan and false teachers.], ... but climbs up some other way, he is a *thief* [Klĕptēs – one who habitually steals by deception; from root word, {Klĕptō – kleptomaniac}] ...and a *robber* [Lēstēs – one who plunders openly and by violence].

But He who enters by the door is a sheep of the shepherd. To him the *doorkeeper* [Thurŏrŏs – *Thura*; a portal or entrance, and *Ŏurŏs*; a watcher; a gate-warden; a guardian. God **is** the door into heaven **and** the guardian of the door, because He owns the sheep. He bought them with a price, and He is responsible for their welfare.] ...opens and the sheep *hear* [Akŏuō – the sensational perception that the Lord's voice is sounding and what He says is not only to be understood but obeyed.] ...His voice and He call His sheep by name {God deals with every person individually; His salvation is a personal and intimate relationship}, and *leads them out* [Ĕxagō– Ĕx – the point of origin from whence motion or action proceeds – the darkness of death; and Agō – to bring out. God's salvation brings every individual person out of the darkness of death into the light of heaven.].

When He passes in front (reveals Himself) to all His own, He goes before (leads the way in the path of God's righteousness) them and the sheep *follow* [Akŏlŏuthĕō –to be in union, likeness, disciple; {John 8:31-32}] ...Him because they know His voice. And a stranger they simply will not follow but will flee from him because they do not know the voice of strangers.'

This *figure of speech* [Parŏimia– parable; graphic illustration.] ...Jesus spoke to them, but they did not understand what those things were which He had been saying to them.

Jesus therefore said to them again, 'Truly, truly, I say to you, I am the door of the sheep. All who came before Me are thieves {kleptomaniacs} and robbers {pillagers}, but the sheep did not hear {comprehend what they hear} them *{sheep without a shepherd}.

I am the door; if anyone enters through Me, he shall be *saved* [Sōzō – Safe, made whole, healed; spiritual and timeless salvation granted immediately by God to those who believe by faith on the Lord Jesus Christ; God's power to deliver from bondage to death; cleansed to be righteous as God is righteous.] ...and shall *go in* (the good shepherd lives with his sheep; he keeps them safe by night by his watch care from the powers of darkness) ... and *go out* (the good shepherd leads his sheep by the light of day; for the sheep to keep him in their sight) ...*to find* [Hĕuriskō – to obtain by perception true spiritual food for spiritual health] ...*pasture* [Nŏmŏ–spiritual food for spiritual health *sheep will drink dirty water and eat poisonous things that cause gangrene. People will follow false teachers with false doctrines that do the same thing to their spiritual health.].

The thief comes only to steal, and kill and *destroy* [Apollumi – destroy fully; to perish; to be lost to God; spiritual ruin; damnation]. ...I came that they might have *life* [Zōē – life as God has in Himself; timeless spiritual Deity] ...and have it *abundantly* [Pĕrissŏs – immeasurable in quantity; highest superiority in quality.].

I am the good shepherd; the good shepherd lays down His *life* [Psuchē – the soul; the life of the physical body; God's Passover] ...for the sheep.

He who is a hireling and not a shepherd, who is not the owner of the sheep, *beholds* [Thĕōrĕō – noun; spectator, to view physically with the eyes. *Verb*; to look at, gaze on, a careful observation with interest.] ...the wolf coming, and leaves the sheep, and flees, and the wolf

God Reveals His Glory [Doxa – True Identity]

snatches [Harpazō – to suddenly take by force. The wolf does not take sheep to save them; but to viciously destroy] ...them and scatters them. He flees because he is a hireling and is not *concerned* [Mĕlō – third person singular used impersonally; not even give them a thought.] ...about the sheep.

I am the good shepherd; and I *know My own* [Ginōskō – this word is used many times in scripture; its basic meaning is to have absolute, infinite knowledge possible only with God.] ...and My own *know* (same word) Me, even as the Father *knows* (same word) Me and I *know* (same word) the Father; and I lay down My life (Soul – the life of the body under God's judgment of death) for the sheep.

And I have *other* [Allŏs – a numerical difference denoting another of the same kind.] ...sheep, which are not of *this* [Tauta – plural; these things] ...*fold* [Aulē – temple worship; the inner courtyard of the temple. The Jews worshipped God in the Holy of Holies with the sacrifice of the blood of animals.] ...Jesus is telling the Jews that the redeemed gentile Christians (the outer court) and the Jews are both God's sheep (the inner courts and the outer courts are the same temple and the same people redeemed by His blood.]; ...I must bring them also, and they (redeemed Jews and Gentiles) shall hear My voice; and they shall become one flock with one shepherd. *In Christ; all redeemed human beings are holy (sanctified) children of God.

For this reason, the Father loves Me, because I lay down My life that I may take it again. No one has taken it away from Me, but I lay it down on My own initiative. I have *authority* [Ĕxŏusia – ability, capacity, freedom, right, liberty, strength and power of the will and commands that must be obeyed.] ...to lay it down, and I have authority to take it up again. This command I received from the Throne of God.

There arose a division again among the Jews because of these words. And many of them were saying, 'He has a demon and is insane. Why do you listen to Him?` Others (Allŏs– Jews in this same group) were saying, 'These are not the sayings of one demon possessed. A demon cannot open the eyes of the blind, can he?` "

*There are two Greek words for this English word *other*. Jesus used the word (Allŏs) in this verse to clarify to the Jews that redeemed Gentiles and Jews are the same holy people to God. The word (Heteros) expresses a qualitative difference denoting another of a different kind.

Jesus was telling these Jews that the Messiah came into this world of death to make atonement for the whole human race. He is the Deity of God to surrender His physical life to death {God' Passover} and raise Himself from the grave. The purpose for God's Passover Sacrifice is to remove His judgment of the power of death which holds humanity in the grave. Every human being who surrenders this physical life of death to God by faith (the power of the mind to die to self) will, through Him; by His heavenly authority, be restored to God's timeless Spiritual Life that cannot die.

John 10: 22-42, Jesus continues His heavenly work to assert His identity as the Deity of God.
"At that time the *Feast of the Dedication* [Egkainia – A compound word meaning the renewal of a religious service. The Feast of the Dedication became the identity of the annual eight-day feast beginning on the 25th of Chisleu (middle of December) instituted by Judas Maccabaeus, 164 B.C.; to commemorate the cleaning of the Temple from the pollutions of Antiochus Epiphanes. Hence it was called the Feast of Dedication. This feast could be celebrated

anywhere. The lighting of lamps was a prominent feature; hence it is also called "Feast of Lights".] ...took place at Jerusalem; it was winter, and Jesus was *walking* [Pĕripatĕō - a compound word meaning to tread around to the public to be seen; to deport oneself in a manner as proof to His true identity] ... in the *temple* [Himatismŏs – a compound word meaning dressed in costly or stately raiment, the apparel of kings.] ...in the portico of Solomon. The Jews therefore gathered around Him and were saying to Him, 'How long will You keep us in suspense? If You are the Christ, tell us plainly.'

Jesus answered them, 'I told you, and you do not *believe* [Pistĕuō – to be persuaded to place confidence in, to trust in, to commit to one's trust] ...the works that I do in God's name, these *bear witness* [Martŭrĕō – to testify as a witness; to affirm the truth of the words.] ...of Me. But you do not believe, because you are not of My sheep.

My sheep *hear* [Akŏuō – to understand in the mind what is heard by the ears] ...My voice, and I *know* [Ginōskō – absolute, infinite knowledge possible only with God] ...them, and they *follow* [Akŏlŏuthĕō – to identify self as one with another one; disciples] ...Me; and I give [Aiōniŏs – timeless] ... [Zōē – spiritual life of God] ...to them, and they shall never *perish* [Apŏllumi – lose the spiritual life given by God] ...and *no way*{*nothing*}[ŏumē – a double negative meaning "nothing is able at all"] ...shall *pluck* [Harpazō– to take something by force to destroy it.] ...them out of My hand.

The God of heaven, who has given them to Me, is greater than all; and *no way* (*nothing*) is able to pluck them out of God's hand. I and *My Father* [Pater – `Ĕlôhîym; the creator of all life rules from His Throne of Life.] ...are *One* [Hĕis – the first cardinal numeral; one - multiplied to infinity. Jesus: the Huios/Christ, is the same Deity of Heaven present in this darkness of death to permanently destroy this spiritual power and restore His timeless Spiritual Life to man created to be the heavenly children of God.].`

The Jews took up stones again to stone Him.

Jesus answered them again, 'I showed you many good works from God, for which of them are you stoning Me?`

The Jews answered Him. 'For a good work we do not stone You, but for *blasphemy* [Blasphēmia – vilification of God; evil speaking against God; defamatory speech of the Divine Majesty]; ...because You, being a man, make Yourself out to be God.'

Jesus answered them, 'It is written (Psalm 82:6) in your *Law* [Nŏmŏ– from Nĕmō; regulations parceled out to Moses and the Prophets] ... "I said you are *Gods* ['Ĕlôhiym – plural; meaning not God Himself, but His divine image] ...and all of you are *sons* [Bēn – son of a builder; from Bânâh – to replenish one's house with children] ...of the Most High." If he {Moses} called them Gods, to whom the word of God came and the *Scripture* [Graphē–the entire holy document written by the inspiration of God to reveal Himself to man] ...cannot be *broken* [Luō -to reject the authority of commandments rendering them not binding.] ...do you say of Him, whom the Father sanctified and sent into the world, "You are blaspheming," because I said, "I am the [Huios- One and the Same Deity of Heaven]?"

If I do not do the works of God, do not believe Me; but if I do them, though you do not believe Me, believe the works that you may know and understand that God is in Me, and I am in God.'

Therefore, the Jews were seeking again to seize Him, and He eluded their grasp. And He went away again beyond the Jordan to the place where John was first baptizing, and He was staying there. And many came to Him and were saying, 'While John performed no miracle, yet everything John said about this man was true.' And many believed in Him there."

Jesus concentrated His final revelation of His Doxa upon the personal relationship of His disciples to the Deity of God in heaven; their relationship to each other; and their relationship to the world. It is still critical to Jesus for His disciples of all the ages to fully comprehend the reality of what it means to be given the timeless Spiritual Life of God's Throne; the identity of His heavenly spiritual beings who are superior to the angels.

Jesus began His teaching with this new concept of His identity. Up to this point the disciples knew Him as a Rabbi and a religious teacher. Along with the Pharisees, they struggled with the deeper concept that Jesus really was the promised Messiah. He changed that by opening their eyes to the fact that they were standing in the presence of the Deity of Heaven. Even this truth did not fully convince them; it was not until their final encounter with Jesus (John 21) that the Holy Spirit was able to move them from being simply believers, to achievers – the transformation of their minds to be one mind with God's mind. The importance of this truth is lost to people who go through the motion of becoming a Christian; but continue to live as a person under the control of death.

John 14:1-31, the Spiritual Oneness of God.
"Let not your _heart_ [Kardia – the chief organ of physical and spiritual life; it stands for man's entire mental and moral nature.] …be troubled; believe in God, believe also in Me.

In God's _house_ [Ŏikia – Heaven is the entire estate of God's dwelling place.] …are many _dwelling places_ [Mŏnē – residence; heaven is the residence of all spiritual beings; God, children of God and angels. "Mansion" comes from the English word "manse", the dwelling place of a minister.] …if it were not so, I would have told you; for I go to prepare a place for you. And if I go and prepare a place for you, I will come again and receive you to Myself; that where I am, there you will be also. And you _know_ [Ĕidō – know by perception of God's mind] …the way where I am going.

Thomas said to Him, 'Lord, we do not know where You are going; how do we know the way?'

Jesus said to him, 'I am the _way_ [Hŏdŏs – the personification of Deity as the means of access to God and heaven], …and the _truth_ [Alēthĕia – the reality of the basis of an appearance; the revealed veritable essence of Deity], …and the _life_ [Zōē – the absolute purity of the holiness of Deity; this is what God created man to be]; …no one comes to God {All human life has its existence as a creation of God} …but _through Me_ {Jesus is the Deity of Heaven Who removed the curse of death on man so he can be restored to the spiritual life of God by the will of God}.

If you had _known_ [Ginōskō – No man can have a true understanding of God's identity by his own mind. By the power of His Spirit {I Corinthians 2}, God reveals Himself to the mind of man. It is up to each individual human being to believe the truth by the God given authority of faith – the will of the mind.] …Me, you would have known God; from now on you know Him and have seen Him.'

Philip said to Him, 'Lord, show us the Father and it is enough for us`.

Jesus said to him, 'Have I been so long with you, and yet you have not come to know Me, Philip? He who has seen Me has seen the Father (Creator of all life); how do you say, "Show us the Father"?

Do you not believe that I am in the Father, and the Father is in Me? The *words* [Rhĕma– scripture verses which reveal the mind of God to love man and redeem him {gospel message of salvation and judgment}.] ...that I say to you I do not speak on My own initiative, but the Heavenly Deity abiding in Me does His works. Believe Me that I am in the Father, and the Father in Me; otherwise believe on account of the works themselves.

Truly, truly, I say to you, he who believes in Me, the works that I do shall He do also; and greater works than these shall He do, because I go to the Father. And whatever you ask in *My name* [Ŏnŏma – the name Christ speaks on equal authority of God because they are *Heis* – one and the same Deity, just as Jesus (the Name) is the *Huios* – one and the same Deity of heaven] ...that will I do, that the Father may be *glorified* [Dŏxazō – God reveals His true identity as the Kingdom of Life; the light of His holiness; all that He is.] ...in the [Huios – the Living God of heaven made visible to man.]

If you *ask* [Aitĕō – a humble petition by a human being honoring the majesty of God.] Me anything in My name, I will do it. If you *love* [Agapaō – Love Christ with the love He has for the Father and the Father has for Him. This word identifies Jesus, the Father/Creator of all life, the Holy Spirit and redeemed Man; are all one and the same heavenly Spiritual Beings of Timeless Life with the Mind of God. *This is the perfect heaven (Revelation 21-22) God will create when He has destroyed death so that it can never exist again and will not even be a memory in the human mind.] ...Me, you will keep My commandments {the ten articles of God's heavenly constitution to govern His people on earth}.

And I will *ask* [Ĕrŏtaō–to speak to the Father on equal footing.] ...the Father and He will give you another (Allŏs) *Helper* [Paraklētŏs – The Holy Spirit of God does not exalt Himself, but is the authority of God to continue the work of Christ on earth to lead God's children in the daily maturing of their minds to worship God, and to undergo trials and persecutions. The Spirit reveals the mind of God to the mind of man; the truth of Christ's identity to the minds of lost humanity for their salvation]. ...that He may be with you [Aiōn – In relationship to God, this word means the timeless rule of Spiritual Life. In relationship to man, it means the unbroken duration of this present Messianic age of salvation until every person is saved who will be saved. The emphasis of this word is not on the length of chronological time, but on what takes place in this period of time for the regeneration of spiritual life in the human being.]; ...that is the *Spirit* [Pnĕuma – The Holy Spirit of God; the unseen breath of God that is His divine movement of light upon the power of darkness;] ...of truth, whom the world cannot receive, because it does not behold Him or know Him, but you *know* [Ginōskō–to have the mind of God to understand spiritual things] ...Him because He abides with you, and He will be within you.

I will not leave you as orphans; I will come to you. After a little while the world will *behold* [Thĕōrĕō – be a spectator] ...Me no more; but you will *behold* {to perceive one's identity; to enjoy one's presence} ...Me; because I live, you shall live also. In that day you shall know that I AM the Deity of heaven {*Hĕis* – one single spiritual Deity}, and you in Me {*Hēn* – one with Christ with His essence of Deity} and I in you {Hēn – one with man with the essence of the holiness of Deity.}.   *Revelation 22, the New Jerusalem from heaven.

He who has My commandments and _keeps_ {lives by} them, he it is who _loves_ {the essential nature of God} Me; and he who loves Me shall be loved by God, and I will love him, and will disclose Myself to him."

John 15:1-11, God empowers His spiritual people to reveal Him to the world.
"I am the _true_ [Alēthinŏs– real, genuine; only timeless Spiritual Life Who cannot die because there is no death in Him.] ..._vine_ [Ampĕlŏs – {Amphi – around} and {Hĕilō – to coil}; the vine draws the nutrients from the earth to feed the entire plant and is the support for the entire extended branches to produce fruit.] ... and God is the _vinedresser_ [Gĕōrgŏs – {Ge – the earth as arable soil - man} and {Ĕrgō – to work the earth as an occupation}. God is the life source of every single person who has been given His timeless Spiritual Life through Christ, and He is the indwelling strength for each one to produce His image in the world.].

Every _branch_ [Klēma – a tender, flexible sprout of the vine. All of the power of the vine is God; the fragile weakness of the branch is man.] ...in Me that does not bear fruit, He takes away; and every branch that bears fruit, He _prunes_ [Kathairō – to cleanse of impurities that kills a plant; to remove useless, unproductive shoots.] ...it, that it may bear more fruit. *{The value of the vine is the quality of the fruit it produces. A branch is cut off if it produces sour - bitter fruit. Galatians 5: 22-25, "But the fruit of the Spirit is love, joy, peace, patience, kindness, goodness, faithfulness, gentleness, self-control; against such things there is no law. Now those who belong to Christ Jesus have crucified the flesh with its passions and desires. If we live by the Spirit {the movement of the Deity of Heaven upon the human mind}, let us also walk by the Spirit."}.

You are already _clean_ [Katharŏs – without blemish, free from the guilt produced by the curse of death] ...because of the _word_ [Lŏgŏs – the spoken revelation of the mind of God to redeem man from the curse of death.] ...which I have spoken to you.

Abide [Mĕnō – verb; to stay in a given place, a state of being, a relationship, and expectancy of presence. God abides in heaven; man expects Him to be there. He also abides in man; we expect Him to be here.] ...in Me, and I in you. As the branch cannot bear fruit of itself, unless it abides in the vine, so neither can you, unless you abide in Me.

I am the vine, you are the branches; he who abides in Me and I in him, he bears much fruit; for apart from Me you can do nothing. If anyone does not abide in Me, he is thrown away as a branch and it dries up; and they gather them and cast them into the fire and they are burned. *{God abides in heaven and earth in the minds of His people. A person <u>produces no fruit</u> if he does not expect God to be here; and neither can he <u>produce fruit</u> if he does not have the mind of Christ}.

If you abide in Me and My _words_ [Lŏgŏs – the revelation of God's mind to sanctify man from the filthiness of death] ...abide in you, ask whatever you wish, and it shall be done for you. By this is God <u>glorified</u> [Dŏxazō – magnified, extolled, honored, esteemed, acknowledged as to His Spiritual identity of the God of all life.] ...that you bear much fruit and so prove to be His _disciples_ [Mathētēs – ones who adhere their minds and actions to that of their teacher; to be imitators of the teacher so as to become teachers.].

Just as heavenly Deity has loved Me, I have also loved you; abide in My love. If you keep My commandments you will abide in My love; just as I have kept God's commandments and abide in His love. These things I have spoken to you that My joy may be in you, and that your joy may be made *full* [Plērŏŏ – to make replete; Jesus fully accomplished the purpose of God in the form of man to transform man to the Spiritual identity of God."

John 15:12-17, the relationship of God's heavenly people to each other.

"This is My commandment, that you love one another just as I have loved you. Greater love has no one than this that one lay down his life for his friends. You are My friends if you do what I command you.

No longer do I call you *slaves* [Dŏulŏs – the original meaning is a verb, to bind two things into one; the noun is properly a "bond man", one who gives himself up to the will of another. The focus of this word is on the relationship and not the service of a servant. Jesus is referring to the willingness of His disciples to dedicate their lives to Him just as He dedicated Himself to God; thereby having a oneness with God.]

for the slave does not know what his *master* [Kuriŏs – {Lord}; in this verse it is a respectful title for one having the authority of a father to care for his children. A child says "Yes sir" in obedience to his father's directions.]

is doing; but I have called you *friends* [Philŏs – primarily an adjective denoting one who is loved, dear to the heart. In this verse it is a noun denoting the disciples are no longer students of the master's teaching, but teachers to continue the master's work. Jesus moved them from being merely physical men who still live on earth; to be responsible spiritual children of God as citizens of the timeless Kingdom of Heaven.]

for all things that I have heard from God I have *made known* [Gnŏrizō – to reveal the mind of God to the human mind; the unknowable spiritual things of God have been made known to the spiritual image of God which can comprehend them.] …to you.

You did not choose me, but I chose you, and *appointed* [Tithĕmi – Verb; in the context of many verses written by the Apostle Paul, it is translated as "*ordained*" – placed in the upright (forthright) position of leadership for the ministry of the gospel. Considering the context of this verse, the Interlinear Bible {Hebrew – Greek – English} used the word "*Planted*" – rooted in God.]

you, that you should go and bear fruit, and that your fruit should *remain* [Mĕnō – Verb; stay in a given place or relationship. When man goes to heaven, he expects God to be there. This word states the authority of God to expect a permanent identity and fellowship with all life He creates in His image.]

that whatever you ask of the Father in My name, He may give it to you. This I *command* [Ĕntĕllŏmai – verb; from {Ĕn – a fixed position in place, time or state} and {Tĕlos – the conclusion of an act or state}. Combined the word means "to charge" or "give charge". It is the declaration of God's authority that what He begins, He finishes. He created man in His image and the end result is man permanently restored to His image] …

you, that you *love one another* [Agapaō – this is a combination of two words which identifies the power of God's bond with man created in His image. The power of this love which bonds the *Father* (the heavenly creator of all life), *Jesus the Huios* (the Deity of God revealed to man) and the *Spirit* (the Deity of Heaven that moves upon the human mind for his salvation) as One <u>Single Deity</u> Who bonds all of His spiritual children to one-another as <u>one single spiritual body</u>. People call themselves "Christians", but for many of them it is a 'self-made identity

God Reveals His Glory [Doxa – True Identity]

according to their denomination' which they self-righteously refuse to allot to anybody else. There is no Godly love in them.]."

John 15:18-27, the disciples' relationship to the world.

"If the *world* [Kŏsmŏs – The Divine creation of paradise for man before the fall of Adam. From that time on it became the place of iniquity under the influence of Satan and the curse of death. It ceased to be known as the abode of man and is now a reference only for the iniquity of man that inhabits it.]

hates you, you know that it has hated Me *before* [Prōtŏn – Adj; first in time, place, or importance. God was hated in heaven by Lucifer and angels, which was the prime motivation for the creation of man as a heavenly being that could be redeemed from the curse of death by the authority of His love for all life He creates.] …it hated you.

If you were of the world, the world would *love* [Philĕō – be a friend to one who is like you; a matter of sentiment or feeling; a matter of the head and not the heart.] …its own; but because you are not of the world, but I chose you out of the world, therefore the world hates you.

Remember the *word* [Lŏgŏs – Jesus' revelation of the mind of God. This is the gospel message of God's salvation the disciples are to take to the world that is under the judgment of death.]

that I said to you. 'A *slave* [Dŏulŏs– Every person who is a "bond man" to God surrenders his own will, to obey the will of God]

is not greater that his *master* [Kuriŏs – Lord, one who is supreme in authority. Jesus is Lord over all life in heaven and earth.]. `…If they persecuted Me, they will also persecute you; if they *kept* [Tĕrĕō – the connotation of this word means to believe and accept the gospel message of salvation taught by Jesus and adhere to it.] …My *word* [Lŏgŏs–the revelation of God's salvation] …they will keep yours also {believe the gospel message spoken by the children of God and adhere to it}.

But all these things they will do to you for My name's sake {persecute Jesus and His disciples because of Jesus' message of His heavenly kingdom rule as opposed to their own kingdom of self-rule; the reason why the Jewish Sanhedrin had Jesus put to death.}, because they do not know the One who sent Me. If I had not come and spoken to them; they would not have *sin* [Hamartia – the governing principle or power of the human mind to think and act through the members of the human body for wrongdoing] …but now they have no excuse for their sin.

He who hates Me hates God also. If I had not done among them the works which no one else did, they would not have sin {not recognize themselves as sinners}; but now they have both seen and hated Me and My God as well.

But they have done this in order that the word may be fulfilled {Psalms 35:19; 69:4} that is written in their *Law* [Nŏmŏs – the laws given to restrain the evil tendencies natural to man in his fallen estate; but because of the sin nature they are ineffective and provokes these tendencies to greater activity.] … 'They Hated Me Without a Cause.`

When the Helper {Holy Spirit} comes whom I will send to you from God, that is the Spirit of Truth who proceeds from God; He will *bear witness* [Marturĕō- teach the glory (Doxa of God) by divine revelation; reveal the deity of Jesus to the minds of unredeemed humanity and convict the children of God of their sins.] ...of Me, and you will bear witness also, because you have been with Me from the beginning."

John 16:16-22, Jesus foretold His death and resurrection to His disciples.
"A little while, and you will no longer behold Me; and again, a little while, and you will see Me.

Some of His disciples therefore said to one another, 'What is this thing He is telling us, A little while, and you will not behold Me; and again, a little while and you will see Me; because I go to the Father?'

So, they were saying, 'What is this that He says, A little while? We do not know what He is talking about.'

Jesus knew that they wished to question Him, and He said to them, 'Are you deliberating together about this, that I said, A little while, and you will not behold Me, and again a little while, and you will see Me?'

Truly, truly, I say to you, that you will weep and *lament* [Thrēněō – to wail in anguish, to mourn in great sorrow.] ...but the *world* [Kŏsmŏs – the place of man under the judgment of death in contrast to heaven.] ...will *rejoice* [Chairō – be glad, joyful, cheerful, happy, at peace within themselves.]; ...you will be sorrowful, but your sorrow will be turned to joy.

Whenever a woman is in *travail* [Tiktŏ – the pain of bringing forth a child; childbirth.] ...she has sorrow, because her *hour* [Hōra – an appointed action begins] ...has come; but when she gives birth to the child, she remembers the *anguish* [Thlipsis – pain that burdens the body.] ...no more, for joy that a child has been born into the world. You too now have sorrow; but I will see you again, and your heart will rejoice, and no one takes your joy away from you."

John 16:23-33, Jesus promised the prayers of the disciples will be answered.
"And in that day, you will *ask* [Erotao – Jesus' normal relationship to His disciples questioning Him as equals] ... Me no question. Truly, truly, I say to you, if you shall *ask* [Aiteo – humble petition honoring the majesty of God] ... the Father for anything, He will give it to you in My name.

Until now you have *asked* (Aiteo) for nothing in My name; *ask* (Aiteo), and you will receive; that your joy may be made *full* [Plērŏō – to make replete; to complete the ministry of the gospel.].

These things I have spoken to you in figurative language; an *hour* [Hōra – an appointed time when an action begins] ...is coming when I will speak no more to you in figurative language but will tell you plainly of the Deity of Heaven.

In that day you will *ask* (Aiteo) in My name, and I do not say to you that I will *request* [Ěrōtaō– present the prayers of the disciples to God on an equal footing.] ...the Father on your behalf.

for the Father Himself *loves* [Philěō – God cherishes the life of His children who have been given timeless Spiritual Life through Jesus] ...you, because you have loved Me, and have believed that I came forth from the Father.

I came forth from the Father and have come into the world; I am leaving the world again and going to the Father.'

God Reveals His Glory [Doxa – True Identity]

His disciples said, 'Lo, now You are speaking plainly, and are not using a figure of speech.

Now we *know* [Ĕidō – to know by perception; to understand what you hear.] …that You *know* [Oida– to have absolute divine knowledge] …all things and have no need for anyone to *question* [Ĕrōtaō – interrogate; demand answers] …You; by this we *believe* [Pistĕuō -persuaded, confidence, committed to one's trust] …that You came from God.'

Jesus answered them, 'Do you now believe?' Behold, an hour (Hōra) is coming, and has already come, for you to be scattered, each to *his own home* [Idiŏs – pertaining to one's self, one's own private life], …and to *leave* [Aphiemi – to send forth] …Me alone; and yet I am not alone, because the Father is with Me.

These things I have spoken to you, that in Me you may have *peace* [Ĕirēnē – harmonized relationship between God and His children]. …In the world you have tribulation but take courage; I have overcome the *world* [Kŏsmŏs – the earth, the habitation of man under the judgment of death]."

John 17:1-12, Jesus' High Priestly Prayer
"These things Jesus spoke; and lifting up His eyes to heaven, He said, 'Father, the hour has come; *glorify* [Dŏxazō – bring to light His true identity] …Your [Huios – Jesus; the visible presence of God in human form; the authority of God's Kingdom of Life to destroy the kingdom power of death that rules the earth], …that Christ may glorify You, even as You gave Him authority over all *mankind* [Sarx – the physical human race under the curse of death], …that to all whom You have given Him, He may give timeless life.

And this is timeless life, that they may know You, the only *true* [Alēthinŏs – Deity] … and Jesus *Christ* [Christŏs – anointed High Priest of God's heavenly kingdom rule of timeless spiritual life – Messiah.] …whom You have *sent* [Apŏstĕllō - Jesus was the voice of God's message of truth; He was the light of God to the minds of mankind in the darkness of death.].

I glorified You on the earth, having *accomplished* [Tĕlĕiŏō – made perfect] …the work which You have given Me to do.

And now, you glorify Me together with Yourself{'Ĕlôhîym}, with the *glory* [Dŏxa – God's true identity] …which I had with You before the world was created {Genesis 1:1}.

I *manifested* [Phanĕrŏō – the Holy Spirit made visible God's unknowable and invisible Deity] …Your name to the *men* [Anthrōpŏs– plural; human beings] …whom You gave Me out of the world; they were Yours and You gave them to Me, and they have kept Your *word* [Lŏgŏs– the spoken revelation of the mind of God; the gospel message of salvation delivered with His authority and made effective by His power of presence {Christ}.].

Now they have come to know that everything You have given Me is from You.

for the *words* [Rhēma– scripture which the Spirit brings to our remembrance for use in time of need; a prerequisite being the regular storing the scriptures in the mind.]

which You gave Me I have given to them; and they received them, and truly understood that I came forth from You, and they *believed* [Pisteuō – Faith; the mental persuasion of truth] that You did send Me.

I ask on their behalf; I do not ask on behalf of the world; but of those whom You have given Me; for they are Yours; and all things that are Mine are Yours, and Yours are Mine; and I have been *glorified* [Dŏxazō – honored for their recognition of His true Deity] …in them.

And I am no more in the world; and yet they themselves are in the world, and I come to You, *Holy* [Hagiŏs – sacred, pure, sinless] …*Father* [Deity of Heaven- Who rules from His Throne of Life],

keep [Tĕrĕō – watch over, preserve the life] …them in Your name, the name which You have given Me, that they may be *one* [Hĕn – the same light of holiness that radiates from God] … even as We are."

While I was with them, I was keeping them in Your name which You had given Me; and I *guarded* [Phulassō – to keep in safe custody from harm] …them, and not one of them perished but the son of *perdition* [Apōlĕia – timeless ruin; destruction; death] …that the scripture might be fulfilled."

John 17:13-21, Jesus' Prayer for His Disciples in The World.

"But now I come to You; and these things I speak in the world that they may have My joy made full in themselves.

I have given them Your *word* {the spoken revelation of the mind of God – the gospel message of salvation}; and the world has hated them because they are not of the world {restored to the timeless spiritual life of heaven – not under the judgment of death}, even as I am not of the world.

I do not ask You to take them out of the world, but to keep them from the *evil one* [Pŏnērŏs – the wicked and powerful influence of Satan]. …They are not of the world, even as I am not of the world.

Sanctify [Hagiazō – purify, consecrate, {set apart for God and His timeless Spiritual Life}] …them in the truth; Your *word* [Lŏgŏs – Christ; the Living Bread from the throne of God] …is truth. As You did send Me into the world, I also have sent them into the world.

And for their sakes I *sanctify* [Hagiazō – Jesus gave up His appearance of God in heaven where He radiated the pure holiness of God. On the earth, He radiated His holiness by His actions and words which identified Him as the Messiah – the Lamb of God – the light which penetrated the darkness of death that rules the mind of the human race.], …that they themselves also may be sanctified in truth {be the light of God by words and actions which reveal our oneness with God - Matthew 6:9-13: The Lord's Prayer}.

I do not ask on behalf of these alone, but for those also who believe in Me through their *word* [Lŏgŏs – The public confession of faith in the person of Christ to identify Him as the authority of God to give them a spiritual birth from heaven.].

that they may all be *one* [Hēn– the character of God revealing His children to be the living temple of Christ]; …even as You, Father, are in Me, and I in You, that they also may be in Us; that the world may believe that You did send Me."

John 17:22-26, Jesus' Prayer for The Timeless Glory of His Children

"And the *glory* [Dŏxa – true identity of God] …which You have given Me I have given to them; that they may be *one* [Hĕis – one with the Deity of Heaven by His Kingdom Rule of timeless life] …just as We are *one* [Hĕis – one and the same Deity on His Throne of Life].

I in them and You in Me, that they may be *perfected* [Tĕlĕiŏō – consecrate the character of God's holiness […in unity, that the world may *know* [Ginōskō – the quality of God to have an absolute understanding] …that You did send Me, and You did *love* [Agapaō– God's deep attitude of affection toward man revealed by His gift of sanctified spiritual life.[...them, even as You did *love* [Agapaō– God' attitude of affection for Christ revealed by His action of resurrecting Him from the grave and placing in Him the full authority of His Throne of Life to regenerate the human race only through Him.] ...Me.

Father, I desire that they also, whom You have given Me, be with Me where I am, in order that they may *behold* [Thĕōrĕō – to glorify Jesus true identity as God's sacrificial Lamb.]

My glory, which You have given Me; for You did love Me before the *foundation* [Katabŏlē – metaphorically; the complete conception in the mind of God for the creation of man to be given the holiness of His timeless Deity] ...of the *world* [Kŏsmŏs – the universe that is divinely arranged for the total destruction of death that rules the mind of man, made in the image of God. Death began in the mind of Lucifer before the throne of God. It can only be destroyed in its rule of darkness where God is not known; by the conversion of the human Spirit from death to life.].

O *righteous* [Dikaiŏs – the divine standard of sinless thought and behavior] ...Father, although the world has not known You, yet I have known You; and these have known that You did send Me; and I have made Your name known to them and will make it known; that the love wherewith You did love Me may be in them, and I in them."

The revelation of the Passover established in Exodus is the anti-type of God's prophesy for the selection of the type; God's true Passover Lamb as recorded in His New Covenant. This was the Corner Stone for the foundation of God's Holy City where there is no death; only the Holy Deity of God and His Children. Isaiah 28:16; I Peter 2:6; Revelation 21:14

John 11:47-57,
"Therefore, the *Chief Priests* [Archiereus – The Jewish high or chief priest was the instituted type of Christ in offering gifts and sacrifices for the sins of the people, entering into the Holy of Holies not without blood. The Chief Priests included the high priest, his deputy, and the heads of the twenty-four sacerdotal families. This group comprised the Sanhedrin].

And the Pharisees convened a council and were saying, 'What are we doing? For this man (Jesus) is performing many *signs* [Sēmeion– miracles of God with an ethical end and purpose] ...If we let Him go on like this all men will believe in Him and the Romans will come and take away both our place and our *nation* [Ethnos – this word is usually used for the whole human race as heathens or Gentiles. The Jews call themselves Laos, the people of God or the Israel of God. In this case it signifies the rule of a self-organized people.].

But a certain one of them, Caiaphas who was the high priest that year, said to them, 'You know nothing at all, nor do you take into *account* [Logizomai – to calculate, to consider what you may be answerable for] ...that it is *expedient* [Sumpherō – profitable, advantageous]...for you that one man should die for the people, and that the whole nation should not *perish* [Apollumi- brought to ruin or to be destroyed] `

Now this he did not say on his own initiative but being high priest that year he prophesied that Jesus was going to die for the nation, and not for the nation only, but that He might also gather together into one people the children of God who are scattered abroad. So, from that day on they planned together to *kill* Him [Apŏktĕinō – slay, to put to death by slaughtering the body].'"

The Sanhedrin (the head of the entire Jewish nation) unknowingly selected Jesus (the Messiah) to be God's true sacrificial lamb for His Passover, by handing Him over to the Roman army to kill Him. When the Romans got through scourging Jesus, He hardly resembled a man.

But they could not kill Him. For Jesus to die, He had to yield His body (soul) to the death of the grave by removing His Spirit as a *living sacrifice* [Zebach – Hebrew; to slaughter a victim for a meal]. …The lamb had to be slaughtered, cooked only by fire, and totally consumed.

God's judgment on every man who chooses to be purely a fleshly being is permanent; totally consumed by God's judgment fire. But every person who calls upon the name of Jesus will be restored to timeless life by God's sacrificial atonement.

It was imperative to the Sanhedrin that Jesus be removed from the cross before sundown because the Jewish Passover was more important to them than God's Passover. Thus His body was put in a tomb, but His Spirit descended into Hades to reveal His Deity there and then He revealed Himself to His disciples as the Living Deity of Heaven.

Jesus' followers were devastated by this event but were filled with exuberant joy on the morning of the third day when they discovered He had risen from the dead.

John 20:19-22, Jesus appeared to His disciples the evening of His resurrection from the grave.
"When therefore it was evening on that day, the first day of the week, and when the doors were shut where the disciples were for fear of the Jews; Jesus came and stood in their midst and said to them, '*Peace* [Ĕirĕnē – a harmonious relationship between people.] …be with you`. And when He had said this, He showed them both His hands {nailed to the cross} and His side {pierced by a Roman spear}. The disciples therefore rejoiced when they saw the Living Lord.

Jesus therefore said to them again, 'Peace be with you; as the Father has *sent* [Apŏstĕllō - to send out for a purpose] …Me, I also send you'. And when He had said this, He breathed on them, and said to them, '*Receive* [Lambanō – the self-prompted action to take by force; to lay hold of a heavenly authority. {Dechomai – means to receive something as a gift}.] …the Holy Spirit of God`."

The next verse in the King James Bible says in English, "of whoever you forgive the sins, they have forgiven them; if you *retain* [Kratĕō – strength, power to hold, seize what is owed] …the sins of any, they have been *retained* [Kratĕō]."

*The result of this verse is there are religious bodies which believe they have the authority of the Holy Spirit to act as God on earth and bless and forgive the sins of those who surrender to their authority, and to condemn as heretics those who will not.

The Greek text says: 'Ever of whom you *forgive* [Aphiemi – to let go of; give up a debt owed to you] …*sins* [Hamartia - moral deviations, the offensive action of refusing to pay a debt.] … let go to them the legal obligation to pay the debt; ever of whom you *retain* [Kratĕō] … they are *retained* [Kekratentai- not responsible to you, but to a higher authority.]."

*Forgiveness is God's directive for His people in the "Lord's Prayer". Christ is the Living Bread Who sustains the authority of God's spiritual children to be holy – reflect the identity of God in their own lives to forgive the sins of others.

John 20:30-31, John concludes his revelation of the Epiphaneia of Jesus.
"Many other *signs* [Sēmĕiŏn – the revealed hidden, secret things of God in heaven.] ... Jesus also performed in the presence of the disciples, which are not written in this *book* [Bibliŏn – a small book; the Gospel of John as opposed to the entire Bible.].
But, these have been written that you may believe that Jesus is the Christ, the [Huios – the Deity of God; the anointed Messenger of God from heaven], ...that believing you may have timeless life in His name."

PHANEROO - THE HOLY SPIRIT

THE DEITY OF HEAVEN SPEAKING TO MAN

The Apostle Paul was led by the Holy Spirit to write his epistle to the Ephesians. This letter has one subject: God's revelation of His identity is the Deity of Heaven Who recreates man in His image. Every Jew and Gentile, in whom the Holy Spirit enlightens the mystery of Christ to the mind, is led to be One Spiritual Body as fellow heirs and members of God's Heavenly Kingdom Rule of Spiritual Life.

John 21 is God's transition of knowing His identity by the *Epiphaneia of Jesus* to the revelation of His identify by the Phaneroo, the presence and work of the Holy Spirit to reveal the Deity of Jesus to the lost world and to empower all of God's people to be His ministering Spirits in this physical world.

Jesus taught his disciples for three years. He told Peter He would make him a fisher of men. In that time Peter revealed he had the mind to defend Jesus to the death; but failed to do so because of the weakness of the flesh. This final chapter of John's gospel deals with the dynamics of the Holy Spirit to call and empower the human mind (not just Peter, but every Spiritual Israelite/Christian in the world) to be God's ministering Spirits of the Gospel Message of Christ – to be fishers of men. It was written in the apocalyptic language of the Holy Spirit which reveals the unseen spiritual actions of the Spirit by the physical actions of the disciples. *This is completely unrecognizable in the English language, but is very visible in the Greek language.

John 21:1
"*After* [Meta – a primary preposition denoting something in succession or sequence] ...*these things* [Tauta- the Epiphaneia of Jesus and His resurrection from the grave.] ...Jesus *manifested* [Phanĕrŏō–the purpose for the presence of the Holy Spirit is to "render apparent what has been openly revealed". The Spirit is not here to reveal Himself, but to reveal the Doxa of the Lord Jesus to the minds of the lost world for their salvation. This is the final presence of Deity in this world of death to deal with every individual human being who will believe in the Christ for His salvation.] ...*Himself* [Hĕautōn – a reflective pronoun meaning the disciples have the

same heavenly spiritual identity of Jesus.] ...*again* [Palin – anew; not as He was in the flesh, but as His identity of Deity in heaven.] ...to the *disciples* [Mathētĕs – His pupils; learners who put into effect what they are taught.]

on [Ĕpi – the superimposition of time, place, order, and direction. *Jesus had a very limited, designated time and place [the Roman world] to accomplish His purpose for His physical presence on the earth. He was limited also by the lifespan and location of the eleven disciples who served Him.]

the *sea* of Tiberius [Thalassa – literally the place where the acts of Christ testified to His Deity was in the turbulence of human life under the domain of death; metaphorically it was the nationalistic Jewish religion and the ungodly men dominating the Roman world. This world will literally continue to be the domain of Satan's rule until God stops it.].

and He *revealed Himself* [Phanĕrŏŏ -The Holy Spirit revealing Him] ...*thus* [Hŏutōs – [the Doxa of God {the Christ} to save humanity. It is the Holy Spirit that reveals Him to His disciples and to every human mind who will believe.].

John 21:2

There *were* [Ĕuschēmōn – noble, honorable, of good standing, respectful men] ...*together* [Hŏmŏu – men akin to one another as the body of Christ, being at the same place and time to be empowered by the Holy Spirit] ... **(1)** *Simōn* [a Hebrew name meaning the name of nine, i.e. Simon *Peter* [Pĕtrŏs – a small piece of rock]; Simon {Zelotes}; Simon {father of Judas}; Simon {Magus}; Simon {the tanner}; Simon {the Pharisee}; Simon {of Cyrene}; Simon {brother of Jesus} and Simon {the leper}] ...and **(2)** *Thomas*[Didumōs - a Chaldean name meaning twin – double]...and **(3)***Nathanael* [from the ancient Hebrew word {Phragĕllŏō – the lash as a public punishment}] ...*from* [Apō –away from something or someone near; place, time or relationship] ...*Cana* [Kana – a name of ancient Hebrew origin] ...of *Galilee* [Galilaia – the ancient Hebrew word meaning the heathen region of Palestine] ...and **(4** and **5)** the sons of *Zebedee* [Zĕbĕdaiŏs – father of James and John], ...and **(6** and **7)** two *others* [Allōs – a numerical difference denoting the same sort.]...of His disciples.

* The Holy Spirit intentionally does not name these two but counts them to belong to a group of seven disciples *{Seven being the number for God}. This is important to this chapter because *seven* is inclusive of all the nameless people of the world beginning with Abraham, who are Spiritual Israelites assigned to be God's ambassadors to the wilderness (the world devoid of the knowledge of God). God used the names of five of His disciples to reveal the fact that He has historically called out both Jews and Gentiles to be spiritually empowered, living witnesses of the Living God.

John 21:3

Simon Peter said to them, 'I am going fishing`. They said to him, 'We will also go with you`. They went out and got into the boat; and that *night* [Nux – the period of the day that is the absence of light; metaphorically - the period of man's alienation from God. This is important to this verse because it reveals six of the seven were not spiritually equipped to accomplish the work God had called them to do.] ...they caught nothing.

*The occupation of these men was fishing; to provide food for them and to sell the rest to those who would purchase the fish. They were accustomed to returning home empty handed but it always had the effect of weighing heavy on the mind. To be successful fishermen they had to persevere with all their mind and physical strength. Jesus selected Peter to be a fisher of men because he had the tenacity required to be faithful to serve God until his death – even his death on a cross. Only God knows the mind of His faithful servants who perish as martyrs for their witness of God.

John 21:4
But now early *morning* [Prŏïa–the beginning of a new hour of light / revelation] …was now *breaking* [Ginŏmai–to cause to be to come into existence; to be fulfilled; to be finished; This revelation is the beginning of a new day in the history of man. It is God's revelation of His continued presence for the salvation of man to the end of this age of redemption.].

Jesus stood on the beach (dry land, the abode of mankind. God is the ever-present spiritual power for the spiritual birth and sanctified lives of all His people.) …yet the disciples did not *know* [Ĕidō – to know by the perception of the mind; the Holy Spirit had not yet revealed Him to them] …that it was Jesus.

*The mystery of God's presence in this world was revealed by the Apostle Paul in Hebrews 5:9-10, "And *having been made perfect* [Tĕlĕiŏō – Jesus fulfilled God's plan designed in heaven before creation, for the salvation of man by perfecting it in His own Person, i.e. The revelation that He is the Deity of God by His death, burial and resurrection.].

Jesus became to all those who *obey* [Hupakŏuō – to listen attentively with the mind to comprehend truth and submit to its authority; to conform to its command] …Him, the *source* [Aitŏs – one who causes an event to happen; the timeless salvation of each individual person to be the "Body of Christ"] …of timeless *salvation* [Sōtēria – the deliverance from the power of timeless death by the greater power of God's timeless Kingdom Rule of Spiritual life.].

being *designated* [Prŏsagŏrĕuō – to address; to accomplish; to move forward with purpose. This word is a combination of words revealing the identity of God as one single spiritual Deity of timeless life {the total pervasive power of God as the Kingdom of Life}, separating Himself to three equal powers of the throne for the purpose to not only destroy death, but to recreate man to his original identity of a heavenly being that stands beside His throne in a heaven devoid of death.].

by God as the *high priest* [Archiĕrĕus – the beginning (original) ruling power of God over all spiritual life] …*according* [Kata – a preposition denoting a place or time in opposition and intensity] …to the *order* [Taxis – the divinely appointed character or nature of a priesthood-God's High Priest.] …of Melchizedek."

*Jesus said He is the light, the way, the truth; no one goes to the Father except through Him. This final revelation of Christ is that no one goes through Him; except by the Holy Spirit. This final age of redemption will conclude with the power of death ruling humanity as it was in the day of Noah. The power of this darkness will require the presence of the fullness of Deity to redeem the remnant of people who can be saved.

Revelation 22 reveals that every trace of the presence of death is removed by the *Right Hand of God – Jesus*. Jesus always commanded Peter to cast his net to the right side of the boat. This is God's revelation that every human being redeemed to His Kingdom of Life is the work of Christ, and every person led by the Holy Spirit to be His witness is also the Right Hand of God.

John 21:5

Jesus therefore said to them, '*Children* [Paidiŏn – an immature small child that has not yet reached school age; metaphorically of believers who are deficient in spiritual understanding, having never been taught.] …you do not have any *fish* [Prŏsphagiŏn – "little fish", a compound word meaning something small (a very small fish; a minnow). It is a symbolic word for the newborn children of God.] …do you?` They answered Him, 'No`.

Verse 21:6

And He said to them, '*Cast the net* [Diktuŏn– from the verb Diko; to cast a seine with such small netting that nothing escapes through it] …on the right-hand side of the boat, and you will find a catch`. This is the revelation by the Holy Spirit of Jesus' continued presence in this world. Humanity without the leadership of the Holy Spirit can do nothing to accomplish God's purpose for them. God's authority to give man His timeless spiritual life is in Christ - Alone, who stands by His right hand. Jesus directed His disciples to cast the net only for a specific people.

They cast therefore, and then were not able by their *might* [Ischuō – ability; force; human strength to prevail; *No human being can do what only God can do.] …to *haul* [Hĕlkō – to draw gently by divine impulse; as God draws humanity to Himself.] …it in because of the *multitude* [Plēthŏs – a super large number like the stars and sand of the seashore.] …of the *fish* [Ichthus – singular; "a fish". *This word is representative of all the people - one spiritual body, brought to Christ by the Holy Spirit. Man without the power of the Holy Spirit cannot even begin to accomplish this heavenly feat.].

John 21:7

That disciple therefore whom Jesus was loving (John), said to Peter, 'It is *the Lord* [Kuriŏs – God, who is supreme in authority and the power of His love to redeem humanity. John used this word to remind the disciples that their personal relationship to God is through the Christ, whom they loved and obeyed.].

And so, when Simon Peter heard that it was the Lord, having *girded on* [Diazōnnumi– to wrap tightly around the body; Jesus girded Himself with a towel and used it to dry the disciples' feet. Peter {led by the Holy Spirit} firmly wrapped himself with the spiritual mantle of God to be a true servant of God. *(See verse 18)] …his *coat* [Ĕpĕndutēs – fishers coat; Peter identified himself with Christ as a fisher of men.]

for he was [Gumnŏs –exposed as merely the mind of a man by the absence of spiritual clothing.…and *threw* [Ballō- to thrust oneself forward with force and effort; to give over to another's care.] …*himself* [Hēautŏu – a reflexive pronoun meaning an automatic self-determined action] …*into* [Ĕis – the point reached or entered of place, time, or purpose with the intent of the mind to never perish or come to an end] …the *sea* [Thalassa – the turbulent ungodliness of humanity under the curse of death. In this verse it is indicative of {Peter and the vast multitude of disciples in this time of God's visitation} being led by the Holy Spirit to unit with Christ in His spiritual battle to reach people who have no knowledge of God's salvation.].

John 21:8

But the other disciples *came not* (to the presence of Jesus, nor the commitment Peter made) in the *little boat* [Plŏiarios – a vessel used by physical fishermen for a small catch of fish].

It is indicative of physical minded human beings who do not have the capacity or the vision to serve the purpose of God for the magnitude of His catch of human lives. The world is full of religious minded people who are comfortable only with the firm ground of their own religious beliefs, which produces nothing but buildings with their name on them.

for they were not far from the *land* [Gē – The whole earth occupied by the totality of humanity characterized by the weakness of the flesh.] …but about one hundred *yards* away [Pĕchus – cubits; the measurement of a man's arm. The Holy Spirit used this word to denote the weakness of man's efforts to be identified as a disciple of Christ.] …, *dragging* [Surō – violently struggling by physical means to no avail] …the net full of fish.

John 21:9

When [Hōs – adverb of comparison; in that manner of physical exertion] …*then* [Ŏun – an adverb expressing the certainty of a completed action] …they went up on the land, they *saw* [Blĕpō – a verb meaning to take heed, to perceive, discern, seeing with the eyes and seeing with the mind] …a *coal* [Anthrakia – a heap of burning coals symbolized by the Holy Spirit as one single coal – the holiness of Christ and all of His disciples, revealing the light of God] …of fire *lying* [Kĕimai – the appointment of affliction; this word is used for Jesus lying in a manger and it has the same connotation of predestination of affliction for the faithful believers who commit their lives to serve God as His witnesses in this world of death.]

and a [Ŏpsarion – cooked meat that is salted and dried as a condiment; a dainty relish for other food] …and bread. What they saw when they looked upon Jesus is the harsh physical life of God's servants who are not dependent upon their own resources but are sustained by God to faithfully feed the world the spiritual food of heaven – the living bread.

John 21:10

Jesus said to them, '*Bring* [Phĕo – verb; to bear, to carry; the "little fish" were "borne along" or impelled by the Holy Spirit. Through God's true disciples, the Holy Spirit brings forth good fruit from the seed that He sows; God reaps the harvest.] …*from* [Apŏ– in composition as a prefix, it usually denotes separation, cessation, completion. Jesus said to bring to Him the totality of the redeemed people of the earth.] …the "little fish" you have now caught'.

John 21:11

Now [Nun – a primary particle of present or immediate time; it denotes an immediate response.] …*went up* [Anabainō – the "rise of thoughts and reason"; the activity of the mind to spring into action in obedience to God's command.] …Simon Peter, and *drew* [Hĕlkuō – verb; this is not the violent dragging revealed by the word "Surō". It signifies drawing by the inward power of divine impulse. Peter {empowered by the Holy Spirit} did single-handily what the combined strength of the other men in the "little boat" could not do.] ...the net to _land_ [Ge – the earth God created as arable soil to produce an abundance of food for humanity. Adam was created from this soil to be the arable soil in which God could produce an abundance of spiritual beings created in His image with His timeless life. Jesus had the net of "little fish" {newborn saints of God's creation} brought to Him to secure their relationship and identity with Him.] ..._full_ [Městŏs – replete; the totality of humanity redeemed by the authority of Jesus.] ...of _great_ [Měgistŏs – exceeding greatness; heavenly identity of the holiness of Christ.] ..._fish_ [Ichthus – This word is not physical fish of the sea, but "a fish". Every single sanctified human being has the certain affinity with God as a heavenly creation; "a fish" is the composite body of _all_ the "little fish – newborn saints /Children of God"; which is a resurrected, heavenly, timeless spiritual body.] ...a _hundred_ [Hěkatŏn – an indeclinable number like the sand of the sea; signifying the complete productiveness of all sown seed. It is a number known only to God; the one doing the saving.] ...and _fifty-three_ [Pěntēkostē - Fifty and three are plural numbers written as one word. God's Passover and God's resurrection from the grave is one single action for both the salvation and resurrection of the hundred – the body of Christ".]; ...and although there were so many, the net was not torn.

John 21:12

Jesus [Iēsŏus – ee-ay-sooce' - This name is used 972 times in the New Testament. Jehoshua is used two times. It is from the Hebrew Jehoshabeath, meaning Jehovah-saved. This name is given by the Holy Spirit to emphasize the timeless identity of God revealed in the Old Testament is the same timeless God revealed in the New Testament, and the same timeless God revealing Himself in this final day of redemption; to save every human being who will be saved.

This new age of man cannot end until God has accomplished this single purpose for creating Adam a spiritual being in the image of God. Everything the Holy Spirit reveals about Jesus is the Deity of God Whose Kingdom of Life rules heaven and earth. Jesus is the rightful identity of the God of heaven and every person restored to God's image.]

..._said_ [Lěgo – to lay forth; to relate a systematic discourse for the future salvation of man.] ...to _them_ [Autŏs–to speak backwards; to speak to all of His disciples from the future; He is the timeless Living God Who continually speaks personally to every disciple until He returns.]

..._come_ [Děutě – come hitherto; follow Me] ...*_breakfast_ [Aristaō – The English word "breakfast" is a verb meaning "break the fast". You have slept through the darkness of the night, now it is time to wake up and eat the first meal of the next day.

*Aristaō has a completely different meaning than this English word. It is a verb meaning "eat the primary meal of the new day". It is from the root word {Arrhēn – the strength of the male.} Genesis1:26, [the origin of man] "God said, "Let the heavens make _man_ [`'Âdâm – the image of God] ..._male_ [Zâkâr– the strength of the heavenly spiritual being (Adam) who was given the command from God to rule over the world. The purpose for his existence was to be a living witness to the Deity of God].

Aristaō means "follow Jesus in this New Day; be the New Spiritual Adam (Male - Spiritual Life of God) created in the image of God with the strength of the Holy Spirit to be God's witness of His identity. Peter clothed himself with this mantel of God to be able to reveal Jesus as the one true Living God. He also revealed Jesus by his written word and by his death.

God Reveals His Glory [Doxa – True Identity]

Jesus' word to this future generation of disciples is be a living spiritual witness/testimony to the Living God of heaven. Wake up, eat the spiritual food God provides (Jesus, the living bread) and experience the presence of God in your daily life and in the way you worship and serve Him.

And *not one* [Ōudĕis–This is a very powerful negative statement, meaning; not even one, nothing, never at any time, absolutely none] …of His *disciples* [Mathētĕs – every single person who adheres to Jesus as the one true God; lives a life of holiness reflecting His holiness that is light in the darkness of this world.] … *dared* [Tŏlmaō – extreme negative conduct of the mind and actions] …to *question* [Ĕxĕtazō – to express doubt that Jesus is God] …Him; Who are You? *Knowing* [Ĕidōs – to recognize someone by their consistent behavior and your relationship to the person] …that it is the Lord.].

Everyday Jesus walked with His disciples were a new day to experience the Deity of God and learn the truth of Who He is. In this verse Jesus is speaking to all of His disciples of this new day of God's revelation of His salvation. Wake up; be alive. Hear His voice speaking to you: listen and talk to Him; *worship Him* in the *first person*; make Him the energizing power of God's heavenly Throne of Timeless Life – it is the Kingdom Rule of God; Be the Living Temple of God in this world of death.

John 21:13

Th*en* [Ŏun – therefore] …*comes* [Ĕrchŏmai – present tense verb; is coming; never ceasing presence] …Jesus and *takes* [Lambanō – to get hold of; to offer; to seize; to take or receive. Metaphorically: a self-prompted action of never ceasing to give Himself; and the never-ending action of the disciples receiving Him] …the *bread* [Artos – the shewbread; the Living Bread of God's Passover.] …and *gives* [Didōmai–Himself - the power of God] …to *them* [Autōs- third person; all of God's disciples in this last age of redemption] …and the "little fish – all of God's children given spiritual life from above",] …*also* [Hŏmŏiōs – equally; every person who belongs to God is equipped by the Holy Spirit to live in this world as the Spiritual Being of God's creation; the image of God.

Jesus never ceases to be the presence of the Living Bread; the power of God's Passover to remove the curse of death from His disciples and every newborn Saint. The Holy Spirit never ceases to make this Deity of God applicable to both our physical and spiritual identity.

John 21:14

This is now the third time that Jesus was *manifested* [Phanaroō – revealed by the Holy Spirit] …to the disciples after He was *raised* [Ĕgĕirō –revealed the presence and power of the Living God] …from the *dead* [Nĕkrŏs – death of the body/ the soul.]

John 21:15-17, the Holy Spirit reveals God's power to restore lost humanity to spiritual life is by the authority of His sacrificial love (John 3:16). The Holy Spirit points Peter and all God's disciples to see Jesus as God's heartbeat for the world; to see and understand God's way of salvation is to love people into His kingdom.

The work of the Holy Spirit is to point the minds of every person in the world to visibly see God's love demonstrated for them. If they will look upon Jesus – they will see the one true God. This is the reality Jesus demonstrated by His presence in this world; and it is still the identity of God that must be revealed until He returns from heaven.

These verses define the reality that Jesus is in heaven; but His disciples are not. The simple fact revealed in this dialog is that man can have a spiritual birth from heaven; but he is still a physical being living in a physical world. God wants every person reading these verses to see themselves living in the power of an increasing spiritual darkness.

John 21:15

"*When* [Hōs – adverb of comparison; in that manner of being changed] …*then* [Ŏun - adverb expressing certainty] …they *dined* [Aristaō – started the "New Day" nourished with Jesus` words that projected their minds into the future] …

Jesus *says* [Lĕgō – break-silence; lay-forth; relate the systematic discourse for the future] …to Simon Peter, 'Simon of *Jonah* [Iōram – John, father of Simon] …do you *love* [Agapaō– used of God's sacrificial love for man and vice versa; to love God with His unselfish love; the essential nature of God to sacrifice Himself for the sake of His children {John 3:16}. God's ten articles of His heavenly constitution to govern His people on earth; tells us to love [Agapaō] Him for Who He is (Deity) and to love our fellow man as His creation.] …Me *more* [Plĕiōn – comparative of quantity or quality] …than *these* [Tŏutōn- God's people of the whole world who are filled with the Holy Spirit to love and serve Him; what Peter could never do before]?'…He said to Him, 'Yes, Lord; You *know* [Eidō – to perceive with the mind (God knows the mind of every human being)] …that I *love* You [Philĕō – to be fond of; sentimental feelings for friends]."

This word is never used in God's commands to love Him. Peter revealed that even though he had the gifts of the Spirit; his mind still controlled his actions. God knows the simple fact that man loves himself more than he can love God. This is reflexive of Adam: as the image of God, he had the mind of God, but the weakness of the flesh had more authoritative power over his physical life than God had over his spiritual life.

Revelation 20; reveals the Apokalupsis of Christ will be the power of God to replace our minds with His Mind. Those who refuse to give up their mind declare war on Jesus and are thrown into Hades. Those who surrender their minds to Jesus can enter God's perfect heaven where death cannot exist because He is the only mind there. This is God's assurance that death cannot exist again; furthermore, He erases all memory of death from the human mind (or man will return to it).

"He said to him, '*Feed* [Bŏskō – provide pasture; give nourishment; minister to (be a shepherd to)] … My own *lambs*` [Arnion – sacrificial lamb, designation of the exalted Christ; newborn children of God need the spiritual food that will progressively mature their minds to grow up and eat the meat of His word. Their whole life on this earth and in heaven depends upon it`.]."

God Reveals His Glory [Doxa – True Identity]

John 21:16
"He said to him again a second time, 'Simon, son of John, do you *love* [Agapaō] Me? ` He said to Him, 'Yes Lord; You *know* [Eidō] that I *love* [Philĕō] You`. He said to him, '*Shepherd* [Poimaino – this word implies the office of a shepherd; to guide, to guard, to lead God's people to righteous living}.] …My own *sheep* [Prŏbatŏn – something that walks forward; used by the Greeks for lambs and calves`.]"

Matthew 10:16, this word reveals true followers of Christ have a unique heavenly identity that separates them from all others. They strengthen their faith by walking forward with Christ in their daily living. This is a critical issue with God. He is bringing this world to an end by *separating the sheep* (people who demonstrate the character of God) *from the goats* (people who demonstrate the character of death). There will not be very many sheep left when Christ returns. It is imperative that God's people persevere in their faith to live in a world of increasing spiritual darkness.] `

John 21:17
"He said to him the third time, 'Simon, son of John, do you *love* Me? [Philĕō– have fondness for or a common interest with Jesus]. ` …Peter was *grieved* [Lupĕō – distressed; overcome with sorrow and sadness] …because He said to him the third time; 'Do you *love* [Philĕō] Me? ` 'Lord, you *know* [Eido] all things; You know that I *love* [Philĕō] You`. Jesus said to him, '*Feed* [Bŏskō -Guide the lost people of the world. Feed them the word of God that the Holy Spirit will reveal the truth of God to their minds for their salvation] …My "little sheep"."

Little sheep are new born Christians starting a new life as Spiritual Children of God. They will fall away from Him if they are not taught by the Holy Spirit to persevere by *faith* – a verb; the activity of the mind to adhere to truth and trust God in everything; and reject the Satanic lie that we have the ability and the right to be a "god power – the image of Satan"; to be ruled by the power of death. `

God used the word "Agapaō" twice to denote the power of His presence in the world to penetrate the darkness of death that rules the human mind. Both times Peter responded with "Philĕō", the only love that is originated by the human mind.

God used this word [Philĕō] the third time to denote the end of this "new hour" will be the weakness of the human mind that is devoid of His love to dispel the darkness of death. It reveals the whole world's loss of the ability to Love Him. Peter {a disciple who walked with God) could not confess anything more than his human ability to love Him. Jesus (knowing the stress this put on his mind and the truth of his mind and heart) accepted that confession with His Own humility and Divine Love for him.

This verse reminds us that God's final judgment on death starts in the church. God knows the mind of His people and the pressure death exerts on them. He knows the reality of having to stand alone in the darkness of death. That pressure tested Him the most when He was on the cross. The result of this increasing power of death is the last days of the church will be more wolves dressed in sheep's clothing, than there are sheep.

The world itself will be ruled by goats (lost humanity under the curse of death reveals their true identity by the character of death that is at war with God and His people) while the sheep (redeemed humanity that is ruled by the Mind of God) is at peace with God and reveals their true identity by their love for lost people.

***Reader: make sure you understand. You cannot fool God. He knows who and what you are, and He will reveal it at the proper time. Until then, God's wants the world to know His message in I Thessalonians is that He loves the whole human race that is under the curse of death. He wants to deliver every lost person from His judgment and the immense physical and mental suffering and tribulation death brings upon the world. God wants all people to understand what the Holy Spirit {Deity} reveals about the last days of this world.

John 21:18-25, God reveals the unchanging identity of His people when they grow old and die.

John 21:18
"Truly, truly, I say to you, *when* [Hŏtĕ–while] …you *were* [Ĕn– imperfect of {Ĕimi – I exist}. Ĕn means "what I was", "what I had been"] …*younger* [Nĕŏs – new (youthful), new in respect of time and experience] …you used to *gird yourself* [Zŏnnumi – to bind about with a belt'. When Peter was a young disciple of the Lord; God changed his whole life. He girded himself with the full armor of God revealed in Ephesians 6:10-18]

and *walked* [Pĕripatĕō - {Pĕri – extremity; all over} and {Patĕō – verb; trampled on serpents.} {Matthew 10:1, "And having summoned His twelve disciples, He gave them authority over unclean spirits, to cast them out, and to heal every kind of disease and every kind of sickness."}. God's disciples are engaged in this spiritual warfare until the moment the Lord returns. The Holy Spirit reveals this to be so in Paul's epistle to the Gentiles (Ephesians), highlighted in verses 6:10-12.]

wherever [Hŏpŏu – {Hŏ – an indefinite pronoun; who, which, what} and {Pŏu – an indefinite adverb; somewhere, the magnitude of an unlimited place.}. Hŏpŏu means everywhere Peter was, the vengeance of God was there to destroy the demonic powers.] …you *wished* [Thĕlō – the will of the mind, the power of determination. *Peter's determination was to win the Jews to the Lord. The Apostle Paul's determination was to win the Gentiles to the Lord. The question is: what is your determination?].

but *when* [Hŏtan – whensoever; hypothesis implying uncertainty of a specific time.] . you *grow old* [Ginŏmai – verb; caused to be come into being as a living mediator of Christ.]'…you will *stretch out* [Ěktĕinō – extend an activity; put forth; literally "to completely finish out"] …your *hands* [Chĕir – literally the hollowness for grasping; metaphorically an instrument for channeling the power of God]

and another [Allŏs – a numerical difference denoting another of the same sort; ten of the disciples met the same fate as martyrs and suffered it with the strength of God] …will *gird* you [Zŏnnumi – bind about (a belt); identified by spiritual armor.]. All of God's disciples through "this hour" strengthen one another and identify with one another with the "full armor of God".]

and *carry* you [Phĕrō – to be "borne along" or "impelled" by the Holy Spirit.] …*not* [Ŏuch – an absolute negative] …*where* [Hŏpŏu – an indefinite pronoun; (who, which, what) and an indefinite adverb; (somewhere, wherever). *The Holy Spirit used this word to identify all of

God Reveals His Glory [Doxa – True Identity]

God's disciples as one single body of Christ: and every single one is an individual living mediator. Both their lives and their deaths are unique to each one.]

you *want* [Thĕlō – the will of the mind; self-determined. We can choose the life we live, but the manner of our death belongs to God.]."

*This word of God has nothing to do with physical aging. It means the lives of every disciple who walks with Jesus reveals Him to the world by word of mouth, but most importantly by demonstrating the character of God through the experience of dying. Jesus was the living witness of God that turned the minds of an unknown number of people to know the true identity of God. His greatest and most powerful witness was His identity as the sacrificial Lamb of God. His entire life; from birth all the way through His death; was the living mediator of His Deity. The Holy Spirit is revealing the importance of our lives as His disciples. We are living mediators of Christ from our spiritual birth all the way through our death (which could possibly be our most powerful witness).]

John 21: 19

"Now this He said, *signifying* [Sēmainō– a mark; a sign to indicate the single identity of something] …by what kind of death he would glorify God. And when He had spoken this, He said to him, '*Follow* [Akŏlŏuthĕō – to be in the same way with (to accompany); a companion with the same identity] …*Me* [Mŏi- to Me; from {Ĕmoi – to be mine} `. The Holy Spirit used this word to identify God's disciples as His heavenly personal property."

*The English translation of these verses does not accurately reveal what the Holy Spirit wrote. What the Greek language reveals is that Peter voluntarily finished the totality of his calling as a disciple of Christ by his final action to surrender to the Romans to kill him. It possibly did not mean anything to the Romans to crucify him, but it meant everything to him. This is the resolve demonstrated by Jesus at His crucifixion.

Garcia Benito was the king (and god) of the Kikongo people in Angola, Africa. He inherited this position because he was born in the royal family. He was converted to Christ and gave up his rule to serve the real King of Heaven.

Garcia and Jose Martins were tortured, and their bodies mutilated by the communist army. But each radiated such a powerful passionate love for Jesus that no forces on this earth could stop them from preaching Jesus.

Garcia died from cancer at the age of ninety-five. Jose (in his middle thirties) was captured, tied down and gutted. No one in this real-life true story chose how or when they would die. But through the entire life of Garcia; God brought about the greatest evangelistic movement in the history of Africa. By the explosive growth of new churches in the midst of this mayhem, an estimated six million Kikongo people have been saved and are living mediators of Christ.

While the way and time of our death is not something, we would choose for ourselves, the mind of God should be the determining power of the mind of all His disciples for the totality of their lives. This brings us to the importance of verses 21: 20 – 25.

John 21:20

"And *turning* [Ĕpistrĕphō – {Ĕpi – direction; toward, upon} and {Strĕphō – reflexively turn oneself; to turn the back to someone}. Peter turned God's attention away from himself and focused it upon someone else.] ...Peter saw the disciple John following after Jesus.

John 21:21
Peter therefore seeing him, said to Jesus, 'Lord, and what about this man? `

John 21:22
Jesus said to him, 'If I *desire* [Thĕlō – determine to act in a certain way; to act with purpose] ... him to *remain* [Mĕnō – verb; to be alive with the timeless spiritual life of God; John's entire life (same as Peter's life – from spiritual birth through death) would be a mediator of God's Word.] ...*until* [Hĕōs – an adverb meaning "continuance of time and place".] ...I *come* [Ĕrchŏmai – the future Apokalupsis of Christ written in the present tense] ...*what* [Tis – an interrogative pronoun; direct question to Peter; or indirect question to everyone] ...is that to you? You follow (identify yourself with My life and death) ...*Me*!'

John 21:23
"This saying therefore went out among the *brethren* [Adĕlphŏs – plural; kinsmen, community based on origin of life, spiritually born children of God.] ...that, that disciple would not die; Yet Jesus did not say to him that he would not die, but only, 'If I want him to remain until I come, what is that to you? ` "

You live your life and let everybody else live theirs. John did in fact outlive all the disciples and did not die until he was ninety-five years old. And in that time, he wrote first, second and third John and the Book of Revelation. Jesus was saying to Peter: you accomplish God's will for your life and John will accomplish God's will for his life. Your life is not permanent; but it is what you do for God with your life that has enduring results.

John 21:24
This is the disciple who *bears witness* [Martureō – to testify as a witness] ...of these things; and we know that his witness is true.

Peter wrote the Epistles of First and Second Peter, which reveal everything Jesus taught His disciples about His identity. John wrote the Epistles of First, Second and Third John to reveal the false doctrines that were tearing the churches apart and to correct them with the true doctrines spoken by Jesus. And he wrote the book of Revelation to uncover the Doxa of Jesus to finalize His purpose for creating humanity.

The Holy Spirit [Phanaroō] is God's continual voice in this present world for the redemption of every human being who will be saved. As long as this world exists (it does not have a permanent existence) the Holy Spirit reveals Jesus to the world as God's only Savior.

Satan speaks against the revelation of the Holy Spirit and man believes him. He is described by names which declare him to be the embodiment of death's ruling power in this world (the deceptive power of a lie). God's judgment is that he will be given absolute control of this world (the desolation of the world) for God's purpose of the Holy Spirit drawing the last remnant

God Reveals His Glory [Doxa – True Identity]

of the human race to worship Him. God's judgment of the flood came when there were only eight believers left. Do we have a faith that can persevere in this time when we may stand alone?

John 21:25

"And there are also many other things which Jesus did which if they were written in detail, I suppose that even the world itself would not contain the books which were written."

APOKALUPSIS – THE KING OF KINGS GLORIFIED FROM HEAVEN

Revelation 19

The Book of Revelation is not a history book of the New Testament age. It does not identify any person or event in time, which allows God to be the personal power of deliverance for the life of every believer who must live out their lives in tribulation caused by the curse of death. The seven seals detail God's movement of His Kingdom of Life through His presence in this world for the purpose of destroying death and saving every human being who will be saved.

The power of death which rules over this world has absolutely no power over the action of God's heavenly justice and righteousness. Revelation 19 comprises the revelation of God's personal presence in His creation [Epiphaneia] to execute His wrath on the kingdom power of death. The entire book of Zephaniah reveals the "Great Day - Revelation of The Lord" to be a terrible judgment on the forces of evil.

19:1

"After these things I heard, as it were, a loud voice of a great multitude in heaven, saying, Hallelujah! Salvation and glory and power belong to our God;"

This chapter begins with "after these things." This is a reference to the previous chapters 15-18, the abomination of desolation that brings the world under the complete control of death. Chapter 18 reveals the anguish of the fallen angels when Christ destroys them by the word of His mouth. The Apokalupsis of Christ is God's revelation to the Angels in heaven that causes them to exalt God with great joy.

The actual movement of God for the Apokalupsis of the Christ as revealed in this chapter is announced first to the angels (the elders of heaven; the ancient ones) who have been a first-hand witness to the entire spectrum of God's revelation. The joy they express is directed toward the person of God. They shout an ancient Hebrew word *Hallelujah* [praise you Jehovah (Lord)].

The second coming of the Christ is the ultimate revelation of the *Epiphaneia* [Deity of God in this present created order], promised in Isaiah 40 and 63; Matthew 24; 25:31-42; II Peter 2:7, 10-13; and I Corinthians 15:23.

I Thessalonians 4:14-17, Paul says the *coming* [Parousia] will be a joyous reunion of all God's family from Adam to the last saint living. Some will come from paradise with Jesus and some will be *caught up* [Harpazo -forcible, publicly, seized from the earth] so that all of Spiritual Israel (the Old and New Testament Saints) will be one with Christ.

II Thessalonians 2:1, Paul says that the coming of the Lord (Parousia) will be for <u>gathering</u> [Episunagoge – to assemble together in one place all the saints that belong to Him].

Mark 13:27 Jesus said, "And then He will send forth the angels, and will <u>gather together</u> [Episunago] His elect from the four winds, from the farthest end of the earth, to the farthest end of heaven."

II Thessalonians 1:6-10, Paul says it will be a time of <u>revealing God from heaven</u> [Apokalupsis] …the righteous judgment of God on every power of unbelief and the deliverance of those who have glorified God by their faith.

The angels reveal every facet of God's power with three words which belong explicitly to <u>Elohiym</u> [The Deity of God; the supreme authority of Life which cannot die and rules by the iron rod power of righteousness]:

1. <u>Salvation</u> [Soteria – deliverance; the idea of total preservation]. This work of God was accomplished by the first coming of Jesus [Epiphaneia] to establish the Kingdom of Life as the timeless ruling power over all humanity cleansed by the blood of the Lamb. It is the resurrection of the human spirit from the kingdom power of death to be reunited with its creator. Jesus (by His own resurrection from the dead) destroyed the power of death to hold humanity in the grave.

John 5:24

"Truly, truly, I say to you, he who hears My word and believes Him who sent Me, has timeless life and does not come into judgment, but has passed out of death into life."

John 6:38-40

"For I have come down from heaven, not to do My own will, but the will of Him who sent Me. And this is the will of Him who sent Me, that of all that He has given Me I lose nothing but <u>raise</u> [Anistemi – to stand again; to rise or arise from the dead] …it up on the <u>last day</u> [Eschatos – the final and decisive judgment which concludes the development of God's plan of salvation]. … For this is the will of Elohiym that everyone who beholds the Deity of Jesus and believes in Him may have timeless life; and I Myself will raise him up on the last day."

2. <u>Glory</u> [Doxa – the recognition of the Deity of God for His true identity, which can be completely known only by being in His presence]. Jesus revealed the identity of God by His first appearance [*Epiphaneia*] to destroy the power of death; to take away the sins of the world. The Holy Spirit continues to unveil the glory of God in this age of redemption by the *Phaneroō* [the uncovering of the Deity of Jesus by the Holy Spirit as the One sent by Elohiym to be the Savior of the world; to every person who will be saved]. The second coming of Jesus [*Apokalupsis*] unveils the glory of God coming from heaven with His fierce wrath as the heavenly authority of the Kingdom of Life to totally and completely remove all the powers of death and finally death itself (the culmination of the rule of Christ**).**

3. <u>Power</u> [Dunamis – the inherent authority for total dominion; the self-will of God's mind] uncovered by the breath of Jesus (His spoken word). Jesus revealed the Kingdom of God is not of this world but is Elohiym: The Life-giving Deity of Heaven. The power of this throne is the only power which can destroy death because it is the only power which is not subject to death.

God Reveals His Glory [Doxa – True Identity]

This is the truth Jesus revealed to Pilate at the time of His crucifixion. Jesus could not be killed; He had to yield His body to death by His own volition. That was His purpose for coming into this world of man. Absolutely nothing has any authority over Him. The good news of the gospel is that every person redeemed by Jesus has this same power over death, the power of timeless life.

19:2

"Because His judgments are True and Righteous; for He has judged the great harlot who is corrupting the earth with her immorality and He has avenged the blood of His bondservants on her."

The angels' song of praise for the coming of Christ is for the condemnation and removal of the great Harlot (Satan). This is detailed in Revelation 16-18 and is finalized in Revelation 20:1-3 and 7-10. If the angels rejoice over something of this significance, it ought to be the focus of our minds to do the same. In Exodus 15 (the song of Moses), all the people rejoiced over their deliverance from Egypt. They had just witnessed with their own eyes the fury of God's judgment on the kingdom powers of this world.

The principal theological content of the angels' praise of God is for the triumph of His throne. The ruling power of life over death is _truth_ [Alethinos – real, genuine, one who cannot lie] and _righteousness_ [Dikaios – the character of pure holiness which cannot sin/die]. This is the only judgment which can come from the mind of God. His judgment on evil is according to His own character of justice and rightness. This is a far cry from the injustice which comes from the principalities ruling human courts. True justice is the desperate need of the human mind, but it can be found only in the Christ.

God has _judged_ Satan [Krino – to divide, separate, and make a distinction]. Revelation 20:1-3, Satan will be chained in the abyss until it is time {Kairos} to affect his permanent removal to the lake of fire. The joy that comes from the hearts of God's elect people is not just the fact of Satan's final demise, but the realization that his power of deception has already been removed as a controlling power upon those who have the mind of Christ. Satan has no jurisdiction over humanity filled with the Holy Spirit; the continuing presence of Elohiym in this world. We are free from bondage to the unrighteousness of death, to live lives empowered by the righteousness of Life.

The Holy Spirit is God's guarantee that Elohiym directs our thoughts while we are in the weakness of the flesh as He did with Adam. He will be the same power of our minds in His timeless presence, which is God's guarantee that death will cease to exist.

God's people in this life {His sheep} are identified by the character of His holiness revealed to man by _Jesus_ [the Huios – visible presence of God in this world of death]. He is the Deity working in this world today to separate His sheep from the goats - Satan's people identified by the destructive powers of death which controls their minds.

The angels rejoice because the coming of Christ will _avenge_ [Ekdikeo – to take revenge, to punish] …Satan for the blood of His _bondservants_ [Doulos – one who is in a permanent relationship of servitude to another]. The ruling power of God's throne was not diminished by Satan's rebellion, or the ensuing power of death which separates man from his creator. The coming of Christ as the Lamb and the Lion glorify God by affirming the permanent relationship of Life between Himself and all that He has redeemed to be righteous. Our relationship with God has always been and will always be just as permanent as God's Kingdom Rule of Life is permanent.

19:3-4

"And a second time they said, 'Hallelujah! Her smoke rises up forever and ever`. And the twenty-four *elders* [Presbus– the original angels which ruled the inhabitants of heaven] …and the four living creatures fell down and worshiped God who sits on the throne saying, 'Amen. Hallelujah`!

Revelation 4:4

"And around the throne were twenty-four thrones; and upon the thrones was twenty-four elders sitting, clothed in white garments and golden crowns on their heads."

The angelic powers which surround God's throne are ecstatic with joy when God's judgment on death is made known to them. They rejoice because God's judgment on death is timeless. Satan and his rule will come to a permanent end. In Revelation 18:9, the demonic powers ruling with Satan weep and mourn over his impending destruction because what happens to him happens to them also. They are the first powers of evil that will be thrown into the lake of fire at the appearance of Christ. What Satan does is temporary, but what God does is permanent.

They prostrate themselves before Him in worship with the realization that there will never again be any authority in competition with God for their allegiance. Those angels which rebelled against God can never be reunited with Him; but most importantly to those angels who remained with God is the knowledge that they can never be separated from Him.

19: 5-6

"And a voice came from the throne, saying, 'Give praise to our God, all you His *bondservants* [Doulos – one whose will be altogether consumed in the will of another] …you who fear Him, the small and the great. ` And I heard, as it were, the voice of a great multitude and as the sound of many waters and as the sound of mighty peals of thunder, saying, 'Hallelujah! For the Lord our God, the Almighty, reigns`.""

These verses project the celebration of God's rule to include saved humanity in paradise. Every saved human being in paradise and on earth is commanded to worship God with the highest praise. The saints in paradise are not there to continue the activities of this world (that is the only way people talk and joke about heaven). They are there to never cease in their worship of God. We must not let the activities of earthly life hinder us in our obligation to never cease in praising God.

This command from the Lord is a direct contradiction to Satan's lie that we do not have to obey God. These verses affirm the positive consequences of a faith which chooses to love and obey God. Obeying God is what His Kingdom of Life is all about. It is revealed to us in I Peter 4:12-19, that God's judgment involves His proving the identity of His true people by blessing

God Reveals His Glory [Doxa – True Identity]

them with the power of His love. God's judgment begins with proving that He alone is the power of righteousness for the transformed minds of the redeemed.

We enjoy the blessed life that comes from familiarity with God as His children. We are comforted by Him as we endure the ravages of death upon our frail bodies. We are strengthened by the knowledge that we are not under the condemnation of God but are assured of permanently enjoying the glory of a heavenly existence empowered by life that cannot die {not under the power of death}. We will sit at Jesus' feet in the Rule of Christ and will live in the presence of His throne in His timelessness. Because of our faith in the Living God to be obedient to Him, we join the heavenly choir in singing His praises with Hallelujah! For The Lord Our God, The Almighty, Reigns.

19:7-9

"Let us rejoice and be glad and give the glory to Him, for the marriage of the Lamb has come and His bride has made herself ready. And it was given to her to clothe herself in fine linen, bright and clean; for the fine linen is the righteous act of the saints. And he said to me, 'Write, *blessed* [Makarios – the state of the believer in Christ possesses His character of deity; timeless life] …are those who are invited to the marriage supper of the Lamb'. And he said to me, 'These are *true* [Alethinos – one who cannot lie] …*words* of God [Logos – the intelligence of God's mind to restore His Kingdom Rule of Life to spiritually dead humanity]."

The Apokalupsis of Christ will produce tremendous joy for the redeemed because it is the uniting of two spiritual beings in love with one-another. The time of engagement or betrothal ends with the *marriage feast* of the Lamb [Gamos – the consummation of the marriage; the actual joining of a husband with his wife to identify them as one flesh. God will consummate His relationship with His people by transforming us to spiritual beings completely ruled by the holiness of His Throne of Life. We will no longer be a *shadow of God* but will reflect His glory {His identity} in our perfected lives.].

The second coming of Christ is the consummation of salvation; the uniting of the Savior with the redeemed to be one spiritual body. This is revealed in I Corinthians 15:42-44, when mortal {man under the authority of death} will be recreated to the glory of a new creation; and Immortal {man not under the authority of death} Spiritual beings free from bondage to death; ruled by the mind and holiness of God. We will not be God, but "Godly spiritual beings". We will be restored to the spiritual identity of God by the authority of His perfect holiness, having been cleansed by His blood.

To meet the Lord in the air is God's authority to free His people from bondage to death that rules the earth (the habitation of man as opposed to the habitation of God) to be alive in His presence as a heavenly people with only His mind.

These verses clearly affirm the discerning mind of God as to who will be blessed by His coming and who will not. Only those who "make themselves ready" are identified as the bride.

Because they identify themselves with Christ by their lives, God puts on them the wedding clothes which identify them as having the same character as the groom. The *clean linen* [Katharos – a legal or ceremonial cleanness from the pollution and guilt of sin; free from soil or stain] … is the *righteous acts* [Dikaioma – the legal rights of Saints; the product or result of being justified by God] ...of the *saints* [Hagios – separation, consecration, devotion to the service of Deity, sharing in Gods purity and abstaining from earth's defilement (spiritually minded instead of fleshly minded]. The bride of Christ is every believer who God purifies by the sacrificial blood of the Lamb. Jesus is the sinless High Priest of heaven who takes away the sins of the world. The bride is identified in Revelation 20:4-6, as those who experience the *first resurrection* [Anastasis – to stand again; to be restored to timeless life]. They will not experience the second death because they hate sin as God hates it.

19:10

"And I fell at his feet to worship him {God's messenger}. And he said to me, 'Do not do that; I am a fellow servant of yours and your brethren who hold the testimony of Jesus; worship God, for the testimony of Jesus is the spirit of prophecy`." (Revelation 22:18-19)

This verse presents a contrast to verse nine. Only God knows the number of people in the history of mankind who will not be blessed by the coming of Jesus but will be judged along with Satan for their idolatry.

At the time of John's writing there was a strong tendency for people in the church to listen to false prophets and human precepts. Paul said in Colossians 2:18 "Let no one keep defrauding you of your prize by delighting in self-abasement and the worship of the angels, taking his stand on visions he has seen, inflated without cause by his *fleshly mind* [Nous – the organ of mental perception and apprehension, the organ of conscious life, the faculty of thought]."

John was over-whelmed by the vision of all heaven worshiping God and fell into Satan's trap of self-abasement (false humility) so that he under-valued himself in his relationship with God, and undervalued "God" to be a "god". He fell at the feet of God's messenger to worship him instead of God.

The angel put the situation in perspective. "Do not do that; I am a *fellow servant* [Sundoulos – a servant of the same Lord] ...of you and your *brethren* [Adelphos – a fellowship of life based on identity of origin; born from above.] ...who hold the *testimony of Jesus,* [Marturia– the announcement of the gospel by the person of Jesus] ...worship God! For the testimony of Jesus is the *spirit* [Pneuma– purpose, aim] ...of *prophecy* [Propheteia – the result of God's grace or divine enablement to reveal the true identity of Jesus to the church]."

John was reminded of how powerful false prophecy is to capture the mind of a person who takes his focus off Jesus as the true Deity of God. Man is a religious being by creation and easily deceived to worship religious powers that cannot save. Paul said in II Corinthians 4:4, "...the god of this world has blinded the minds of the unbelieving, that they might not see the light of the gospel of the glory of Christ, who is the Deity of God." Many religious people are captured by the schemes of false prophets to worship "gods" from their own imagination. This has been the work of Satan since he led the angels to rebel in heaven; and the last time he will do it is at the culmination of the Rule of Jesus (Revelation 20).

The words of the angel are a prophetic message to the church that it must be on guard so that it does not lend itself to false prophecy. There is no substitute for Jesus (the Huios of God) or the salvation He provides for man. There is only one kingdom rule in this world or will ever be in this world: It is God's Kingdom Rule of Life (His mind of righteousness) that removes death from controlling the minds of the redeemed. The church must be firmly grounded in this truth and love the truth. The words Jesus spoke are the only words which bear repeating, for they are the words of truth which speaks to the mind of man to believe and be saved. Jesus is the only power of Deity who can set man free from bondage to death.

19: 11

"And I saw heaven opened; and behold, a white horse, and He who sat upon the white horse is called *Faithful* [Pistos – trustworthy; steadfast to fulfill a promise] ...and True; and in *righteousness* [Dikaiosune – justice which fulfills God's claims upon the believer; God's standard of Life to which all created beings are required to conform] ... He *judges* [Krino –separates; makes a distinction] ... and wages war."

John's vision of Christ in this nineteenth chapter is limited to His appearance and the subsequent purpose of His presence. John saw heaven opened to reveal Christ on a "white horse." In battle, horses were used to break enemy formations. In this respect, it is representative of an aggressive charge by the holiness of heaven to bring about an unmerciful victory. No one can hide, retreat or flee to safety. No one can escape the authority of heaven. All the world is a witness to God's character of holiness revealed by Jesus in His first coming; and it will be revealed even more so at His second coming. These words reveal the sovereign authority of Jesus to destroy this world of death and rule over a sinless people.

Revelation 1:7

"Behold, He is coming with the clouds, and every eye will see Him, even those who pierced Him; and all the tribes of the earth will mourn over Him. Even so, Amen."

Matthew 16:27

"For the Christ is going to come in the *glory* [Doxa – true identity] ... of His Deity with His angels; and will then recompense every man according to his deeds."

The emphasis of Revelation 19:11, is upon the awesome might of God as the victorious heavenly Kingdom of Life. The only light (the Epiphaneia – the first coming of Christ) powerful enough to shine in the darkness of death was the truth of God's saving grace revealed by the Sacrificial Lamb. The angels in verse six worshipped God because of it. The second appearance of Jesus (Apokalupsis) will vindicate God's revelation of Himself to be the truth. It will be the righteous judgment of God's throne to execute His wrath on the very existence of death and all under its power.

Demonic powers and unbelieving man do not look for God to act in this world and will be surprised (astonished) when He does. The white horse declares to all these unbelievers of the entire history of this world that the one riding it has proven Himself to be victorious in His warfare with death. His Word spoken from the very beginning is the only true word for life. For the first time in human lives, unbelieving man will know the fear of God and will acknowledge Jesus to be God.

19: 12

"And His eyes are a flame of fire, and upon His head are many *diadems* [Diadema – flags or filaments (banners) of silk or linen]. And He has a name written upon Him which no one knows except Himself."

In Daniel 10:6 and Revelation 1:14, the eyes in the visions of God have the appearance of lightening. This is a symbol of deity which imposes the power of security for those in a right relationship with God. He sees all and He knows who is pure in heart for He sees to the most inner thoughts of the mind. The words spoken by lips are not always the same as the words of the heart. God secures the one who speaks truth from the heart; but His fierce judgment is on the lying tongue.

Diadems are not the crowns worn by a king sitting on a throne, but the symbols of victory flown by a conquering king returning from battle. In this sense, Jesus is the commander of a victorious army riding a white horse into the city of his own people. His appearance is a message that the enemy has been vanquished and they who belong to Him are safe from harm. This king cannot be defeated. By His judgment on death, He has safely secured every person who would be saved and has vanquished everyone who will not be saved.

The name engraved on Christ is fixed as a legislative act of the Person of God to denote that the Person of Jesus is the same as Elohiym: The One God. The name Jesus has a greater authority in heaven than any name given Him by man. The name is of vital importance to God because it is the embodiment of God in all His holiness. It is revealed in writing to emphasis the fact that God brings to remembrance everything He has revealed about Himself. His judgment is upon all who defame this name, to make it unholy. God will vindicate His name because He gave up His glory in heaven (true identity) to suffer the will of God in this world of death.

19: 13

"And He is clothed with a *robe* [Himation – a large, loose outer garment that can be used as a covering for sleeping]…*dipped* [Bapto – to immerse, baptize]…in *blood* [Haima – the substantial basis for life]; …and His *name* [Onomar – the confession of man to his unique identity; to be baptized into the faith of that person; to be totally identified with his character and purpose]…is called 'The *Word* of God` [Logos – the intelligence of the mind, the utterance of God's mind which can be understood only by those who want to hear with understanding]."

Christ is immersed in His own blood; His offering of Himself on the heavenly altar. This verse reveals the preplanned purpose of God to give His own timeless life to redeem humanity. This royal robe identifies Christ as the Deity of God who came to earth to establish the heavenly rule of righteousness (Life), to cover each and every human being which identifies itself with God. Jesus is Elohiym, the creator of all life in heaven and on the earth, all life physical and spiritual. His blood is spiritual life that cannot die, and it purifies heaven and earth.

The life of the human soul is in the blood of the body. The life of the human spirit is in the blood of Christ. This verse declares the preplanned purpose of God to restore timeless life to all those redeemed from the curse of death, by the sacrificial blood of the Lamb. The robe covers all the sins of redeemed man; those who are "asleep" (wrapped in His robe through the

God Reveals His Glory [Doxa – True Identity]

ages), and all the saints who are alive at the return of Christ; for they will not experience the death of the grave.

The Word of God is the voice of the throne declaring God's will. Human life is not godless random; but is loaded with information about the reality of the creator and His will for man to be totally immersed in His authority of Life. Humanity was created with this Life by God's Word, and every human being who wants to be saved will be restored to this Life by the Word of God. He will not lose even one who believes His word.

19: 14

"And the armies which are in heaven, clothed in fine linen, white and *clean* [Katharos– a legal or ceremonial cleanness; pure in a spiritual sense from its previous pollution and guilt of sin] …were *following* [Akoloutheo – to cling to Christ by a total identity with Him] ...Him on white horses."

Those who come from paradise with Christ are an army of all the saints of world history. They have experienced the grave (the death of the soul) and the resurrection of the spirit to Paradise. Many people adhere to the belief that there are many ways to God and life. But only those who have died to themselves (live in obedience to the righteousness of God) are alive in Christ.

The white horses are a tribute to their own personal battle of faith and their victory over sin and death. They are identified as soldiers of God {Spiritual Israelites} in this world by their adherence to the gospel and their character of living morally clean physical lives. The Spirit of God ruled over their physical lives and God glorifies them by His witness of Paradise. They share the one and the same identity of God as victors over death.

I Thessalonians 4:14

"For if we believe that Jesus died and rose again, even so God will bring with Him those who have fallen asleep in Jesus."

19: 15-16

"And from His mouth comes a sharp sword, so that with it He may smite the nations; and He will *rule* [Poimaino – the whole office of the shepherd] …them with a rod of iron; and He *treads* [Pateo – a beaten path; to trample upon or have in subjection] …the wine press of the *fierce* [Thumos – a violent action of the mind] …wrath [Orge– an outburst of that state of mind with the purpose of revenge] …of God, Almighty. And on His robe and on His thigh, He has a name written, 'King of Kings, And Lord of Lords.'"

A sword comes from His mouth, not His hands. This is a metaphor for the glorious supernatural power of the Kingdom of Life to separate and establish the authority of Christ's Rule upon saved humanity as it is in heaven. God reveals Himself as ELOHIYM- KING OF KINGS AND LORD OF LORDS - Supreme Ruler of all life in heaven and earth. He speaks His Will (His judgment of justice) that the forces of death have come to an end; not one person under its power will be left alive.

These verses declare the universal destruction of the natural creation and the unbelieving human being as a creation of flesh (the abode of death). These verses are meant to reveal the savagery of God in the execution of His wrath upon death and everything under its power.

This is the revelation of God's judgment by the action of His presence. The person of God is the power of His throne. The presence of God is the power of His throne enacted. The grand entrance of the victor unleashes the superior power of God's throne of Life over the inferior power of the kingdom of death. Just as death could not hold sway over Jesus at His first coming, it falls away in defeat at His second coming. It has no power over God or the Saints (those who are under the authority of Life by virtue of being alive in Jesus).

These verses in Revelation 19 are the transition point in God's plan for redeemed man to no longer live under the rule of death, but to live by the authority of Christ's ruling Kingdom of Life as it will be in a perfect heaven. It will bring about His final judgment on death. Every person in world history who professes salvation in Christ will worship Him face to face; many will adhere to Him by perfect obedience (sinless mind of Christ) and will enter into a perfect heaven where there will not even be a remembrance of death. But many will not. There will no longer be forgiveness for their sins. Everyone who withdraws their mind from Christ's rule (Gog and Magog) will be thrown into Hades for the Great White Throne Judgment.

19:17-18

"And I saw an *angel* [Aggelos – an angel designated by God to announce or proclaim His immediate actions] …standing in the sun; and he cried out with a loud voice saying to all the *birds* [Ŏrněŏn – odious birds; vultures] … which fly in midheaven, 'Come, assemble for the great supper of God; in order that you may eat the *flesh* [Sarx – the bodies of men, beasts, fish, or birds; our present weak and corruptible state subject to the ruling power of death] …of kings and the flesh of commanders and the flesh of mighty men and the flesh of horses and of those who sit on them and the flesh of all men, both free men and slaves, and small and great."

19:19-21

"And I saw the *beast* [Thēriŏn – a venomous viper] …and the *kings of the earth* [two potentates with Satanic power. Revelation 13:1-10 is the sea beast; the power of the Satanic lie given to fallen angels to destroy the identity of Christ; and Revelation 13:11-18 is the land beast; the power of fallen angels to raise up false prophets to exalt Satan] …and their armies, assembled to make war against Him who sat upon the horse and against His army.

And the beast was seized, and with him the false prophet who performed the *signs* [Semeion – miracles which indicates connection with a higher spiritual world (they appear in the heavens in the last days / they are identified by unbelieving minds as aliens come to save the world.)] …in his presence; by which he deceived those who had received the *mark* [Charagma– image of Satan, total character of death that identifies them as Tares and Goats] …of the beast and those who worshiped his image; these two beasts (Revelation 18 - fallen angels) are thrown *alive* [Zaō – they deceive men by having the appearance of gods with the power of life {God gave life to Moses staff as a serpent; the fallen angels did the same for Pharaoh's court magicians}; God will demonstrate the truth that He is the only one who can give life.] …into the lake of fire which burns with brimstone. And the rest (all the host of humanity empowered by death)

God Reveals His Glory [Doxa – True Identity]

were killed with the sword which came from the mouth of Him who sat upon the horse, and all the birds were filled with their flesh."

The complete picture of the demonic war with Christ is found in Revelation 6–18. Jesus opens the first six seals of the scroll in heaven. The first six trumpets define the movement of the *Holy Spirit* [Phanaroō - revealed in John 21:1; the second revelation of God's presence in this world to reveal God's salvation only through The Christ] …. This is the sunteleia as related in Matthew 24. Satan's rule increases in this time with the aid of the fallen angels (sea beast and land beast) to the point that God in II Thessalonians 2:1-12, withdraws the Holy Spirit for the short-lived Mowed of Satan and his desolation upon the earth.

The abomination of desolation is this time Satan is allowed to rule the world. Satan, called (Babylon the great, the mother of harlots and the abominations of the earth) is allowed to sit in the *earthly temple* [Naos of God-His temple in the mind of man]. Satan is given freedom to bring seven woes upon the earth for the purpose of identifying and collecting to him all men who reject the gospel message of Christ. This spiritual battle is so intense that God has to end it, lest not even one single human being will be left alive; eight were left alive in the day of Noah.

The sixth bowl is to assemble all the forces of death to do battle with Christ. In Hebrew, this battle is called Har-Magedon. Over two hundred battles have been fought on the Plain of Jezreel. In the Old Testament, Har (Hill)-Magedon became the symbol for the victory of God over all the forces which came up against Israel. Since the defeat of Judah under King Josiah by Egypt under Pharaoh Neco, the word Har-Magedon became a symbol for defeat. The symbol is a combination of words: *Epiches* (at the time of) and *Periecho* (astonishment). Har-Magedon came to mean "the time of astonishment".

Satan gathers all his powers of death for this eschatological battle with Christ, but all it takes for their instant destruction is for Christ to speak and God's judgment is instantly accomplished. The fallen angels are so astonished (Revelation 18) that they *weep* [Cărôsheth – cut themselves] and *lament* [Koptō–to strike or beat one's breast with the hands expressing grief]; …because (Revelation 19:20) they are thrown alive into the lake of fire and (Revelation 20:1-3) Satan is bound and thrown into the abyss. These verses make it very clear to humanity and to the satanic powers of Hades that;'ELOHÏM IS THE LORD. Death and hell can do absolutely nothing except what God empowers them to do. People on earth under the authority of death are killed with the sword which comes from the mouth of Him who sits upon the horse, and all the birds were filled with their flesh."

James V. Holland

Chapter 9

GOD'S FINAL JUDGMENT ON DEATH

THE RULE OF CHRIST

REVELATION 20

20: 1-3
"And I saw an angel coming down from heaven, having the key to the abyss and a great chain in his hand. And he laid hold of the dragon, the serpent of old; that is the devil and Satan, and bound him for[chiliŏi ětŏs –the appointed worship of Jesus in His timeless presence.]…and threw him into the abyss, and shut it and sealed it over him so that he should not deceive the *nations* [Ethnos –the human race Jesus gathers to Himself; considered in a noble or enlarged view as one nation (Isaiah 2:1-4)] …any longer, until the (chiliŏi ětŏs) is *completed* [Teleo –to bring something to perfection or its designated goal; this word is not a measurement of time but the revelation of a completed purpose]; …after these things he must be released for a short *time* [Chronos – not the movement of chronological time; but the designated moment in God's progressive revelation for Satan's final act of deception; to deceive the people [Gog and Magog] who have drawn away from Christ in their minds. This is God's final judgment on the power of death to separate all created life from Him. Following the Great White Throne Judgment; Hades and everyone in it, and Satan and death are thrown into the Lake of Fire.]."

The purpose and the subject of the entire Book of Revelation is the supernatural uncovering of Jesus from heaven to bring His fierce wrath upon death, so that all the redeemed men of world history may worship Him free from its power. These two words [chiliŏi ětŏs] define the absolute power of God's righteousness in heaven (His Mind) to rule over man in a sinless and timeless environment outside of heaven.

The purpose for the Rule of Christ is to perfect the obedience of the saints and reveal those who will not surrender their minds to God. Ezekiel 38-39 calls it the Adamah of God (habitation of God in man). Isaiah 2 calls it simply the mountain (the high place of God over all creation); but Ezekiel reveals the mountain is surrounded by a vast plain (the habitation of man that is still subject to the power of death – Gog and Magog).

The Rule of Christ [chiliŏi ětŏs] is God's final voice to humanity which can still choose death over life. The purpose of Satan's confinement is directly related to the purpose of the third *Parousia* [Apokalupsis -the unveiling of God from heaven for the purpose of Gods final judgment on death and all its powers]. Christ will *rule* [Phthêggômai – to utter a clear sound; to proclaim with an authoritative voice with the intention of swaying the hearers; to speak, to make known the thoughts of the mind] …. It is the open manifestation (Epiphaneia) of God's heavenly throne in a newly created sinless realm of man; designed for Christ to separate His righteous people from the pretenders.

Satan will be silenced because God's final voice of revelation will be to the last vestige of created life that can still reject the iron rod rule of God's righteousness. Satan will be released when it is God's purpose that he should speak for the last time to the minds of those who will still listen to him. The emphasis of these verses is that the revelation of God's kingdom rule which is designed to speak to the human mind without interference from the power of death will be accomplished at God's predestined opportunity. The purpose of God's final judgment on death at the conclusion of Christ's rule is to completely remove every vestige of created life which can fall away from Him. Death began at the throne of God – it will end at the throne of God.

20: 4-6

"And I saw *thrones* [Thrŏnŏs – the place of royalty; the ruling power of Christ and His court of angels] … and they that sat upon them and *judgment* [Krima – the result of making a legal judgment is to pronounce the sentence of innocent or guilty. This is the realty of God separating the sheep from the goats revealed in Matthew 25:31-46] …was given to them.

And I saw the *souls* [Psuche –the life element from God that gives animation to the body; the physical lives of every human being] …of those who had been beheaded because of the testimony of Jesus and because of the word of God, and those who had not worshiped the beast or his image, and not received the *mark* [Charagma – the revelation of Satan's rule; the visible character of death that rules the human mind] …upon their *forehead* [Mĕtōpŏn– Meta (with) and Ŏptanŏmia (eyes); to gaze with wide open eyes as at something remarkable; voluntary observation / participation of the mind]…and upon their *hand* [Chĕir – an instrument to channel power; "by the hand of", "by the agency of"]…but lived by the spiritual power of God and they reigned with Christ for His timeless rule.

The rest of the *dead* [Nekros - every spiritually dead person of the whole human race were cast into Hades. They will be raised up to stand before the Great White Throne judgment of God] …did not come to life until the timeless worship of Christ was *complete* [Teleō – not merely to end something, but to bring it to perfection]. …This is the *first resurrection* [Anastasis- to cause to stand up on one's feet again; to be raised from the power death has on mortal flesh; to be alive again as spiritual (heavenly) beings untouched by death; to be restored to the perfection of God's throne of Life] …of spiritual man. *Blessed* [Makarios – possessing the characteristic of deity – having the sinless mind of Christ] …and holy is the one who has a part in the first resurrection; over these the second death has no power, but they will be *priests* of God [Hiereus– a sacred position, set apart or consecrated for serving at God's altar; an honored position higher than the angels in heaven).] …and of Christ and will reign with Him for His timeless heavenly rule."

The *first resurrection* [Anastasis]is the designated goal of God as defined in I Corinthians 15:21-26, "For since by a man came death, by a man also came the resurrection of the dead. For as in Adam all die, so also in Christ all shall be made alive. But each in his own *order* [Tagma – to place in one's proper order by a designed method. This word is only used in this verse]; …Christ the first fruits, after that those who are Christ's at His *coming* (Parousia -the

God Reveals His Glory [Doxa – True Identity]

Apokalupsis); then comes the end when He delivers up the kingdom to the God and Father, when He has abolished all *rule* [Arche – the beginning of a ruling power. The power of death began its rule in the mind of Lucifer in the presence of God's throne. It will be abolished by the presence of Christ's heavenly rule] ...and all *power* [Dunamis – the basic meaning of being capable of action; inherent power of the mind]. ...For He must *reign* [Basileuo– to be king; to have predominance] ...until He has put all His enemies under His feet. The last enemy that will be abolished is death."

    This present natural world is where God destroyed death's power to permanently separate human life from His rule of righteousness. He accomplished this by His own *resurrection* [Ĕgĕirō– to collect one's faculties; the resurgence of Christ's mind to return to His original identity of ʾĔlôhîym. He left His throne in heaven and gave up His glory (identity of ʾĔlôhîym) to be a sacrifice; His resurrection is His action of restoring Himself to the Throne of God as Supreme Ruler]. This permanent Rule of Christ will be demonstrated as the truth of God's revelation of a Savior by the first resurrection of every person He has saved; then and only then can God finalize the total removal of death when it is completely erased from their minds as if it had never existed and will be incapable of ever existing again. Then, and only then, can God create a perfect heaven where absolutely everything exists under the sovereign rule of His mind; revealed in Revelation 21-22. The fulfillment of this goal is known only in the mind of Elohiym and can only be accomplished by revealing the true belief that controls every person's mind.

    Christ's rule over the mind of this final generation of man began in this world of suffering. John's vision describes the identity of those who experience the first resurrection by their Godly character of righteousness while living under the burden of death.

Philippians 2:5-8
    "Have this mind in yourselves which was also in Christ Jesus, who, although He existed in the form of God, did not regard equality with God a thing to be grasped, but emptied Himself, taking the form of a bond-servant, and being made in the likeness of men. And being found in appearance as a man, He humbled Himself by becoming obedient to the point of death, even death on a cross,"

Philippians 3:7-11
    "Whatever things were gain for me, those things I have counted as loss for the sake of Christ. More than that, I count all things to be loss in view of the surpassing value of knowing Christ Jesus my Lord for whom I have suffered the loss of all things and count them but rubbish in order that I may gain Christ and may be found in Him not having a righteousness on my own, but that which is through faith in Christ. The righteousness which comes from God on the basis of faith; that I may know Him and the power of His resurrection and the fellowship of His sufferings, being conformed to His death; in order that I may attain to the resurrection from the dead."

I Corinthians 15:50
    "Now I say this brother, that flesh and blood cannot inherit the kingdom of God; nor does the *perishable* [Phtharta–under death; an unredeemed body incapable of avoiding suffering,

sickness and the power of death which controls the mind to sin.] ...inherit the *imperishable* [Aphthartos–not under death; a body that is subject to the greater power of Christ to establish His righteousness as the controlling power of the mind]."

I Corinthians 15:53, 54
"For this perishable [Phtharta] ... must put on the imperishable [Aphthartos] ...and this *mortal* [Thnĕtos – to die; from Thnĕskō; created to die a natural death.] ...must put on *immortality* [Aphthartos – life that cannot die] .... But when this perishable will have put on the imperishable, and this mortal will have put on immortality (the rule of God's mind of righteousness), then will come about the saying that is written, '*DEATH* [Thanatos –the kingdom power which cannot live] ...IS SWALLOWED UP IN VICTORY'."

Romans 6 describes Spiritual Israel as that part of the whole human race which overcomes the curse of death established by Adam; by the authority of the second Adam who is from heaven. Romans 9:1-18, clearly defines Spiritual Israel as all people of this world with the spiritual mind of God as their Father. They are called "Saints" – "Sanctified Ones". They will worship Christ in His final revelation by right of living as martyrs of the faith. In Romans 4-8, and Hebrews 11-12, the word "martyr" means "the witness of an over-comer". Every Saint (Spiritual Israelite / Christian) is a martyr; a witness of God; an over-comer, whether they are called upon to die physically or not. They have proven by the testimony of their own lives the reality of God's Kingdom of Life given to them as a free gift. Every Saint dies to self in the battle with sin, and lives by obedience to God's commands.

John 3:35-36; John 5:21-27, and John 6:27,33,35-40,53-58, are all adamant statements by God that He is the heavenly Kingdom Power of Life and He has given the power of His Life to every person in this generation of man who claims it by faith in Jesus, the Savior. Revelation 20:6"Blessed and holy are those who have part in the first resurrection. The second death (God's final judgment on death – the Lake of Fire) has no power over them."

I Thessalonians 3:13
"May God strengthen your hearts so that you will be blameless and holy in the presence of our God and Father at the *coming* [Parousia– presence of God]. ...of our Lord Jesus with all His Saints".

20:7-9
"And when the chilioi ĕtŏs (the final event in the Jewish calendar when God will establish the timeless worship of Christ) is *completed* [Teleo – not merely to complete something, but to bring it to perfection as its designated goal], ...Satan will be released from his prison and will come out to deceive the *nations* [Ethnos – the very last vestige of the entire human race that turns away from worshipping Jesus is designated in this context by the governing power of death] ...which are in the four *corners* [Gōnia – extreme outer limits] ...of the *earth* [Gē – the whole habitat of man surrounding the throne of Christ], ...

Gog [Gōwg– the symbolic name for the spirit of antichrist - people who withdraw from Christ in their minds] ... and *Magog* [Magōg – the symbolic name for the total embodiment of people who are ruled by the darkness of death – referred to as Reubenites.], to gather them together for *the war* [Pŏlĕmŏs – to fight a single encounter with full expectation of complete victory]; …the number of them is like the sand of the seashore. And they came up on the *broad plain* [PlatŏsGē- the vast low land that surrounds the high place of Jesus and His people] …of the earth and surrounded the *camp* [Parēmbŏte–military term for the open encampment of an army.] …of the *saints* [Hagios– the sanctified, set apart holy ones worshipping Christ.] …and the *beloved* [Agapao – God's love which indicates the direction of His will to find joy in something] …*city* [Pŏlis – the visible (unwalled) capital of a kingdom – the ruling place of Jesus] …and *fire* [Pur – the holiness of God which purifies] …came down from God out of *heaven* [Ŏuranŏs – the holy abode of God; it cannot be entered by man until death has been permanently destroyed.] …and *burned* [Katĕsthiō – to devour or consume to complete obliteration] …them (Gog and Magog)."

*Please note that all the powers of death and this present world ruled by death will be violently removed by the Apokalupsis of Christ; however, death itself will remain to serve God's purpose of completely identifying and removing the last vestige of created life that can possibly be tested by death. The release of Satan from the abyss is not designated as the time which ends the rule of Christ (a theological precept taught by men). His release is God's designated opportunity to fulfill Satan's final role as the great deceiver before he is thrown into the Lake of Fire.

He will reveal that death is a latent power in the minds of men who will secretly choose to reject the iron rod rule of God's Kingdom Power of Righteousness. Death is the ultimate enemy of God because it is the authoritative power of self-rule of the mind and rejection of God's righteousness. Through the Rule of Christ, God will reveal the truth that death has no power over the person of God nor can it reclaim humanity which is governed by the mind of Christ. Satan is released to call out every person surrounding the throne of Christ who will not believe this revelation spoken from God's own mouth. They will withdraw from Christ in their minds, but they cannot act overtly toward Christ until Satan speaks to them and death is given its power for the last time.

In verses 20:8-9, Satan is released to "deceive" the *nations* [Ethos – the totality of mankind surrounding the throne of Christ and His people, which by context proves itself to be godless.] Gog and Magog were real people. Gog was a grandson of Reuben (Jacobs first born who rejected the God of Abraham). He created a nation in Asia Minor named *Magog* [people of the north / people of darkness] …that was always at war with Israel.

I Chronicles 5:1-6
"Now the sons of Reuben, the first born of Israel (Jacob), because he *defiled* [Châlal – to profane a person by an illicit sexual act] …his father's bed, his *birthright* [B^{e}kôwrâh or B^{e}kôrâh, fem. of root word B^{e}kôwr – first born individual in a family] …was given to the sons of Joseph, the son of Israel (Jacob); so that he is not enrolled in the genealogy according to the birthright. The sons of Reuben were Hanoch, Pallu, Hezron, Carmi and Joel. The sons of Joel were Shemaiah, **Gog**, Shimei, Micah, Reaiah, Baal, and Beerah. Joel was leader of the Reubenites whom Tilgath-pilneser king of Assyria carried away into exile."

Ezekiel 38:2-4

"And the _word_ [Dâbâr – the essential content of God's revelation] …of the Lord came to me saying,' _Son_ [Bên – from Bênâh; builder of the family name; legal children who give life to the future established by what exists] …of _man_ [Adam – humanity created in the image of God] …_set_ [Sîym – to appoint someone with a task] …your face toward Gog of the _land_ ['Erets - the earth created as the domain of man under the curse of death] …of Magog, the _prince_ [Nâsîy` - an exalted person of a particular family] …of Rosh, Meshech and Tubal, and _prophesy_[Nâbâ - speak by inspiration] …against him, and _say_ [Âmar – command] …'Thus says the Lord God, behold, I am against you, O Gog, prince of Rosh, Meshech and Tubal. And I will turn you about and put hooks into your jaws and I will bring you out, and all your _army_ [Chayil – strength; used also for the entourage of the queen of Sheba (I Kings 10:2)] …horses and horsemen, all of them splendidly attired, a great _company_ [Qâhâl–This masc. Heb. noun is considered to be one of the most important terms in the entire Old Testament. It is convocation, a congregation, an assembly, a crowd, a multitude, an army, a gathering of the Hebrew people for deliberation, the whole assembly of Israel; also, an assembly of any kind for the purpose of plotting war. The Greek Septuagint usually translates Qâhâl with ekklêsia, but it uses sunagôgê thirty-six times. This word is God's revelation for the identity of the masses of people (like the sands of the seashore) who claim to be the body of Christ (the church) but reveal they are Reubenites who do not have the legal birthright of Israel.] …with _buckler_ [Tsinnâh – a large shield with extended sharp hooks] …and shield, all of them wielding swords`."

In Ezekiel 38:7-13, God reveals that everything about this group (Magog) is under His direct and determinative control. He controls their minds and hardens their hearts (like Pharaoh who refused to make a proper decision).

Ezekiel 38:10-11

"Thus, says the Lord God, 'It will come about _on that day_ ['Yôwm – this is not a period of time but a theological category; what is designated by God.] …that _thoughts_ [Dâbâr – mental recognition to carry out the will of the heart (Ideas which reveal the purpose of their actions)] …will come into your mind, and you will devise an evil plan. And you will say, I will go up against the land of unwalled villages. I will go against those who are at _rest_ [Shaqat – perfect tranquility, living securely without protective walls, bars, or gates. *The camp of the Saints (Revelation 20:9) is not a geographical location; but the identity of all those who will not turn away from their perfect security in God. Death has no power over them.].''

Ezekiel 38:14-16

"Therefore, _prophesy_ [Nâbâ` - speak the will of God by divine power] …son of man and say (command) to Gog, 'Thus says the Lord God, on that day (an activity designated by God for His purpose) …when My people Israel are living securely, will you not _know_ it? [Y^{e}da 'yâh – give recognition to the sacred name of God Who possesses His people.]. …And you will come from your place out of the remote parts of the [tsâphôn – darkness; gloomy unknown, death]. …you and many peoples with you, all of them riding on horses, a great assembly and a mighty army; and you will _come up_ ['Âlâh– ascend up as you are commanded] …against My people Israel like a _cloud_ ['Ânân – a dark storm cloud] …to cover the land. It will come about in the *last days* [`Achărôwn – after the last days; at the extreme back which has no future] … that I will bring you against *My land* [`Ădâmâh – the entire world God created to bring forth and support life. Adam was created from this soil and is owned as a holy possession of God. Every person born to God's kingdom of life is God's holy ground; the camp of God's saints.] …in order that the *nations* [Gôwy – all the unbelieving people of Magog and all the people in Hades] …may know Me when I shall be *sanctified* [Miqdâsh–consecrated by His holiness to be worshipped as the living Deity of God] …through you before their eyes, O Gog."

Ezekiel 38:18-19
"And it will come about on that day when Gog comes against the land of Israel, *declares* [Nâ`am – God utters a judgment of His mind] … the Lord God that My fury will mount up in My *anger* [`Âlâh – an explosion of passionate emotion]. …And in My zeal and in My blazing *wrath* [`Ebrâh – out burst of rage] …I declare that on that day there will surely be a great [Râ `ash – fierce uproar] … and My fury will mount up in My anger."

Ezekiel 39:6-8
"And I will send fire upon Magog and those who inhabit the coastlands in *safety*; [Betach – an overconfident mind; Magog is the totality of all those individuals whose security is in themselves. God sets them apart for destruction.] …they will know that I am the Lord. And My *holy name* [Qôdesh– a most holy, sacred name that is apart from every other name] …I shall *make known* [Yâda – to cause to make known by an intimate knowledge gained by the mind] ….in the midst of My people Israel; and I shall not let My holy name be *profaned* [Châlal –the action of death to do violence to the established rule of God; as Satan did] …anymore. And the *nations* [Gôwy – the totality of people in Hades and all the people of Magog will face the Great White Throne judgment and consignment to the lake of fire] …will know that I am the LORD, the *HOLY ONE* [Qâdôwsh – pure righteousness that cannot be defiled] …in sanctified Holy Spiritual Life – Israel, My People. Behold, it is coming, and it shall be done declares the Lord God. That is the day of which I have spoken."

Satan's deception serves the purpose of God to expose the power of death that is hidden in the mind of every life it possesses. This is the last enemy of God to be completely destroyed. God wants us to know that death originated in Satan's mind in the presence of God's throne. There was no temptation for Lucifer to sin other than the desire of his own mind to glorify himself above God. A multitude of the angels had the same hidden evil in their minds. They had no fear to follow Satan's lead and provoke God to His face. Gog and Magog; these people under Christ's Rule will be like the angels in heaven; like Adam and Eve who fellowshipped with God face to face and like Judas with Jesus at the Passover table. Satan will uncover the evil hidden in their minds and they will act in its power.

God uses Satan's deception to reveal that death does not come from a being's environment or the power of temptation. It comes from our desire to be secure in ourselves (to act as gods – the reason Adam was barred from reentering the Garden of Eden). The clear prophecy of Ezekiel 38-39 and Isaiah 65:17-25, is that when God again places man in a heavenly environment without a tempter (the rule of Christ), many *"pretenders"* (from the context it will be numbered as the sands of the seashore) will still be disposed to unbelief and the lust of the flesh to rebel against Him. But this time there will not be the Christ who says, "ĔliHλi - Deity of Heaven; forgive them for they do not know what they do."

Those who reveal themselves to be unbelievers in the presence of Christ are burned with the *fire* [Pur– Hebrews 10:27, "the fury of a fire {the natural significance of burning} which will consume the adversaries"] …of God's wrath and consigned to Hades with all the spiritually dead; to await God's judgment of the second death.

The destruction of this entire body of people and angels is God's final witness to heaven and earth that HE IS THE LORD. They will see the security of those under God's protective care who enter His perfect abode (Revelation 21-22). Death can never again exist in their minds, because His Mind is the only mind in His perfect heaven. Life without death is Holy because God is Holy. What every unbeliever would not believe (truth revealed by the Holy Spirit) they now fully understand from His judgment that their death is just as permanent as His gift of life is for believers.

The great tragedy of Revelation 20 is the story of Paradise Lost. No human mind can grasp the magnitude of God's grief at the loss of practically the entire human race (Genesis 6:5-7). The tragedy of human life is not just what every lost person feels at their time of judgment; it is also the reality we are witness to in our own experience of living. We see our friends and family members (inside and outside of the church) who will never, even for a moment, experience the joy of having God in control of their minds. No matter what they profess to believe, they remain spiritually dead and without hope for knowing the purity of life in God. They are totally ignorant of the truth that they are in bondage to the power of death by their own unceasing war with God.

The pain we share with God is the fact that there is nothing we can do about it. They are dead and gone. Jacob had twelve sons. Exodus 49 is his judgment on eleven of them (all but Joseph}; each one of them according to the reality of their individual character – whether it was good or evil. What grief must have broken his heart to know that this people (Gog and Magog) are his descendants called Reubenites. It is the conviction of this author that judgment on the people we dearly love must be left up to God, the only one who knows the truth of their minds. Our duty is to love them with God's love and pray for His love to win their hearts, whether He succeeds or not.

20:10

"And the devil that deceived them was thrown into the *lake of fire* [Pur – the holiness of God which consumes their minds so that they have no self-identity. God creates spiritual life, and He can cause it to cease existing as if it never existed.] …and *brimstone* [Thĕiŏn – burning sulfur; referred to as "fire from heaven" because fires started by lightening have a sulfur smell] …where the beast and the false prophet are also; and they will be *tormented* [Basanizō – when used as a verb it means to torture; in the passive voice it means to be harassed, distressed] …*day* [Hēmĕra – timeless existence] …and *night* [Nux – the total absence of light] …*forever and ever* [Alon – a timeless duration; timeless alienation from God]."

Satan is not consumed by the fire of God's wrath in verse 9. That fire was meant for the removal of Gog and Magog to Hades. When Satan has accomplished his work of revealing the hidden rebellion in the human mind, then he is removed permanently from further evil. His

God Reveals His Glory [Doxa – True Identity]

function was not to originate sin in man, but to reveal it and develop it as the power to work against the will of God. Its power of rebellion is to destroy the life it controls; while the power of God's kingdom rule is to produce life that is obedient to do His will (righteousness).

This verse reveals truth about Satan which should be known by every saint of God. Satan is called "the great serpent" and many other names which describe his character of evil. But Satan is not a god power, nor is he in any sense a rival to God. God tells us that we are not to fear him. He cannot go beyond the permissive will of God in his actions and at the appointed time he will cease to exist as a self-determinative being.

God's judgment on Satan and sin is just (Romans 6:23, "For the wages of sin is death"). Satan is personally responsible for his own action of separating himself from God. God's judgment on man as a sinner is equally just (Romans 3:23, "for all have sinned and fall short of the glory of God."). Our sins move us from the security of God's kingdom of life that cannot die, to a kingdom power that cannot live. Death becomes our master by our choice of a self-serving mind. In the Lake of Fire, absolutely nothing will have a self-determinative mind so that death ceases to exist.

The judgment of God's Kingdom of Life is also the action of a righteous mind. The Kingdom of Life and the kingdom of death cannot co-exist as competing powers. Good and evil cannot sit upon the same throne. God's character is Righteousness, Holiness, and Perfect Justice. He is just in His actions to destroy that power (death) which destroys life He created; and He is just in His actions to destroy all life that puts itself in submission to this opposing authority.

God's judgment to restore the spiritually dead to His timeless life is equally just, because it is the action of His righteous mind (there is no death in God's mind). God made it possible for man to once again be placed in the security of His Kingdom of Life. By our choice of a believing and submissive mind (repent), we can return to the authority of His Kingdom Rule.

Romans 3:22, "...the righteousness of God has been revealed through faith in Jesus Christ, for all those who believe". John 11:25-26, Jesus said to Martha, "I am the resurrection and the life; he who believes in Me shall live even if he dies, and everyone who lives and believes in Me shall never die. Do you believe this?"

The justice of God's throne is revealed in that: (1) the redeemed of God are secure under the authority of His Timeless Kingdom of Life, (2) all unbelieving humanity will face the Great White Throne judgment and the second death, and (3) every angelic being which promotes and glorifies the kingdom of death will suffer its fullest curse; to be consumed in the Lake of Fire (to cease to exist as a self-determining power of life). This is the authority of God's Throne of Life: to destroy every single self-determining mind under the power of death as if it never existed. This is God's guarantee that death can never exist again.

20:11

"And I saw a great white throne and Him who sat upon it, from whose presence *earth* [Ge – The physical part of creation which denotes man's domain and the history transacted between God and man. It is the habitation of death.] ...and *heaven* [Ouranos – God's original dwelling place where death began.] ...fled away, and no place was found for them."

In Revelation 15:1, "And I saw another *sign* [Semeion – miracle with an ethical end and purpose; the fingerposts of God which indicate the grace and power of His higher spiritual world] ...in heaven, great and marvelous; seven angels who had seven plagues, which are the <u>last</u> [Eschatos – primarily with reference to the extreme, most remote place in time which concludes everything. It denotes the time when the complete development of God's plan of salvation shall come to a close; the time of the final and decisive judgment.] ...because in them the <u>wrath</u> [Thumos – a violent motion or passion of the mind] ...of God is <u>finished</u> [Teleō – to bring something to perfection or its predestined goal]."

The final act for the Living God to cleanse creation of death is to bring all lost humanity before His Great White Throne, the judgment seat of heaven. The time has passed for God's revelation of Himself seated on the mercy seat of salvation. The realm of natural man (the place of death) has served its purpose. God permanently and completely removes heaven, earth, and the universe; everything that has been contaminated by the presence of death. Unbelieving man is now purely physical beings held in Hades for judgment. They can now stand before the Living God and see Him with absolutely nothing to distort their knowledge of Him. With everything spiritual removed, so are all man's hopes of reincarnation, evolution, aliens and every religion they have trusted in. There is no place to hide from the God they claim does not exist. They will know the truth about God, and they will know the truth about themselves. There will be no place for argument about God's justice when sentence is passed upon them.

20:12-13
"And I saw the <u>dead</u> [Nekros –man as a physical being separated from the power of life; one who has no hope of regaining life], ...the great and the small, standing before the throne, and books were opened; and another book was opened, which is the book of life; and the dead were judged from the things which were written in the books, according to their deeds. And the sea gave up the dead which were in it, and <u>death</u> [Thanatos – natural death of the soul (the soul is the life of the body), this is the death of the grave. The earth/physical life yields up every dead soul] ...and <u>Hades</u> [Sheol in Old Testament Hebrew -the intermediate confinement of the soul until it is called forth for the judgment of the second death] ...gave up the dead which were in them; and they were judged, every one of them according to their deeds."

Every spiritually dead human being in world history will stand before the Great White Throne for their personal accountability. Every single unbelieving human being will have experienced the death of the body and Hades. The basis of God's judgment on the spiritually dead is twofold: the book of works in which man's deeds are recorded, and the Book of Life.

The significance of this double check means that the judgment of the Throne is not the arbitrary decision of God, but the action of injustice and unbelief which clearly separates the lost from the saved. The dead now stand before the One who knows their minds.

John 2:23-25
"Now when Jesus was in Jerusalem at the Passover during the feast, many believed in His name, beholding His signs which He was doing. But Jesus on His part was not entrusting Himself to them, for He <u>knew</u> all men [Ginosko – to know experientially; to perceive with understanding] ...and because He did not need anyone to bear witness concerning man for, He Himself knew what was in man".

First, the dead are judged according to their <u>deeds</u> [Ergon – performance; usually denotes comprehensively what a person is and how he acts] …. Works are unmistakable evidence of the loyalty of the heart. Rejecting the power of goodness enhances and glorifies the evil that is the real treasure of their heart.

Matthew 7:16-10
"Jesus said, 'You will know false prophets by their fruits. Grapes are not gathered from thorn bushes, nor figs from thistles, are they? Even so, every good tree bears good fruit; but the bad tree bears bad fruit. A good tree cannot produce bad fruit, nor can a bad tree produce good fruit. Every tree that does not bear good fruit is cut down and thrown into the fire`.'"

God's judgment is not a "balancing of the books"; weighing good works against bad works but is a balance between disobedience and obedience. What is recorded in the book of works reveals what is in the heart. Luke 6:45, "Jesus said, 'The good man out of the good treasure of his heart brings forth what is good; and the evil man out of the evil treasure brings forth what is evil; for his mouth speaks from that which fills his heart`.'" The book of works reveals the choice of the unbeliever is to live separated from God's control. The penalty for rejecting the person of God and His salvation is permanent death.

Secondly, the dead are judged for the absence of the person's name from the "<u>Book of Life</u>" [Zoë – the principle of life in the spirit and soul which expresses all the highest and best character of God]. The Book of Life distinguishes spiritual life from *bios* (purely physical life). A person whose name is in the Book of Life has believed God and is obedient to live under His authority of righteousness. This person produces the good works that comes from a cleansed heart and will never cease in living the timeless existence of God's own holiness.

John 3:17-21
"Jesus said, 'For God did not send the *Christ* [Huios – Deity] into the world to judge the world, but that the world would be saved through Him. He who believes in Him is not judged; he who does not believe has been judged already because he has not believed in the name of the only begotten [<u>Huios</u> – Christ]. And this is the judgment, that the light is come into the world and men loved the darkness rather than the light; for their deeds are evil`.'"

20:14-15
"And death and Hades were thrown into the lake of fire. This is the second death, the lake of fire. And if anyone's name was not found written in the Book of Life, he was thrown into the lake of fire."

These verses reveal the finality of the second death. Absolutely nothing God created which lives with the power of a rebellious mind will continue to exist. The judgment of Revelation 20:12-13 reveals God's mercy to save is extended to every human being, but His mercy is not limitless. God's love for man will never reject anyone who will trust in Him; but His righteousness will not force Himself on any who chooses to live without Him. The power of the second death is God's ability to permanently remove the free will of every created being, so they cease to exist.

Every lost person in the history of creation will be a witness to the power of the second death. They will be thrown into the lake of fire along with death and Hades. Death and Hades are God's witnesses relegated to the purpose of this present natural creation. At the point they are thrown into the lake of fire, the purifying work of Christ is completed. This is the culmination of all life outside the heavenly presence of God. It is now possible for Jesus to return to His glory of `Ĕlôhîym. The second death closes the door on even the most remote possibility that there will ever again be the darkness of death. It is now time for God to create a new kind of abode for man as a spiritual being in the light of His timeless presence (Revelation 21-22).

Chapter 10

THE FINAL STATE OF GLORIFIED HUMANITY

REVELATION 21-22:9

John's visions are the magnificent sight of the final state of God's presence with redeemed and glorified humanity. At this point in God's progressive revelation, man has now become a natural part of all the holiness of God's own person and has a timeless fellowship with Him and the angels in a Throne room designed for this purpose. The New Jerusalem is not a physical city, but glorified man himself, referred to as the Bride of Christ; just as the Church is not a building, but the people who compose the body of Christ.

The earthly temple and the city of Jerusalem in this created earth were revelations of the security afforded to every person who experienced the inward reality of a transformed heart and life (Jeremiah 7:1-7). God revealed the identity of such a person as one who has been liberated from the curse of death through God's own person: the Christ. Through Christ, man is restored to a righteous relationship with God's Kingdom Throne of Life and will be empowered in His presence with His Mind as a spiritual being superior to the angels (Hebrews chapter one).

The rollcall of faith in Hebrews 11-12 is a promised resurrection at the second coming of Christ. Hebrews 11:40 through chapter 12, says the promise is fully realized in the perfecting work of the Rule of Christ; to be a kingdom people which cannot be touched by death. God's Kingdom of Life offered as a promise is guaranteed by Christ for this purpose.

Hebrews 4:9-10
"There remains therefore a Sabbath rest for the people of God. For the One who has entered His rest has Himself also rested from His works, as God did from His."

Ephesians 2:4-7
"But God being rich in mercy, because of His great love with which He loved us, even when we were dead in our transgressions, made us alive together with Christ (by grace you have been saved), and raised us up with Him and seated us with Him in the heavenly places in Christ Jesus, in order that in the _ages_ [Aion – refers to a specific time to come – permanent life in God's timeless presence.] …He might show the surpassing riches of His grace in kindness toward us in Christ Jesus."

The new creation of Revelation 21-22 is a vision of the oneness of man and God. We are a very privileged people who have the revelation of this heavenly rule of God beyond this time of our present world. The new heavenly abode for man is the creation of a new and rightful place for man as a holy spiritual being; the perfect image of God which shines with the light of His Righteousness.

21:1

"And I saw a _new_ [Kainos – qualitative new use; not a new one numerically, but a different kind] …_heaven_ [Ouranos – the residence of God where death can never exist again] …and _earth_ [Ge – sphere of man's domain as a spiritual being]; …for the first heaven and the first earth passed away, and there is no longer any _sea_ (the universe created outside of heaven; created for the place of death which separates God from His created beings. It is a turbulent power of destruction to the peace of God)."

The original creation of the world was in the darkness of the universe. God created this darkness for the removal of Satan and death from the holiness of heaven. It was in the darkness where the light of God (Jesus) destroyed the power of death. Now that Satan and death have been thrown into the lake of fire, the physical creation has now served its purpose and is totally removed as if it had never existed. In its place is a new kind of existence, ruled by the authority of God's timeless presence. Both God and man are now spiritual beings united as one with the same mind and character of perfect holiness. No trace of evil in any form can ever again exist in the mind of man or angels. The new domain of God and man is a unity (oneness) of His holiness in the power of His perfect peace.

Please note the finality expressed by this verse. No longer can there ever be even the most remote possibility of another Lucifer or an Adam and Eve. Death is so completely removed that it cannot even be a remembrance. It will be as if death had never existed.

21:2-4

"And I saw the _holy city_ [Hagios – sanctified; its fundamental idea is consecration, devotion to the identity of Deity, sharing in God's purity], …new Jerusalem, coming down out of heaven from God, made ready as a bride adorned for her husband. And I heard a loud voice from the throne, saying, 'Behold, the _tabernacle_ of God [Skeen – a movable habitation of God] …is among _men_ [Anthropos – sinless humanity which focuses timeless attention upward away from self; toward God], …and He shall dwell among them, and they shall be His _people_ [Laos – humanity joined together as a single unit by a common power; the kingdom power of God's Throne of Life gives all life one single holy identity], … and God Himself shall be among them and He shall wipe away every tear from their eyes; and there shall no longer be any _death_ [Thanatos – the power of separation from God]; …there shall no longer be any mourning, or crying or _pain_ [Ponos – labor to exhaustion]; …the first things have passed away (ceased to exist).'"

The new domain of God and man is described as a Holy City, a social community of God, man and angels. It is the perfect, holy environment of God's throne room. The city is presented as the movable abode of God, coming down out of the present abode of God. This present abode of God will be replaced with this new creation; a Throne room which includes glorified man. God's new and permanent abode is both a gift to man to exist in His presence, and it is His movement towards man to make him an extension of Himself (His children). Humanity as spiritual beings will no longer exist outside of God's visible presence and will be one mind with His mind.

God Reveals His Glory [Doxa – True Identity]

God's first dwelling with Israel was in a tent which could be stolen by the Philistines. He dwelt in Solomon's temple which was destroyed by the Babylonians. When in Jesus, "the Word became flesh and dwelt (tented) among us", it is this time He empowers man to be His light in the darkness of death. Everything that was temporary and destructible is past. The Holy City of heaven is a picture of perfection and permanence. Redeemed humanity (God's Bride is consummated with the Groom) is adorned with the glory of God – true identity as one spiritual being.

The Holy City of God is the timeless presence of God's bride. It is the glorious estate of spiritual humanity which reflects the wealth of God to love His people in a tender and joyous relationship of oneness. God will not just remove man from suffering the pain of this present world of death; He will totally transform man so that he cannot experience pain of a body or grief of the mind. There can only be the expressing of an intimate love a bride and groom have for one-another. Agape love will be the absolute power of both God and man.

21:5-6

"And He who sits on the throne said, 'Behold, I am making all things new`. And He said, 'Write, for these words are *faithful* [Pistos – certain, worthy to be believed] ...and *true* [Alethes – absolute truth that is possible only with God and heavenly man] `. ....And He said to me, 'It is done. I am the Alpha and the Omega, the beginning and the end. I will give to the one who thirsts from the spring of water of life without cost."

21:7 is the pinnacle of revelation concerning the glorification of humanity.
"He who *overcomes* [Klēronomeō – receive the promise of God as a birthright] ...shall inherit these things, and I will be his God and he will be my [Huios – not a shadow, but timeless spiritual life identified with the holiness of Deity.]."

The New Jerusalem is a radically new kind of existence prepared especially for a radically new kind of man. Humanity is described as a new spiritual creation to the last detail, befitting the entire scope of God's redemptive plan created in His mind [Genesis 1:1-2; 26].

God command John to *write* down His words [Grapho – engrave in stone; unalterable]. Writing the words of a king declared them to carry his full weight of legal authority. The truth of what He says is that (v.6) "it is done". God confirms in writing the fact that:

1. The permanent removal of death is a task which could only be accomplished by the power of God's own kingdom power of Life. God identifies Himself as the:
   A. *Alpha and Omega* [the first through the last letters of the Greek alphabet].
      This signifies total and perfect knowledge, and the perfect ability of the
      Spiritual Deity of God to communicate absolute truth with spiritual man.
   B. God is the *beginning* [Arche – the only timeless ruling power of life who can create
      Life, and the only one who has the legal responsibility to create a heavenly existence
      for the spiritual man that began with Adam.
   C. And He is the *end* [Telos – goal achieved]. God continues to be the unchanging

ruling power of timeless life after the completion of the task as He was before and during the task. The completed task is restoring man to His image, completely free from the curse of death. Christ is the Deity who accomplished this.

2. What God has accomplished is the creation of an honored existence for man which is identical to His own. Man may drink from the *spring* [Pēgē – free flowing, non-ending fountain of life-giving knowledge; the full extent of the mind of God; the Spirit of God] …of the *water* [Hudatŏs– timeless, pure, holy spiritual life {Genesis 1, God's reservoir of water used by the Holy Spirit to create all life is not contaminated by death} …of *Life* [Zoe –spiritual life in its purist form cannot be contaminated by death]. Now that death has been removed so that it can never exist again, man is empowered to be a heavenly spiritual being with the fullest character of God's righteousness that cannot die.

In the new creation of the abode of spiritual man; there is no trace of the kingdom power of death which rules this physical world. Man will no longer be identified with the natural creation as God's sons (Teknons) under the limitations of the flesh. In this new heaven, man will be a spiritual creation *uniquely* [Monogenes – the only ones of a family] …God's spiritual family. Man will reflect God's perfect identity of "Spiritual Life" by the light of holiness {God's glory–His true identity of Deity shining from within them}.

God does not change His identify by moving heaven toward man. He changes man's identity to His own; by bringing man close to Him. This honored position before God is given only to that segment of humanity which loves, honors, and glorifies God in the darkness of this sinful world; just as Jesus did. What greater love and justice can God have for man than (Revelation 22:4) to glorify him as timeless before His face and say as He said to Jesus (Matthew 3:17), "This is My beloved *Huios* [Holiness of Deity] in whom I am well pleased".

21:8

"But for the cowardly and unbelieving and abominable and murderers and immoral persons and sorcerers and idolaters and all liars, their part will be in the lake that burns with fire and brimstone, which is the second death."

This verse is a contrast to verses 1-7. It identifies the character of the sinful person who cannot be acceptable to God as His Son. This verse emphasizes that God does not want any distortion of the fact that the fate of all people is determined by personal choices of right and wrong. People who love God accept His wisdom and His discipline. Those who hate God despise His wisdom and love evil.

John 3:19-21

"And this is the judgment that the light is come into the world, and men loved the darkness rather than the light; for their deeds were evil. For everyone who does evil hates the light, and does not come to the light, lest his deeds should be exposed. But he who practices the truth comes to the light, that his deeds may be manifested as having been wrought in God."

21:9

"And one of the seven angels who had the seven bowls full of the seven last plagues, came and spoke with me, saying, 'Come here, I shall show you the bride, the wife of the Lamb.'"

This verse personalizes the glorious spiritual, heavenly city of Jerusalem by its description as the pure bride of the Lamb of God. This is in contrast to the great prostitute of the earthly city which was a mockery of the righteousness of God. People who lived in that city loved the power of Satanic evil. They loved the idea of God as long as they could play the role of God.

This heavenly city is identified by those who remain true to the *Lamb* [Arnion –the exalted sacrifice which rules by the inherent power of Spiritual Life]. The Lamb restores man to the righteousness of God and the Life which comes from Him. The inhabitants of the heavenly city are there by authority of their spiritual birth from above which makes them children of the heavenly Father. He is pleased with His Holy Children. No father can have a greater value and love for his children than God. And no earthly child could have a more secure home than that which God prepares for His children.

The city is characterized as the Bride of the Lamb because this is the only people who can inhabit it. God will consummate His marriage relationship with His bride when Jesus comes to rule over all of redeemed humanity, free from the rule of death. The throne room of God is the most holy place because of the Most Holy One who occupies it. The city is holy because its occupants are holy. This is a judgment of the righteousness of God. It is verified by one of the seven angels which poured out the seven bowls of God's wrath. The Heavenly City is not a place of punishment, but the prized reward for loving God, like He loves man. There is no greater blessing for man than to be at home with the Lord. The long-awaited desire of the bride is to be one with the bridegroom in the security of their own home.

Verses 21:10 – 22:5, are the vision of the progressive construction of the city by His progressive revelation of His Deity in this world of spiritual darkness.

21:10 -11

"And he carried me away in the Spirit to a great and high mountain, and showed me the holy city, Jerusalem, coming down out of heaven from God having the *glorying* [Doxa – the uncovering of God in heaven to see His true identity] …Her brilliance was like a very costly stone, as a stone of crystal-clear jasper."

John is carried by the Spirit to a high mountain from which he is shown the holy city. This is symbolic of the separation between heaven and earth. John could only see heaven in a vision.

John saw this vision "in the *Spirit*" [Pneuma – the authority within man which focuses on God to see and know Him in truth (1 Corinthians 2:1-16)]. John's vision reveals knowledge of spiritual things that cannot be known by the fleshly mind of man. This vision reveals the true meaning of glorified human life. Our physical life is real to us while we live on earth, but in this verse, we are given the ability to "see" beyond it to a greater reality of spiritual life.

The human mind as a physical instrument for reasoning is limited in its ability to identify truth. Natural man identifies truth only by what he can experience physically. His gods are the product of the human mind. Thus, the gods of human thinking are identified only with this natural creation. All man-made religions rob us of our ability to see the true glorified life of our final existence as the Holy Spirit reveals it.

Hebrews 1:1-3, Jesus is the perfect revelation of God. He gave up the glory which identified Him as Spiritual Life and entered the created world. He identified Himself as God by the power of a sinless life and doing the things only God can do. To speak on a human level of understanding, He relegated His teachings of spiritual things to the use of parables. The religious powers of humanity (the Jewish priests in Jerusalem) only measured Him by their own human expectations. He was not the conquering king they demanded of the Messiah; thus, He could not be the presence of the Living God He claimed to be. In their minds He was just a man who posed a threat to their own self-glorification. Unable to recognize spiritual truth, they hated Him and used the Romans to dispose of Him.

All that has been written thus far concerning this verse is meant to move our minds to the same spiritual power of understanding as was given to John. We need to see this vision of the domain of God and man through God's eyes. This is not "spiritualizing" scripture. It is the recognition of truth spoken by the mind of God and revealed to our minds by the Holy Spirit.

John was taken to a high place to experience the holiness of God beyond any earthly influence. This vision of progressive revelation enables us to see life after death and everything of the first natural creation no longer exists and most importantly, is not even a memory. The New Jerusalem cannot even remotely be described by the theologies of the world or the wildest fantasy of the human mind associated with this natural world. What is before us is an entirely new kind of Spiritual existence that has never been known before. It is God's new throne room designed to include man as a spiritual being like to Him, reflecting the glory of His holiness.

What John saw with spiritual eyes was the glory of God. Absolutely everything about this Holy City magnifies the presence of God to the extent that it is filled with His glory. It is a *brilliant* light [Photos – a light from within God which illuminates Him and His family. No light on earth has such power.]. John describes this glory in earthly imagery as the glitter of light reflected by a very costly, crystal clear jasper stone. This stone may be comparable to a flawless diamond which reflects every facet of light. John's vision is not that of a physical city, but God's revelation of every facet of His glory which is given off by the purity of glorified man.

Isaiah 35:2
"…they will see the glory of the Lord, The majesty of our God."

Children of God in this present time of revelation are guarded and protected by the indwelling glory of the Holy Spirit. Matthew 5:14-16, "You are the *light* of the world [Phos – light never quenched]. …A city set on a hill cannot be hidden. Nor do men light a lamp and put it under the peck-measure, but on the lamp stand; and it gives light to all who are in the house. Let your light shine before men in such a way that they may see your good works and glorify your Father who is in heaven." We are light-bearers to reveal the majesty of God to men of this world. They cannot see Him because their minds are darkened by death. God's glory shining in glorified man in the holiness of His presence means we will never again dwell in the darkness of our minds.

This light of God shining in our physical identity is nothing compared to the unquenchable light of God that will shine from within His children in His holy presence in the celestial city. Each and every one is bathed in the light of holiness and can see God in all His glory. All are of one mind {God's mind}; to be "light bearers," to glorify Him with worship like the four beasts which never cease to cry "Holy, Holy, Holy is the Lord God, the Almighty." All are under the care of God's glory with such a force of holiness that death can never, ever, come into existence again.

21:12-18

"It had a great and high wall, with twelve gates, and at the gates twelve angels; and names were written on them, which are those of the twelve tribes of the sons of Israel. There were three gates on the east and three gates on the north and three gates on the south and three gates on the west. And the wall of the city had twelve foundation stones and on them were the twelve names of the twelve apostles of the Lamb. And the one who spoke with me had a gold measuring rod to measure the city and its gates and its wall. And the city is laid out as a square, and its length is as great as the width; and he measured the city with the rod, fifteen hundred miles; its length and width and height are equal. And he measured its wall, seventy-two yards, according to human measurements, which are also angelic measurements. And the material of the wall was jasper; and the city was pure gold, like clear glass."

John's vision projects the Holy dwelling of God as a bastion of security, surrounded by the host of Angels. The great high wall surrounding the city forms a perfect cube that has no weakness. An angel measures the city with a golden rod. The act of measuring signifies God's securing something (or people) for blessing and to preserve it from spiritual harm or defilement. This measuring reveals the perfection, the strength, the fulfillment and completion of all God's purposes for His elect bride.

John expressed by symbols the vastness, the perfect symmetry, and the splendor of God's fulfillment of all His promises to transform us from death to the light of His own kingdom. The security of the city is further enhanced by the deliberate use of the number twelve. Jesus fed five thousand people and had specifically twelve baskets of bread and fish lift over. This meant each of His twelve disciples received a full basket of food. God established this number as His authority for bringing all His spiritual creation to completion as a new kind of existence in the presence of His ruling power of life. *These verses reveal that God's salvation is not a religion or a theology of human origin.

The twelve gates reveal God's provision for opening heaven to every Old and New Testament saint. The gates are guarded by twelve celestial gatekeepers. In Genesis 3:24, God placed angels on the east side of the Garden of Eden to keep sinful man from eating of the tree of life. Three is a number for God. Three gates are on each side of the four walls of the city. God has provided a wide-open entrance for all of humanity that will enter through Him.

The gates have the names of the twelve tribes of Israel written on them. The Old Testament covenant of the sanctification of Spiritual Israel declared they were not pagan idol worshipers, but a people who would worship only the living God. It was God, Himself, who spoke the words of His Heavenly Constitution to govern His people on earth as He governs all life in heaven. It was God who commissioned the Israelites to build the only Temple in this world which brought a unique people into existence with a new message to the world. The Holy of Holies was the revelation of God's power to transform the life of believers by the authority of the One who sits on the Throne of Judgment, the Mercy Seat. The living God is the supreme authority for cleansing man of his guilt of sin and death. Humanity cannot make itself righteous to be in favor with a god of its own making.

Twelve gates are God's revelation that only He can make a true Israelite. God makes man righteous by submission to His authority of Life and then empowers him to live a transformed life of holiness. God's people will always be in control of their own lives.

The walls of the city are built on twelve foundation stones and on them are the names of the twelve apostles of the *Lamb* [Arnion – little lamb; sacrificial lamb; designation of the exalted Christ. This is the progressive revelation of God's Living Temple that is the only open door to heaven. I Peter 2:5, "Behold I lay in Zion a choice stone, a precious corner stone, and he who believes in Him shall not be disappointed."

The foundation of the city is a graphic picture of the strength of mans' salvation designed by God. It is a people built upon Christ, the cornerstone. The revelation of salvation is no longer found in stone temples; but in the temple God established in the heart of every person who carries His message of salvation to the whole world. The resurrection of the person of God from the dead produced a spiritual Israel which turned the world upside down. God's revelation to the

power of His Kingdom of Life was given by His Deity, the Messiah. Man's security for timeless life can only be found in the Deity of God who personally destroyed death's power of separation. God's covenant of grace guarantees that every person who trusts in the authority of God to raise Himself from the grave; that person's spirit will also be raised from the domain of death. That person's spirit will not enter Hades but will ascend to the Father in Heaven. They will never be separated from God again.

The twelve gates and twelve foundation stones identify the continuity, unity and totality of God's work through Christ to perfect man as a heavenly being. The unity of the people of the old and new testaments (one body in Christ) was established by their lives as bearers of the testimony of the Messiah – the Christ.

The true Israel of God's own making is the sanctified faithful martyrs to the truth of His unique revelation given to each one. The names of the twelve tribes of the Old Testament Israel are written on the twelve gates. This is God's witnesses that the spiritual nation God created from the descendants of Abraham have His authority to enter the city. The names of the twelve apostles under the New Testament covenant of the Lamb of God are written on the twelve foundation stones of the city. They bear the full weight of the whole city because they are a unique identity of Israel. They are a personal witness to the God-given revelation of salvation for sinful man through the resurrection of the Christ, who is the Kingdom of Life. This is the strength of the foundation on which God establishes the city (His people; His bride; all who have life in Him) as the presence of the Living God. This city is the timeless, heavenly *Naos (Holy of Holies)*.

The unity of the Old and the New Covenants finds its purest and ultimate expression in John's vision of the glorious throne room of God. The city is *pure* gold [Katharos – clean in the sense that it is lawful; it is legally and ceremonially cleansed; pure from the pollution of the guilt of sin] ... like *clear* glass [free from stain; purified by the blood of the Lamb].

21:19-20

"The foundation stones of the city wall were adorned with every kind of precious stone. The first foundation stone was jasper; the second, sapphire; and the third, chalcedony; the fourth, emerald; the fifth, sardonyx; the sixth, sardius; the seventh, chrysolite; the eighth, beryl; the ninth, topaz; the tenth, chrysoprase; the eleventh, jacinth; the twelfth, amethyst."

The main idea of this vision of the foundation stones is to convey the revelation that the ruling power of God's Throne of Life is theologically perfect. These precious jewels adorned the breastplate of the high priest in Exodus 28:17ff and 39:10ff. This breastplate was the authority for the high priest to make decisions for the nation of Israel when he was before the Lord. No other people in the whole world have a true theological foundation for their religious beliefs, because they did not come from the throne of God. Every religion in the world is apostate idolatry, including unbelieving Judaism.

The jewels on the foundation of the Holy City are listed in a reverse order than that of Exodus and, also of the signs of the Zodiac by which the ancient world traced the times and seasons of the year. This reversal is significant. It establishes the sovereign authority of God to be the only decision maker, and He has established the Holy City (His people) on the perfect order of the Lamb who took away the sins of the world. The very imperfect humanity is transformed to the perfect people of God by the *Word* (the perfect mind of God) who revealed His name as the only authority given under heaven by which man can be saved from the authority of death.

These twelve jewels give emphasis to the fact that every person who calls upon the name of Jesus should be praising God with thanksgiving of the heart. It is God alone, who makes it possible to praise His name in His Holy Presence.

21:21

"And the twelve gates were twelve pearls; each one of the gates was a single pearl. And the street of the city was pure gold, like transparent glass."

The twelve gates each consists of a single pearl and the one street in the city is made of the purest gold. The purpose for magnifying the singleness of the pearl which composes each gate is to visualize the love of God's heart for man. He moves the decision-making power of the throne from the legalism of law (Romans 6:23a, "For the wages of sin is death") to salvation by grace (Romans 6:23b, "But the free gift of God is timeless Life in Christ Jesus our Lord"). The pearl of great price is the person of Jesus; this is the foundation and strength of Life that cannot die. The salvation of man is purely the work of God's grace to cleanse every person who would choose to love Him.

Matthew 7:13, Jesus said, "Enter through the narrow gate. For wide is the gate and broad is the road that leads to destruction and many enter through it. But small is the gate and narrow the road that leads to life and only a few find it."

Men struggle in this life of darkness to find that small gate, but the portals of God's heavenly glory are open wide to all His children who come to Him from the "four corners" of the earth. God has provided an open door for everyone who would by their own volition, enter the city through Jesus, and indeed few there are who enter through it. For only those whose name is written in the Lambs Book of Life is declared righteous before the Great White Throne of God's final judgment on death. Everyone else is <u>unclean</u> [Ischuo – to be powerless before the awesome pull of the gates of Hades].

The street of purest gold like transparent glass is an invitation to <u>walk barefoot</u> before God on His holy ground. Moses was required to take his shoes off to approach God because the shoe leather of a slain animal was not sufficient to protect him from God's wrath. It only identified him as a sinner. Only the blood of Christ can purify man to be sinless before Him and walk the path of righteousness barefooted; justified by the Holiness of God.

The revelation of the street of transparent gold is the glorious truth that in heaven there is no sacrificial death of animals or man because God took the judgment of death upon Himself to justify man in His presence. The city of God is glorified man walking freely before God without judgment. He now exists by the power of righteousness and may eat of the tree of life without fear or restraint. It is not the power of death that rules his mind, but the holy, pure righteousness of God's throne. Only that which is as pure as God can exist in this city of holiness.

21:22-27

"And I saw no temple in it, for the Lord God, the Almighty, and the Lamb, are its temple. And the city has no need of the sun or of the moon to shine upon it, for the glory of God has illumined it, and its lamp is the Lamb. And the nations shall walk by its light, and the kings of the earth shall bring their <u>glory</u> [Doxa – true identity of God's saints] …into it. And in this light its gates shall never be closed; and they shall bring the glory and the honor of the nations into it; and nothing unclean and no one who practices abomination and lying shall ever come into it, but only those whose names are written in the Lamb's book of Life."

There is no <u>temple</u> in the heavenly city because it is the pure holiness of God and everyone in it. The temple in the old covenant was the revelation of God's Deity as the authority to forgive sins. This was necessary for this world under the curse of death. It was replaced by the reality of God's Deity as the heavenly ruling authority for Timeless Life (Christ – the Messiah – Living Temple).

In this present world, the saved person is the place of God's presence, guaranteed by the indwelling of the Holy Spirit {Deity}. In the New Jerusalem, a temple for man to worship is no longer needed because God has gone beyond judgment to the glorification of man as sinless.

In John's vision the whole city is the Naos (the heart of God), for it is filled with the presence of the Lord God Almighty and the Lamb. In verse 23, the life-giving, light-shedding glory of God's character of righteousness makes all other light sources (physical universe) unnecessary. The glory of God was the light of heaven before the darkness and its luminaries were created. This glory is the power that could not be dimmed nor replaced by a greater light in the created order. This glory is the timeless Jesus. Just as He was the light of God in the darkness, He is the prevailing light of God's glory in His domain of the celestial city.

In verse 24, the kings of the earth add their glory to the city. What an incredible thought it is that God should honor the Saints by recognizing the glory of Christ which shines in their lives. The saints of God's creation will be heavenly light-bearers to the truth of Jesus.

What an inspiration this is to make the glory of Christ fill the darkness of this sin-ridden world which is our present domain. It seems as though our redeemed lives are more important to God than to us. It would be wise of us to live honorably before the Lord as soul winners and let God bestow honor when honor is due.

In verse 25, God's glory provides a perpetual light so that the present earthly concept of darkness is completely unknown. The glory of God is revealed by His power to glorify mankind and make them timeless light bearers. Man, in this physical life is a shadow of God (without glory), but man in the throne room of God is a spiritual being which, like unto God, radiates the glory and holiness of God from within himself. We owe a debt of gratitude to God for the magnitude of the "pearly gates" which, not only gives us entrance into the timeless day'; but also identifies us with Christ as children of God. Those whose names are written in the Lamb's book of life are cleansed by the blood of the Lamb. There is no trace of death upon them. They bring to the throne room their unique _glory_ [Doxa – their true identity of oneness with God, the holiest of all God's created life; above even the holiest of God's angels] ... by which God calls them [Huios – Holiness of Deity]. God's throne room is a place of such purity and power of Life that it is impossible for the darkness of death to enter it.

22:1-2

"And he showed me a river of the water of life, clear as crystal, coming from the throne of God and of the Lamb, in the middle of its street. And on either side of the river was the tree of life, bearing twelve kinds of fruit, yielding its fruit every month; and the leaves of the tree were for the healing of the nations."

The angel shows John sparkling clear water flowing from the throne of God. In scripture "waters" and "living waters" are used to symbolize spiritual life and the blessings which freely flow to humanity from the person of God. The pristine water is the holiness of God that cleanses humanity of death. God created everything from the deep reservoir of water and everything He made was sinless, pure and holy. The water of life is the power of salvation to transform man from being totally dead, enslaved to the evils of death; to spiritual life characterized by the God powers of righteousness and holiness. The only pure water comes from God, Himself, and blesses us with His timeless holiness. Life can come only from the Kingdom of Life which creates life in everything which exists. The Holy City (God's sanctified people) is empowered with God's Throne of Timeless Life.

The addition of the Lamb to the Godhead is an affirmation that the _nations_ [Ethos - the whole redeemed human race identified as one nation (Spiritual Israel – the body of Christ)] ... will live at the source of the life-giving stream. This vision identifies saved humanity with the oneness of the Godhead as Jesus declared in His prayer of John 17. He prayed for the time man would be one with God. We will share the same honor given to Jesus (21:7), [Huios – Holiness of Deity].

The vision continues with the Water of Life flowing down the middle of the street of purest gold. On both sides of the street is the Tree of Life bearing twelve crops of fruit every month; and the leaves of the Tree are for the healing of the nations. In John 15, Jesus said He is the Tree of Life which bears its fruit by the authority of the Father. The Tree of Life bears fruit because Jesus and the Father are the same spiritual life (`Ĕlôhîym). All human beings cleansed by the Word of Jesus are the branches of the Tree. We bear the same fruit as that of Jesus because we abide in Him and the Father.

Jesus produced the perfect character of God by His total obedience to the Father. It was His will to do so. The scene in 22:2 is that of the Tree of Life and all of its branches (twelve is the number for the full redemption of man) producing the perfect character of God by their timeless obedience to the Father. It will be our perfect will to do so. So powerful and abundant is the flow of Living Water through the Tree of Life to its branches that the Saints of God's own making will be empowered by God to be His Holy Children.

The healing leaves of the Tree are a testimony to the complete absence of the power of death that produces sin in us today. So powerful is the salvation of God that the power of sin is completely removed. The authoritative power of Life that flows from the throne of God will sustain us and permanently cure us of ever sinning again. We will never cease from glorifying God because He will never cease producing the fruit of the Tree of Life in us.

22:3
"And there shall no longer be any curse; and the throne of God and of the Lamb shall be in it and His bondservants shall serve Him;"

There shall no longer be any curse (death) is a judicial decree from the Throne of Life. Elohiym (one spiritual being- one single mind) makes the judicial decree that for all life in His heavenly city (man and angels), there will only be one ruling power (one mind). All life will be in total submission to His iron rule of Holy Righteousness; the power of life that cannot die. All life –man and angels - will be of one mind in subjection to His rule. *There will never again be a Lucifer in heaven. The Holy City will be governed by:

(1) God's Kingdom rule of Life. It is His righteousness that ensures His holiness that radiates from His children.
(2) The unifying power of the resurrected sacrificial Lamb. All have been purified by His altar in heaven. The power of His perfect love permeates the mind of all life in heaven.
(3) The authority of God's mind controls the will of man to produce the perfect character of God; a humbleness that has never been known on earth. Everyone loves and serves everyone.

Philippians 2:1-15, Jesus was a _bondservant_ [Doulos- a slave; one who voluntarily submits himself to a permanent relationship of servitude to another; one whose will be totally consumed in the will of the other] …to the will of the Godhead in Jesus, man is no longer governed by the self-serving power of physical, but the authority of God's Timeless Spiritual Life which issues from the Throne of God.

God Reveals His Glory [Doxa – True Identity]

22:4
"And they shall see His face, and His name shall be on their foreheads."

This verse is the culmination of mans' glorification. It expresses two blessings of being a bondservant to God. The first; "They shall see His face." This is an expression of God's pride of ownership because of the value He places on redeemed man as His own family. In Matthew 5:8, Jesus spoke to the multitudes and said, "Blessed are the pure in heart, for they shall see God." In this verse, the bondsman will be exalted to the position of the King's family. God will value glorified man not as adopted sons, but as His *begotten sons* [given spiritual life from God – our Father]. The blessing of seeing the face of God is the joy of being able to love Him with the same perfect love that God has for His children and the children have for their loving father.

The second blessing is the expression; "His name shall be on their forehead." Because God now considers us to be His family, He identifies us to all of heaven as His kin. His name identifies us with His perfect character of holiness. Thus, the face of glorified man will reflect the unmistakable likeness of God. This verse stresses ownership and likeness as the metaphor for "oneness." There can be no greater achievement for relating created man to the throne of God than this concept of oneness. Nothing else in heaven can have this personal relationship with God.

Hebrews 1:2-4
"In these last days God has spoken to us in His [Huios – Deity of Christ], whom He appointed *heir* [Kleromomos – one who holds a possession in his own power, the birth-right of the first-born son] …of all things, through whom also He *made* [Poieo – to endow a person or thing with a certain quality of an independent existence of its own] …the *world* [Aion– people of timeless existence]. …And He is the radiance of His glory and the exact representation of His nature and upholds all things by the power of His word. When He had made purification of sins, He sat down at the right hand of the Majesty on high; having become as much better than the angels, as He has inherited a more excellent *name* [Onoma – the representative word used for the person himself] …than they." *The heavenly birth-right given to man through Christ is the name; "HuiosTheos" – the Deity of God.

22:5
"And there shall no longer be any night; and they shall not have need of the light of a lamp nor the light of the sun, because the Lord God shall *illumine* [Phŏtizō – spiritual enlightenment of God's identity-`Ĕlôhîym – the One Spiritual Deity of God.]. …them; and they shall reign with the shining light of Holiness as His Timeless Spiritual Children."

This verse is the final and complete revelation of God. In the first verse of the Bible (Genesis 1:1), we are given the full revelation of the identity of God before creation. He is [`Ĕlôhîym – a singular, supreme ruler or judge - "Deity"; the one and only power for the existence of life]. His glory is the light that reveals His true, timeless identity. Because death came into existence in heaven, Elohiym created darkness as its abode. He created luminaries to give light in the darkness. These luminaries reveal the glory of His presence.

The Kingdom Rule of Life rules over everything which came into existence by the executive authority of His Throne. In Genesis 1:26, Elohiym created man, a spiritual being like Himself with His authority to be His decision-maker but separated from Him by the flesh. This verse also reveals the separation of Elohiym {One Spiritual Being} into a plurality of His Deity for the purpose of destroying death so that it cannot exist again. This plurality of life was only revealed by the *coming* [Parousia] of Elohiym into His creation to destroy death's power of separation. The coming of Jesus into the world was the *visible presence* [Epiphaneia] of Elohiym. Jesus could say to His disciples in John 14, "Look at Me, you see Elohiym". Jesus ascended back into the heavens where the glory of Elohiym continues to shine as His authority to destroy death ruling the mind of man.

This verse (22:5) tells us that; with the completion of the unification of man with God in the new heaven and the complete destruction of death, there is no longer any darkness or need for any luminaries. There is no longer the need for Elohiym to be the saving God (revelation of Himself as Lord, Huios – Christ, and Holy Spirit). The light that shines in God's new throne room is the glory [true identity] of His Throne of Life that was in the beginning (Genesis 1:1). His final revelation of Himself *illumines* [Photizo – to enlighten, to instruct, to make to understand] …the minds of the Saints. It will be the brightest light of revelation ever to shine from God. It is the uncovering of God that has no equal. Elohiym will reveal Himself as He has always been and always will be One single spiritual power of Deity, the supreme judge over all life. Man's oneness with God will be as permanent as the unchangeable oneness of Elohiym. This perfect and final uncovering of Elohiym is the objective for all that He does through His revelation of the Christ.

EPILOGUE

REVELATION 22:6-21

This very important concluding section presses home two practical lessons of God's redemptive work through Jesus. They are the authenticity of the message of God's salvation in Christ and the nearness of the fulfillment of God's removal of all life outside of heaven.

22:6-7
"And he said to me, 'These words are faithful and true; and the Lord, the God of the spirits of the prophets, sent His angel to show to His bondservants the things which must shortly take place.' 'And behold, I am coming quickly. Blessed is he who heeds the words of the prophecy of this book.'"

The *words* of this book [Logos – the expression of intelligence of the mind; the thought of one mind to another] …communicate the mind of God to the spiritual mind of man. All true prophecy originates from God. II Peter 1:21, "For no prophecy was ever made by an act of human will, but men moved by the Holy Spirit spoke from God." We cannot know the deep thoughts of God expressed in this book unless He explains them to us. God's revelation of these mysteries is *faithful* [Pistos – proven to always be true, worthy to be believed, steadfast] …and *true* [Alethines – genuine, truth that cannot be tainted by a lie].

The revelation of this book came from "the God of the spirits of the *prophets*" [Prophites – one to whom and through whom God reveals Himself and His purposes in the context of the lives of the ones spoken to] …. Prophecy is not fortune-telling or future-telling; but the directive God gives us to live our lives according to His Will and purpose –Jesus fulfilled all prophesy.

The message of this Book was delivered to John by God's *angel* [Aggelos – announcer, proclaimer; the heavenly being which has the unique office of speaking for God]…. "*Blessed* [Makarios – possessing the characteristic of deity; to be indwelt by God because of Christ] …is he who heeds the words of the *prophecy* [Propheteia – to tell forth God's word] …of this book."

The message of the church is not future telling of historical events, but the gospel of salvation for the conversion of the lost. These are the only words that come from our mouths which are empowered to glorify God. We are "prophets," for we are admonished to be busy prophesying the gospel during the time God has allotted for it.

The Saints of God's making are those who are obedient to the will of God. They heed His warning that time is both short and chaotic. These people adjust their manner of living accordingly. We are to study this book and teach it; grounded by a belief in God that it is the Holy Spirit which is guiding our minds. We are warned in I John 4:1-6, that spirits of the antichrist have produced many false prophets who speak lies and unbelieving men are quick to believe lies. We are charged with the responsibility to separate ourselves from false prophets and denounce their prophecies. The person who belongs to God must recognize the spirit of truth and the spirit of error, and boldly speak the word of God with confidence.

22:8-9

"And I, John, am the one who heard and saw these things. And when I heard and saw, I fell down to worship at the feet of the angel who showed me these things. And he said to me, 'Do not do that; I am a fellow servant of yours and of your brethren the prophets and of those who heed the words of this book; worship God.'"

These two verses present a unique warning against idolatry. John states that he had actually seen and heard all the things recorded in this book. The uncovering of God was more than he could comprehend; it was over-whelming to the mind of a man still earth bound by the weakness of the flesh. The angel glowed with the brilliance of heaven and John identified it with the spiritual power of God. He fell on his knees and worshiped it. This is the second time in writing this book that John admits to doing this.

The irony of these verses is that they give us the basis for understanding why the lost world is so quick to clamor after false prophets. John was not led of the Holy Spirit to worship the angel; it was the desire of his own mind. In II Corinthians 11:14, Paul warns us that, "Satan disguises himself as an angel of light" and false prophets do the same thing. Humanity is easily led to worship everything but the right thing because they consider what they worship to be "holy".

To put it in perspective; the angel defines himself as John's _fellow servant_ [Sundoulos – equal servants to the same Lord]. The angel is not a superior power to John, but one who takes his orders from God just as John does. This heavenly being is a companion in the worship of God with John and his _brethren_ [Adelphos – from the womb; a fellowship of life based on identity of origin *spiritual beings]; …those who prophesy and _heed_ [Terco- obey a command] …the words of God. Both the angels in heaven and man (a timeless spiritual being on earth) must give the same reverence and obedience only to the Deity of Heaven.

John committed the sin of misplaced worship just like Adam did in the Garden of Eden. Adam talked with God on a daily basis and was on familiar ground with the angels. He had a fear of God, but he was not prepared in his mind to surrender his will to the more persuasive and deceptive words of Lucifer (the most glorious and dynamic angel created). He demonstrated his misplaced fear when he hid from God instead of trusting Him. God put His finger on the problem when He asked Adam the question, "Who told you that you were naked?"

These verses serve as a poignant reminder that there are powerful spiritual forces at work in this world to pervert the truth of God's word and to silence His prophets. The saints of God must be just as much a powerful, spiritually minded people in today's world as we expect to be in the future when we serve God in His presence. We need a reverent fear of God that causes us to fall on our faces in worship of Him in all His glory. If we are a people who believe in and expect God to gather us to Himself, then we ought to prepare ourselves by growing daily in the grace and knowledge of God, to worship Him with joy, to resist the apostate voices that lead men to worship idols, and to speak the true gospel message to believing minds.

22:10-11

"And he said to me, 'Do not seal up the words of the prophecy of this book, for the time is near. Let the one who does wrong, still do wrong; and let the one who is filthy, still be filthy;

and let the one who is righteous, still practice righteousness; and let the one who is holy, still keep himself holy.'"

John is told not to seal what he has written but share it with the churches. The people were at a critical moment in history and they were the ones who had to live it. God has done His part; He has finished His work to prepare us for timeless life. The *time* [Kairos – not a succession of moments that mark the passing of time (chronos), but that moment which time gives an opportunity to do] …is *near* [Eggus – close; figuratively used of cementing spiritual relations] … for each of us to also prepare our own lives for the timelessness of God's presence.

Unbelieving people alive at the return of Christ will reap the consequences of the kind of life they live. If they die before Christ returns, they will reap the same consequences. The time arrives for all of us when change is impossible because our character has already been determined by the choices of our minds. The arrival of the end forecloses any possibility of alteration. The deliberate choice of every person fixes his fate for the timeless future.

There is a real sense of urgency pressed upon the unbelieving person. The end time will come for them before they know it. It is a tragedy for every person who is unprepared for the consequences of unbelief.

22:12-13
"Behold, I am coming quickly, and My reward is with Me, to render to every man according to what he has done. I am the Alpha and the Omega, the first and the last, the beginning and the end."

God announces a second time that Christ is coming without delay. This means it is totally unrelated to chronological time and the chaos of this world. There is nothing related to this world that can stand in God's way to divert Him to do something else. The continuance of God's movement is to completely finish His course of action that He established before He created anything – Genesis 1:1-2.

Inherent with Christ's return is His *reward* [Mistos – wages] …for our labor of faith. We will be paid appropriately for our work. God is not telling us we will be saved by our works. He is telling us that the quality of a person's life provides the ultimate indication of what one really believes. If our character of life reflects the character of God, then we will receive the same power of life which identifies the person of God.

The authority of God to reward man comes from the ruling power of His throne of Life. It is completely apart from the entire created order. God is the *Alpha and Omega* [the complete embodiment of all knowledge] …the *first* [Protos – before time] …and the *last* [Eschatos – the extreme conclusion of time; after time ceases to exist] …the *beginning* [Arche – the primary and ultimate authority of kingdom rule] …and the *end* [Telos – the sole concluding authority of His kingdom rule] …. The only kingdom which has ever existed or will ever exist in heaven and the earth is <u>God's Kingdom of Life</u>. The Person of God and the Throne of God is one and the same. He is the ruling power which rewards man with His own power of timeless Life.

22:14-15

"Blessed are those who wash their robes that they may have the right to the tree of life and may enter by the gates into the city. Outside are the dogs and the sorcerers and the immoral persons and the murderers and the idolaters, and everyone who loves and practices lying."

God expresses the ability of a Saint to enter His holy sanctuary is a *blessing* [Makarios – possessing the characteristic of deity; indwelt by God] …and a *right* [Exousia - permission, authority granted by the executive power of God's throne] …. The blessing and right belongs to those who; Revelation 7:14 "…have washed their robes and made them white in the blood of the Lamb." This demands a salvation which involves obedience, discipline and sacrifice. The people who have the will to believe God and commit themselves to His rule will eat of the Tree of Life as a sanctified, heavenly spiritual being in God's presence. In contrast to the pureness and holiness of the Saint is the evilness of the unbeliever.

Verse 15 does not intend to teach they have a presence just outside the heavenly city. Like verses 21:7 and 8, it is a contrast between the blessedness of those inside the city and the horrible fate of the wicked that are in the lake of fire.

22:16

"I, Jesus, have sent My angel to testify to you these things for the churches. I am the root and the offspring of David, the bright morning star."

Jesus speaks for Himself in this verse. He authenticates the angel as His personal messenger. He also authenticates the message of His personal revelation to the *church* [Ekklesia – the called-out congregation of the people of Spiritual Israel; all who were called by and to Christ in the fellowship of His salvation; the church world-wide and in all times].

Jesus identified Himself as the true "root and offspring of David, the bright morning star." In Isaiah 14:12-13, Lucifer laid claim to be "the star of the morning," ruler over all the heavens; to be like the Highest God. But he and all he called out are cast into the lake of fire. Jesus is the (Isaiah 9:2-27) great light of revelation from heaven who establishes the kingdom of God as the ruling power upon the earth. He also calls out His body of followers. In Isaiah 11:1-10, the ruling power of heaven is a "green shoot" coming from the "stump of Jesse." Jesus is the [Epiphaneia - visible Deity and audible voice of the Throne of God on earth; the revelation of God's salvation which establishes peace between God and man. At His second appearing, He will prove the prophetic Word of God to be true.

22:17

"And the Spirit and the bride say, 'Come.' And let the one who hears say, 'Come.' And let the one who is thirsty say 'come'; let the one who wishes, take the water of life without cost."

This verse is directly related to verse 16. It is an invitation addressed to the whole world to believe the prophecy of God's own mouth. The *Holy Spirit* [Phaneroo – God's self-witness to the truth of Jesus is revealed by the Holy Spirit] …is calling all people to come to God through Christ.

The "bride" is the church which joins with Christ in calling men to repentance. Matthew 25:1-10, the Kingdom of God is compared to those who are pure and have prepared themselves to meet the bridegroom. They eagerly await him and are the only ones allowed into the throne room of God. The church body is the personal voice of God revealing His efforts to save every human who will be saved. Empowered by the Holy Spirit, it constitutes the great evangelizing force of the age.

The one who "hears" is not just one who hears the book of Revelation read aloud, but one who hears the gospel message and is converted. These people add to the number inviting others to "come to Christ," to invite the "thirsty" to take the water of life freely, without price.

The threefold use of the present imperative "come/let him come" is the work of the church to continually extend the invitation until that very moment when salvation history is past and there will be no further opportunity for making decisions.

22:18-19

"I testify to everyone who hears the words of the prophecy of this book: if anyone adds to them, God shall add to him the plagues which are written in this book; and if anyone takes away from the words of the book of this prophecy, God shall take away his part from the tree of life and from the holy city, which are written in this book"

Revelation draws to a close with a severe warning against anyone who in any way distorts the prophetic message of God. The apostle Paul gives the same warning in Galatians 1:6-8, "…there are some who are disturbing you, and want to distort the gospel of Christ. But even though we, or an angel from heaven, should preach to you a gospel contrary to that which we preached to you, let him be _accursed_ [Anathema – estranged from Christ and His salvation by an indissoluble vow]."

This warning is so severe that it seals an offender to the confines and punishment of death in the lake of fire. The grace of God seals the believer to His timeless life in His presence. The righteousness of God's judgment seals the unbeliever to permanent separation from Him.

It is our appointed place to stand reverently before our God in worship and to stand obediently beneath His Word. It is not our place to presuppose correct theology. It is the supreme authority of God to speak His mind and teach us truth by His Spirit.

There are many who proudly sit in judgment on the truth of scripture. There are many who covet high positions and demand obedience to their private precepts. There are thousands of church members who will not obey God's Word themselves, but every Sunday they pass judgment on the Minister's message. The God of truth does not like to be called a liar by liars.

People who obey God's Word are those who study it; and being led by the Holy Spirit to understand truth, they are empowered to live it. Every person must understand the personal nature of these two verses. Every person (without exception) is either cursed for the distortion of God's Word or is being blessed for belief in and obedience to it.

22:20

"He who testifies to these things says, 'Yes, I am coming quickly.` Amen. Come, Lord Jesus."

God tells us that time is not on our side. The prophetic revelation of this whole book ends with the testimony of Christ that His coming will be quick -- without delay. John's response is an expression of agreement and eager expectation; "Amen, Come, Lord Jesus". This is an affirmation that God is doing and will do everything He says. It does not subject that event to any kind of earthly measuring rod, neither chronological time nor the theological reasoning of man. It is not our place to prove it or to hold God accountable to human demands. It is only our place to eagerly await the blessing of it.

The early church expressed that same affirmation at the close of the Lord's Supper. The conclusion of the Lord's Prayer was: "Maranatha", meaning "O Lord Come." Paul used the same word to conclude the book of I Corinthians. People expected Jesus to be present in their daily lives; and they expected Him to appear in all His glory every day, as if it was the last day.

We also are blessed by the companionship of the Lord. The Holy Spirit has already confirmed and granted that living presence to everyone who loves to be in His presence. These people are secure in the knowledge that they will be with Christ at the end of their physical lives and they rejoice that Jesus will bring this age to its end.

The revelation of the second coming of Christ enables us to have a meaningful understanding of history (which is His Story). This world was created for God's purpose to destroy death. God accomplished that by His personal intervention into human life by the first appearance of Jesus. God will consummate His relationship with all the redeemed of the world by the second appearance of Jesus. This event is God's sure hope for the timeless future of every person who has committed himself to God by faith. Redemptive history remains incomplete until God appears personally to put an end to it. Our expectation and hope are that He will do that without delay.

22:21

"The grace of the Lord Jesus be with all. Amen."

To conclude a book written in apocalyptic language with a benediction is thought to be unusual by those who study it only as literature. Those who see Revelation as a prophetic, personal word from God understand this verse to be a continuation of John's response to Jesus' final words, "Yes, I am coming quickly." John praised God with "Amen! Come Lord Jesus." Then he reminds us that it is nothing less than by God's grace that Jesus comes, and it is nothing less than by God's grace that any of us can be a witness to it. We all need to be blessed by the grace of God. What better ending can God give to redeemed man than the affirmation that it is His will that "The grace of the Lord Jesus be with all." What better conclusion can be ours than:

Amen! And Amen!" Come Lord Jesus!

BIBLIOGRAPHY

Berry, George Ricker. <u>Interlinear Greek – English New Testament, King James Version</u>.
    Nashville, Tennessee: Broadman Press, February 1992.

Graham, Billy. <u>Angels: God's Secret Agents</u>.
    New York, New York: Pocket Books, April 1977.

Graham, Billy. <u>Death and the Life After</u>.
    Dallas, Texas: Word Publishing, 1987

Green, Jay P. Sr. <u>The Interlinear Bible, Hebrew - Greek- English</u>.
    U.S.A.: A. H. Hendrickson Publishers, September 2008.

Lemonick, Michael D. "How the Universe Will End".
    <u>Time</u>; 25 June 2001 / Vol. 157 NO.25, pp.48-56.

Newport, John P. <u>The Lion and the Lamb</u>,
    Nashville, Tennessee: Broadman Press, 1986.

Thompson, Frank Charles. <u>The New Chain-Reference Bible</u>.
    Indianapolis, Indiana: B.B. Kirkbride Bible Company, Inc., 1964.

Strong, James. <u>The New Strong's Concordance</u>.
    Nashville, Tennessee: Thomas Nelson Publisher, 2001.

Zodhiates, Spiros. <u>The Hebrew-Greek Key Study Bible. New American Standard</u>.
    Chattanooga, Tennessee: AMG Publishers, June 1990.

APPENDIX

On August 16, 1962, President John F. Kennedy named Brigadier General Robert Preston Taylor United States Air Force Chief of Chaplains. General Taylor wrote a book entitled <u>DAYS OF HOPE AND DAYS OF GLORY</u>. My personal copy was a gift, autographed and presented to my son on the day of his birth. Another book was given to me, written by the Japanese Ace in WWII. His book revealed his awesome respect for the American soldiers, but more importantly the conversion of his whole family to Christ.

I discovered that only a small number of General Taylor's book were printed, and none can be found for purchase. However, a much more detailed book about the life of General Taylor was written by Billy Keith; entitled <u>DAYS OF ANGUISH, DAYS OF HOPE</u>; printed by Doubleday & Company, Inc., Garden City, New York, 1972. The only copy I could find was from Driftless Books and Music; Box 302; 117 W. Commercial; Viola, WI 54664; phone number (806) 627-1132.

God Reveals His Glory [Doxa – True Identity]

EXODUS FROM ANGOLA

August 1975

Because of the build-up of tensions in Angola, as the three liberation movements vied for power, the Angolan Mission faced the possibility of evacuation and formulated plans for when it should become necessary. The Misson took into consideration the difficult situation in which we were all living in a background of war and shortages; and voted to combine vacations with medicals and spend some time in South Africa. For both vacations and the event of evacuation, we chose the overland route: Luanda, Nova Lisboa, Sá da Bendeira, Pereira d'Eça, South West Africa border.

The decision was made at our Annual Mission Meeting on July 22, 1975. In order to keep part of our Mission on the field Missionary Journeyman Tress Miles, mission office secretary; Bo Jackson, BSU Summer Missionary from Texas, and career Missionaries Harrison and June Pike would remain in Luanda. Carolyn and I with two-year old Loren were to remain in Nova Lisboa where we had been living since early May when we were evacuated from Luanda and could continue language study. Curtis and Betty Dixon and Bert and Jenny Sutton along with their families (three children each), traveled together to Johannesburg (Joburg). The rest of our Mission personnel would take our trip to Joburg when they returned.

On Friday morning, August 8th, a letter from the Consul General advised the Pikes that all Americans leave Angola because of the intensity of the fighting erupting in all areas of the country. They immediately put our Mission plans into action. At 11:30 AM on Sunday, August 10th, the Luanda Mission personnel started out to Nova Lisboa (450 miles south-east of Luanda) where my family would join them. From there our convoy of four vehicles would travel another 860 miles to the Southwest African border. Without a shadow of doubt, we all knew we were not running away. We were transferring our headquarters outside of Angola to continue our work until things were more settled. Our hearts would remain in Angola. As upon many other occasions our Misson staff was comforted by the words "Yea, though I walk through the valley of the shadow of death, I will fear no evil". These words gave us the assurance of the presence of the One who said, "I am with you always, even to the end of the world".

Nova Lisboa had been the center of intense fighting for four days. The three factions had converged on the city at the same time. They reduced one of the most beautiful cities in the world to a massive pile of rubble. The Luanda staff knocked on the door of my house at 10:30 that night. They had been through hundreds of soldiers and 24 checkpoints where they had been stopped and searched by representatives from all three liberation groups. Miraculously, they had done what others had deemed impossible. All of us knew why. They had given out thousands of Gospels of John and tracts with friendly conversation to soldiers and civilians alike. God had made this Sunday an incredible evangelistic opportunity. If God had not delayed them by the 24 check points they would not have made it to my house. By God's providence, that night was the first quiet night in the city.

When that door opened and Carolyn saw Harrison, she hugged his neck and said, "I knew you'd come!" When Harrison told us our evacuation plans, I related the terrible reports I had heard of people trying to get to the South West African border; of confiscation of cars, looting and raping and beatings. Yet Harrison was not deterred; he said their experience from Luanda to Nova Lisboa gave them the faith to believe that our God would continue to be sufficient. Our only hope to evacuate would be to reach that border.

Carolyn and Loren had been sick for several days. Though weak, Carolyn prepared something for the four of them to eat. Then we all began packing and repacking. The truck was a real gas burner and would be left in Nova Lisboa. The Luanda vehicles were refueled and prepared for the next day's journey. It was by God's providence that we had diesel vehicles that were fuel efficient and I had managed to store away a few gallons in all the chaos. While the four of them slept for two hours, Carolyn and I packed our things and added to the water and food supply. When they awoke at 4:30 AM, Carolyn was making pancakes so that we could begin our day on full stomachs.

That night June had seen Loren's little American flag. Carolyn told them that just four days earlier Loren had seen the flag on the drier in the kitchen and said, "Mom, that's a beautiful flag". Harrison said, "God can use that flag to get us out of this country". At 6 AM we were own the way again, this time with a convoy of four vehicles. That flag was draped from the sun visors in the Peugeot; since Harrison was now driving it as the lead vehicle (it had the green plates of a state vehicle and would prove to be the most difficult one to get through). The second vehicle was Carolyn driving my 1968 Mercedes Station Wagon. The third vehicle was me driving my Mission Land Rover and the fourth was Bo driving the Toyota Land Cruiser. Leaving the city, we passed through areas where the heavy fighting had completely destroyed vehicles in the street, businesses and homes. Once again, we were subjected to checkpoints every few miles. Without exception when we were asked for our party cards, Harrison would point to Loren's little American flag as our "cartão", explaining that our country had requested that we leave Angola until peace would be restored and that we were missionaries, and we would return. Time and time again he explained that the women in the second car (Carolyn and Tress) spoke very little Portuguese and that the child could be frightened; therefore, would the soldiers please not upset them? One soldier asked permission to look into the window of that car. Without exception the soldiers were polite and respectful to us.

Once we felt we were out of the danger area, Harrison left the convoy in order to reach Sá da Bandeira in time to transact business at the bank before noon closing time. The rest of us reached the city at noon and parked on a side street near the bank. June went to find Harrison so he would know we were safe. When she neared the entrance of the bank two soldiers standing in front of the bank crouched with their guns ready. She froze. The soldiers then ran across the street and one of them dropped his gun to his side and motioned for her to go ahead. About that time someone inside the bank unlocked the door and motioned her to come in. She entered and was told that Harrison was up-stairs. Then one of the bank directors informed her that he had left. She asked him how she should go to get out with soldiers engaged in a crossfire in the streets. He said, "Lady, breathe a prayer and run".

Our convoy left that area as rapidly as we could. We saw soldiers from other groups advancing on that point from every direction. We thought Harrison would go to the home of Don Lutes (a Canadian) on the southern outskirts of the city; so that is where we went. We drank cold water and ate sandwiches (all their Portuguese neighbors supplied us with what little bread they had) while the men refueled the vehicles with 40 liters Don had managed to have in reserve. We could only pray we had enough fuel to drive another 600 plus miles.

The Lutes insisted that we stay with them for they had also heard terrible reports from those attempting unsuccessfully to flee. We had already been through fighting in the city of Caála that morning and wanted no more of it. Knowing what we had just seen on the streets of Sá da Bandeira forced us on; for we all had that sweet peace in our hearts that God was with us. Surely, we would encounter nothing ahead that could be worse than what we had already come through.

"Kilometer 16" outside the city of Sá da Bandeira was a checkpoint said to be impossible to pass. When we arrived there, a car was already being searched and everything from it was on the ground being opened. Two state vehicles driven by Angolans were being confiscated. After some discussion our cars were examined but not touched. (The other five people in our convoy were unaware that the Lord had directed me to talk to the soldiers in such a way that it completely diverted their attention from us. However, it created a very tense moment for them when they saw me doing it.) Bo was ordered to move the Toyota over to the group from which their vehicles had been confiscated so that all those people could load their possessions and themselves into it. This done, we were on our way again with Bo taking these people to their destination several hours drive down the highway.

The afternoon's journey over almost deserted paved highway was at a reduced speed and was actually very enjoyable. At one point we passed a convoy of Portuguese people in trucks and cars stopped on the road for lunch and a rest. Our hearts cried out for them considering the uncertainty of them getting out of the country. Later Harrison and June did meet some of these people again in South West Africa.

We knew that we would have three very difficult checkpoints in the Roçadas area; many stories had circulated about what was happening there. At the first checkpoint we were met by many soldiers with guns ready to fire. At first, they wanted to confiscate everything we had and turn us back. After insisting that we were following our government's orders, they let us go on but warned us we would not get pass the next checkpoint controlled by a different liberation group.

The difficulties at this second checkpoint turned out to be minimal. We did pick up a rider there who was going to Pereira d'Eça. Once again Bo had a passenger in the back of the Toyota. The soldiers gave us an order to pass but assured us that we would not get past the third checkpoint on a bridge ahead.

Harrison had no way to communicate this message to the others, but we knew that all of us were united in prayer of supplication and this checkpoint would be no exception. As we came near the bridge, we saw cars coming down a dirt road off to our left (heading south) which intersected the main highway just past the bridge. It was Portuguese fleeing in a group of hundreds of cars, bumper to bumper, with huge dust clouds engulfing the entire convoy. The bridge was long and at the other end we could see soldiers on both sides of the highway. All we could do was cry out to the Lord to help us. As we reached them one soldier waved us through. Incredibly, we drove within inches of the soldiers amassed at that point, but it appeared they could not see us. We had seen many miracles on our exodus, but certainly this Biblical event was the greatest to this point (there was more to come).

Our convoy did not stop. We cut through a small hole in the other convoy as we kept on the pavement and they continued on their dusty escape route without slowing down. (That entire convoy bogged down in a river at the border and there were many reports of the tragedy of it in the American newspapers.) Later that afternoon we drove up to a filling station to ask information and hopefully to buy fuel. Once again, we were told that there was no fuel. One of the attendants suggested that we follow a little dirt road; but we were certain God's road for us was the legal way out on that main highway.

We watched the antelopes and other wildlife along the road and rejoiced in the Lord. The Lord gave us this opportunity to relax our minds and bodies and enjoy the beauty of southern Angola. We were not traveling with any speed because we knew that every vehicle had to get at least one hundred miles more than normal consumption for us to reach the border. There was no fuel to buy along the way and every drop we had was in the gas tanks. As night came on, we continued to travel though all of us were exhausted. Carolyn had driven since 6 AM without a break as weak as she was, though the Lord had temporarily healed her body (she was hospitalized in Windhoek for a week after we crossed the border). We traveled way up into the night looking for a place to camp. We had to go as far as Pereira d'Eça to deliver Bo's passenger; then we would be just forty kilometers from the border.

Harrison decided that the best place to sleep would be on the pavement in front of the airport where he and his son Dan had camped the previous year. Thus, we drove to the outskirts of Pereira d'Eça, left the passenger and returned to the airport. When we reached the airport, we turned off all headlights and maneuvered the four vehicles into a square so the men could sleep in the middle while the women slept locked in the cars. All of us got out of the cars talking and laughing relaxed in the cool of the evening. Peace and calm surrounded us. Then Carolyn heard someone approaching and mentioned it to June. She, in turn, spoke to Harrison, but by then all of us could see silhouetted around us perhaps twenty-five soldiers with guns ready. Harrison immediately identified us and discovered Christians in the group. Soon he was giving a report of the trip from Luanda (which he had done at nearly every stop along the way). Tress laughingly called this the "7:30 News Report". The soldiers immediately agreed that we could camp there, but they felt we would be safer within the barbed wire fence of the airport and between buildings to give us even more protection. They assured us that they did not look for an attack that night and they did not plan to attack the next day.

A very tall, handsome, well-educated Canyama (the very southern-most Angolan tribe) was in charge of these soldiers. We gladly shared with him and his men gospels of John and some other tracts. Without a doubt we had the opportunity in our two days of travel to give out over 2,000 gospels of John to representatives from many tribes we had never reached before; and we had contacts with soldiers from the four corners of Angola (which is twice the size of Texas).

We slept without fear under the Milky Way with the Southern Cross shining brightly in the middle of it. *(This is a work of God in itself. The cross is the only thing in a circle in the Milky Way and it revolves 365 degrees in 365 days.) At 6 AM a mortar followed by shooting served as our alarm clock. We broke camp as quickly as possible and had to bribe the soldiers to let us go. We made our way the fifteen miles into Pereirad'Eça to find a restaurant, and hope-fully a good breakfast meal. Alas, the local café had only hot water, sugar and bread to offer us. That was good enough; we provided the tea bags, margarine, jelly and peanut butter.

Before we ate our hearty breakfast, Harrison pulled one of the gospels of John from his jacket pocket, opened it at random to John 10:7-10, and read it to us in Portuguese. That was a beautiful and encouraging revelation to us. All of us were certain that we would get through that legal gate out of Angola into Southwest Africa and those forty kilometers straight to the south was God's road leading us out. Our comings and goings were being determined by Him, and we had nothing to fear. (The waiter graciously accepted the gospel of John when we had finished with it.)

Though the customs house was to open at 8 AM, no one had appeared for work. We were informed that all banks in Angola were closed. The customs office would not be opening that day or possibly any other day until order could be restored. We had not been able to get the $50,000 certified check in Sá da Bandeira and now we could not get the legal documents to take our cars out of the country; yet we chose to go on to the border. I had nicknamed Harrison "Moses" as he led our exodus. He said he had all the confidence he needed that God would part the "Sea".

Harrison had taken us through territory known to him. Near the border we passed a side road and he revealed to June that he had wire cutters behind his seat. If necessary, we would come back to this road and take it to the border; however, it was very sandy and, in all probability, we would not have enough fuel. First, we would try it through the legal gate.

We saw no Portuguese flag at the border, nor the thousands of people we had been led to believe would be there; only one minor Portuguese border official using men from the liberation groups to help him. There were two of the liberation flags flying. Within minutes all of the legal work was done. We were free to pass without having to make the $50,000 deposit on the vehicles. We were calm and relaxed because there was nothing to fear. That legal gate was open to us and all our passports had legal re-entries into Angola.

However, this was still checkpoint number 42, and the Angolan soldiers wanted to see what we had. We willingly took out our suitcases one by one in an orderly fashion, working our way from one vehicle to the next. Loren was handing out hard candies to the children who were curiously watching us while Carolyn was handing out tracts and gospels of John. June taught the children the song "My Best Friend is Jesus" and promised to return to teach them more songs and Bible stories. Bo played his guitar and all of us conversed in a relaxed fashion. Even the official invited Harrison to come back through on September 3rd to attend his wife's birthday party. What we anticipated to be the most difficult part of our trip; turned out to be a celebration.

God opened that gate for us; and forty-eight hours, 1310 miles, and forty-two checkpoints after June and Harrison said goodbye to the Christians in front of the First Church, Luanda; Carolyn, Loren and I, Tress, Bo, Harrison and June were standing on South West African soil.

By the providence of God, we stood next to the gas pump that had just received fuel that morning; they had been without fuel for three months. With our hands joined, we sang the "Doxology" to the Holy One Who had saved us and Who had been responsible for our comings and our goings. All of the gas tanks were empty, but the gas gauges were stuck at the one-half mark.

The South African soldiers had been watching us with their binoculars the whole time and were ready to go get us if necessary. Looking at the American flag; the only thing they said was, "You really advertised it, didn't you"?

This war had been raging for over ten years and would go on for many more. However, it could not stop God from feeding the hungry.

Ordination service: celebrated by over a thousand happy people. They overflowed into the street and sang as they rode around town in pickup trucks.

God Reveals His Glory [Doxa – True Identity]

James V. Holland

Organizing new churches.

God Reveals His Glory [Doxa – True Identity]

Baptisms

James V. Holland

Check Point 42

God Reveals His Glory [Doxa – True Identity]

We finally made it to the South West Africa side of the border.

It was a sad day to say goodbye to our adopted son "Chimp". He was put in jail for having an FNLA party card in MPLA territory.

The Angola Mission disbanded several months after our exodus. Carolyn and I remained in Joburg for five months to work with the Portuguese refugees. South Africa was involved in its own conflicts which erupted into a shooting battle in the suburb of Soweto. This is where the Lord sent me to do a little "street preaching".

BOTSWANA

The Foreign Mission Board moved us to Francistown, Botswana on Carolyn's birthday in January 1976. Our main task for several months was to get familiar with the Setswana language, which is a derivative of Chinese. It is a very difficult tonal language. I quickly learned I could not hear the deviations in sound, and I could not make the guttural sounds of animals and the Bushman clicks.

Our most productive work was in Selebi-Pikwe ("place of the big snakes"). The Botswana Mission had the only dentist in the country. Three days a week we ran a dental clinic located at my house. Usually, the people's teeth were in such bad shape he usually just pulled them and cleaned the wood out of their jaw bones. They did their own root canals with sticks. God gave us four young men who were on fire to serve the Lord; and it was through them that I organized church services to reach people all over eastern Botswana. We built several new churches, one in which the President of Botswana attended. God used this work to train these young men to be missionaries for their own country. I am thankful for their dedicated work and God's blessings to make them His personal emissaries. My most memorable personal event was the opportunity to preach to over five thousand people who were Satan worshippers under the absolute control of the most powerful witchdoctor in Botswana. There were 37 "Satan churches" in Pikwe. They wept with joy to hear for the first time the message of God's love for them and His gift of salvation through faith in the Lord Jesus. God's most visible and far-reaching work was to bring this witchdoctor to Him for his salvation (page 160).

My proudest moment was the day Dr. Robert McNamara (President of the World Bank and Secretary of State when Richard Nixon was President) gave Carolyn an award for her work with the African women.

She taught them as best she could how to cook healthy food (which was very scarce) and avoid diseases (boil all usable water and do not eat rotten meat) and how to make their own clothing. Finding food was a real problem because it had to be shipped in by train and trucks and it was always stolen by the soldiers fighting their civil wars in Rhodesia and South Africa. Stores would have a few cans of one item and that was about it. The street markets would have some vegetables but most of it was uneatable. I had some fruit trees, but it was all stolen at night and eaten green. I never had any of it to ripen enough to eat. There was no bread of any kind and flour was so full of weevils you just picked them out until you got tired. You could cut a piece of meat off a cow hanging in a tree and beat it until it was chewable. Usually there was no electricity for refrigeration so I would kill a zebra and immediately cook what I needed. The rest of it was a welcome meal for the villagers because they rarely ate meat. The kids ate the bugs that would swarm around any light. It was a time for a national celebration when the mopone worms hatched. They would squirt the juice out of them and eat them raw. Fortunately for us it was only a one-day drive in my Landrover (a dirt trail and a river to ford) to South Africa where we could get some good canned food. I could drive the paved road to Gaborone, but it was a real all-day hassle to fight the long lines in the stores. Each person would tell the clerk what they wanted, and they would wait for the clerk to get it from a back room.

Carolyn taught Bible lessons and had a number of conversions of both the African women and the European women whose husbands ran the copper-nickel plant. But she was best known by the Botswana President and the national government for teaching women working as secretaries how to type (maybe ten words per minute was the best they could do, and they did not know how to center a page). Her work was a tremendous breakthrough for their advancement in the business world; plus, it reduced the strain and frustration of the government workers from having to deal with very poorly written paperwork.

The Lord gave me an unusual ministry in Botswana that turned out to be a blessing. It was to minister to African women suffering the trauma of burying their still-born babies, either wrapped in rags or put in milk cartons. It opened the door for the Lord to reveal His salvation of the women and their babies.

Grocery shopping.

Self-serve gas stations. (Bring your own gas.)

Highway maintenance.

The President of Botswana at the dedication of a new church.

Thirty-seven churches in the surrounding area worshipped Satan.

Satan's royal priesthood.

Regrettably, we had to leave Botswana in August 1977, for our daughter to be born in the United States. Otherwise, she would have a South African passport which would create enormous problems for us any time we needed to travel. She was born October 28, 1977, and in December the Foreign Mission Board transferred us to Mexico. We had six months schooling in Guadalajara to learn Castilian Spanish. We gave room and board to a medical student from Bolivia. He spoke English, Russian and Japanese, but would only speak Spanish for us to learn to hear it in a normal conversation. I enjoyed an interim pastorate for three months. I learned from experience to write my sermons to make sure I was using the correct words. I was asked to speak and pray at schools and church services and got a lot of laughs when I would use a wrong word.

MEXICO

God has an interesting way of preparing people to serve Him. While having a root canal at a dentist office in Mexico City, I got a call from the American Consulate to get out to the airport and welcome President Jimmy Carter. For two hours I was on live TV with him. As a result of this I was recognized everywhere I went as "friend of the President". The Lord moved us to Acapulco, which expanded my work to several hundred miles of the pacific coast and mule rides to the villages in the mountains.

God Reveals His Glory [Doxa – True Identity]

Message of the Virgin of Guadalupe in Mexico City

I am the (single / always, only) Virgin Mary, Mother of the (real / authentic / genuine) God; author, perpetrator from the beginning to the end of all life; creator of everything in heaven and Lord of the earth to gather together everything in the whole earth. I desire; have a burning passion; a sense of emergency that you build a temple on this spot. A temple where the Mother of Love for you and your fellow man reveals Me. Have mercy and compassion that is natural to you and all that are here; that you love Me and seek after Me.

Construction of the building began in 1895 and was completed on October 12, 1945. The building is currently sinking sideways into the ground and is a hazard for people to enter it.

The following pictures are of the Virgin of Zapopan which resides in Guadalajara. It took four days for Mexico to welcome her back from a pilgrimage to bless all the Catholic churches; to give them protection from storms and earthquakes. *Most of the Catholic churches in southern Mexico were destroyed by earthquakes shortly after these pictures were made. The Bishop led the procession and proclaimed that any person who could touch the Virgin would be granted eternal life – however men surrounded the bier with clubs to prevent anyone from doing it.

God Reveals His Glory [Doxa – True Identity]

James V. Holland

Medical issues were a serious problem for my family the whole time we were in Mexico. Twice we had to have my children's stomachs pumped and Carolyn was hospitalized with hepatitis. We were there for only three years before it became a necessity to return to Texas. I got a job in the business office at Texas Christian University as Director of University Services. This was another providential work of the Lord to heal a rift between the three divisions of the University and to live in the home of the University Chaplin. For two years we endured bimonthly arsenic treatments to kill the amoebas destroying us. *Arsenic is a very painful way to die. We suffered the result of it for a good ten years. We would not have survived it if it had not been for God's merciful intervention. <u>GOD IS LOVE</u>. Believe it! Live it!

Milton Keynes UK
Ingram Content Group UK Ltd.
UKHW021551260324
439986UK00005B/117